Organizations, Uncertainties, and Risk

Organizations, Uncertainties, and Risk

EDITED BY
James F. Short, Jr., and Lee Clarke

Westview Press

BOULDER • SAN FRANCISCO • OXFORD

Copyright © 1992 by Westview Press, Inc., except Chapters 4, 5, 8, 13, 14, and 15, previously published in *Law and Policy* (Special Issue on Social and Legal Aspects of Risk and Risk-Related Behavior) II:3 (July 1989), copyright © 1989 by Blackwell Publishers

Published in 1992 in the United States of America by Westview Press, Inc., 5500 Central Avenue, Boulder, Colorado 80301-2877, and in the United Kingdom by Westview Press, 36 Lonsdale Road, Summertown, Oxford OX2 7EW

A CIP catalog record for this book is available from the Library of Congress.
ISBN 0-8133-8562-8

Printed and bound in the United States of America

The paper used in this publication meets the requirements
of the American National Standard for Permanence of Paper
for Printed Library Materials Z39.48-1984.

10   9   8   7   6   5   4   3   2   1

Contents

PART FOUR
Institutional Responses to Uncertainty

PART FIVE
Choosing Technologies, Managing, and Regulating Risks

PART SIX
Institutionalizing Risk

Foreword

Sociology is a second-guessing science. Much of its work consists of examining how people account for their own actions, then confronting those accounts with ostensibly deeper explanations of the same actions. Some of sociology's subversive reputation results from this will to challenge people's own cherished beliefs about their behavior. In this regard, nonetheless, sociology resembles political science, anthropology, history, plus those shrinking segments of economics and psychology that take conscious intentions seriously . . . if only to unmask them. It differs greatly from biology and chemistry, where the actor's consciousness and intentions rarely come under scrutiny, and even in those rare cases constitute objects to be explained, not potential explanations.

Second-guessing does not mean second-rate. When we watch Erving Goffman describing how inmates of total institutions create stories about their fall from freedom and competence or George Homans identifying the circumstances in which men in Western Electric's Bank Wiring Observation Room "binged" each other--traded punches on the upper arm--we suddenly gain insight into opaque social processes. Second-guessing can be brilliantly hermeneutic, radically reductionist, or aggressively critical. The common ground is an alternative account of social action to that provided by the actor. Viable views of reality result from the deconstruction of motives.

The authors in this volume concentrate on two kinds of situations: (a) those in which identifiable people within organizations make decisions affecting the probability of rare but dangerous events, notably preventable illness and death, and (b) those in which observers make estimates of such a probability. They deal especially with cases where the decision-makers or observers have at least a dim awareness of possible consequences of the actions in question-- making Corvair automobiles more or less safe, continuing to sell contraceptive shields when news about their deleterious effects is seeping in, preparing to launch an orbiting rocket, and so on. Broadly speaking, their most general model of the problem looks like this:

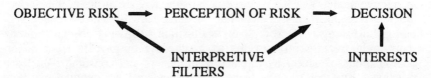

In such a scheme, a single actor (who may, of course, be a collective actor) makes a decision influencing the likelihood that a harmful event will occur on the basis of two factors: her perception of the risk and her interests. Interpretive filters intervene in the relationships between objective risk and perception of risk, on one side, and between perception of risk and decision, on the other. The objective risk is the actual probability that a harmful event will occur under a specified set of conditions; when it comes to automobile accidents, contraceptive shields, and rocket-launching, actors often have inadequate or faulty information; in many such cases, indeed, no one knows the odds. (In this book, some authors speak of "hazard" in this way, reserving the term "risk" for *estimates* of hazard.) If something very harmful happens, if someone else estimates the odds very differently, or if the odds become known later, however, interested observers of the decisions have strong incentives for second-guessing.

Interested observers include harmed parties, lawyers, and other members of the decision-making organizations. They also include sociologists. In this book, the sociologists differ considerably in which elements of the interpretive scheme they emphasize: relations between objective risk and perception of risk, the overriding of perception by interest, the character and strength of interpretive filters, or something else. Many authors focus their second-guessing on the processes by which organizations arrive at their official perceptions of danger, their "risk assessments." But all take for granted that they are dealing with something like the situation the diagram describes. The situation is strikingly individualistic; it concerns a single actor's decision.

To a student of war and political conflict, this way of organizing the problem comes as a surprise. War and political conflict certainly involve risk. Nuclear war, for example, has only occurred in military scenarios and the U.S. bombing of Japan. But its analysts have now and then asked whether a nuclear holocaust could occur by accident, as a result of faulty decision-making under stress and uncertainty (e.g., Fischhoff, 1991). Students of revolution, rebellion, and political violence have occasionally, although decreasingly, portrayed them as expressing the wills, irrepressible urges, or calculations of single actors-- scheming revolutionaries, frustrated masses, indignant workers (for reviews and critiques, see Aya, 1990; Kimmel, 1990; Rule, 1989). In those versions, analyses of war and political conflict resemble individualistic risk analysis. But on the whole, recent specialists in war and political conflict have treated them as interactive phenomena involving at least two parties. That is why, for example, two-person game theory has enchanted so many strategic analysts. Similarly, more and more analysts of collective action reject one-actor models in favor of models portraying strategic interaction among authorities, challengers, and competitors.

In principle, there is no reason why observers of risk could not develop interactive models of what they see. Certainly they are aware of interaction, as the sensitive portrayals of neonatal intensive care by Carol Heimer and of biological testing by Dorothy Nelkin illustrate. Drawing on that awareness, they could treat harmful events as a schedule of payoffs from different combinations of action by interacting producers and consumers--at least in principle. But that sort of scheme would draw analysts in quite a different direction from that followed by most authors in this book. In general, this book's authors want to offer alternatives to the risk assessments that organizations now generate, alternatives informed by social science. They want to second-guess organizational decisions, especially those that involve self-conscious estimates of danger.

It would also be possible, in principle, to analyze what features of social structure affect how much danger individuals face--to trace, for example, whether the higher industrial accident rates of Hispanic workers in the United States result from their concentration in high-pressure jobs on poorly-maintained equipment. Though limits of this sort of analysis are formed in these pages, that enterprise falls outside most of the "risk analyses" practiced here. The authors in this volume focus primarily on how people in organizations assess risks and/or act on those assessments, without systematically addressing stratification effects. In that sense their approach is quite individualistic.

Within those limits, however, they differ substantially in their emphasis, even in their epistemologies. All combat the mythologies of rational cost-benefit analysis, but their sociological weapons vary enormously. Some authors, such as Hilgartner and Manning, attempt to analyze decision-making in the face of risk but give large weight to interpretive filters, so much so that the idea of objective risk practically disappears from view. Others, such as Sanders, turn away from interpretive filters to scrutinize the organizational logics and processes by which agents can and do arrive at estimates of the costs of different possible courses of action. Still others, such as Jasper, aim to understand the ways in which certain interpretive filters become dominant. The result, then, is not only a fascinating array of case studies in the assessment of risk, but also a catalog of competing approaches to its analysis. Second-guessing obviously has its rewards.

Charles Tilly

Acknowledgments

This book began when Jim Short organized a session on "risk" for the 1988 meetings of the Law and Society Association. The session included papers by Bill Felstiner and Peter Siegelman, Diane Vaughan, Peter Manning, and Keith Hawkins, with Al Reiss as discussant. Hawkins, an editor of *Law and Policy*, subsequently asked Short to edit a special issue of that journal. Short recruited additional papers from Susan Shapiro and Joe Sanders and added an introduction titled "Toward a Sociolegal Paradigm of Risk." As the title suggests, the focus of the issue was on sociolegal scholarship relating to risk, rather than organizational decisions and decision making.

Peter Manning first suggested the *Law and Policy* issue should be expanded into a book. In the course of exploring the idea Short wrote to several people, including Lee Clarke, who suggested the focus of the book might be on organizational decision making under conditions of risk and uncertainty. Noting that the literature in this area was sparse and lacking coherence, Clarke suggested several potential contributors.

Clarke's ideas were so appealing that he was asked to co-edit the book. With the help of Keith Hawkins, who identified other British researchers, contributors were contacted and we were on our way.

Some of our contributors had not yet analyzed their data sufficiently to permit early closure, and several continue field work even as the book is published. A few were unable to complete chapters we had hoped for.

When all the contributions were assembled, it became apparent that a final chapter was badly needed to draw together the ideas and findings from an extremely wide-ranging collection of theoretical and empirical essays. In addition, we faced the problem that few publishers are willing to undertake multi-authored projects such as this. Only after we located Westview, through the good offices of Charles Tilly, was publication assured.

All of this is by way of explaining the book's appearance at this time, following a long and sometimes arduous process. We are grateful to the initial group of authors who stuck with us throughout this process. We are particularly indebted to Tammy Small, secretary extraordinaire, without whose help the book would have taken years longer to produce, and to our other chapter authors, whose work strengthens and helps to define an amorphous field. Charles Tilly not only wrote a thoughtful Foreword but critiqued earlier versions of Chapter 1, in particular, and worked with Westview to bring the book to fruition. From Westview, Editor Dean Birkenkamp, Julie Seko, and Lynn Arts have been unfailing in their efforts on our behalf. Colleagues Gene Rosa and Bill

Freudenburg have been especially helpful. Finally, Kelma Short and Patricia A. Roos have been supportive throughout, and it is to them, our children, and future generations who, above all, must cope with the legacy of risky decisions, that we dedicate this book.

James F. Short, Jr., and Lee Clarke

PART ONE

Introduction

1

Defining, Explaining, and Managing Risks

James F. Short, Jr.

We live with a profound and troubling paradox: that the potential for the destruction of life is as much a product of the crowning achievements of science, technology, and social organization as is life enhancement and enrichment. The paradox is all the more perplexing because new knowledge--of harmful substances in the food we eat, the water we drink, and the air we breathe-- heightens the sense that living on planet earth involves terrible risks even as it makes possible protection from many hazards.

Science and its applications permit effective control over many of the hazards that plagued past civilizations. By epidemiological criteria, life is now less risky than in the past. Yet, science and technology--and the uses to which we put them--add to our anxieties by creating new hazards and by developing more sophisticated and precise methods of detection of both old and new hazards. The result is an uneasy balance between protection and cure on the one hand, and vulnerability to threats of global hazards never before experienced by humankind.

Expertise narrows and becomes more esoteric, and embedded in remote organizations and institutions, even as it becomes more necessary. The role of experts and their fiduciary responsibilities (and those of the aforementioned organizations and institutions) become increasingly problematic. So, too, the reliability and validity of their knowledge. Hazards on a global scale, such as nuclear holocaust (see Sagan and Turco, 1990), are added to those associated with

I am grateful to Lee Clarke, Eugene Rosa, Albert J. Reiss, Jr., and Charles Tilly for their careful reading and critique of earlier drafts of this chapter.

smaller-scale endeavors, many of which previously were considered benign. Cherished beliefs and common practices--even "the persistence and fulfillment of the natural and the moral social orders" (Barber, 1983:9)--seem challenged and threatened.

Why Focus on Organizations and Institutions?

How did all this happen? What can, and is, being done about it? Who decides, and how are decisions reached concerning hazards and their attendant risks? This book deals with these types of questions. The primary focus is on organizational and institutional contexts of risk analysis, because it is primarily in these contexts that hazards and their attendant risks are conceptualized, identified, measured, and managed.

What about individuals? Do we not assess the hazards and estimate the myriad risks of daily living? Individuals must, and do make such assessments, and we know a good deal about how individual decisions are made under conditions of risk (see Kahneman, et al., 1982; Heimer, 1988). Individuals also assess current social and political issues involving hazards and risks. Information about such issues is acquired in a variety of ways, from media such as television, newspapers, and magazines, in conversations and meetings of interested parties. Individuals participate in debates and vote, and some take other actions such as joining voluntary organizations and taking part in organized protests against risks they believe should not be taken (see Chapter 11, below).

"One person, one vote" does not govern most important risk decisions, however. Increasingly, organizations--often very large organizations such as national and international business firms--and institutions such as governments and regulatory bodies--set the parameters and the terms of debate of risk decisions. Businesses make decisions regarding production processes, products, and services. Governments pursue policies, enact laws, and set up procedures to regulate risks. Standards are promulgated and enforcement agencies established. Laws designed to provide relief or recompense to the victims of hazards are passed and agencies are established to administer them.

Institutions of higher learning and the professions become involved, as producers and communicators of knowledge, designers of products and trainers of professionals. Media of mass communication, aided by new technologies, make news of these discoveries, their costs and benefits. "The public" (more appropriately "publics"), informed and misinformed, are affected and implicated as consumers, workers, voters, and protesters, often in highly organized ways.

What are we to make of this complex and often confusing picture? The organizing theme of this book is that institutions and the organizations that comprise them provide the primary contexts for the assessment and the management of risk. It is within these contexts, therefore, that answers to many of the most critical questions about risk-related decisions and decision making must be found.

Hazards, Risks, and Risk Analysis

Conceptual problems plague the study of risk. Commonly used terms acquire technical meanings and technical terms are used far beyond their generating domains, both problems conducive to misunderstanding. In common parlance, risk and hazard are sometimes equated (see the Shorter Oxford English Dictionary definition of risk, at the beginning of Chapter 15). Technical definitions view these terms as related, but distinct: "Hazards are threats to people and what they value and risks are measures of hazards" (Kates and Kasperson, 1983:7027). Dietz, et al. (forthcoming:1) define risk as "a compound measure of the probability and magnitude of some event or adverse effect." This definition has the advantage that it allows for "desired risks" such as are involved in many recreational pursuits and in entrepreneurial activity in which thrills or "highs" associated with risky behavior are said to be an important part of their attractiveness (see Machlis and Rosa, 1990; Mitchell, 1983).

Note that the distinction between risk and uncertainty becomes blurred in risk analysis (see Chapter 16; also Knight, 1921). Indeed, as a leading figure in risk analysis notes, "identification of the most likely failure scenarios and the major sources of uncertainty is an essential part" of Probabilistic Risk Assessment and Probabilistic Safety Assessment (Apostolakis, 1990: 1359).

Much human behavior--by individuals, groups, organizations, and institutions--requires that decisions be made in the absence of calculable probabilities of both desired and undesired outcomes. Many such decisions involve "ordinary people"--parents, workers, and consumers--as well as risk professionals and members of other professions. Varied as they are, cases analyzed in this book are but a sampling of risk-related decisions and decision making by organizations and institutions: manufacturing firms' decisions regarding worker and consumer health and safety (Chapters 4, 5, 7), decisions by corporations to file for Chapter 11 bankruptcy (Chapter 6), news organizations' consideration of libel law in determining what to print or broadcast (Chapter 8), the management of information by neonatal intensive care units and parental response to such information (Chapter 9), criteria for decisions used by British Agricultural, Factory, and Industrial Air Pollution, Railways, and Nuclear Inspectorates, and by OSHA inspectors in the United States (Chapters 10, 14, 15), governments' use of expert advice and public participation in risk-related decisions (Chapter 11), French nuclear energy decisions (Chapter 12), and NASA and NASA contractor decisions related to the Challenger tragedy (Chapter 13).

These few examples are sufficient to suggest that risk and uncertainty are generic features of social life and integral to it. Risk analysis is an extension of formal and informal ways of assessing and dealing with hazards and risks, powerfully augmented by science and technology. Science and technology have decreased risks and uncertainties associated with many traditional hazards (e.g., famine and pestilence), discovered others and aided in their assessment and mitigation, and created still others. While understanding some risks requires highly specialized, technical knowledge, others are routinized by convention, rule, or law, or distributed through markets. Our thesis here is that much can be learned by study of the organizational and institutional contexts within which both routine and esoteric risks are identified and managed. Humankind has, after all, been living with risk and uncertainty for a very long time.

Risk Analysis, Risk Management, the Law, and the Public

Risk analysis is customarily divided into risk assessment and risk management, though these processes are often quite indistinct. The assessment of risks has been viewed as an objective, technical, and scientific enterprise, identified predominantly with the physical and biological sciences, economics, statistics, medicine and engineering. Risk managers also have come from these disciplines, but other professions such as operations researchers, lawyers, and others frequently are found in such positions (Dietz and Rycroft, 1987). In its modern manifestations, risk analysis is a recent phenomenon, and it has grown rapidly. Technical demands vary a great deal, depending on the types of hazards, risks, and uncertainties that are at issue. Many of these are legal, economic, and more broadly social, rather than technical from an engineering or scientific perspective. Organizational and institutional goals and uncertainties in the risk climate of a corporation, local, state, or national government often determine the role and the nature of risk analyses.

The chapters that follow, as Albert J. Reiss, Jr. notes in Chapter 16, focus primarily on risk managers, thereby drawing attention to decision making processes. But we learn a great deal about risk assessment, as well, particularly as practiced "on the job." Bridget Hutter and Sally Lloyd-Bostock, for example, note that inspectors in OSHA and in the British agencies they studied "continually operated with notions of risk and uncertainty. While risks were by definition theoretically calculable, they were not necessarily calculated, nor was it necessarily only explicitly calculated risk that informed inspectors' decision making."

Distinctions between risk and uncertainty, and between risk assessment and management thus become blurred in both theory and practice. Political interests, inherent uncertainties in scientific inquiry, the lack of attention to and resources for careful study of the effects of introducing new substances and technologies into the environment (into the work place, the food chain, ambient air, the atmosphere, water delivery systems and aquifers, for example), and a host of other considerations (information overload, blocked communication channels, profit, reputation, venality, etc.) cloud measurement and management at every level. Individuals and organizations sometimes act not because they understand risks, but because they feel they *must act*. Risk objects are identified and defined out of a variety of motivations (see Hilgartner, 1985 and in this volume). So, also, are risk assessment and management. As we shall see in the chapters to follow, each step in this process is problematic.

Risk objects and activities associated with them often provoke organized protest and legal threats. This is particularly the case among western democracies; and especially in the United States (see Jasanoff, 1986). Victims of hazards, and those who fear victimization either personally or on behalf of broader constituencies or causes, often seek to prevent actions they perceive as threatening or to obtain redress. Threats of legal suit occur across an extremely broad spectrum of risks and organizational activities, from common and traditional work environments such as construction, farming, manufacturing and transportation, to mass media of communication and cutting-edge scientifically advanced and highly technical fields such as neonatology and the space program. Legally responsible regulatory bodies may also be targeted by protest and legal actions brought by regulated industries and/or their workers, consumers of their products, or public interest groups.

A common thread of chapters throughout the book is concern with the legal context of risk analysis--with legal definitions and regulations applied to broad classes of hazard, with legally established agencies designed to carry out those regulations, their rules and procedures, with legal responsibilities and liabilities. Equally important is the "legal climate" within which work, consumption, and citizenship take place. The legal climate of a community or nation--even of the world--influences how business is conducted, how science and engineering are carried out, how workers are treated and consumers served, and how governments and other institutions respond to human needs.

The legal climate of risk-related issues is complicated in many nations by conflicting interests. Anthony Barker (in Chapter 11) discusses the mechanisms and functions of "expert advice and formal public involvement in public policies involving risk." Though scientific and technological advice to governments is both common and increasingly intensive, surprisingly little attention has been given to such matters (but see Golden, 1991). Barker's conclusion--that "the divide between expert and general citizen perceptions of risk, or of the merits of major new hazardous projects or developments" is unlikely ever to be bridged--is modified by the caveat that the "shared decision advice processes" he analyzes offer hope in this respect.

The view that risk-related problems stem primarily either from ignorance or from narrowly defined self interest oversimplifies and distorts the nature of risk analysis, public perceptions of risks and their acceptability, and decision making with respect to risks. Social scientists who have studied general-population samples find that differences in risk perceptions cannot be explained by differences in information levels, but that they are correlated with differences in personal values (see Dietz, et al., 1989). Additionally, careful studies of groups that have organized to resist hazardous conditions or proposed developments report that members of such groups typically search actively for technical information and are frustrated by their lack of access to credible scientific information. (see, e.g., Freudenburg, 1991a; Fowlkes and Miller, 1987; Brown, 1987).

Many in the science community, including science advisors to governments, testify to the need for better understanding of uncertainties that are inherent in science and technology, of the self-correcting nature of science, and for countering political and economic considerations that lead to short-term decisions and neglect of long-term considerations. As we learn from the chapters that follow, however, risk-related decisions often are embedded in organizational and institutional self interest, messy inter- and intraorganizational relationships, economically- and politically-motivated rationalization, personal experience and "rule of thumb" considerations that defy the neat, technically sophisticated, and ideologically neutral portrayal of risk analysis as solely a scientific enterprise. Risk analysis, which in theory should precede and inform management decisions, may occur in the course of these decisions, or even follow them in rationalization of management decisions (Clarke, 1988).

Science, Risk Analysis, and Public Policy

There is much confusion as to what can be expected of risk analysis, how it is carried out, who benefits and who pays, how much, and in what ways. The object of risk analysis typically is phrased in terms of safety, for example, as in "probabilistic safety assessment," noted above, or "margin of safety" or "safety factor." As Bernard Goldstein (1990:7) notes, however, "safety" may improperly communicate "an *absolute degree of freedom from risk* that is not implicit in the science, and confuses regulatory activities" (emphasis added). As is so often the case with semantic problems, confusion, unrealistic and unwarranted expectations follow. Concern for safety (as in the Hippocratic oath: "above all do no harm") and recognition of "the fallibility of science and technology," Goldstein argues, are associated with "approaches to risk that lead to the setting of standards more stringent than those apparently required by direct estimation" (Goldstein, 1990:7). The acceptability of margins of error associated with risk estimates often is a more appropriate consideration for social policy issues than is the acceptability of risk (see Reiss, 1989 and below; also Lowrance, 1976).

Risk assessment methodology is controversial in many circles, nowhere more than within the scientific community. Philosopher of science, Kristin Shrader-Frechette, is highly critical of "fallacious inferences" and "methodological value judgments" that creep into risk identification, risk estimation, and risk evaluation, under the guise of science (Shrader-Frechette, 1991; 1985). Agencies responsible for the regulation of risks are criticized for being both too cautious and too bold, and for using out-dated scientific information. Philip H. Abelson, a distinguished scientist, member of the National Academy of Sciences, and long-time editor of *Science*, charges that the Environmental Protection Agency "still sets guidelines on carcinogenic risks based on the limited information available during the 1970s." While conceding that the Clean Air Act passed by the U.S. Congress in 1990 "will eventually have some limited beneficial effect in reducing chemical risks to human health," Abelson is concerned that its implementation will be regressively expensive to consumers who will be taxed "because industry will pass on to them increased costs" including "substantial hidden costs" related to "uncertainty in corporate planning" and probable job losses due to "weakened ability to compete globally." "Principal beneficiaries," he concludes, "will be lawyers and entrepreneurial engineers" (Abelson, 1990; see also Abelson, 1991).

Abelson's thesis is not universally shared among scientists, and it is vigorously contested by EPA administrators, as noted in contributions to the "Letters," "News and Comments," and "Research News" sections of *Science* in which the extent and fervor of disagreement is evident. The notion that the law impedes implementation of the most advanced scientific knowledge, or permits such knowledge to be ignored, is echoed in many fields, however (see Clarke, 1988). A recent (U.S.) National Research Council report concludes, for example, that the rigidity and specificity of laws governing "Crew Size and Maritime Safety" inhibit technological innovation and the achievement of greater efficiency (Turner-Lewis, 1990-91). Note, however, that had the Exxon Valdez not been so efficient, there would have been more human slack in the system to counter the human errors than occurred in that disaster (Clarke, 1990; see also Perrow, 1984).

"Legal inertia" is a prime illustration of what William F. Ogburn termed "cultural lag," in that one aspect of culture (science and technology) changes more rapidly than does another (in this case, law). This type of cultural lag is complicated by widespread disagreement within the scientific community regarding proper standards for protection against many risks and uncertainties. Disagreement often extends to scientific methods and interpretations, as for example, with respect to hazards posed by toxins used or generated in production processes, or in products such as pesticides, building materials, food preparation and/or enhancement for commercial purposes. Disagreement is, of course, inevitable (and probably necessary) in science. Misunderstanding of this point is common among all parties in risk analysis, by scientists, risk assessors and managers, as well as by others, thus exacerbating problems of risk analysis.

Public policy analyst, Aaron Wildavsky (1988, 1989; see also Douglas and Wildavsky, 1982) has studied the political, economic, and legal framework of risk-related social policy. "Searching for Safety" as an absolute value, he argues, has resulted in greater risks for more people. The effort to insure safety has focused too much on avoiding error by means of *anticipation*, and not enough on encouraging *resilience* through trial and error. That is, preventive actions taken in anticipation of danger may result in losing potential benefits from a line of research or a new technology.

"Trial without error" toward the solution of risk-related matters clearly is impossible. Wildavsky bases his argument on "the principle of uncertainty, the axiom of connectedness, and the rule of sacrifice" (1988:4). Uncertainty is an integral feature of virtually all scientific inquiry as it is in the course of human events. The complexity and inter-connectedness of the environment, human behavior, health, and life, ensure that introducing change in one part of these systems is likely to produce changes in other parts, not all of which can be anticipated. Thus, we cannot be certain about all possible effects of the discovery or the applications of new knowledge. So far, so good.

The rule of sacrifice is more controversial, however, for it raises questions of equity and fairness. The rule stipulates that "if the parts of a system are prevented from facing risks, the whole will become unable to adapt to new dangers" (Wildavsky, 1988:6); and "whole systems cannot be stabilized unless the parts are destabilized in adapting to environmental change" (Wildavsky, 1988:72). In principle, the rule is surely correct. Safety as an absolute value is impossible. Risks are by definition probabilities, even when carefully and accurately measured. Some will suffer, no matter what decision is made. Given uncertainty, mistakes, accidents, and errors are sure to occur. But which parts of systems are to bear the burden of risks and/or to be destabilized? Who is to decide? Are the losers--those who are victimized by risks decreed by others--to be compensated, how and by whom (see O'Brien, 1987)? Ignoring these questions and asserting an overarching utility function for an entire society glosses conflicts of interest that shape risk creation and distribution.

Wildavsky addresses these questions only indirectly. He insists that risk policies be based on aggregate benefits and harms, emphasizing that insofar as possible all costs and benefits must be factored in to considerations of social policy with respect to risk. The point is well taken, though full accounting is impossible due precisely to uncertainty and connectedness. If it were, the argument goes, "trial and error" unfettered by government regulation will most efficiently and effectively promote safety. Capitalism is the engine that drives Wildavsky's search for safety. "The best process known to mankind for using our mistakes to do better is the decentralized, trial-and-error system of people coordinating their own efforts called capitalism" (Wildavsky, 1989:4).

Wildavsky places his faith in entrepreneurs. It is they who should decide. Yet surely others also have interests in choices and in their consequences. The argument is that redundancy in the form of backup parts and systems and competitive markets "works (as long, of course, as the failure of any single part is independent of the failure of its backups) because it divides risks" (Wildavsky, 1988:72). The caveat is critical. Large, complex, and tightly coupled systems, such as nuclear power plants, are prone to "normal accidents," as Perrow's research (1984) strongly suggests. Moreover, it is apparent that resilience may also be encouraged by strong public resistance to and stringent government regulation of existing technologies. Evidence is mounting, for example, that new technologies may well diminish both the tight coupling and the complexity of nuclear power production, making it much less prone to "normal accidents."[1]

Wildavsky's dismissal of public resistance to hazardous undertakings (e.g., nuclear plants and waste facilities) is cavalier: "How will the costs of change be borne if everyone says 'Not me'? The NIMBY reaction (Not in My Back Yard) of those faced with necessary but inconvenient facilities is a potent example" (Wildavsky, 1988).

The Fairness Issue

That some must suffer in the search for safety is undeniable. Accidents will happen, no matter how reliable or remote the prospect of accident or failure, and uncertainties abound. Yet one must ask, how *fair* is safe enough? (Rayner and Cantor, 1987). Who is to suffer, and who to gain? Are these decisions also to be left to trial and error? Wildavsky's vision of resilience and fine-tuning through trial and error would leave such decisions to entrepreneurs. If the principal beneficiaries of the Clean Air Act will be "lawyers and entrepreneurial engineers," who will be the principal beneficiaries of unregulated trial and error?

Sheila Jasanoff is also highly critical of risk-related decision making in the United States, but her position differs from Wildavsky's. She singles out the adversarial legal climate in the U.S. and political control of regulatory agencies as being particularly ill-suited to "dealing with problems of scientific uncertainty" and risk management as social policy (1985:156). She contrasts the "law-obsessed vision" of the U.S. with regulatory policies in western European countries which are legitimated "by building up bureaucratic and technical expertise in the executive branch" and where civil servants are shielded from partisan politics (Jasanoff, 1985:157).

"Working through consultation and negotiation," Jasanoff observes, "European decision makers prevent the polarization of divergent viewpoints and encourage consensus building. Scientific judgments, in particular, are developed through private deliberations among experts, so that expert disagreements are not exposed to public view. Although decisions are made behind closed doors, the public's trust in the legitimacy of administrative action is maintained through

---

1. The Public Broadcasting System series, "Race to Save the Planet," aired in the Fall of 1990, featured this technology.

institutional stability and the assurance that the rules of the regulatory game will not change drastically with changes in political leadership" (Jasanoff, 1985:157-58).

Here, of course, is the rub. Jasanoff acknowledges that the U.S. approach is attractive because it is "inherently democratic," and because the "politics of pluralism" serves "the instrumental functions of the law" (Jasanoff, 1985:174). For a variety of reasons change in the direction of the European model seems unlikely in the U.S. Jasanoff concludes that the results of that model are quite similar to those achieved in the U.S, without the rancor and additional economic costs brought on by litigation and other types of controversy in this country. However, Jasper's analysis (1990 and in this volume) of French energy policy demonstrates that the European model may result in political decisions that run rough shod over opposition, even from powerful economic forces. Moreover, if Barker (Chapter 11) is correct, the European model may be breaking down in response to increased public concern with risks and uncertainties.

Though it is not always acknowledged as such, fairness is an important issue underlying most of the chapters to follow. The nature of science and the gravity of modern risks, coupled with repeated instances in which the judgements and the trustworthiness of governments, their agents and agencies, and of other institutions and their agents and agencies, highlight the issue. Asking "How safe is safe enough?" as risk analysis traditionally has done, begs issues in which considerations of technical competence and of confidence that the fiduciary obligations and responsibilities of organizations and institutions will be properly discharged are linked (Barber, 1983). Both of these types of trust seem likely to increase in importance as public acceptance of fateful risk-related decisions becomes more problematic.

Effective management of highly publicized risks such as nuclear power and storing nuclear wastes, global warming and the greenhouse effect depends heavily on public trust in science, in technology, and in managing institutions. Public opinion surveys and case studies demonstrate that large segments of the public do not trust government agencies responsible for such matters (see, e.g., Freudenburg, 1991a; Finsterbusch, 1989; Freudenburg and Rosa, 1984). The critical importance of trust in science and technology, as well as in private business and the federal government, is suggested in surveys undertaken to determine citizen's concerns and willingness to support local citing of nuclear waste repositories in Nebraska and Nevada. Lacking trust, respondents were far more likely to oppose local construction. Trust variables far outdistanced traditional sociodemographic variables and cost-benefit considerations (Kunreuther, et al., 1990).

Institutional legitimacy rests to a considerable extent on trust. Yet, as Barber notes, *distrust* is not always destructive. "The public is now more competent and more knowledgeable, more capable of effective distrust. . . . a certain amount of rational distrust is necessary for political accountability in a participatory democracy" (Barber, 1983:166). Ample evidence exists that distrust in the organizations and institutions responsible for risk management often is warranted (see previous citations in this section; also Erikson, 1976; Levine, 1982). The balance between trust, distrust, and other social control mechanisms thus is critical to public acceptance of risk-related decisions and their implementation.

Organization of the Book: Theoretical and Empirical Perspectives

Sections of the book are divided roughly according to their focus on four aspects of organizational decision making: (1) rationality and the identification of risk objects; (2) corporate contexts of decision making concerning risks; (3) institutional responses to uncertainty (4) choosing technologies and assessing, managing and regulating risks.   The final section discusses the institutionalization of risk and social organization and risk.

Part One, consisting of Chapters 2 and 3, examines two theoretical and conceptual areas that are critical to risk analysis: the rationality of decision making and the identification of risk objects. These chapters set the stage for the empirical analyses of particular institutional and organizational contexts of risky decision making in Parts Three through Five. Lee Clarke critiques theories that have traditionally guided risk analysis, focusing on rational choice theory drawn from economic analysis, and on critiques of rational choice based on work in cognitive psychology. After critiquing the critiques, Clarke outlines elements of a theory of contextual influences on organizational decision making, emphasizing the importance of networks of decision makers, especially among those who occupy positions of power in the organizations that make decisions of consequence in risk-related matters. He argues the importance of ideology and culture, and of organizational position, rather than personal characteristics, in explaining decisions. He finds illustrations of these factors in the localized, substance-specific studies in several chapters in the book.

Stephen Hilgartner's deep constructivist examination of the manner in which risk objects are identified, and of the consequences of risk object identification, completes Part One. His primary focus is on "networks of risk" that follow from identification of particular objects as risky. Risk objects direct public attention, as well as risk analysts' and policy makers' attention, to the objects so identified. Hilgartner urges that networks of risk should be "pried open," as a challenge to passive acceptance of risk objects that are identified by networks of sociotechnical systems. His primary example is auto-based transport and Ralph Nader's dramatic portrayal of the Corvair as "unsafe at any speed," challenging "the driver" as the predominant risk object in matters of auto safety.

The consequences of identifying particular objects as risky can be seen throughout the book, as authors probe the manner in which various parties to risk assessment and management go about their business. What they discover is that risk analysis is characterized by complex motivations, relationships, and procedures--and consequences that often are unanticipated and quite different from the goals and purposes that ostensibly guide the enterprise. Miscalculation, misunderstanding, confusion, and neglect of other "risky objects" that are unattended because not identified as such are found to be commonplace. Both Clarke and Hilgartner, despite their very different approaches, agree that research attention should be directed toward institutional elites whose participation in sociotechnical systems identifies and defines risk objects and powerfully shapes risk analyses, public attention, political debate, and social policy.

The Clarke and Hilgartner chapters highlight a pervasive problem in risk analysis, in social science analysis and in the objects of analysis. All are extremely diverse, risk analysis and the objects of social science analysis by necessity; social science approaches by tradition, historical development, and conviction (some might say perversity). The sections of the book are to some extent arbitrary, and there is a good deal of overlap between chapters assigned to each section. Theoretical and methodological perspectives brought to these concerns also differ widely among the chapters, again with much overlapping. It is instructive, however, to note certain broad categories of the approaches taken in various chapters.

Clarke (Chapter 1), Sanders (Chapter 4), Felstiner and Siegelman (Chapter 5), and Heimer (Chapter 9), each direct specific attention to models of *rationality in decision making*. Clarke, and Felstiner and Siegelman, are especially critical of economic models of rational decision making, pointing to serious flaws in underlying assumptions and empirical realities. Heimer calls for modifications of both economic and psychological models, based on situational qualities of information transfer and different meanings of risk among parties to risky undertakings (see also, Heimer, 1987). Sanders bases his analysis of firm risk management on neoclassical economic principles, as modified by organizational decision making research and theory.

Several chapters are based on a frankly *social constructivist* approach: Hilgartner (Chapter 3), as previously noted, Delaney (Chapter 6), Shapiro (Chapter 8), Hutter and Lloyd-Bostock (Chapter 10), and Manning (Chapter 14). Each of these researchers describes the social construction of risk and the consequences for risk management, within specific domains. Note, however, that all of the chapters in Parts Two through Five can be *interpreted* in terms of their consequences for the social construction of hazard, risk, and risk assessment and management.

The social construction perspective does not deny the objective reality of hazards, risk objects, and risks associated with them. Rather, it draws attention to alternative ways of identifying hazards and risk objects, and of assessing and managing risks, as Chapter 3 demonstrates. Examples are not hard to find, though careful documentation is rare (see, e.g., Levine, 1982; Clarke, 1988; Szasz, forthcoming).

A third approach, taken by several contributors to the book, is an emphasis on *social policy and power relationships that influence social policy.* Six chapters have this broad area as their primary focus. Barker (Chapter 11) and Jasper (Chapter 12) are concerned with central government decision making; Hawkins (Chapter 15) studies British factory inspectors' decision making concerning health and safety matters. Delaney (Chapter 6), Nelkin (Chapter 7), and Vaughan (Chapter 13) study large firms that are faced with quite different risk-related decisions.

Despite widely differing theoretical and methodological perspectives, and substantive interests, certain concerns and conclusions are common to nearly all of the chapters. Principal among these are concern for the legal context of organizational decision making and, closely related and intertwined with them, economic concerns.

The legal context is ubiquitous, often appearing to overdetermine organizational decision making. The threat of suit is a common denominator for virtually all risk assessments and for risk management. Three of the papers take this threat and related matters as a primary concern for their research. Felsteiner and Siegelman examine the adequacy of tort law for insuring consumer and worker safety with respect to latent injuries, i.e., those for which considerable time elapses between exposure to a hazard and the occurrence of harm. They find that tort law provides neither an optimal level of safety nor an adequate incentive for employers to take precautions toward that end. Shapiro focuses on the effects of libel law on news organizations. She finds that the pursuit of constitutional protections of free speech by media lawyers subtly chills and shapes the social construction of news. Finally, Sanders studies corporate risk management strategies in dealing with products liability law. Firms vary a great deal in their attitudes toward products liability law and toward risk management. In sketching a theory of risk management strategies, Sanders places special emphasis on certain characteristics of firms and the law. Firms, as has often been noted, are constrained by existing organization and characterized by bounded rationality. Driven by the bottom line of profit, they must guard against illegal or otherwise improper behavior by opportunistic managers. The advent of strict legal liability for injuries caused by defective products and the increasing complexity of legal requirements combine with uncertainty in application of the law, court handling of cases, and jury decisions to produce even more uncertainty. One result of these uncertainties is that the ability of firms "to engage in pre-accident, prospective risk management" is limited.

Other chapters, though focused on very different types of risks and decisions, likewise document a high level of concern with the threat of legal suit and with short-term risks. Heimer notes that documentation of procedures in neonatal intensive care units "is fundamentally about risk--the risk of being sued." Since "parents can sue hospitals and their staff members for performing inappropriate procedures, failing to perform appropriate procedures, or performing procedures ineptly," procedural matters tend to be thoroughly documented and carefully communicated, in contrast to information about diseases and their possible consequences.

Concern with the risk of being sued is not the only law-related reason that organizations tend to focus on risks that are immediate and observable, as opposed to those that are less observable and may have longer term consequences. Keith Hawkins reports that the English Factory Inspectors he studied were especially concerned that their decisions not reflect badly on their own competence or on "the agency's sense of credibility." For these inspectors decisions regarding observed occupational hazards--particularly those of a routine nature--were transformed into legal risks to the inspectors themselves. He also notes, however, that employers and employees, as well as inspectors, responded more readily to hazards that posed immediate risks than to those for which the risk was projected into an uncertain future. Again, the result was neglect of long-term health consequences associated with the work environment.

Historically, focus on safety in the workplace was motivated by concerns with the economic consequences of absenteeism and compensation for injuries sustained on the job. Job-related consequences to health were more difficult to identify and posed less immediate economic demands. In some sectors of the economy this clearly is changing, as Dorothy Nelkin's chapter demonstrates. Introduction and use of more and more chemicals in production processes has exposed increasing numbers of workers to toxic hazards. Union pressures, absenteeism, costly medical services, litigation and increasing regulatory pressures have combined to force many companies to seek remedies to these hazards. Most of these remedies, as Nelkin notes, have "centered on the individual" (changing worker behavior by means of training programs, rotation of workers in high-risk jobs, providing masks or special clothing, and excluding classes of workers from jobs involving hazardous exposure). Among the latter are various types of biological testing in order to identify "hypersusceptible" workers, such as pregnant workers. Nelkin's chapter is a far-reaching discussion of uncertainties in the scientific basis for biological testing and of problematic issues related to their use as a risk management tool.

Organizational v. Individual Concerns with Risk

While our primary focus is on organizational decision making, the risk concerns of individuals, individual rationality and decision making also recur as themes in several chapters. Concerns for the future assume special importance. Some of these are for the short-term, much as most corporate concerns appear to be. Some, however, are for futures projected into the long term, in anticipation of or as a result of latent injuries, for example; or with the futures of neonatal intensive care patients and their parents. In both of these instances, organizational and individual interests diverge considerably, as the chapters by Felsteiner and Siegelman, and by Heimer demonstrate.

Recent studies of Chapter 11 bankruptcies offer another contrast between organizational and individual interests and decision making. Both corporate and individual bankruptcies often result from entrepreneurial risks. Kevin Delaney focuses on large corporations who have used Chapter 11 reorganization to achieve organizational goals far beyond those envisioned by the framers of modern bankruptcy law (for example, to gain concessions from labor unions or to protect themselves from damage awards). In contrast, the individual entrepreneurs studied by Teresa Sullivan and her colleagues (1989) were small business people. For others--single women and middle-class wives who do not work were also overrepresented--entrepreneurial behavior had nothing to do with their financial problems. The vast majority of the single filers had tried desperately to avoid bankruptcy.

Commenting on these findings, Lisa McIntyre (1989) theorizes that individual bankruptcy is viewed as a violation of trust, while corporate bankruptcy is more likely to be viewed (by both debtors and creditors) as simply "good business." Personal credit and corporate economic behavior both signify far more than economic solvency, but guiding principles differ. Paying one's debts was a moral as well as a contractual responsibility for the bankrupt individuals studied. For Delaney's corporations bankruptcy was a strategy for complying with the law while achieving economic and other goals.

Concern for the Future and the Moral Dimensions of Risk Analysis

The moral dimensions of risk analysis are profound but not well understood. The morality of some risk-related decisions are tied to concerns for the future. Heimer observes that meetings called by hospital personnel for the purpose of conveying "bad news" to parents "don't work well . . . because what families have to say is not morally neutral." Nor, of course, are many risk assessment and risk management decisions. Yet they are often posed in just this way, as merely "good business," or as inevitable, given the lack of alternatives (see Jasper, Chapter 12). The decisions that Heimer's parents make regarding their infants' health and survival may have profound implications for their future lives. Survival of an infant may be achieved at the cost of great personal and financial sacrifice.

The issues are equally profound in the realm of public policy. An intellectual impasse between risk perceptions and decision making is created, Mary Douglas (1985) argues, when the technology of risk analysis and the theory of rational behavior are brought together in support of the machinery of administration that is necessary to modern society. Nowhere is this more evident than in the search for ways to dispose of nuclear and other toxic wastes. Here the future--for some risks the very long-term future--is very much at issue. A survey of Nevada residents concerning location of a high-level nuclear waste repository in that state found that concern for "serious risks to future generations" was "critical in determining one's willingness to support a local repository" (Kunreuther, et al., 1990:476). Anthropologist Willett Kempton reports that "a desire to preserve the environment for one's descendants" was "the strongest environmental value to emerge" from his ethnographic interviews of a diverse group of U. S. residents (Kempton, 1991:183, 196-98).

Not surprisingly, there are moral claims on both sides of such issues. Bernard Cohen, for example, expresses moral outrage at placing limits on the use of nuclear energy for power generation on the grounds that traditional uses of fossil fuels results in *"killing extra people"* (1985, p. 2; emphasis in original).

Institutionalization as Context

We cannot here address all of these issues, but they must remain on the agenda if the social and behavioral sciences are to participate meaningfully in the generation of knowledge concerning risk, and in related policy debates. Risk and risk analysis have been institutionalized as technical matters, and they are surely that. In technical terms the phenomena at issue have also been interpreted as being more predictable than in fact they often are, and as manageable on the basis of the criteria and methods of the physical and biological sciences and their applied counterparts. In practice, as the following chapters demonstrate repeatedly, undertakings that involve hazard are often quite unpredictable; and decisions regarding risks often are made with little regard for the technicalities of risk assessment. Instead, "rules of thumb," based on experience or on political and economic considerations, dominate much risky decision making. Insidiously, many of these considerations focus on short-term, more immediate problems than on longer-term, often more serious hazards.

This chapter and Part Two review the history and critique the theoretical perspectives that have dominated risk analysis. New perspectives that challenge the framing of risk in these terms are offered. These emerging perspectives, as yet neither fully developed nor institutionalized, have been forced on the old by theoretical and empirical weaknesses in earlier formulations. Skepticism and misunderstanding remain, but the need for greater knowledge of human--especially organizational and institutional--response to risk is clear.

More is at stake in these debates than the intellectual agenda of risk analysis. The fundamental issue is one of control of resources and their allocation, and of the means by which control is achieved. Institutional elites have great power to define problems and promote particular responses. Institutional power is magnified when decisions involve highly specialized knowledge to which few have access (see, especially, Heimer's analysis of parental and medical decision making in neonatal intensive care units, and Vaughan's case study of the Challenger space accident). Yet, as Jasper's (1990, and in this volume) examination of nuclear politics demonstrates, political and economic elites may override scientific/rational considerations in the determination of social policy.

Institutions and their constituent organizations routinize responses to problems and determine the nature of events and objects on which data are to be collected.   They see to the collection of data, and distribute data and/or information based on data.   Such information is heavily influenced by considerations of legal liability, political, economic, and other organizational interests, ideology, and even national pride. By framing public perceptions and political debate concerning hazards, risks, and uncertainties, institutionalized information determines in large measure what is considered real and possible.

Institutionalization is, above all, a process of rationalization. Increasingly, as the universe has become "disenchanted," to use Weber's felicitous phrasing (Weber, 1919), rationalization has emphasized rationality rather than--and often opposed to--tradition, religious or magical beliefs.   Mary Douglas' (1985) argument that contemporary society is dependent on administrative machinery based on the theoretical discipline of rational behavior makes the theory itself an important context for organizational decision making.   Clarke notes that the theory rests heavily on assumptions about individual preferences; for example, that each individual holds "a set of preferences which are clearly-defined, well-understood, and rank-ordered" in order that logical tradeoffs can be made among preferences.[2] A large body of research demonstrates that individual preferences often meet none of these requirements.   Instead, preferences are heavily influenced by the contexts within which choices are made, contexts such as the types and amounts of information that are available, the range of available options, predispositions based on experience, and whether a choice involves the prospect of gain or loss.

The importance of the rational choice paradigm for risk analysis owes much to a 1969 article by risk analysis pioneer, Chauncey Starr. Comparing funds spent on such high risk behavior as cigarette smoking with those spent on insuring the safety of nuclear power facilities (which he felt was easily demonstrated), Starr argued that public expenditures reflected "revealed

---

2. Economists George Stigler and Gary Becker (1990) argue "that tastes neither change capriciously nor differ importantly between people" (Stigler and Becker, 1990:191). Most economists and other social scientists, however, appear to agree with philosopher Robert Goodin's (1990) assessment that while this position pushes back the limits to rationality by "showing that some of the differences and changes in taste that we observe are amenable to analysis in ordinary economic ways . . . the formation and reformation of tastes still remains largely outside the rationality model" (Goodin, 1990:221).

preferences" regarding risks. This notion is an obvious oversimplification, both because it ignores the complexity of human behaviors (such as smoking) and because it assumes a higher degree of agreement on social policies than exists, particularly in controversial matters such as those involving risk and uncertainty. Nevertheless, Starr's article and reactions to it were early harbingers of what has become a major--perhaps *the* major--issue in risk analysis; that is, the role of the public in risk analysis. Starr also fueled perceptions in the risk analysis community that many public preferences were irrational, as in the example of fears associated with nuclear power.

The rationality of individual and organizational choice behavior remains a topic of great controversy, despite decades of research and theory (see Cook and Levi, 1990). Different rationalities result from different interests and contexts; and conflicts in risk assessment between rationalities (e.g., workers v. corporations, doctors v. hospitals v. patients, scientific v. legal, scientific/technological rationality v. the "social rationality" of ordinary citizens) often lead to risk management policies that satisfy no one.

Additionally, as James March (1991) observes, many organizational decisions are "not as central to an understanding of decision making (and vice versa) as might be expected." Instead, organizational decision making often becomes ritualistic and symbolic; recent organizational research emphasizes "concepts of decisions and decision making that emphasize overlapping networks of linkages within and among organizations rather than coherent hierarchies, temporal orders rather than causal orders, loose coupling rather than tight coupling between decisions and decision making, and the role of decisions and decision making in the development of meaning and interpretations" (March, 1991:108). These factors combine to compromise (and often to complement) the rationality of "an ecology of actors trying to act rationally with limited knowledge and preference coherence; trying to discover and execute proper behavior in ambiguous situations; and trying to discover, construct, and communicate interpretations of a confusing world" (March, 1990:111).

Concerning High Reliability Organizations and Systems

The temptation to conclude that contributors to this book are pessimistic about science, technology, social organization, and risk should be resisted. We are drawn to understanding system failures and human limitations by worry about danger and intellectual curiosity about things that go wrong. This is an intellectual choice, not a premise of the field. The hope is that careful study will result in improvement--that margins of error will be reduced and safety increased, and that greater fairness will be achieved.

Hope is nourished by documentation of "high reliability organizations and systems" (HROs; see LaPorte, 1991; Tamuz, 1988; Pfeiffer, 1989)--and by the hope of "Learning from Samples of One or Fewer" (that is, learning from experience, tradition, and rare historical events; see March and Tamuz, 1991). Among the HROs that have been studied are air transportation information safety systems, a major electrical distribution system, and aircraft carrier operations.

For present purposes, we focus on organizations in air traffic control, as reported by Michal Tamuz.   These systems successfully operate multiple information gathering and risk assessment systems.   The success of these systems does not depend on high motivation, altruistic employers, or human perfection.   The systems thrive on, rather than attempting to avoid, human limitations such as bounded rationality, cognitive and self-interested biases, and other organizational limitations.

Aviation safety information systems collect reports of potentially dangerous incidents from pilots and air-traffic controllers which are then analyzed by decision makers.   The major problem for safety regulators is that information about potential causes of aircraft accidents is sparse.   To increase effectiveness, and to gather high quality information about possible accidents, aviation safety systems collect data on *near* accidents and situations that under slightly different circumstances could have resulted in accidents. The systems are voluntary; pilots' identities are kept confidential. Institutional mechanisms have evolved that over-ride barriers to relaying bad news. One system offers limited immunity for air traffic violations, so it is in pilots' self and professional interests to report potentially hazardous mishaps. Because definitions of incidents or near accidents are ambiguous, pilots enjoy considerable interpretive latitude when identifying a near accident (other systems define near accidents more narrowly).

When an accident occurs, multiple reporting systems kick into high gear. Pilots increase the frequency with which they report near accidents. Safety analysts search their data bases for near accidents that might be similar. Two consequences follow: (1) safety inspectors analyze the accident within the framework of previous similar events. Thus conceptually equipped, inspectors have a better understanding of the accident at hand; they also have more opportunity to identify system failures that may have previously been overlooked. (2) Because the overall system opens itself to a wide range of possible accidents rather than relying only on what has actually happened, institutional learning about plausible accident scenarios is enhanced. Rather than focusing narrowly on problems with a particular accident, risk managers respond to the increased attention created by the accident by rectifying more generic problems that might otherwise go unnoticed in the uproar surrounding an accident.

HROs, it bears pointing out, are structured very differently than the NASA safety system that Vaughan analyzes (Chapter 13 and 1990), or the regulatory systems studied in other chapters. It is far from clear as to how the lessons from studies of HROs might be applied to other, less intense, safety systems, or to such high-hazard tasks as nuclear plant operation, or toxic waste disposal and clean-up. Study of HROs also pose challenges for organization theory and research (LaPorte, 1991).

Conclusion

"People problems" increasingly dominate risk analysis and risk-related decision making. The social and behavioral sciences have been slow to respond, though much pioneering work has been done, as evidenced by the empirical and theoretical work cited and reported in these chapters.

The professional concerns of risk analysts focus more and more on people problems and on the work of social and behavioral scientists. Most of this research has focused on individuals--their perceptions, fears, and other concerns, and on ways to communicate more effectively with them. The thesis of this book is that greater attention must be focused on organizations and on institutional analysis.

There are other reasons to urge more, and more rigorous, attention to risk by the social and behavioral sciences. Technical risk analyses pose profound challenges. The state of knowledge concerning risks from indoor air, water, and food chain exposure to a dozen classes of pollutants, for example, suggests that background cancer risk resulting "from widespread global pollution from a multitude of widely dispersed sources . . . cannot be reduced significantly by controlling emissions associated with production and use. . . . *If we do not want to change our style of living*, the only way to reduce global chemical pollution is to make production and consumption processes more efficient, thereby lowering the necessary levels of production of these toxic chemicals. Thus, the only reasonable solution to global pollution . . . (lies in) . . . decreased production, achieved through improved process design, waste reduction, and material recycling" (Travis and Hester, 1990:465; emphasis added).

We know that life styles are difficult, but not impossible to change. Making production and consumption processes more efficient will require more than recycling and other conservation measures by individuals. Institutional and organizational decisions will determine in large measure the objects of attention and the terms of debate over such issues. Though scientific data are inadequate, and debate among scientists is intense, margins of error for some risks such as global warming, the green house effect, and ecological scarcity appear to be narrowing (see Catton, 1980; 1989). The questions thus posed are profound at many levels--for all the sciences and learned disciplines, all institutions, and for the type of world in which all must live.

Whatever answers are discovered or constructed to these types of questions, it is certain that institutional elites and organizations will play the most critical roles in their formulation and investigation, and in their interpretation and resolution. We need to know a great deal more about "how institutions think," in the words of Mary Douglas, because individuals "have no other way to make the big decisions except within the scope of institutions they build" (1986:128).

PART TWO

Decision Making Contexts and Networks of Risk

2

Context Dependency and Risk Decision Making

Lee Clarke

Sociological voices now shape intellectual discussions about risky decisions, but in many ways the sociology of risk and decisions is a reaction to scholarship in psychology and economics. Psychology has been especially important in drawing attention to technological risks, while economics has long provided general theories of decision making under conditions of risk and uncertainty. My goal here is mainly critical and programmatic: to evaluate economic and psychological theories of choice and to suggest some elements of a sociological replacement. I briefly outline economic decision theory, then analytically review psychology's critique of economics. I then use psychology's main finding--that actual choice behavior is notoriously unstable--as the basis of a sociological critique of psychology. Finally, I propose some issues for institutional theories of risky decision making. Both my critique and program are centered on the importance of contexts for giving choices meaning. Indeed my central argument is that we need institutional theories of context regarding risky decisions.

Economics' Rational Chooser

Economic decision theory, premised on the primacy of individual choice, is the premier explanation for decision making, even as it strains under a steady

---

For helpful critiques, thanks to Patricia Roos and James F. Short, Jr.. Some of the ideas in this paper were developed when I was a visiting scholar at the Russell Sage Foundation.

barrage of criticism. The core of microeconomics is a theory of rational choice. The most forceful critiques of economics have come from psychology, experimental economics, and sociology, although these fields remain indebted to traditional economic analysis. For whatever its faults, economic decision theory is unusually clear about its assumptions, implications, and predictions. This clarity no doubt contributes to the theory's resilience, despite the mounting evidence against it. Another reason for the staying power of rational choice is its normative vision of how individuals *should* make choices and how society *should* be organized--a vision in accordance with dominant ideologies in the U.S.[1] Critiques of the politics of economics have been advanced by others (e.g., Hirschman, 1982; Perrow, 1986; Block, 1990). Here my primary concern is with conceptual deficiencies in economic decision theory in accounting for how people make choices regarding risk.

"Preferences" and "rationality" are the central concepts for rational choice theory. The theory requires that decision makers hold a set of preferences which are clearly-defined, well-understood, and rank-ordered so that people can make logical tradeoffs among them. Preference sets serve as menus of alternatives on which information is gathered and evaluated. Once the preference set is constructed, agents maximize utilities (or profits). The collective consequence of the multitude of self-interested decisions is Pareto optimality (i.e., where no one can be made better off without hurting someone else), or efficiency for the economic system. Rationality characterizes a decision making process that maximizes an actor's utilities.

Problems With "Preferences" and "Rationality"

Assuming rationality (and utility maximization) and asserting preferences makes a black box out of how decisions are actually made. Cognitive psychology initially demonstrated the importance of peering into the box; indeed much of that work was designed to rectify the excesses of economics.[2] In particular, psychology has subjected the notions of preferences and rationality to empirical scrutiny and found economic decision theory seriously deficient.

---

1. Particularly the prescription that society be organized around the pricing systems of competitive markets (Davis and Kamien, 1970).

2. I would be remiss not to mention that criticizing economic logic has a long, venerable history. Space limitations and substantive focus prevent a treatment of those criticisms. Important works include: March and Simon (1958), Ellsberg (1961), Gorman (1967), Morgenstern (1972), Moe (1979; 1984), Elster (1979), Hadari (1987), and especially Hirschman (1977; 1982).

Preferences

That decision makers have stable and ordered sets of preferences is central to rational choice. Although economics holds that preferences are exogenously given (and therefore presumably socially constructed), they are nevertheless relatively immune to situational circumstances. Research contradicting this tenet is important because to the extent that uncertainty and ambiguity regarding preferences is normal, rather than deviant, the image of choosers ordering values and rationally maximizing utilities obscures and mystifies decision making.[3]

Recent work in psychology, risk, and experimental economics has demonstrated that preferences can change, or even *reverse*, depending on a problem's frame of reference (Lichtenstein and Slovic, 1971; Grether and Plott, 1979; Thaler, 1980; Slovic and Lichtenstein, 1983; Kahneman, et al., 1982; see also Whyte, 1989). Plott and Levine (1978) show that preferences, values, and decisions can shift in a systematic manner with how committee agendas are structured. Tversky and Kahneman (1981:453) demonstrate that when faced with a set of logically identical choices, decision makers will nevertheless evince different preferences depending on how the alternatives are structured. For example, consider the following problem (from Tversky and Kahneman, 1981): An outbreak of an unusual disease will probably claim 600 lives, and two programs have been proposed in response.

A) If this program is adopted 200 will be saved.
B) If this program is adopted there is 1/3 chance that 600 will be saved, and 2/3 chance that none will be saved.

Of 152 experiment subjects (college students), 28% chose program B, while 72% chose program A, the *risk aversive* alternative (Tversky and Kahneman, 1981:453). Another group of subjects was presented the same problem, but new programs.

C) If this program is adopted 400 will die.
D) If this program is adopted there is 1/3 chance no one will die, and 2/3 chance that 600 will die.

---

3. All theories are unrealistic to some degree. At issue here is not the simple charge that economics over-simplifies, but that it does so in an unproductive way. There is a point on the real-unreal continuum where one must conclude a theory is not only unreal but wrong.

In this trial (N=155), 22% chose program C while 78% chose program D, the *risk taking* alternative. Yet, the two decision problems are obviously equivalent in terms of their probabilities of preserving life. Research such as this, which has an enormous replication record, essentially makes preferences a function of the situation in that a fairly simple rewording of alternatives imparts an entirely different meaning to the choices. These findings directly contradict economic theory.

Or consider the problem of preferences concerning seat belt use. Nearly 50,000 people die each year on U.S. roadways, and despite the effectiveness of seat belts only about 10 to 20% (net of legislation) of automobile passengers wear them (Kunreuther, et al., 1985; Schmidt, 1985; see also Svenson, 1981). Yet Slovic and colleagues (1982:91) found that experiment subjects were more likely to express a preference for using seat belts once they knew that the lifetime risk of dying in an auto accident is .01 (assuming 50 years of driving), and .33 of injury if seat belts were not used. Again preferences change with context, in this instance the context of information on the risks of driving without seat belts.

Another way decisions are context dependent concerns the role of information. Although economic theory need not assume full information, it does assume actors are reasonably unconstrained by biased information regarding alternatives; rather, a classical free market governs the flow of information. Yet summarizing the experimental literature on information processing, Slovic, et al. (1982:85) note that "new evidence appears reliable and informative if it is consistent with one's initial beliefs; contrary evidence tends to be dismissed as unreliable, erroneous, or unrepresentative." In other words, information becomes data for decisions when it confirms or appears consistent with positions already held.

In fact, preferences are not stable, bedrock entities but unsteady variables whose meaning is transformed in different situations (Elster, 1979:116); they may even follow rather than precede behavior.[4] In other words, preferences shift and change with a variety of extra-individual influences (Gorman, 1967). To the

---

4.   One implication of the idea that preferences are context-dependent is suggested by a branch of cognitive reasoning usually neglected in critiques of economics. Karl Weick (1979) argues that action frequently precedes preference formation. Since we cannot assume that what people do accurately reflects their preferences (Bem, 1967; Fazio and Zanna, 1981), and we cannot assume that what people say they think is an accurate reflection of what they actually do (Schuman and Johnson, 1976; McMahon, 1984), it may be that preferences are largely beside the point in decision making. From this view, preferences are little more than devices that tell people what they have done rather than what they desire.

extent that decision frames, rather than individual tastes, are responsible for preference formation, the generality of economic theories of decision making is called into question. There may, in fact, be as many preference orderings as there are decision-frames. If that were true, we would need a theory of preferences for every individual in each decision making context, robbing economic theory of explanatory power. Indeed, as Friedman and Hechter (1988:214)--themselves rational choice theorists--point out:

> Until the time that significant progress is made toward an understanding of preferences, the scope or power of rational choice analyses is clearly limited. Since preferences are given rather than explained in rational choice analyses, these analyses are far better suited for social phenomena that are the outgrowth of individual preferences that are strong (relative to competing), stable (over time), and uniform (across actors).

Friedman and Hechter's diagnosis suggests there *are* conditions under which economic decision theory is helpful in explaining how choices are made: in situations of low ambiguity, familiar situations in which individuals can easily understand the future consequences of their choices (March, 1978:580). But under unfamiliar conditions, such as those associated with nuclear power (Erikson, 1990), genetic damage, and toxic chemical contamination (Edelstein, 1988), preferences are more flexible, more likely to shift as frames of references shift (Slovic, et al., 1985:249). Perhaps economic decision theory is least useful in situations involving choices regarding important risks.

Rationality

The other concept central to economic models of decision making is rationality,[5] which is reasonably well defined: decision makers are rational if they systematically evaluate information that is relevant to utility maximization, and then maximize. As March and Shapira (1987:1402) describe them, "rational models see decisions as being made by the evaluation of alternatives in terms of their future consequences for prior preferences." Diverging from this portrayal is, therefore, irrational.

Rational choice assumes a constant environment and choosers' understanding the environments in which they are situated (Simon, 1955). Irrelevant information and preconceived biases regarding information are regarded as insignificant influences on choice processes. The theory requires that decision makers systematically gather and/or process information (for example, on some

---

5. For searching critiques see Moe (1979) and Elster (1979).

technology or activity) while ignoring or discounting issues based on incomplete or irrelevant information or preconceived ideas.

As with preferences, there are severe limits on how well this conception of rationality captures processes of choice. For example, people living in flood prone areas have been reluctant to purchase even highly subsidized flood insurance, doing so only after the government "required coverage as a condition for subsidized disaster relief and Federally funded mortgages" (Kunreuther, et al. ,1985:2). Similarly, studies of denizens of the Los Angeles area show a remarkably low level of preparedness for earthquakes (Turner, et al., 1986).

Much evidence demonstrates that people do not typically gather large amounts of information even on risks they regard as important and immediately threatening (Soelberg, 1967; Quinn, 1978; Maher, 1986; Hickson, 1987). Rather than being inveterate data collectors, most people are fairly passive receivers of information. Moreover, people do not systematically evaluate the information that does come their way; nor do they organize information in such a way that allows them to discern between that which is objectively relevant to a risk and that which is not. Instead, decision makers depend on cognitive heuristics to order information regarding risks (Kahneman, et al., 1982). There is now a relatively large catalogue of such heuristics. For illustrative purposes, I am mainly concerned here with the *availability heuristic* (for an extended treatment see Heimer, 1988).

The availability heuristic was one of the first Tversky and Kahneman (1974) identified. It has been frequently rediscovered, cited, and put to a great deal of use and misuse. Essentially, the availability heuristic is used when people estimate frequency or probability by ease of recall. For example, if I witness a murder in the subway I might be led to overestimate the dangers of subway riding. Or, if some errant government official is discovered and exposed as an agent of illegality, I might be led to think that immorality or illegality is a modal characteristic of politicians.

The availability heuristic turns out to be quite useful in managing information because frequent events are typically easier to remember than infrequent ones (Slovic, et al., 1979). But because recall can be influenced by phenomena not directly associated with frequency or probability of hazard, the availability heuristic can lead to inaccurate perceptions, and hence irrational decision making processes. For example, using the availability heuristic to interpret information on murders and dissembling politicians distorts evaluation processes to the extent that base rates or the frequency of these phenomena are not taken into account.

If recall is fundamentally shaped by heuristics such as availability, the logical question becomes what, in turn, shapes availability? What is the mix of heuristics and rationality that determines decision making, and what determines that mix? Understanding the mechanisms that make information available is clearly vital to decision making theory (Slovic, et al., 1985).

The mechanisms that most affect availability are the media. We know from previous work that there is a low correlation between the types of death-causes most frequently reported in newspapers and their real frequency (Combs and Slovic, 1979). We also know that, apparently because of the media, people underestimate threats from chronic, prosaic risks such as those posed by lawn mowers and botulism compared to sudden, dramatic ones such as those posed by airlines crashes and nuclear power accidents (Slovic, et al., 1979; see also Mazur, 1985; Covello, 1986; Singer and Endreny, 1987; Nelkin, 1987). It appears, then, that people do not evaluate large numbers of alternatives on the basis of valid and reliable information, at least partly because a major source of information on risks is biased (see also Lindblom, 1958; Simon, 1955:110).

In short, economics ultimately fails to explain how decisions are made regarding risk because preferences and rationality are context dependent rather than global attributes of the human condition.

Critique of the Critique

The work reviewed above contributes greatly to modifying rational decision theory, questioning its basic assumptions and amassing disconfirming evidence. The core of the critique from psychology is that we ought to be researching how people actually think and behave (Kunreuther, 1986), rather than wondering why people do not conform to a normative theory. Yet, there are a number of problems with the psychological critique.

First, there is a striking irrelevance to reality in much of the work, especially the experimental work, as Perrow has argued (1984:Ch. 9). Part of the trouble is what we might call the "improbable problem" problem, by asking people, for example, whether "absinthe is...a precious gem or liqueur" (Lichtenstein and Fischhoff, 1977:160), or the frequency with which words begin with, or have as their third letter, the letter R (Tversky and Kahneman, 1982:167). By using improbable problems in its research, psychology recommits economics' sin of being unproductively unrealistic.

Second, and more important, is the questionable correspondence between choices in experiments and choices in *institutional* settings. As Henrion and Fischhoff (1986:791) note:

> The premise of laboratory studies of human judgment is that all judgments are governed by a set of core cognitive processes. If those can be understood in experimental settings, then reasonable speculations can be made about human performance in the real world.

Although this may be true, it seems unwise, and quite possibly wrong, to assume that "core cognitive processes" are immune to the constraining forces that social structures exert on behavior. I lack the space for an extended treatment, but it should be noted that a recent collection of essays on rational choice (Cook and Levi, 1990) contains a number papers that recognize the larger problem here (neglecting institutional context) and suggest a variety of responses that, it is claimed, might save the theory of rational choice while according institutional context its due (see especially Plott, Taylor, and Stinchcombe, all in Cook and Levi, 1990).

Third, it is now commonplace for researchers in this area to acknowledge that people are "boundedly rational"; that is, limited in cognitive ability. This is a welcome practice, as it draws attention to the situational dependency of behavior and cognition, allowing us to understand behavior that would otherwise appear irrational (at least from the view of economic decision theory). Yet there remains a lingering bias in the direction of behavioral and perceptual consistency, attenuating psychology's contribution to explaining risky decision making.[6]

Consider Thaler's (1980; 1983) use of the availability heuristic and his more general musings on distortions of judgment concerning risks. Thaler considers it a judgmental error when people prefer, for example, reducing the risk of a nuclear meltdown from .001 to 0 over reducing it from .004 to .003. Although quantitatively there is no difference between these two reductions, this preference is not a "cognitive illusion," as Thaler calls it, but a recognition that the two choices do not represent equivalent amounts of risk reduction. Goldman (1987:623), reporting a Department of Energy study, estimates an additional 28,000 worldwide cancer fatalities from the Chernobyl disaster. There is a vast *qualitative* difference between reducing to zero the probability of 28,000 deaths and reducing it from 4/1000 to 3/1000. More generally, the conclusion that popular distrust of nuclear power is a cognitive illusion itself involves several illusions. It neglects the frequency and probability of expert errors (Freudenburg, 1988). It neglects the history of secrecy and propaganda from those in the nuclear industry. It neglects the biases of organizational leaders, the institutionally shaped information they disseminate about nuclear risks, and their unfailing conviction--which has never been based on hard data--that nuclear power can be cheap, lessen dependence on foreign oil, and so on (Clarke, 1985, 1988a). Were researchers to consider *these* illusions the phenomena of interest, a different research agenda and arsenal of theoretical concepts might result.

Heuristics such as the availability heuristic should be placed in a broader frame of reference (Heimer, 1988). The multitude of studies documenting, refining, renaming, and cataloguing this heuristic leads researchers to focus on

---

6. Oddly, when situational complexities reveal organizational elites to deviate from the rational model the tendency is to invoke bounded rationality; when the general public so deviates the rhetoric is more likely to invoke irrationality.

how experiment or survey subjects get things wrong. When it comes to real world problems, the media constitute the chief culprit in distorting people's decision making processes. It is now a popular sport to bash the media, accusing them of sensationalism, out of context quotations, a focus on probabilistically trivial threats, and so forth. All of these charges have some merit. But when considering the larger context of political debates concerning risks, these faults are probably trivial. More importantly:

- The media are insufficiently attentive to the biases of experts and officials.
- When systems fail, the media are as quick to blame operator error as are engineers, ergonomic specialists, and those who have an institutional stake in system maintenance.
- The media depend heavily on public statements from government and corporate officials for their information concerning risks (see Shapiro, this volume).

Critiques of rationality, biased information regarding risks, and individually oriented studies overly concerned with emotional publics and sensational media, neglect larger issues involving the structural connections between those who are most influential in risky decisions and those who actually bear the risks. The critique of economics has been insufficiently attentive to its principle finding: while building a convincing case against the economic mainstream, the attackers have failed to elucidate a theory of context. Thus, the critique finds itself in the unproductive position of either (1) modifying received economic theory or (2) recommitting the sin of searching for stable and given characteristics of human character (specifically of cognitive functioning).[7] I argue that modifying error should not be confused with, or substituted for, correcting error, and that the search for fixed human characteristics neglects the situationally dependent nature of behavior.

Some Elements of a Theory of Context

If the behavioral critique has failed to provide a theory of context, what should such a theory look like? I have no definitive answer to this question, but I think the following six issues and questions will move us far down the road to one. (Carol Heimer [1988] has adequately dealt with the issue of the sociological relevance of heuristics, including the key question: if risk perception, and presumably decision making, depends on the decision frame, what leads people to adopt one frame rather than another? She concludes that

---

7. On this point see Miller (1956).

social location, production pressures, rhetorical manipulations, and symbolism provide the keys to a reasonable answer to this question.)

First, preferences are not independently formed by atomized individuals but shaped by social networks. A number of researchers have demonstrated that high-level decision makers systematically violate prescriptions of rational choice (e.g., Rasmussen, 1987). Mintzberg (1973:118), for example, shows that top level executives prefer "face-to-face interaction and even hearsay and gossip to analysis of factual reports." Networks of meaning and association are important even at an individual level of analysis. Kunreuther, et al.'s (1985:3) studies of flood insurance, noted above, show that people depend on "personal contacts" for their information on flood hazards. As Hadari (1987:347) argues, scholars should "...retrieve the webs of significance within which individual preferences are formed and transformed."

Second, we need answers to the question "What are the decision making processes of those who make important choices regarding technological risks?" The phrase "important choices" in my question is deliberate. Elsewhere, I have criticized psychology for failing to account for key organizational forces that impinge on decision making (Clarke, 1988a). Neglected in the field of risk are the decision processes of those who run powerful organizations. By "important," I mean those choices having the greatest consequence for allocating resources toward and away from risks. Obviously, my assumption is that organizations are the arenas within which the most consequential decisions are constructed. Focusing on non-organizational, individual decision makers leads researchers to miss those who:

- Sit atop hierarchies that allocate resources toward and away from risks and technologies.
- Frequently set the terms of debate regarding risk acceptability.
- Make social choices regarding risk that have implications well beyond their immediate environs.

The latter point extends beyond organizational decision making. Larger institutional arrangements influence both individual and organizational decisions. As Cole and Withey (1981:146) pointed out a decade ago, "one might legitimately question what it means at the individual level to ask about one's willingness to pay for auto transportation or electrical energy...in a society that is structured around the availability and frequent use of both." Thus, the technological base, and institutions related to it, set parameters within which decisions are framed and limits the discretion of decision makers.

Third, theories of context will benefit from attending to what McCloskey (1985:Ch. 7) has called, "the problem of audience." Decisions are, among other things, dramaturgical and rhetorical accomplishments, and all dramas and rhetorics are directed toward particular audiences. Ann Langley (1989) demonstrates the importance of audience in a study of how organizations use formal analyses. She notes:

> formal analysis studies are carried out within specific social contexts involving different people linked together in hierarchical relationships: some people request analysis, some do it, and some receive it. [Further,] the purposes of analysis and the political dynamics surrounding it depend on who does what for whom, and...it appears that the types of uses of formal analysis favored by an organization may depend on that organization's structural configuration (Langley, 1989:626).

More generally, decision making is a social, relational phenomenon. Explaining choice as the result of properties of individuals, or even of decision "events" is ultimately futile. Explicitly theorizing the audiences for decisions will highlight the role of interaction in decision making processes.

Fourth, ideologies are important in accounting for the contexts of decisions, even though arguments about ideology often neglect structural explanations. Fischhoff (1975:72) speculates that "...when we learn about an outcome, we immediately make sense of it by integrating it into what we already know." Ford (1982a,b), Hertsgaard (1983), and Jasper (1990), among others, have demonstrated the near-overwhelming role that pro-nuclear ideology played in the development of atomic energy in the United States. Each of these authors, along with a great many others, shows how important the ideas and worldviews of elites are in explaining how technological choices are made (Jasper, this volume). Especially interesting in this regard is the *degree of openness* of an industry or organization (Clarke, 1988b). That is, the degree of insulation from outside scrutiny covaries with ideological homogeneity among decision makers. Thus we are likely to find that the greater the degree of structural isolation among elites, the more narrow will be their consideration of alternatives.

Fifth, we need to distinguish between private and public decisions: some decision makers make choices that affect primarily their own milieu, while others (primarily because of their locations in positions of organizational authority) make choices that strongly affect the life chances of others. Externalities are crucial, and it is the *organizational position* of those who make choices regarding externalities--not their personal characteristics--that is the key to understanding their decisions (Vaughan, this volume and 1990). Moreover, some decision makers have a strong, institutional incentive (as distinguished from personal preference) to thwart the dissemination of valid information regarding risks. Such incentives are completely missed by both neo-classical economics and cognitive psychology. As Fischer and Merton (1975:83) point out:

The fundamental point is this: the incentive structure punishes any entity which discloses its bads. If a manager of a public or private enterprise called in the resources of an advertising firm to detail a new malefit, the manager might soon be out of work.

Sixth, we need work on institutional illusions. "Organization theory," writes Mary Douglas in a book that both devastatingly attacks and benevolently extends psychological theory on risk perceptions, "is poor in explanations of institutional blindness" (Douglas, 1985:85). Organizations systematically ignore, or are ignorant of, certain types of risks, and systematically attentive to others. We need to know the conditions under which organizations are, as Feldman and March (1981) have bluntly put it, "systematically stupid" (cf. Starbuck and Milliken, 1988).

I shall end with the following diagnosis and prognosis. One of the major difficulties with nearly all theories of decision making--whether from psychology, economics, or sociology--and whatever their substantive interest, involves the attempt to create a general theory of choice. Although social science claims as one of its central goals the development of general laws, given the present state of knowledge, progress toward adequate understanding of decision making is more likely via local, substance-specific studies. The substantive chapters in this book are illustrative of this point in a variety of ways. With accumulated research, we can legitimately hope to draw more general conclusions about decision making processes. These conclusions are likely to focus explanations on various contexts of decision making. The mainstay of those explanations will lie in structural factors, with significant contributions from scholarship on culture and ideology as well.

3

The Social Construction of Risk Objects: Or, How to Pry Open Networks of Risk

Stephen Hilgartner

Why do different individuals perceive the risks of the same technology differently? Why do different social groups develop conflicting definitions of the same technological risks? Such questions stand at the center of much social research on risk. But the predominant questions are poorly framed, in light of recent work in the history and sociology of technology. The emphasis on people's *responses* to hazards holds within it an unduly static view of technology. Treating perceptions and definitions of risk as the dependent variable, the typical approach in psychological and social research,[1] leads to a one-way analysis that neglects the dynamics of technological change. Perceptions of risk are not things that get tacked onto technology at the end of the day. Definitions of risk get *built into* technology and shape its evolution.

I would like to thank Ned Woodhouse for his critique of an earlier draft.

1. For psychologists, risk perception is the dependent variable, something to be explained by looking at the nature of the hazard and at social-psychological factors. Although sociologists and anthropologists make groups, rather than individuals, the units of analysis, their explanations often have a similar structure. The way a social group defines risk is a dependent variable to be explained in terms of the nature of the hazard and some mix of institutional factors, interests, organizational structures, and so on. For a review of the social science literature on risk, see Douglas (1985). See Misa and ElBaz (1991) for a recent bibliography.

To succeed in explaining how risk gets embedded in the social fabric (Short, 1984), the sociology of risk needs to be rooted in a much more dynamic framework.

Developing such a framework requires addressing two deficiencies in the social science literature on risk. First, social scientists have made little effort to examine the conceptual structure of social definitions of risk. Few analysts have paid close attention to the conceptual objects that appear in these definitions, the linkages among these objects, or the process through which these objects are constructed. Second, in general, risk analysts have employed an antiquated, artifact-centered view of technology. This view--which conceives of technology primarily in terms of machines, hardware, materials, industrial facilities--has been abandoned by most sociologists and historians who study technological change. Nevertheless, this view of technology remains entrenched, at least implicitly, in the risk literature.

This paper addresses these deficiencies and outlines a dynamic framework for the sociology of risk. Drawing on insights from the "new" sociology of science and technology (Star, 1988), I develop a system/network perspective on risk. This framework is thoroughly constructivist, and should be seen as an effort to extend the work of those who are analyzing risk as a social construct.[2] I begin by discussing the problem of studying the conceptual structure of risk definitions, and then describe an alternative to the artifact-centered view of technology. Next, I discuss the construction and control of entities that are deemed to pose risks, and sketch out how the sociology of risk can address the dynamics of technology. I use as an example the familiar technological system of automobile-based transportation. Because readers have direct experience with this system, the paper can tightly focus on conceptual issues, rather than on the workings and history of an esoteric technology.

Conceptual Networks

Definitions of particular risks include at least three conceptual elements: an *object* deemed to "pose" the risk, a putative *harm*, and a *linkage* alleging some form of causation between the object and the harm. I will refer to objects (whether things, activities, or situations) that are deemed to be sources of danger as "risk objects." Thus, to take a simple example, in the phrase "the risks of

---

2. Researchers who view risk as a social construct are pursuing many diverse approaches, as can be seen by examining the work of Bradbury (1990), Clarke (1989), Douglas and Wildavsky (1981), Gamson and Modigliani (1988), Nelkin (1985), Rayner (1987), and Stallings (1990).

driving," the risk object is "driving."[3] Risk objects are the things that pose hazards, the sources of danger, the entities to which harmful consequences are conceptually attached.

Most research on risk has treated risk objects as relatively unproblematic, and little effort has been directed at examining the social construction of risk objects. For engineers and natural scientists who take a technical approach to risk, risk objects--like the hazards they pose--are simply objective features of reality. When psychologists conduct psychometric studies of people's subjective responses to hazards, they also treat risk objects as objective pieces of the world (Bradbury, 1990). A study that asks people to estimate the risks posed by, say, driving a car, traveling in commercial aircraft, and riding hang gliders implicitly treats these activities as well-defined entities that can simply be taken for granted. People's responses to the objects, not the objects themselves, are what such research sees as problematic.

For sociologists and anthropologists who view risk as a social construct, matters are not so simple; it is dangerous to take anything for granted when one is trying to analyze the social construction of reality. (See the discussion of pattern construction in Stallings (1990).) Nevertheless, studies of the social definition of risk have paid insufficient attention to the social construction of risk objects. Similarly, studies also have failed to examine systematically the construction of networks of causal attribution that link chains of risk objects to harm. In other words, the conceptual structure of risk definitions--and the social construction of these structures--has been largely ignored.

Neglecting the social construction of risk objects restricts the power of social science approaches to risk analysis. To assume that objects are simply waiting in the world to be perceived or defined as risky is fundamentally unsociological. Even less can one assume that linkages among objects simply exist "out there" in reality. Nor should we assume, even implicitly, that definitions of objects or the linkages among them are invariant, either historically or across social groups. Finally, we cannot assume that the process of linking an object to a putative harm is independent of the process that defines the object as an *object*. Abandoning these assumptions--and applying constructivist analysis to the structure of risk definitions--opens up a line of research that can advance the sociology of risk.

---

3. As we will see below, risk objects are more typically linked into complex networks; moreover, they can be nested within one another. These linkages can be studied through the examination of texts.

Ambiguous Objects, Ambiguous Linkages

For analytic purposes, the construction of risk objects can be divided into two levels. The first level entails constructing the objects themselves, since an object cannot very well be defined as risky unless it is also defined as an *object*.[4] As constructivists, symbolic interactionists, and others have shown, the world does not present itself prepackaged into unambiguous and clearly-differentiated objects. On the contrary, the division of the world into objects is a conceptual achievement. The world can be parsed in many different ways, and category systems used to classify objects are fundamentally ambiguous (Barnes, 1983).

The second level of the social construction of risk objects consists of defining objects as *risky* by constructing linkages between objects and putative harm.[5] These linkages are always problematic because a risk can always be attributed to multiple objects. One can always construct many potential branches to the chains of causation that lead to disaster. Moreover, the length of each branch can in principle be extended indefinitely; there is no unambiguous endpoint. Thus, the risk of motor vehicle accidents can be attributed to unsafe drivers, unsafe roads, or unsafe cars (Irwin, 1985; Gusfield, 1981). The risks posed by unsafe drivers, in turn, can be attributed to inexperience, irresponsibility, fatigue, or alcohol consumption. Inexperience, in turn, can be attributed to inadequate driver education programs, which can be attributed to shortages of funds. The networks of objects deemed to pose risks can abruptly terminate, can wind their way back to common causes, or can diverge. The set of possibilities, in principle, is infinite.

Of course, people do not construct endless chains of causal attribution when they think and act about the sources of risks.[6] No individual or group can make sense of the world using the notion of causation set out in the nursery rhyme "for want of a nail . . . a kingdom was lost." The issue, then, if we want to understand people's sensemaking about risk, is to understand the networks of risk objects and causal linkages that people *do* construct.

---

4. Indeed, defining an object as an object is logically (although not necessarily temporally) prior to defining it as dangerous.

5. A third level, which for reasons of space will not be discussed here, is the process of defining harm.

6. One important research topic for understanding the social construction of risk is the investigation of what one might call "chain terminating objects"--entities (such as "human error," or "acts of God," or "bad luck") that are considered to be final causes that are not worth investigating further, and that thus serve as endpoints in networks of causation.

Moreover, we need to understand the process through which these networks get constructed, not least because the construction of risk objects has important political implications. Gusfield (1981) has shown how the "killer drunk" was singled out as *the* cause of traffic fatalities that involve alcohol. As he argued, this way of framing the problem allows car makers and the alcoholic beverage industry to "disown" the problem, shifting causal, moral and political responsibility for traffic deaths onto other actors. Directing attention at the individual drunk driver as the risk object deflects attention from alternative risk objects--such as unsafe cars, or land use and transportation policies that permit bars to be sited in locations accessible only by automobile.[7]

In sum, understanding risk requires that the conceptual networks that make up risk definitions be pried open, and the construction of risk objects be explored. These tasks are necessary to improve our understanding of how risks get embedded in technology as technologies evolve.

Sociotechnical Networks

The risk objects that social scientists have selected for study reflect the artifact-centered view of technology, with the literature tending to emphasize such objects as toxic chemicals, nuclear reactors, genetically engineered microorganisms, aircraft, and so on. Moreover, risk analysis tends to treat these artifacts as static entities, stable "things" that individuals perceive or social groups define as more or less risky. This approach to technology, thus, contributes to the tendency to treat risk definitions in a *post hoc* manner.

A variety of recent work in the history and sociology of technology has developed ways of conceptualizing technology that are richer and more powerful than the artifact-centered view. The perspective of the sociology of scientific knowledge has been brought to bear on technology (Pinch and Bijker, 1984), and increasingly, researchers are conceiving of technology not as isolated artifacts or machines, but as intricate systems that weave together the technical and the social. These systems connect diverse collections of components--including hardware, organizations, management procedures, personnel, laws and regulations, research programs, and so on--into functioning technological networks. Things once classified as "technical," "economic," "social," "political," and "legal" are now often seen as being part of a fabric. Technology is a "seamless web" (Hughes, 1986).

---

7. Given the stakes--for organizations seeking to "disown" or "own" risks, for inter-professional competition for turf (Abbott, 1988), for policy, and for the careers of organizations and individuals--it is not surprising that intense conflict often surrounds efforts to construct risk objects.

The research that defined this new approach (e.g., Hughes, 1983, 1986, 1987; Callon, 1980, 1987; Latour, 1987) shares an underlying theoretical core that one might call the system/network perspective.[8] Central to this perspective is the view that people and organizations construct technological networks out of a wide variety of components, and that these networks span and blur the traditional categories of the technical and the social.[9] Among other advantages, the system/network perspective simultaneously avoids the reductionism of both technological determinism and social determinism: causality is distributed throughout the network and is not under the complete control of any single type of "actor" (to use Callon and Latour's terminology).[10]

Viewed from the system/network perspective, auto-based transportation is a technological network--or, more accurately, a *sociotechnical* network--of enormous scale and incredible complexity. Its billions of components include cars, drivers, and interstate highways; manufacturing firms, trauma centers, and investment banks; carbon monoxide and the Clean Air Act; and even iron mines and oil fields. The system also includes government agencies involved in everything from building roads to controlling air pollution. Some of these entities, such as tires and engines, have a solid physical existence; others, such as the traffic laws of the State of New York, are less tangible.[11] Some, such as

---

8. The technological system approach of Hughes and the actor-network theory of Callon and Latour differ on some crucial points. These differences will be largely ignored here, and I will use the terms system and network more or less interchangeably. However, it is worth noting the most important points of contention. First, a system has a boundary and exists in an environment, whereas a network is, at least theoretically, unbounded (Law, 1987; Hughes, 1986). (This difference does not seem to be of much practical importance, however, so long as one recognizes that locating the boundary of a system is in practice problematic, as is deciding how far to go in developing an account of a network.) Second, the perspectives differ on the extent to which they consider the properties of system components (or actors) to be socially constructed. The approach to risk developed here relies most heavily on the work of Latour, Callon, and Law.

9. Other works that express the system/network perspective include: Bowker (1987), Callon (1986), Callon, Law, and Rip (1986), Law (1987), and Mackenzie and Spinardi (1988a, 1988b). For a related, but distinct approach, see also Pinch and Bijker (1984, 1987) and Bijker (1987).

10. See especially the discussion in Law (1987). See also Misa (1988).

11. Even entities that future analysts will eventually conclude never really existed can play important roles in sociotechnical networks.

street lights, are unproblematic, off-the-shelf components that can simply, and quite literally, be "plugged in" to the system; others, such as old laws or new machines, need to be tinkered with before they can be fitted into place.

As auto-based transport evolved, the people and organizations that assembled the system managed to weave its components together into a functioning network. This task entails controlling the behavior of a diverse mix of human and non-human actors, enrolling them into the network and inducing them to perform their assigned roles, overcoming any resistance they offer. Law (1987) calls such work "heterogeneous engineering," the process of assembling functioning technological systems out of indifferent or hostile elements of the natural and social world. Like the systems they create, heterogeneous engineers (or "system builders" in Hughes' [1987] terminology) are an eclectic lot, linked together by complex and shifting alliances and struggles. Auto-based transport, for example, has been shaped by such diverse actors as engineers and managers, corporations and environmental groups, scientists and investment bankers, lawyers and government officials.

Measures to control risks are directly and materially built into the auto-based transportation network. As the network evolved, numerous efforts to reduce risks were incorporated into it.[12] Early in the history of the car, concerns about risks led to the codification of traffic laws, the requirement that drivers be licensed, and the substitution of safety glass for the plate glass initially used in windshields (Flink, 1970; Rae, 1965). More recently, concerns about risks have led to seat belts, driver education, speed traps (and radar detectors), catalytic converters, unleaded gas, and road blocks to detect drunk drivers. As these examples suggest, efforts to reduce the risks of this system involve a complex interweaving of things that traditionally would have been classified as "technical" or "social" controls.

---

12. Another advantage of the system/network perspective is that it provides the basis for dynamic accounts of sociotechnical evolution. Often technological change is described in linear terms, as if it were a journey down a single road. But a more apt metaphor is provided by the evolving network of roadways in an expanding highway system. Changes in network structure occur as system components are added, deleted, connected in new ways, as they are reconstructed, recombined, and refined--all for the purpose of changing the power of the system and the distribution of power within it. As troublesome actors emerge in the network, and as people seek to push the system in new directions, struggles over the future shape of the network often take place. Macro-level transformations of technological networks can result from what start out as micro-level changes in network structure (Latour, 1983).

Constructing Risk Objects

As a system evolves, how do new risk objects, and efforts to control them, take shape? From the system/network perspective, constructing risk objects involves chopping up the seamless web of sociotechnical networks. Because these networks are more continuous than discrete, many alternative boundaries can be drawn that define particular "objects" as *figure* and the rest of the system as *background*. In auto-based transport, one can choose many different risk objects, including drivers, vehicles, roads, speed limits, engine emissions, understaffed trauma centers, giant tire piles, dependence on foreign oil, the absence of bicycle paths, or any combination of the above.[13] Far from being limited to artifacts, *any* entity--whether biological, physical, legal, organizational, or wholly conceptual--can be a risk object.[14]

In its simplest form, the process of constructing a risk object consists of defining an object and linking it to harm. This task is a rhetorical process, performed in texts that are displayed in specialized organizations or in public arenas, and it usually involves building *networks* of risk objects.[15] As an example, Ralph Nader's (1965) *Unsafe at Any Speed* played an important role in crystallizing support for the National Highway Traffic Safety Act of 1966, a law that for the first time brought federal regulation to automotive design (Irwin, 1985).[16] Nader's book dramatically presented a new perspective, which had emerged gradually since the Second World War, on how to reduce traffic injuries. Nader constructed for a popular audience a network of new risk objects associated with motor vehicle accidents. His book mounted a frontal assault on the notion that "driver failure" was the cause of traffic casualties.

"The driver" had long been the dominant risk object in road safety policy. In its place, Nader offered many alternative risk objects. He redefined the General

---

13. See Renner (1988) for a critical discussion of auto-based transport that discusses many risk objects.

14. Case studies of the social construction of risk objects, thus, should take as their topics not only technological artifacts, but a huge range of entities, including laws, regulations, organizational structures, characteristics of technological systems (see Perrow, 1984), monitoring systems for averting disaster (Morone and Woodhouse, 1986), management systems, and so on.

15. See Hilgartner and Bosk (1988) for a discussion of how social problems are defined in public arenas. Regarding the texts in which risk objects are constructed, in keeping with recent sociology of science, these texts may involve "inscriptions" (Latour and Woolgar, 1979) produced by laboratory instruments.

16. Nader, of course, did not act alone; he had numerous allies.

Motors *Corvair* as a car with a built-in tendency to roll over or to go "unexpectedly and suddenly out of control." Then, he opened up the sociotechnical networks that were connected to the *Corvair*, revealing for the reader many more risk objects. Looking inside the *Corvair* itself, he found a dangerous "rear axle suspension" that created a severe tendency toward "oversteer," placing "impossible demands" on the driver, and sometimes leading to "extreme tuck-under" and "rollover." Inside the group that designed the car, he found decisions that violated sound engineering principles, stemming from constraints imposed by "cost-cutters" and marketing-oriented "stylists." Inside the wider General Motors organization, he found "a breakdown of the flow of authority and initiative," "bureaucratic rigidities," and "abject worship of that bitch-goddess, cost-reduction." Outside in the wider world, he found an absence of any federal regulation of automotive design, a situation that allowed the American automobile to come "into the marketplace unchecked." He found cars that were not crashworthy, and described a deadly event called "the second collision," which occurs a few milliseconds after a car crash when the auto's occupants slam against its interior. He found a lack of commitment to saving lives by designing cars with occupant protection in mind.

The network of risk objects that Nader constructed was quite heterogeneous, including everything from the *Corvair*, to built-in oversteer, to the second collision, to complacent engineers, to corporate irresponsibility, to the absence of federal regulation. As Nader and his allies pushed such objects into public discussion of automotive safety, they fundamentally changed the actor-world connected to motor vehicle accidents by linking accidents to a new network of deadly risk objects. The transformation of auto safety policy in the mid-1960's cannot be attributed simply to the Congress growing more concerned about the risks posed by a static entity called "motor vehicle accidents." One must look beneath the surface of the category "motor vehicle accidents" and examine the heterogeneous collection of entities that are deemed to be sources of danger. Much can be learned about why people define the "same" risk differently simply by taking *inventories* of risk objects at different times or among different social groups.

Controlling Risk Objects

As the example of the transformation of auto safety policy in the mid-1960's suggests, changes in the definition of risk objects can redistribute responsibility for risks, change the locus of decision making, and determine who has the right--and who has the obligation--to "do something" about hazards. Efforts to construct new risk objects, or redefine old ones, thus often take the form of intense struggles.

Struggles over the construction of risk objects are complemented by struggles to *control* risk objects. Consider a mundane, but troublesome intruder into the world of auto-based transportation: snow. This dangerous material can silently blanket an entire network of roads, causing cars to suddenly spin out of control, skid across lanes, careen into ditches. What efforts are taken to control this deadly risk object? It would be possible to ban the use of motor vehicles during the winter months, but this is not the preferred strategy. Instead, state and local governments levy taxes to finance an army of snowplows. Trucks dump tons of salt and sand on highways. People fit their cars with snow tires. Manufacturers install anti-lock brakes. Motorists are instructed in winter driving skills. Thus, a rather extensive sociotechnical network for combatting snow has co-evolved with the larger system of auto-based transportation.

In the case of snow, much of this network is directed, quite literally, toward displacing the risk object from the system. A key strategy is to eliminate the risk (that is, the social definition of danger) by eliminating the risk object in so far as possible. But for some risk objects, displacement from a technological network is neither possible nor desirable. The explosive properties that make gasoline extremely hazardous also make it an excellent fuel. In such cases, heterogeneous engineers attempt to contain the risk object within a network of control capable of displacing the *risk* from the system, while leaving the *object* in the system. At every point in the long journey from the oil field to the spark plug, fuel flows through a network of pipelines and procedures intended to prevent premature combustion.[17]

Building a network of control around a risk object is often a complex task of heterogeneous engineering, involving struggle with a variety of human and non-human actors. Sometimes, heterogeneous engineers manage to enclose the risk object in a network of control that is deemed so successful that it eliminates the risk (as a matter of concern), decouples the risk object from danger, transforms the risk object into a mere object, and turns this whole process into an arcane episode in the history of technology. Perhaps more typically, networks of control are only able to mitigate concerns, to weaken the linkage between a risk object and danger. Sometimes, of course, the networks break down, and systems are "dissociated into their component parts" (Law, 1987:147)--perhaps with a bang and a burst of flames.

Emplacing and Displacing Risk Objects

Constructing risk objects is a two-way process, propelled by efforts to *emplace* risk objects within, and *displace* them from, sociotechnical networks. To emplace a risk object means to make the object, and its risks, into significant

---

17. See the discussion in Latour (1987) of how science and technology consist of long, thin networks.

actors in a sociotechnical network. In other words, to emplace a risk object means to turn it into something to be reckoned with, something that is capable of influencing the future of the network. To displace a risk object means precisely the reverse: to strip the object, and its risks, of their significance; to neutralize them; to remove their capacity to influence the evolution of the network.

Risk objects can be emplaced from two directions: First, they can be emplaced through construction; that is, entities get emplaced as risk objects if people (1) successfully define them as objects, and (2) successfully link them to harm. Second, risk objects can be emplaced through resistance to control; that is, risk objects get emplaced if heterogeneous engineers cannot remove them from the system or enclose them in networks of control. Risk objects can also be emplaced if the networks of control that surround them come to be seen as unreliable.

Displacement, the mirror image of emplacement, also can occur from two directions. On the one hand, risk objects can be displaced through deconstruction; that is, a risk object can be displaced if people successfully challenge the existence of the object, or successfully sever the linkage between the object and harm. On the other hand, risk objects can be displaced through control; that is, they are displaced if the heterogeneous engineers are able to enclose the objects in networks of control, or to remove them from the system entirely.

Struggles over the construction and control of risk objects take place constantly as sociotechnical networks evolve, and unpredictable developments in these struggles propel objects back and forth along a continuum of emplacement and displacement. New objects can be created, old objects can be defined as risky, and new data can sever the linkage between an object and a harm. New systems of control can transform a risk object into something deemed to be harmless, or an accident can suddenly raise doubts about the reliability of systems of control.

Often struggles to emplace and displace risk objects involve collecting reams of data or building new sociotechnical systems. Consider the efforts of Nader and his allies to emplace a new chain of risk objects into the world of auto-based transportation. In laboratories, in forensic examinations of accidents, in scientific papers, in courts, in *Unsafe at Any Speed*, Nader and his allies marshalled data and rhetoric in order to define as risk objects such entities as "the second collision." General Motors and its allies, for their part, tried to resist this effort and displace these definitions.

Nader and his allies wanted to impose significant changes in the structure of the auto-based transportation network, a fact that accounts for the intensity of the struggle. Specifically, Nader sought to surround certain risk objects (such as built-in oversteer and irresponsible corporations) with new networks of control intended to eliminate them or mitigate their harm. Accomplishing this--in the face of resistance from the largest corporation in the United States--would be no mean feat. Success depended on firmly emplacing the new risk objects in the conceptual worlds inhabited by actors, such as the Congress, powerful enough to tell General Motors what to do. The goal of mitigating the devastation of the second collision, the dream of eliminating it entirely--these depended, first of all, on emplacing "the second collision" in the conceptual networks powerful people used to think about motor vehicle accidents.

The struggle to construct and control risk objects is fundamentally a struggle over the future shape of sociotechnical networks. When new definitions of risk objects get emplaced within the conceptual networks that people use to think about a technological system, they *act* on that system. Often, definitions of new risk objects become reified into material form, as new networks of control are constructed around them.[18] The victory that Nader and his allies won in 1966 is a case in point: The National Highway Traffic Safety Act greatly accelerated the process through which "the second collision" grew from a phrase coined in the late 1940's by an Indiana state trooper (Irwin, 1985) into something to be studied using standardized crash dummies and standardized collisions; something to be attacked with air bags and automatic seat belts; something that today is surrounded by an extensive network of engineering and regulatory controls.[19]

The Social Distribution of Risk Objects

This dynamic two-way traffic of emplacing and displacing risk objects does not occur in some abstract location, such as "society," but in specific social arenas. In which arenas is this traffic heaviest and fastest? In which social worlds are the inventories of risk objects largest? Where do the conceptual networks that link objects to harms reach the greatest complexity? From what kinds of arenas are new risk objects most likely to emerge? In general, the answer to none of these questions is "the public" or the mass media (although the media at times play a major role),[20] despite the emphasis on these actors in

---

18. This point parallels the observation in the new sociology of science that new facts and theories get incorporated, directly and materially, into new scientific instruments. See Latour and Woolgar (1979); see also Knorr-Cetina (1981).

19. Struggles, of course, continue about whether this network is "adequate," how it might be improved, and at whose expense. For a case study of the controversy over the air bag, see Reppy (1984).

20. Obviously, the media at times play a crucial role as a vehicle for mobilizing protest or as a tool for engineering consent. But the sociology of risk cannot neglect the many other kinds of engineering--that is, the heterogeneous

the risk literature. On the contrary, the most important arenas for constructing risks are those that devote *sustained attention* to constructing facts and machines, laws and regulations, organizations and management systems, research programs and data collection systems, risk objects and networks for controlling them.

As an example, consider the activities that surround one of the risk objects connected with the auto-based transport system: carbon dioxide. Not long ago carbon dioxide--a colorless, odorless, non-toxic gas--was not a risk object at all; it was a harmless byproduct of combustion. But over the past few decades, the carbon dioxide spewed forth by the world's 386 million cars has been transformed into a risk object of global proportions.[21] Carbon dioxide has been linked to an entity called the greenhouse effect, which threatens to increase the average temperature of the earth's atmosphere. Such global warming, in turn, threatens to melt the polar icecaps, flood the largest cities on the planet, disrupt terrestrial ecosystems, and turn rich croplands into deserts.

The linkage between carbon dioxide and global peril began when scientists first speculated about the climatic effects of an increase in the atmospheric concentration of the gas. At first, the linkage was a weak one, but over the years, scientists have developed conceptual and material tools for assessing the dangers of global warming. They have constructed new facts and designed systems for monitoring the atmosphere. They have made measurements and built computer models of the earth's climate. They have studied the dynamics of polar ice buildup and projected global fossil-fuel consumption. They have mapped the planet's energy balance and studied the earth's carbon reservoirs. They have argued about the severity of the threat and debated the options for control. Governments, environmental groups, and transnational organizations have joined in the debate. Thus, a growing collection of actors is struggling about what, if anything, should be done to control the network of risk objects now linked to carbon dioxide, and to "open the way to a world in which the greenhouse century exists only in the microchips of a supercomputer" (Schneider, 1989).

Within the specialized communities that are most intensely involved in manufacturing knowledge about global warming, there is a vast inventory of risk objects that remains largely outside of public view. The distribution of risk objects among different social groups and locations in sociotechnical networks is extremely uneven. In general, the size of these inventories, and the average speed with which risk objects are emplaced and displaced, are highest within

---

engineering--involved in constructing risk. Mass media are by no means at the center of risk construction, they are merely one point in the network.

21. Cars, of course, are only one source of carbon dioxide. The number 386 million cars is a 1986 figure.

communities of specialized professionals, such as scientists, engineers, lawyers, medical doctors, government officials, corporate managers, political operatives, and so on. For this reason, analysts of the social construction of risk who start with "the public" are beginning their work at the wrong place. The most important action takes place in organizations (Clarke, 1989) and in arenas that are populated by communities of specialists--not among the individual members of the general public. Indeed, many technologists spend their professional lives trying to emplace and displace risk objects that most people never hear of; and usually, only a handful of other specialists care to know about all of the calculations and tests involved in constructing a new risk object, bringing it under control, and deciding that the controls are "adequate."

Social analysis of the construction of risk must recognize that the resources (e.g., the cultural authority [Starr, 1982:13], the conceptual tools, funds, and laboratories [Latour, 1987]) needed to take part in defining risk objects are very unevenly distributed. Members of the public lack such resources, and even mass media organizations have finite "carrying capacities" (Hilgartner and Bosk, 1988) for constructing and displaying risk objects. As a result, the general public plays a limited role in constructing risk objects. Indeed, much of the time, risk objects and the networks of control that are built around them get embedded in the social fabric with almost no one noticing. Alternatives disappear even more quietly. Technical experts and other system builders are the central players in constructing and controlling risk. If risk is to be understood, and if more effective policies for controlling it are to be developed, then social scientists need to focus on system builders.

Conclusion

Risk is not something that gets attached to technology after the engineers go home, when the press and the public arrive. Risks are constructed constantly as technological networks evolve. Social scientists must abandon their *post hoc* approach to risk, and move analysis upstream to the arenas where specialized professionals are working most intensively to extend sociotechnical networks. Studying risk objects offers a way to pry open networks of risk, and look at the dynamics of the process through which risks are created, controlled, and distributed.

Research on the construction of risk objects can also contribute to improving risk management by revealing blind spots in the ways we conceptualize risk. For example, in the system of electric power production and use, there is a supply-side bias in the construction of risk objects. The dangers of power plant emissions are regulated and endlessly debated, but there has historically been little attention directed at, say, the hazards of inefficient light bulbs, which--from a demand-side perspective--are also a cause of air pollution.

Social scientists can contribute to strategies for risk management by working to identify ways that social organization restricts the kinds of risk objects that receive attention, and policy studies that explore different ways of constructing risk objects can help bring "non-objects" into the open.

The analytic edge of the sociology of risk can be sharpened by future research that explores: the conceptual structures that people use to think about risk; the interplay between the construction and the control of risk; the shifting fate of risk objects and the struggles to emplace and displace them; the uneven distribution of risk objects; and the processes that cause inventories of risk objects to change over time. Research needs to "follow the actors" (Latour, 1987), concentrating on those who are trying to direct the evolution of technological networks. Analyzing the social construction of risk objects can speed progress toward understanding how networks of risks, and efforts to control them, get embedded in the social--and sociotechnical--fabric.

PART THREE

Corporate Contexts of Decision Making

4

Firm Risk Management in the
Face of Product Liability Rules

Joseph Sanders

The last twenty years have witnessed a substantial increase in governmental regulation of products and processes believed to impose a health threat to citizens. Simultaneously, the courts have extended the tort law to hold companies liable for injuries caused by their products. Both courts and agencies now find themselves in the business of assessing the risk of products and weighing these risks against other technical, economic, political and social considerations.[1] They find themselves in the business of risk management.

This is a revised version of a paper presented at the 1988 Law and Society Association meeting. Work on the paper was supported by the Environmental Law Program at the University of Houston. I wish to thank Ann Ross-Ray for her research assistance and James Short for his many helpful comments.

1. Federal safety statutes vary in terms of risk assessment requirements of firms (for example, compare Toxic Substances Control Act, 15 U.S.C. Sec. 2601 (1982) with Federal Water Pollution Control Act, 33 U.S.C. Sec. 1251), and in terms of what benefits they will allow the agency to balance against product risk (compare the No Risk Standard of the Delaney amendment to the Food, Drug and Cosmetic Act, 21 U.S.C. Sec. 348 (c)(3)(A) (1976) with the balancing test of the Federal Insecticide, Fungicide and Rodenticide Act, 7 U.S.C. Sec. 135 et seq. (1980). Occasionally, the appropriate standard has been a matter in dispute as in the Benzene Case, *Industrial Union v. American Petroleum Institute*, 448 U.S. 607 (1980). See generally, Coodley (1984).

Most discussions of risk management have focused upon agency decisions.[2] Others have compared agency versus court enforcement of product and environmental safety standards.[3] Less attention has been given to risk management activities of firms themselves, especially as a reaction to common law liability.[4] Firm risk management is the topic of this paper.

Existing Knowledge

Eads and Reuter (1985) interviewed corporate product safety officials in nine large manufacturing concerns as well as insurance company product safety personnel. The firms were acknowledged to be safety leaders. Eads and Reuter asked, "how innovative corporations responded to changes in their environment" (1985:2). The interviews were guided by two questions; what factors shape firm responses to pressures for product safety, and what responses are effective? As to the first question, responses were shaped by the existing organization of the firm, the culture of the firm, and the inherent seriousness of the safety problem faced by the firm (1985:14).

The firm's product safety office must adopt a structure similar to the existing organizational structure or risk impotence. One attempt to develop a centralized corporate-level product safety office in a firm that was strongly decentralized apparently cut the office off from day to day decisions at lower levels and thus limited its influence.

Corporate culture is reflected in the chief executive officer's commitment to safety. The corporate product safety organizations in some of Eads and Reuter's firms were the legacy of "missionary" personalities that had long "preached the gospel of product safety" (1985:19).

Eads and Reuter separated organizations into three categories based on the seriousness of their product safety problem: firms making inherently hazardous products such as certain drugs, firms making moderately hazardous products, and firms making low-hazard products. The product safety organization in the firms

---

2. See, Crandall and Lave (1981), Hawkins (1984), Kagan (1978), Lave (1981), Nelkin (1979), Perrow (1984), Rodgers (1980), Scholz (1984), Wilson (1980).

3. See, Coodley (1984), Huber (1985) Katz (1969), Pierce (1980), Rodgers (1979), Rosenberg (1984), Yellin (1981).

4. Engineers have made some efforts to inform firms how to manage risks generated by common law rules. The American Society for Quality Control held Product Liability Prevention Conferences for a number of years. See, e.g. Colangelo and Thornton (1981), Product Liability Prevention Conference (1979), Seiden (1984).

making low-hazard products was directed at compliance with agency regulations (here CPSC), and with the defensive goal of defending product liability claims. In firms with inherently hazardous products officials were concerned with safety, and there was nearly always a strong regulatory agency influence as well as a substantial volume of product liability litigation.

Importantly, unlike other firms in the study, the two high risk firms treated product liability settlements as part of the cost of doing business. In one firm liability settlements were treated as overhead expenses. In the other liability costs were allocated to products only for the purpose of pricing and deciding whether to continue a product line (not for measuring specific safety efforts). Product safety efforts were organized in part to shield engineers from product liability issues. Separate litigation or regulation "specialists" dealt with liability problems. Shielding engineers served two purposes; it minimized costs that would arise if everyone in the firm had to become involved in product cases, and it minimized potential morale problems that would arise from involving designers and engineers in the endless flow of litigation, especially when the firm believes that the designers and engineers are doing their job properly (Hoenig, 1981).

In one of the two firms with moderately hazardous products there was a small risk management organization backed by the company president. In the other an assistant general counsel was working to develop a corporate organization in the face of a relatively hostile corporate attitude. It is worth noting that the latter firm manufactured industrial products and, therefore, almost all product safety pressures came by way of product liability suits.

The effectiveness of a firm's product safety program must be assessed within the context of multiple goals. These goals include helping in design trade-off decisions, establishing and implementing design audit procedures, preaching product safety throughout the organization, coordinating product liability defense efforts and providing an interface with government regulatory agencies. These goals may conflict.

Are certain organizational forms more effective in pursuing these multiple goals? Eads and Reuter concluded that while some product safety organization is necessary, the specific structure is less important than is informal power.[5]

---

5. In a very useful study of mine safety in five coal companies Braithwaite (1985a) discovered some patterns across firms that were similar to those of Eads and Reuter.

    In the final analysis, the conclusions about what these five companies had in common could be regarded as mundane. They were companies which: (1) gave a lot of informal clout and top management backing to their safety inspectors; (2) made sure that clearly defined accountability for safety performance was imposed on line managers; (3) monitored that performance carefully and let managers know when it was not up to standard; and (4) had mostly formal programs for ensuring: (a) that

Most respondents believed that safety decisions could not be left to the design engineers because of product complexity and hazard subtlety. Some type of formal organization for safety is necessary.

Two more findings are particularly important. First, Eads and Reuter had expected to find that product safety personnel, especially at the corporate level, would play an important role in the firm's product liability litigation. They would develop litigation and settlement strategy and would appear as expert witnesses on the firm's behalf. Instead, they found that product liability defense is treated as a legal problem best handled by the law departments of the firms. The corporate lawyers reach past the corporate level safety officers and down to operating units to find individuals to assist in litigation. Second, except in a few highly regulated industries such as drugs and aircraft, product liability considerations outweigh regulation as an influence on product design decisions. The effect, however, is very indirect.

> Although product liability exerts a powerful influence on product design decisions, it sends an extremely vague signal. Because the linkage between good design and a firm's liability exposure remains tenuous, the signal says only: 'Be careful, or you will be sued.' Unfortunately, it does not say *how* to be careful, or, more important, *how careful* to be (1985:28).

The Eads and Reuter study provides an enticing glimpse into corporate product safety efforts. It also raises a number of questions about firm response to product liability rules. First, what internal factors influence the way firms respond to legal and economic pressures for product and environmental safety? Answering this question requires a more complete *theory of the firm.*

Second, are questions of *legal impact.* How is firm risk management behavior influenced by law? Eads and Reuter note that products liability rules are more uncertain than agency rules. There is still much to learn, however, about the nature of legal uncertainty.

Third, how do the attributes of the firm and of products liability rules interact to influence *risk management strategy?* Those against whom legal rules are directed may devote their efforts toward obeying the directives of the rule or toward avoidance of the rule. From the point of view of the firm, the combination of efforts that minimizes the total costs (including such costs as

---

safety training and supervision [by foremen in particular] was never neglected; (b) that safety problems were quickly communicated to those who could act on them; and (c) that a plan of attack existed for dealing with all identified hazards (1985b:52-53).

See also Braithwaite (1984), Fisse and Braithwaite (1983).

good will losses arising out of adverse product liability findings) is the most effective response (see Zacharias, 1986). Within the area of products liability risk management this involves two related, but separate goals--product safety and loss reduction. To what degree do these objective differ; and what is there about rules and firms that causes greater or lesser effort to be devoted to each objective?

Determinants of Risk Management Behavior

The remainder of the paper examines the literature concerning how organizational contingencies and legal rules combine to produce risk management strategies. The goal is to develop hypotheses concerning the compliance/avoidance choice as a response to law. Risk management strategies are the dependent variable, not the independent variable.[6]

Attributes of the Firm

The firm from a transaction cost perspective. Oliver Williamson's "transaction cost approach" views institutions as transactions between agents and institutional behavior as efforts to minimize transaction costs.[7] An important part of those costs derives from the fact that humans are not perfectly rational economic actors. They exhibit "bounded rationality" and they engage in "opportunism"[8] (Williamson, 1981: 554).

---

6. Existing studies have moved too quickly to make risk management strategies the independent variable designed to explain such things as the level of product safety, without developing an adequate understanding of the causes of these strategies.

7. Williamson (1975). The transaction cost approach fits within a group of theories that includes the organizational theory of Simon (1952-3), Cyert and March (1963) and March (1978), the X-efficiency theory of Liebenstein (1966, 1976, 1982), the "exit-voice" theory of Hirschman (1970) and the game theory model of Aoki (1984). All of these theories differ from neo-classical economic theories in the ways suggested in the text. A closely related literature on corporate crime also rejects a neo-classical view of the firm. While transaction cost theorists generally adopt the point of view of corporate principals trying to control agents (Ross, 1973) corporate crime theorists often adopt the point of view of the agent and his potential co-optation or exploitation by the firm. Perhaps the leading book in the area is Stone (1975). See also, Braithwaite (1984), Clinard (1983), Vaughan (1982, 1983).

8. Williamson (1981: 554) summarizes these two differences by saying:

Because individuals do not have perfect analytical and data-processing skills, they fail to take account of every contingency. Their rationality is "bounded," as a result of which decisions:

> will be made in terms of localized disturbances to which abbreviated analyses will be applied with short-term recommendations as the result. A search for more stable solutions... is unlikely; consequences are not given much attention, and apparently logical solutions may prove faulty as their consequences ramify (Weick, 1969: 10).

Infrequent events with remote consequences are particularly difficult to plan for and control. They will have relatively little impact on decisions. For most firms products liability suits are infrequent events that cannot themselves be used as measures of product safety. Alternative measures must be developed.

Opportunistic managers are not fully trustworthy. They will not always do what is promised, or they may obey the letter of a promise and not its spirit.[9] Coffee (1981) reports the following opportunistic behaviors by middle management: falsification of emission data supplied to the EPA by Ford engineers and the falsification of reports to the Army Corps of Engineers by low-level officials of Allied Chemical with respect to the dumping of Kepone into Chesapeake Bay. In both cases the activity apparently occurred without even the tacit approval of people higher in the firm.

Controlling opportunistic behavior is difficult for several reasons. Because it is often difficult or impossible for firms to distinguish between those who will behave opportunistically and those who will not (Pratt and Zeckhauser, 1985), institutional rules must arrange matters as if everyone will be opportunistic.[10] Yet rules promulgated to guard against opportunism may be

---

> "A different way of putting this is to say that while organizational man is computationally less competent than economic man, he is motivationally more complex."

Traditional law and economics analyses have often been accused of assuming perfectly rational economic actors when modelling the effect of liability rules on actor behavior. There have, however, always been exceptions and the behavioral assumptions of law and economics analyses have grown increasingly more sophisticated. See Calabresi (1970), Kornhauser (1980), Landes and Posner (1987), Shavell (1980, 1987).

9. Arrow (1985) notes, there are two main types of nondisclosure, hidden action and hidden information. Economists, borrowing from insurance language, sometimes call these two problems moral hazard and adverse selection.

10. Economists sometimes model the situation as a type of principal-agent problem. The firm (the principal) must try to arrange incentives so that it is in

difficult to construct and costly to implement. It is difficult to define reward systems that favor desired behaviors and to measure unacceptable behaviors. Moreover, constructing rules to deal with opportunistic agents is costly. Transaction costs rise with greater rule system complexity--there is more red tape (Grandori, 1987: 37). The firm must strike a balance between rules that guard against opportunism and rules that allow those who will not act opportunistically to act with maximum freedom and efficiency.

Human asset specificity further constrains control efforts. Some assets are not easily moved or replaced. Part of their value is specific to their current use. Asset specificity assumes various forms, site specificity, physical plant specificity, and, of most relevance in the present context, human asset specificity (Williamson, 1985: 55). When workers have skills specific to a given job they are not easily replaced. It is not to the firm's advantage to discharge an employee for less than perfect performance because replacement costs would be substantial. Structures developed to control product safety often must operate within the context of a protective governance structure designed to tie the individual to the firm (Williamson, 1981: 563).

Moreover, human asset specificity is often a group phenomenon. A large variety of "skills and knowledge can be formed only in an organizational context and embodied only in a team of employees" (Aoki, 1984: 25).

> [P]erformance in some production and most managerial jobs involves a team element, and a critical skill is the ability to operate effectively within the given members of the team. This ability is dependent upon the interaction of the personalities of the members, and the individual's work "skills" are specific in the sense that skills necessary to work on one team are never quite the same as those required on another (Doeringer and Piore, 1971: 15-16).

Ouchi (1980) argues that group assets are most likely to exist in those parts of the organization engaged in scientific and industrial research, the same groups that often play a central role in the design of new products.

Group asset specificity raises a special set of problems for the firm. Individual level performance monitoring is less effective and it may undermine the group based asset. Because of this Ouchi (1980) has noted that circumstances where there are group specific assets are ripe for a "clan" type of organization; a governance structure based on social conditioning and appeals to

---

the interest of the agent to act in the best interests of the principal. See, Epple and Raviv (1978), Holstrom (1979).

organizational culture rather than on legal and economic sanctions.[11] Nevertheless, this type of organization, too, has its risks, for by creating greater autonomy the potential for undetected opportunism is increased.

Limits to organizational change and control. Existing arrangements impede change. They represent past investments that insulate programs from displacement by alternatives that might be chosen if one were starting from scratch. Eads and Reuter noted, for example, that existing organization constrains product safety programs. Why should this be the case? Pratt and Zeckhauser (1985) observe that most changes are retroactive with respect to organizational structure, and because of this they have redistributional effects.

> To the extent that capital is in place, contracts drawn, and commitments made, any rule change will have retroactive implications. That is, it will have effects that, if anticipated, would have affected previous decisions. This feature of rule changes has redistributive consequences. The more important the retrospective implications of a change relative to its efficiency gains, the closer it comes to being purely redistributive in its consequences (1985: 19).

The redistributive effects of retroactive change may create a sub-group within the organization with a set of goals and payoffs different from those of the total organization. In common parlance, protecting one's turf is a typical response to the distributional consequences of retroactive changes.

When bounded rationality and opportunism are added to this equation the result can be a particularly pernicious type of persistence called a sunk cost effect. The sunk cost effect describes a tendency to continue a course of action in which one has invested time and capital even when it is economically irrational from the firm's point of view. Organizational change is called for, but is resisted. The effect is especially relevant to the problem of risk management given the numerous examples of firms that have become trapped in a course of action in which they continue to support an inadequate product long after its inadequacies are revealed. The Ford Pinto, the Firestone 500 and the Dalkon Shield are examples of such situations. Both laboratory experiments (Fox and

---

11. The attraction of Japanese management style is, in part, its ability to create governance structures that recognize group based assets and to nurture teams rather than undermining them by excessive individual monitoring. See Vogel (1979), Williamson and Ouchi (1981).

Staw, 1979; Staw, 1976; Staw and Fox, 1977), and examples from everyday life document the robustness of this effect.[12]

Bounded rationality offers a partial explanation of this effect. Payoffs from prior decisions create a framework for new decisions and, perversely, when these payoffs are negative individuals may become risk seeking, literally throwing good money after bad (Arkes and Blumer, 1985).

Opportunism also explains sunk cost effects. A firm's organization can increase the potential of opportunistic behavior and thus the likelihood of a sunk cost effect (Fox and Staw, 1979). Employees finding themselves in an administrative situation with low job security are most likely to engage in justificatory escalation of their commitment to a failing policy. The need to account for actions already taken is likely to produce a retrospective rationality designed to explain and justify past decisions in order to save one's position in the organization Tetlock (1985). Firms may attempt to minimize this effect by constructing a governance structure that provides greater job security and protects employees from certain consequences of their actions. This alternative, however, may decrease the firm's ability to monitor and detect opportunistic behavior. The problem of sunk cost again reveals the tension between control structure and autonomy.

Ideally the firm may minimize this tension by constructing mechanisms that will cause actors to consider risk management issues before taking action, engaging in prospective rationality. However, as Eads and Reuter note, product liability law, because of its open texture and uncertainty, imposes special burdens on a firm attempting greater prospective rationality. It says "be careful," but not how careful or how to be careful (1985:28). This leads to the question of legal impact.

Attributes of the Law

From the point of view of the state the central legal impact question is how to draft an effective rule that produces certain results.[13] From the point of view

---

12.   Arkes and Blumer (1985: 124) provide as an example the following comment of Senator Sasser in 1981.

"Completing Tennessee-Tombigbee [Waterway Project] is not a waste
of taxpayer dollars. Terminating the project at this late stage of
development would, however, represent a serious waste of funds already
invested."

13.   Some of the most insightful law review literature on the control of corporate behavior works from this premise and attempts to construct a set of effective rules given an understanding of the firm. See, e.g., Coffee (1981), Huber (1985), Kraakman (1984), Roe (1986), Siliciano (1987), Stone (1975, 1980), Zacharias (1986).

of the firm, the central question is how to respond to law. Because firm behavior is not solely a response to formal legal rules it is useful to divide legal impact into two parts, the nature of the law--the set of substantive and procedural rules that comprise product liability law; and the nature of legal rationality--the set of assumptions and decision rules legal actors bring to the decision as to whether a firm has committed a tort.

The nature of products liability law. Modern products liability was born in the early 1960s with the decisions in *Henningson v. Bloomfield Motors*, 161 A.2d 69 (N.J. 1960); *Greenman v. Yuba Power Products, Inc.*, 377 P.2d 897 (Cal. 1963); and the promulgation of the Restatement of Torts 2d Section 402A (American Law Institute, 1965). Henceforth, the manufacturer became "strictly liable" for injuries caused by a defective product.[14] The plaintiff no longer had to prove that the defendant was negligent in the manufacture or sale of a product that caused injury.

Proponents of strict products liability had hoped that this rule would cause corporations to internalize the costs of defects and thus build safer products. As Justice Traynor had said in his seminal concurring opinion in *Escola v. Coca Cola*, 150 P.2d 436 (Cal. 1944):

> [P]ublic policy demands that responsibility be fixed wherever it will most effectively reduce the hazards to life and health inherent in defective products that reach the market. It is evident that the manufacturer can anticipate some hazards and guard against the recurrence of others, as the public cannot.... It is to the public interest to discourage the marketing of products having defects that are a menace to the public.

---

14. As Shavell (1987:59) observes, strict liability for defective products is different from strict liability for injuries caused by products. A "defectiveness" test is a lesser standard in the sense that the manufacturer is assured he will not be responsible for injuries caused by his products unless they can be shown to be defective. Within the context of economic analysis, Shavell argues that manufacturers may under-invest in safety with respect to "non-defective" products. It is not surprising, therefore, that the greatest single amount of doctrinal energy in the products liability area has gone into defining "defective." The bitter disputes over the "state of the art" defense, and whether some products are unavoidably unsafe and therefore not subject to strict liability (see, e.g., *Brown v. The Superior Court of the City and County of San Francisco*, 751 P.2d 470 [Cal. 1988]) are understandable from this perspective. Ultimately, they are disputes over the extent of the difference between "strict liability" and "defect liability." This paper adopts the widely used term "strict liability" to define product liability rules not based on negligence principles.

Traynor's intuition about legal impact was based in part on the assumption that strict products liability would create a simpler and more certain rule system than the negligence system it replaced (Shavell, 1987). As the law developed, however, complexity increased, especially with respect to the concept of "defect." The courts distinguished three general ways in which a product could be defective: a product may be defective in its manufacture (e.g., a bottle with a hidden flaw); in its design (e.g., an automobile gas tank located in a dangerous place); or in its marketing (e.g., a bottle of medicine with inadequate instructions or warnings) (Shapo, 1987). Each type of defect has its own slightly different set of rules.

With complexity comes increasing uncertainty of application.[15] Many would agree with Eads and Reuter that the signal tort law sends out is frequently difficult to interpret (Burrows, 1984; Henderson, 1983). Siliciano (1987) employs the concepts of inevitability and predictability to capture the nature of this uncertainty. Tort rules, like other rules, may not be enforced, because for example the injured party does not know his legal rights. Lack of inevitability would not matter to the firm if there were a known set of transition rates from injury to litigation and from litigation to judgment. However, the rate of litigation itself is a variable, introducing uncertainty as to the probability of litigation given a defect produced injury. The volume of products liability suits increased three-fold between 1975 and 1985, and in certain areas at a much faster rate. In 1981 there were 7,500 Dalkon Shield cases while in 1986 there were over 300,000 such claims (Hensler, 1987). Often, therefore, the question of inevitability is part of the question of predictability.

Even a constant set of rules produces uncertain outcomes if their application in specific cases is problematical. Products liability rules are problematical in this sense because, like most common law rules they are very general in nature. The result of the movement to strict liability has been that the ambiguity surrounding the concept of negligence (a person should behave reasonably under the circumstances) was replaced by ambiguity surrounding the concept of defectiveness (a product is defective if it is unreasonably dangerous to the consumer). In either case such rules offer little guidance in particular cases (see Epstein, 1982). The traditional common law source of specificity is the law of the case, the individual prior cases that serve as precedents for other cases with similar facts. Here, however, from the point of view of the firm there is too much specificity. The system is one of "tailor made justice in every case" (Henderson, 1982). It is difficult to know whether a particular case or a particular problem is sufficiently similar to assure a similar outcome. Products

---

15. For general discussions of the effects of legal uncertainty see Calfee and Craswell (1984).

liability law, like most tort law is simultaneously too general in its rules and too specific in its application to provide clear guidelines for risk managers (Epstein, 1987).

A more appropriate level of specificity is often available in the standards of regulatory agencies.[16] Most courts, however, have adopted the position that compliance with governmental regulations is only some evidence that a product is not defective.[17] At times this leads to surprising results. Consider *Turner v. General Motors*, 584 S.W.2d 844 (Tex. 1979), an automobile crashworthiness case in which the plaintiff alleged that the roof of the car in which he was driving crushed too easily in a rollover accident. The Supreme Court of Texas approved a trial court's exclusion of defendant's evidence that subsequent to the first trial of the case the National Highway Traffic Safety Administration adopted a standard requiring vehicle roofs to bear a 5,000 pound load, and that plaintiff's vehicle passed the test at 13,000 pounds. The jury found the roof to be defectively designed and awarded the plaintiff, who had been paralyzed, $1,140,000.[18] Thus, from the point of view of the firm there is often a conflict, at least in terms of resource allocation, between the goals of diminishing common law product liability and conforming to agency regulations. An organization that devotes all of its energies into compliance with agency behavior may be disappointed in the outcome of some litigation. See, e.g., *Dawson v. Chrysler Corp.*, 630 F.2d 950 (3rd Cir. 1981), cert. denied 450 U.S. 959.

The argument against adopting a rule that regulatory compliance should be per se exculpatory has been that some regulatory standards are inadequate. Plaintiff experts have sometimes presented evidence that ordinary newspaper could pass federal standards for rapid and intense burning set out in the

---

16. For a discussion of optimal specificity in administrative rules see Diver (1983).

17. See *Wilson v. Piper Aircraft Corp.* 577 P.2d 1322 (Ore. 1978). For an argument that regulatory compliance should be per se exculpatory, see Schwartz (1988).

18. A typical reaction to this type of case is expressed in the following passage from General Motors' chief products liability attorney:

It is patently absurd that the machinery of governmental standard setting should be observed through vigorous procedures, and that designers should be required to meet the mark of that standard, only to have their designs second guessed and their responsibility expanded case by case, perhaps inconsistently, in courtrooms by jurors with little or no expertise and in emotional settings affected too often by pitiful injuries and heartrending human suffering (Raliegh, 1977: 261).

Flammable Fabrics Act.[19] In such situations the standard is not a valid indicator of defectiveness. As Epstein (1987) notes, however, the price of increased validity is increased unreliability as to the standard of care required of the firm. There is no determinate rule around which the firm can organize behavior.

Unpredictability is created by rule instability as well as a lack of an appropriate level of specificity. In several areas the courts have found it impossible to maintain a consistent strict liability standard, the most important being design defect cases. From time to time courts have adopted a consumer expectations test,[20] a knowledgeable seller test,[21] a risk-utility test,[22] or exotic combinations of these tests.[23]

Most states have adopted a risk-utility test in which the adequacy of a given design turns on whether there is an alternative feasible design.[24] Henderson (1973) among others, argues that at least in the case of conscious design decisions the design problems are polycentric and therefore not appropriate for traditional adjudication under any test.[25] Few would disagree with the

---

19. See *Howard v. McCrory Corp.* 601 F.2d 133 (4th Cir. 1979).

20. *Cronin v. J.E.B. Olson Corp.*, 501 P.2d 1153 (Cal., 1972); *Vincer v. Esther Williams All-aluminum Swimming Pool Co.*, 230 N.W.2d 794 (Wis., 1975).

21. *Phillips v. Kimwood Machine Co.* 525 P.2d 1033 (Ore. 1974).

22. *Turner v. General Motors*, 584 S.W.2d 844 (Tex. 1979).

23. *Henderson v. Ford Motor Co.*, 519 S.W.2d 87 (Tex., 1974); *Barker v. Lull Engineering*, 573 P.2d 443 (Cal. 1978). In Barker, for instance, there is a two-prong test for measuring defectiveness. First, the plaintiff succeeds if he can show that the product does not meet reasonable consumer expectations as to safety. If this cannot be done the plaintiff can propose some alternative design and the burden shifts to the defendant to show that the risks of the alternative outweigh the benefits.

24. The standard for design cases may differ from the standard for manufacturing or marketing defect cases where the courts maintain 402A's reasonable consumer test. As one might expect, many cases can be analyzed as fitting in more than one category. For instance, is a product that barely fails to meet manufacturing tolerances defective in manufacturing, or in design because the design tolerances were not sufficiently rigorous to assure that products that slightly failed to meet tolerances would be adequate to their intended purpose?

25. For a useful response see Twerski, et al. (1976).

observation that jurors are relatively unprepared to conduct any type of sophisticated analysis of the risks and benefits of design choices (Schwartz, 1988).

Unpredictability is increased when there has been a passage of time since the product was made. While some unpredictability is unavoidable when rules change in a common law system, uncertainty is minimized by the fact that usually a new rule is made to apply only to the present and future cases. In the products liability area, however, future cases arise that concern products designed or manufactured in the past. From the point of view of the firm, or the firm's insurer, a new rule is ex post facto with respect to the stock of existing products. Thus the "tail" of new liability may stretch a into the future for as long as the product remains in the marketplace.[26] The result, according to the president of an aerospace products firm is that:

> We're defending suits involving ancient products, with claims that were totally unforeseen when the products were designed and sold and when insurance was purchased. It is impossible to predict what future application of product liability law will be made in today's products (McGuire, 1988:1)

Uncertainty is created by changing technology and changing information as well as by changing rules. What should be done with a product that was as safe as any of its kind when it was made, but is no longer so?[27] How should a product be judged when these defects were unknown at the time it was sold? The

---

26. See Henderson (1983), Page (1983), and Schwartz (1983) on the effect of the passage of time on liability. Recently, insurers have attempted to minimize this source of uncertainty by writing "claims" insurance rather than "event" insurance. Under a claims insurance policy the insurer promises only to defend and pay claims that accrue during a given period of time. Under an event insurance policy the insurer promises to defend and pay any claims that eventually arise for events that occur during a given period of time. In the case of injuries such as asbestos exposure no claim may be made until the plaintiff has suffered an injury such as lung cancer many years later. Event insurance is a more uncertain proposition when legal rules are prone to change between the event and the claim. Recently in a suit filed by several states against the insurance industry one allegation is that the industry has conspired to refuse to write event insurance in several areas. Product Safety and Liability Reporter (April 1, 1988:318-319).

27. See *Bruce v. Martin-Marietta Corp.*, 544 F.2d 442 (10th Cir. 1976), Henderson (1983), Epstein (1986).

courts have had a difficult time deciding what to do with state-of-the-art information in both design defect and marketing defect cases.[28]

One further source of uncertainty is the size of damage awards. Recent work by the Administrative Office of the United States Courts, the Rand Corporation Institute for Civil Justice, the National Center for State Courts, and researchers at the American Bar Foundation indicates that products awards are higher than most other tort awards. In Cook County, for instance, median automobile accident awards in the early 1980s have been in the $10,000 range while median products liability awards were over $180,000 (Hensler, 1987:488).[29] These awards have increased over the years. In the period 1960-1964 the median products liability award in San Francisco was $27,000. In 1980-1984 it was $200,000 (Peterson, 1987). When compared to non-products liability awards, the size of products awards cannot entirely be explained by the nature of plaintiff's injury or the presence of a "deep pocket" defendant (Chin & Peterson, 1985; see Black, 1987).

Increasing awards result in increasing variance as well, and with it increasing uncertainty with respect to the expected value of a lawsuit. The "danger value" of an increasing percentage of product suits causes risk averse defendants to settle cases that might be won on the merits (McGuire, 1988: 11; cf. Ross, 1970). To the degree products liability law sends uncertain liability and damage signals to the firm it creates what the insurance industry tellingly calls the legal hazard.

The nature of legal rationality. A second dimension of product liability law might be called legal rationality: that is, the rationality used by legal actors in making liability decisions. A recent collection of articles on risk and decisions presents the following questions:

> When different professionals use the term 'risk,' are their apparent differences of approach due merely due to the different jargons which they use or are the jargons obscuring more fundamental differences in

---

28. Compare *Beshada v. Johns-Manville Products Corp.*, 447 A.2d 539 (N.J. 1982) and *Feldman v. Lederle Laboratories*, 479 A.2d 374 (N.J. 1984). In the first case the New Jersey Supreme Court refused to recognize a "state of the art" defense, that is it refused to allow the defendant to argue that it could not warn the plaintiff of certain risks because at the time they were unknown. In the latter case the court allowed a state of the art defense. In distinguishing the cases the court said "The rationale of Beshada is not applicable to this case. We do not overrule Beshada, but restrict Beshada to the circumstances giving rise to its holding." 479 A.2d at 388. What those circumstances are, is anybody's guess.

29. The mean awards are much higher, between $800,000 and $1,000,000 (Hensler, 1987:490).

meaning? Are these fundamental differences to do with objectives and values? (Singleton and Hovden, 1987: xiv)

In the same collection Glendon (1987: 87) addresses this question and notes that risk analysis exists in three levels. The first level involves the type of risk appraisal traditionally found in mathematics, economics and engineering; including the calculation of probabilities of risks, cost/benefit analysis and risk analysis. The middle level is concerned with perceptions of risk, and of behavior in the face of risk. Analyses at this level typically fall within the field of psychology, although they occur within engineering as well (e.g, human factors analysis). The third level is concerned with the social and political dimensions of risk. Analyses at this level typically fall within the fields of sociology and political science. The great weight of analysis in books on corporate risk analysis is directed at the first level.[30] Legal rationality, however, also includes components of the second and third levels. Higher levels of legal rationality are more likely in a system where lay people (judges and juries) ultimately must assess whether a product is defective. They are especially likely in cases where the plaintiff's political agenda that is of equal or greater importance than is the recovery of damages (Douglas and Wildavsky, 1982).

The perception of risk.[31]   Middle level rationality involves the perception of risk and of the reasonableness of behavior in the face of risk. The central observation is that perceptions do not always correspond to the measured hazards of various activities or products. There are at least two dimensions to perception of risk. First, assessments of risk are often based on a wide variety of factors. While lay people can assess risks in terms of measures such as annual fatalities, and can do so with some measure of accuracy, their judgement of risk is sensitive to other factors such as the number of people exposed to the risk, the degree to which the risk is understood,[32] and the degree to which it evokes a feeling of dread.[33] On the contrary, experts tend to rate risks primarily on the

---

30. See, for example, Crouch and Wilson (1982), Doherty (1985), Hertz and Thomas (1983, 1984), Lalley (1982), Whipple and Covello (1985). This is also true of environmental auditing books (see Harrison, 1984; but see, also, the recent collection of articles in Lave, 1987).

31. This section relies heavily on the discussion in Slovic, et al. (1987).

32. This includes things such as whether the risk is observable, whether those exposed to it are aware they are being exposed, whether the risk is known to science, and whether its effects are delayed in time.

33. This includes things such as whether the risk is controllable, and voluntarily encountered; and whether the damages it may produce are fatal, inequitable, potentially catastrophic, global in scope, and not easily reduced.

dimension of annual expected fatalities (Slovic, et al., 1979; 1987).[34] This difference in perception creates the potential for different conclusions concerning the appropriate level of safety. When a risk is encountered involuntarily, not understood, and dreaded people look upon it more unfavorably and thus want it reduced to a greater degree (Slovic, et al., 1987:33; Reschler, 1983). In these situations a risk/benefit analysis based upon first level considerations will produce a level of safety that appears to be inadequate to lay judges.[35]

Second, the perception of risk can be influenced by the way information is presented. Some judgments are biased by what is called the availability heuristic (Tversky and Kahneman, 1973; Nisbett and Ross, 1980). People judge an event to be likely if they can imagine or recall past instances of the event. Ability to recall is also influenced by factors such as the size of a disaster and publicity. The frequency of dramatic and sensational deaths is overestimated (Lichtenstein, et al., 1978). From the point of view of the firm, when a product failure becomes a public issue the increase in vividness may increase the probability that lay decision makers will find it to be defective.

Judgments may also be influenced by the decision frame in which they are placed. Tversky and Kahneman (1981) call this a lack of invariance; choices vary depending on how they are framed. A key component of framing is whether, in situations of risk, choices are described as either a gain or a loss relative to the status quo. In a choice between "gains" people tend to be risk averse and to choose "sure things;" in a choice between "losses" people tend to

---

This analysis helps us to understand the substantial opposition to nuclear power. Opponents believe that its risks are unknown, uncontrollable, inequitable, catastrophic, and likely to affect future generations (see Slovic, et al., 1987:35; Fischhoff, et al., 1983).

34. Were all to agree that human injury and death should be the appropriate measure of costs, problems would remain since estimates of the value of human life still vary widely (see Pierce, 1980; Viscusi, 1983). Moreover, cost calculations that place a dollar value on human life open a firm up to charges of callous disregard for the sanctity of life (see Calabresi and Bobbit, 1978; Owen, 1982).

35. The problem posed for firm risk management strategies is that, given one's premises, other perspectives appear to be "irrational" and therefore illegitimate. This tendency is exacerbated by the fact that people are often overconfident in their judgments, especially in their ability to estimate the probability of uncertain events (Lichtenstein, et al., 1982). This is as true of experts as it is of lay people once the experts are forced to go beyond their data and rely upon judgments (Hynes and Vanmarke, 1976). The firm must attempt to defend its products in an environment of differing, strongly held opinions.

be risk seeking and to choose the gamble (Kahneman and Tversky, 1984). Similar instability in judgments can be observed when choices are framed as losses vs. costs. Consider the choice between a sure loss of $50 and a 25% chance of losing $200. Slovic, et al. (1982), report that 80% of the subjects in one experiment chose the gamble over the sure loss (people are risk seeking in the domain of losses). However, only 35% of a group of subjects refused to pay $50 (a cost) for insurance against a 25% risk of losing $200. Kahneman and Tversky report:

> The failure of invariance is both pervasive and robust. It is as common among sophisticated respondents as among naive ones, and it is not eliminated even when the same respondents answer both questions within a few minutes. Respondents confronted with their conflicting answers are typically puzzled. Even after rereading the problems, they still wish to be risk averse in the [gain] version; they wish to be risk seeking in the [loss] version; and they also wish to obey invariance and give consistent answers in the two versions. In their stubborn appeal, framing effects resemble perceptual illusions more than computational errors... The moral of these results is disturbing. Invariance is normatively essential, intuitively compelling, and psychologically unfeasible (Kahneman and Tversky, 1984: 343-344).

Part of the legal hazard confronting the firm is that lay legal decision makers also are likely to be susceptible to framing effects. They may make efforts to overcome the failure of invariance, but there is reason to expect that this is difficult to achieve in the context of a products liability lawsuit. Kahneman and Tversky (1984) argue that to be successful such efforts must cause decisions to be framed as choices in states of wealth (total assets) rather than gains and losses. Such a choice requires a common, agreed upon metric, for without such a metric people cannot compare alternatives. Are a million cars that costs $15 less each worth an additional 10 human lives? In situations where a metric is difficult to construct or situations where individuals lack access to formulae to compute the impact of various designs they may resort to what Fischhoff, et al. (1981) call bootstrapping approaches; they judge the acceptability of proposed risks against the baserate of the level of risk that has been tolerated in the past. In such a decision making environment any change in product design is risky.

The social and political context of risk. The third level of risk analysis is the political and social context of risk.[36] When firm risk assessment

---

36. For examples of articles that are part of this literature see Abel (1982), Chubb (1983), Nelkin and Pollack (1980), Perrow (1984), Short (1984), Rule (1978).

processes come under attack part of the challenge is to the legitimacy of first level risk analysis. The criticism is that the level of analysis done within the firm is too narrow because it fails to give adequate consideration to psychological, political and social concerns. Any consensus that may exist among engineers about the risks of some process is discounted as the ideological bias of a shared culture that prefers technologies with risky potential (Hertsgaard, 1983; Wildavsky, 1988).[37]

It is difficult to assess the effect of such arguments on specific cases. It does seem, however, that products do become less acceptable because of a general belief that their risks have not been assessed properly. The product and its producers lose public trust (Short, 1984). When trust is lost a firm's first level risk analysis is more vulnerable to political attack.

The social context of risks may also influence risk assessment. In some cases, for instance, the courts and juries appear to rate human autonomy as the central consideration, and therefore to find a product to be defective because of a lack of a warning even though most people would agree that had a warning been given it would not have influenced the behavior of the plaintiff (Sagoff, 1982). The clearest examples of this phenomena are the polio vaccine cases. Typically, a young child contracts polio from the ingestion of the Sabin oral polio vaccine. The probabilities of this result are very small, but measurable. No warning has been given to the plaintiff or the plaintiff's parents. In early cases, because the plaintiff's area was experiencing a polio epidemic, the risks from taking the vaccine were orders of magnitude smaller than the risks of refusing. Even on these facts the courts have been willing to create a presumption that plaintiffs would have refused the vaccine if warned, and juries have rejected defense efforts to overcome this presumption by showing the relative risks of taking the vaccine and refusing it. The cases are best understood as examples where risk/benefit considerations (here risk benefit calculations of plaintiffs) are subordinated to considerations of human autonomy and victim compensation.[38]

---

37. In turn, supporters of complex technologies have argued that the legal system itself is flawed because it offers no clear rules about how to weigh such considerations. DeLong notes that:

> [T]he legal system does not have any clear concept of how to deal with risk issues. In part, this reflects the general confusion in society over the question of "how safe is safe enough?" and the general reluctance to look explicitly at issues that appear to involve trading lives for money (1984:363).

38. See, for example *Reyes v. Wyeth Laboratories*, 498 F.2d 1264 (5th Cir.), cert. denied, 419 U.S. 1096 (1974). As a consequence of this group of cases drug manufacturers refused to market flu vaccines because of unknown liability. The federal government passed a statute promising to indemnify the companies for all tort losses not attributable to manufacturer negligence. This immunity

The concept of mental accounting helps to explain the decision making process in such cases. Thaler (1980) describes three levels of accounting. A *minimal* account makes a decision with respect to the difference between two options. One disregards any features the options might share. A *topical* account judges the consequences of possible choices based on the context within which the decision arises. Topical accounting occurs when we find we will drive to a different shopping mall to save five dollars on the purchase of a fifteen-dollar pocket calculator, but will not drive the same distance to save five dollars on a $1,500 personal computer. By minimal accounting one would look only to the five dollar difference in each case. Finally, there is *comprehensive* accounting in which the relative advantage between two options is calculated within some larger context such as monthly expenses. The results in the polio cases reflect court and jury unwillingness to limit the analysis to a minimal account based upon the difference between two options. The issue of autonomy and perhaps the apparent inequity of one person being injured while many others are protected, cause the courts and jurors to adopt a different level of accounting. To the degree that certain products are judged by a comprehensive accounting standard general social contexts become part of the products liability case.

Which type of products or product defects will be treated this way? A plausible hypothesis is that those cases in which the injury scores high on the dread and unknown dimensions will be judged by a topical or comprehensive mental accounting and thus present the firm with a legal rationality most dramatically different from the first level rationality of traditional risk/benefit analysis.

Toward a Theory of Risk Management Strategies

To repeat, those against whom some legal rule is directed may devote their efforts toward compliance with the law or toward arranging their affairs so as to avoid the application of the rule.[39] Within the area of risk management for

---

has been expanded to all childhood vaccines through the National Childhood Vaccine Injury Act of 1986, tit. III, Pub. L. No. 99-660, 100 Stat. 3755 (1986).

39. An extreme, strategic type of avoidance is the counter-mobilization of law. Counter-mobilization can involve efforts to change rules through the legislative process or through the courts. In the area of products liability there have been repeated efforts on the part of defense interests to turn to the legislature for relief from onerous products liability rules. The movement is beyond the scope of this paper, but is an important part of a risk management strategy. For a review of some of the developments in this area see special issues in the Ohio State Law Review (1987) and the San Diego Law Review (1987). Counter-mobilization may also occur within the judicial system. Occasionally manufacturers, like any repeat player, may play for rules, and pursue a case with

product safety, a firm's response involves two related, but separate goals--product safety and loss reduction. The central theoretical question of this paper is, how is the balance between avoidance and compliance influenced by the nature of the firm and the nature of the legal rules? At the outset two caveats are in order.

First, compliance is not an either/or decision. Many behaviors may be the result of mixed (or even confused or conflicting) motives. Equally important, compliance and avoidance are not mutually exclusive investments. At some rate of return, investment in product safety produces loss reduction. One determinant of a firm's risk management strategy is the degree to which compliance behavior is, reliably, also avoidance behavior.

Second, both avoidance and compliance behavior can occur within and outside the context of a given case. Although there are no pure types, distinctions can be made. For instance, at the end of his book *Product Safety Engineering for Managers,* Seiden (1984:340-341) lists the ten commandments of product safety, some of which involve pre-accident behavior. They cover both general and case related behaviors, including: thou shalt properly apply risk-utility analysis; thou shalt not use warnings and instructions in place of feasible built-in safety hardware; thou shalt not plead the state-of-the-art defense when thou knowest thou should have known better; thou shalt not bear false witness against thy adversary's expert opinion when thou knowest damn well it's right. Each of these commandments either explicitly or implicitly rejects avoidance behaviors on the part of engineers.[40]

---

the objective of altering existing product liability law (Galanter, 1975). DiMento (1986), for instance, reports the following comments of one auto company executive as to why they pursued a low probability defense in a case against the EPA. "Quite frankly, what we were looking for in litigating that particular case was kind of a no-harm, no-fault decision. It might have been a longshot. .... We didn't get it" (1986:87).

40. Attorneys are less likely to feel bound by any such commandments. Thus, to the degree that attorney effort is concentrated in case-specific efforts we might expect a greater percentage of those efforts to be devoted to avoidance behavior (DiMento, 1986). In turn, to the degree the firm's response to product liability is concentrated in litigation-related activity it is likely to be weighted toward avoidance behavior. It is important to note, however, that attorneys often play an active role outside the context of a case. In part this is because attorney involvement may offer the firm protection from certain discovery efforts in the event of trial. Upjohn v. United States, 449 U.S. 383 (1981) protects internal corporate documents from discovery under the attorney-client privilege in cases governed by federal law. Chayes and Chayes (1985) note, however, that corporate counsel remain concerned that state law may offer a narrower ambit for the privilege. For a more complete discussion of confidentiality issues see Eizenstat and Litan (1984), Price and Danzig (1986).

With these two caveats in mind, following are some hypotheses concerning ways in which the nature of the firm and the nature of product liability rules interact to affect risk management strategy. Whenever possible these ideas will be related to the findings of Eads and Reuter.

The nature of the firm sets the background conditions within which legal impact must operate. If the firm wants to invest in compliance with safety rules, bounded rationality and opportunism place limits on attainable levels of compliance.

In the boundedly rational firm the more infrequent the potential of a lawsuit the more costly it is to construct structures that incorporate products liability rules. The firm will use alternative methods to govern and assess safety. Most of the firm's attention to products liability rules will be within the context of avoiding liability in specific cases. This apparently is the course of action taken by the firms studied by Eads and Reuter that produced "low hazard" products.

When safety efforts are costly to the individual the firm must establish procedures to guard against employee opportunism. Human asset specificity, however, constrains the range and severity of available governance structures. Constraints are greatest when asset specificity exists at a group level. If, as some have argued, group asset specificity is most likely to exist in those parts of the organization that play a role in the design of new products (Ouchi, 1980), the firm's weakest governance structures should exist with respect to design decisions. It is here that serious sunk cost effects are most likely to occur, including the use of retrospective rationality designed to justify what has already been done. The most egregious examples of firm avoidance behavior do in fact appear to be associated with design decisions.

Ford's famous cost/benefit memo justifying the location of the gas tank in the Pinto was apparently a retrospective analysis, generated after production decisions had been made (Kinghorn, 1984). Likewise, the great majority of the studies conducted by A.H. Robins with respect to the safety of the Dalkon Shield IUD were conducted after the product was in the marketplace and were designed to justify Robins' decision (Bureau of National Affairs, 1988a). Eventually sunk cost effects may invade the legal department as well. In a particularly extreme case a plaintiff won a reversal of a jury verdict for Robins by successfully arguing that Robins' expert perjured himself. In discovery proceedings the expert hid the fact that he had done a study on the safety of the shield, but testified to the results at trial (*Harre v. A.H. Robins Co.* 750 F.2d 1501 [11th Cir., 1985]). The expert subsequently was indicted on eight counts of perjury. The research was apparently part of a group of seven or eight secret studies of the Shield that were paid for by Robins' attorneys. The results were never reported to the company's medical department, making it possible for members of the department to testify that they were unaware of any studies questioning the safety of the Dalkon Shield.

By sending a vague signal, product liability law causes the boundedly rational firm to lean toward avoidance behavior. The uncertainty of products liability law limits the firm's ability to engage in pre-accident, prospective risk management. The uncertainty generated by the product liability rule system is of two types (see Grandori, 1987). There is uncertainty due to the cost of information. The effort required to analyze the ways in which a product may be found to be defective or how a specific type of defect will be treated by the court taxes the limited information-processing capacity of the firm.[41] There is also uncertainty due to lack of knowledge about cause and effect relationships. Even with full knowledge, i.e. a full understanding of all legal precedents on point, the firm may be unable to predict the legal effect of certain risk management behaviors. This is not simply a cost of information problem, but more nearly approaches a state of the environment problem.

In the face of increasing rule uncertainty that makes it difficult to construct specific compliance rules the firm's risk management effort will become bifurcated. The effort to design and market a profitable product will be separated from the effort to limit liability losses. Recall that Eads and Reuter found that in many of the firms they studied such a split has occurred. Product safety personnel and products liability defense efforts operated on parallel tracks, with limited interaction with respect to ongoing litigation.

The greater the rule uncertainty the more the firm will engage in pre-litigation avoidance behavior. A larger percentage of effort will be directed toward constructing a viable defense, even when this may come in conflict with constructing a safer product. Such conflict can occur both by acts of omission and acts of commission. The company may choose not to create or maintain certain records for fear they may later be discovered and used against it in litigation (Kent, 1987). In extreme cases it may choose to hold back on safety decisions because of legal considerations.[42]

---

41. In the face of this complexity the firm may generate simplifying structures that allow it to typify the legal meaning of various situations (Lempert and Sanders, 1986). Routinizing processes are difficult to achieve, however, in an environment of rule uncertainty, increasing damage awards and ever-changing technology (see Grady, 1988).

42. Recently United States District Judge Robert Renner released a set of G.D. Searle & Co. documents relating to the Copper-7 IUD. Among the materials was a note from a manager that alleged as follows with respect to the introduction of an improved model of the product:

> Hold-up on IUDs is legal cases--Legal dept. does not want us coming out with "New & Improved" product design--hurt our chances--FYI--this is slowing everything down regarding IUDs. (*Simon v. G.D. Searle & Co.*, DC Minn No. 4-80-160, 4/28/88; as reported in Bureau of National Affairs, 1988b)

Affirmatively, uncertainty encourages the firm to construct a "process defense" that is directed more toward defense than toward safety processes per se.[43]

> [I]f the liability consequences of various production decisions become too unpredictable, manufacturers may find it more cost-effective to invest in the appearance of safety and the intensive litigation of safety issues, rather than in safety itself (Silicaino, 1987: 1830 n. 36).

> But audits differ, and some might be more defense-oriented than others. An audit may be designed primarily to ascertain that specific procedures have been followed and that required documentation exists (or does not exist if not required)--a defense orientation. Or, an audit may be designed to examine whether safety-related decisions were reasonable, regardless of specific procedures followed--a more operational orientation (Eads and Reuter, 1985:11).

When legal rationality moves beyond a first level risk-utility analysis this, too, will cause the firm to be less likely to respond with compliance behavior. It is relatively difficult to build higher order rationalities into a firm's risk management program. Moreover, a decision to accept legal outcomes based on higher level rationality as appropriate measures of successful performance invites increased opportunistic behavior. Employees are likely to view such rules as aberrations to be overcome rather than goals to be pursued. Because higher level rationality is most likely to occur in situations where the risk is "dreaded," it is here that we should observe firm reluctance to use products liability rules to judge employee performance. Eads and Reuter's finding that firms engaged in the manufacture of inherently hazardous products treated products liability costs as overhead rather than as indicators of product failure is consistent with this hypothesis.

Finally, increases in rule uncertainty and higher level legal rationality cause the products liability rule system to lose legitimacy within the firm. There is some evidence that corporate managers and the population at large hold much of tort law in low repute (Insurance Information Institute, 1982). A loss of

---

43. The proposal by Twerski, et al. (1980) that products liability law should formally adopt a "process defense" can be viewed as an effort to keep firms from divorcing their product safety efforts from their loss reduction efforts by allowing their safety process to be a defense to product claims. This proposal has not been adopted in any jurisdiction, but the growth of environmental audits suggests that firms may find a process defense useful in defending suits. The initial process defense proposal was opposed by Henderson (1981), with a rebuttal by Twerski, et al. (1981).

legitimacy provides the psychological justification necessary to pursue a risk management policy that focuses on avoidance behavior. Perceptions of illegitimacy may eventually cause the firm to move beyond avoidance behavior to active counter-mobilization and work for rule changes in the legislature.

Conclusion

This paper has attempted to sketch a general perspective that combines elements of a transaction cost perspective on the firm with an understanding of the nature of legal rules and the nature of legal rationality to generate hypotheses concerning firm risk management strategies. Beyond this first effort, further theoretical refinements are in order and more data are essential. One useful place to begin empirical work is to study the role of corporate counsel in various legal and corporate environments (see Chayes and Chayes, 1985).

At a more general level, a theory of firm risk management strategies can be part of a theory of effective response to legal rules. The theory of efficient breach in contract law is part of such a theory as is recent work on criminal decision making processes (Piliavin, et al., 1986). The question of why firms make certain risk management decisions given a set of rules is not unlike the question of why criminals choose to commit crimes in certain locations and at certain times given the criminal law. Closer to the present topic, a good part of the regulation literature rejecting the application of rigid safety rules is premised on the idea that they encourage avoidance behavior to a greater extent than does a more cooperative environment (Scholz, 1984). Thus the larger agenda is to understand the ways in which rules and the objects of those rules interact to produce legal (and illegal) consequences.

5

Neoclassical Difficulties:
Tort Deterrence for Latent Injuries

W. L. F. Felstiner and Peter Siegelman

The deterrent effect of tort compensation is a pressing social issue and has spawned an immense literature. The particular difficulties posed by latent injuries have generally been ignored in the academic and political struggle although such injuries have affected large numbers of people (Boden and Jones, 1987:321) and are likely to plague even larger numbers in the future (McCulloch, 1986:231-33).

By latent injuries we mean those for which the lag between exposure to the injurious agent and manifestation of harm is measured in years at least, and frequently in decades. Three classes of victims are afflicted with latent injuries caused by business firms--users of business-produced products, workers who make those products, and bystanders. Illustratively, in the first class have been victims of thalidomide, acutane, bendectin, the Dalkon shield, Agent Orange and asbestos; in the second class are workers in asbestos factories and employees of chemical and nuclear plants; bystanders have been victims of nuclear leaks and tests, dioxin leaks and non work-related asbestos exposure. Because of the bar to employee tort claims theoretically imposed by workers' compensation, our analysis is primarily directed to the first and third classes. The situation of workers is introduced because (a) workers injured by asbestos do have a tort remedy against asbestos manufacturers; (b) the theory about the relationship between tort compensation and safety measures for workers is supplemented by the theory of compensating wage differentials; (c) the exclusivity of workers'

We acknowledge thoughtful comments on earlier drafts by Ian Ayres, Mary Coyne, John Braithwaite, Robert Dingwall, John Donohue, Tom Durkin, Wendy Espeland and Mark Grady.

compensation is under attack (Barth, 1984:570); and (d) partial experience rating of workers' compensation makes the economic theory applicable to tort compensation potentially relevant.

The thesis of this paper is that latent injuries introduce empirical complications that overwhelm the assumptions on which the deterrent effect attributed to tort law by neoclassical economic theory is based.[1] This point is essentially negative. We are not suggesting that regulation, social insurance, or other schemes are superior to tort as a means of securing an optimal allocation of resources for accident prevention. Rather we argue that the theoretical model of tort as the baseline for comparison of alternative systems is misleading because, at least in the context of latent injuries, it cannot work as predicted by the neoclassical model.

Although the main argument of this paper is that in calculations about safety precautions firms cannot take the long term into consideration, we begin by reciting the case that today's firms and their managers frequently do not even want to do so.[2] This argument has three strands: that American firms are increasingly short run optimizers; that they have conflicting goals and structures that interfere with coordinated efforts at maximization; and that managers confronted by uncertainty often seek personal goals at the expense of organizational ones.

Hirsch (1987) and Drucker (1986) have argued that it has become increasingly irrational for American corporations to make decisions based on long-term considerations. The main effect of investment banker and arbitrageur involvement in corporate ownership is that a corporation's value now depends on its ability to maximize the short-term return on shareholder investment.[3] Hirsch's (1987:18) case studies demonstrate that the favored path to this goal is the elimination of long term planning, development, and capacity through

---

1. Deviations from perfect maximizing behavior need not to be large to have significant effects. In a highly provocative article, Akerlof and Yellen (1985) asked "Can Small Deviations From Rationality Make Significant Differences to Economic Equilibria?" and conclude that they can. The intuition behind this theoretical result is difficult to explain, but its consequences are profound. No longer is it reasonable to claim, as many Chicago school economists do (see, e.g., Landes and Posner, 1987:12-13) that "nearly-maximizing" action produces virtually the same results as maximizing behavior.

2. Even in the case of harms with immediate effect some analysts (e.g. Braithwaite, 1984; Fisse, 1983) believe that sanctions (such as fines and tort damages) imposed on corporations are ineffective in controlling the behavior of corporate officials who are themselves unaffected by the penalties.

3. Stein (1988) presents a neoclassical model formalizing these conclusions.

downsizing, dismantling, and increasing debt. Executives of nearly all large American corporations have responded to this market pressure (Hirsch, 1987:45-47). As divisions have been summarily eliminated, and company officials fired, often without regard to productivity and experience, managers have responded with a new ethos -- that of Free Agent, concerned far more with their own future than the company's (Hirsch, 1987:xvi, 109-10) and ready to leave the company whenever a better offer is at hand.[4] Peters and Waterman (1982:43-52) have argued that a short-term focus also follows from an over-reliance on superficial analyses and a bias against innovation. American firms rely on cost-benefit analyses that undervalue or ignore long term efforts and benefits (research and development, productive capacity, high morale, company goodwill) that are difficult to quantify in favor of readily available figures (material costs, inventory turnover, sales) that are more easily obtained. The capacity to measure only short run projects precisely leads to analyses that focus on monthly, quarterly, or single year goals. Thus future values are not just discounted to present value, but further discounted because the benefits are so difficult to quantify.[5]

The link between future profits and present actions is further weakened by the so-called "agency problem"--the fact that managers of most firms make decisions rather than the owners, and the interests of the two parties do not always coincide. There is a vast literature on the ways in which firms are structured to reduce this divergence of interests and no consensus about the degree to which efforts to enforce maximization are successful. It is, however, clear that the problem is likely to become more acute as the planning horizon gets longer.

Organization theorists long ago abandoned the idea that firms acted toward a single, coherent goal (see, e.g., Allison, 1970; Scherer, 1980:29-41). Not only do organizations seek multiple and often conflicting goals, but employees use their power to convert resources to secure sub-organizational objectives. Allison's "governmental politics model" (1970:ch. 5) recognizes that results are determined by the interplay of influential actors holding influential positions. Players enter the game with different agendas, levels of formal authority, skill,

---

4. Hechinger (1988:25) has identified the same short-term focus in business schools and their students. A recent report of the American Assembly of Collegiate Schools of Business reported that training "focused too much on the short term at the expense of taking a broader, deeper, long-range perspective." Corporate executives reported that new MBA's were "afraid of actions that cannot be backed up with a detailed quantitative analysis" (Porter and McKibben, 1988:99).

5. Economic models of criminal justice have also been criticized for ignoring information quality and availability problems and hidden transaction costs (see Coffee, 1980: 440-49).

power, and control of crucial information. As in the Cuban missile crisis, the politically modified "score of the game" is often distinct from what any group or person intended, and far from the organization's best interest.[6]

Many neoclassical economists would object to the way these propositions overpersonalize corporate decision-making. Their analysis assumes that firms are forced by competition to try to maximize the present discounted value of future profits. Managers may disagree on goals and seek short-run objectives, but market forces curtail such behavior so that deviations from profit maximization are limited.

Market discipline is said to arise from two sources: competition in the market for the products that firms sell and the market for capital in which virtually all firms participate. The basis of product market discipline is simple: "In the austere environment of complete and perfectly competitive markets, there is no alternative desideratum left against which the value of the firm might be traded off" (Nelson and Winter, 1982:54). Thus, firms which do not minimize costs, for example, cannot generate the market rate of return on their capital at the market price for output, and will sooner or later go bankrupt. Using some ingenious simulation techniques, however, Nelson and Winter (1982) have demonstrated that firms that follow non-maximizing heuristic decision rules can nevertheless survive in the long run, even in industries where many firms are strict profit maximizers. Thus even ignoring changing business conditions and organizational and psychological theory, the neoclassical view that product market competition guarantees that firms will be maximizers is not necessarily correct.

The second source of discipline is the market for capital. In this view, "it is to the external discipline provided by the takeover raider, rather than the internal discipline imposed by [the owner] that society looks for the effective functioning

---

6. The psychological literature on the dilemma of the commons (Hardin, 1968) also makes one skeptical that actual behavior follows neoclassical economic logic. In a series of experiments Brewer and her colleagues have shown that in the absence of any of a set of unusual conditions people will destroy a common resource on which they all depend in the long term in order to maximize short-term gratification. These studies imply that managers would sacrifice current profits by instituting safety measures against latent injuries only when assured that managers of rival firms or rival divisions of the same firm were adopting the same course (Messick, et al., 1983) or when forced to do so by external controls (Messick and Brewer, 1983) or when limited social distance between decision makers and victims reduces distinctions in managerial welfare calculations (Brewer, 1979). In other words, in a context of intense competition for short-term results, weak regulation, and hierarchical labor relations, which is the general situation of American industry, this research predicts that managers do not incorporate the very long-term into their profits and safety calculations.

of the [firm]" (Nelson and Winter, 1982:54). If a firm fails to maximize profits, its stock price will be depressed; it will then be a tempting target for take over by new owners who will be able to make a profit by buying at the low price, restoring profit maximizing behavior, and raising the price of the stock they own. Even in theory, however, recent work (e.g., Grossman and Hart, 1980) demonstrates that it is not at all clear how much discipline takeovers, or capital markets in general, can provide.[7]

Furthermore, notions of bounded rationality and statistical ignorance also suggest that firms fail to maximize profits over time horizons as long as those involved in many latent injuries. The uncertainty and complexity of the profit-maximization problem increase exponentially as the planning horizon expands. Simon (1957) and others have argued that such complexity leads to "satisficing" behavior even in the short run because the problem of achieving maximum profit is simply too difficult to solve. Rules of thumb or extrapolation from past practice, rather than an optimizing calculus, govern business decisions, especially those whose consequences will be felt in the distant future. The body

---

7. In addition, maximization theories must confront "the optimality problem." Although neoclassical models frequently seek to demonstrate that markets produce optimal results, no model can be a model of everything--thus, any demonstration of optimality is at best only a showing that given certain externally generated assumptions, an optimal result is achieved. Consider, for instance, a change in legal procedure that might have an effect on the costs of bringing or defending a suit, on the awards to successful plaintiffs, and so on. If firms act in accordance with traditional economic models, this hypothetical change will lead them to alter their behavior--for instance, to increase their spending on safety or reduce their labor force. Assuming that there are no distortions, the new levels of safety and labor will be optimal given the new rule. However, the original level of safety was also optimal given the old rule. The key point, then, is that "mere" optimality given the existing rules may not be very interesting, even were it consistently attained. To evaluate the social utility of the tort system, one thus needs to look not only at how firms respond, or fail to respond, to any given set of rules, but whether the rules themselves are optimal. Landes and Posner (1987) have recently argued that most rules of tort law are indeed optimal. But, just for example, whether the statute of limitations in asbestos cases should be five years, or fifteen years, or whether indeed there should be any statute of limitations at all, is far from obvious. Green (1988) and Epstein (1986), for instance, look at this question and derive dramatically different answers. If the statute of limitations is set "incorrectly" and firms make maximizing calculations on the basis of the "wrong" rule, the system may appear to be producing optimal results, but will in fact be failing to do so. Moreover, firms attempting to make decisions about how much to spend to prevent latent injuries must optimize not only on current rules, but on expected future rules as well.

of this paper is a demonstration that the level of complexity in the latent injury context virtually guarantees the impossibility of long-run maximization.

Finally, further doubts about the profit maximizing assumption in the context of latent injuries stem from the nature of the uncertainty involved. Virtually all economic models treat uncertainty in a convenient, but highly stylized fashion. The paradigmatic example is flipping a coin, a case in which the exact outcome (heads or tails) is not known in advance, but the range of possible outcomes and the probabilities of each are given (or can be learned over time). This kind of uncertainty poses little difficulty for model makers. If the agent being modelled is risk neutral, the expected value of the uncertain outcome can be substituted for its uncertain range of outcomes.[8]

Rather than choosing a single action which produces the best average payoff under a range of known circumstances, decision makers for long-term projects such as spending to avoid latent injuries know neither the range of possible outcomes nor the probabilities associated with each. However such choices are actually made, it seems clear that they can not be made as they are modeled in mainstream economics, since the range of possible outcomes and the level of ignorance are far greater than any planner could contemplate.[9] Moreover, most business decisions are

> unique, in the sense that [they] are most unlikely to replicated anywhere else in the economic system, and...can never [be] repeated. Actuarial or statistical probability has no application to an experiment which is non-divisible and non-seriable [not repeatable]; it makes no sense to apply the arithmetical processes which belong to actuarial probability to a purely subjective estimate of probability. Carter (1972:30).

Causal Assumptions and Empirical Reality

There is no single authoritative neoclassical analysis of the working of the tort system.[10] Here we abstract what we take to be the key assumptions or

---

8. If the agent is risk-averse, then the problem becomes slightly more complex, but still easily manageable.

9. See Arrow and Hurwicz (1972) and Carter (1972) for some alternative views on decision making under ignorance.

10. For recent surveys of the economics of tort, see Landes and Posner (1987) and Shavell (1987).

requirements of this style of modeling that are particularly problematic in the context of latent injuries.

Most work in mainstream economics assumes that firms maximize the present discounted value of (expected) profits from the present through the infinite future. Suppose a firm is considering whether or not to spend money today on product safety that will prevent some injury that becomes manifest thirty years hence. The benefits of making this expenditure are the damages the firm will avoid having to pay to injured parties and the litigation expenses it will escape. If these benefits are properly measured and weighed in the firm's calculations, then the neoclassical analysis leads to the conclusion that the firm will decide to spend the socially optimal amount on safety. If there are distortions in the way the firm factors these distant benefits into its decisions, however, then the amount spent on safety will depart from the optimum.

Now let us examine the operation of these neoclassical assumptions. First, future damages would be discounted to present value. A $100,000 adverse judgment thirty years in the future would at a 10% discount rate approximate a $6000 current penalty. A firm ought not then spend more than $6000 to avoid the harm that thirty years from now will underlie the $100,000 judgment (Viscusi, 1986:322).[11]

Second neoclassical theory does not consider workers exposed to toxic substances to be random casualties of capitalist production, but rather people who have to some degree bargained for the harm by accepting extra compensation for the extra risks that they assumed at the workplace (Rosen, 1986:642). There is considerable empirical support for the proposition that people are compensated to some degree for job risks (see Smith, 1979; references cited in Landes and Posner, 1987:309). But there are several factors that suggest that we should not abandon our concern for the worker on this account. What is the evidence about the relationship between risk and wages in the latent injury

---

11. The theory assumes that the tortfeasor itself pays the damages. If the tort liability is covered by insurance, then the firm ought not spend on safety more than the amount that the liability will increase the insurance premiums discounted from the date of the increase. If insurance premiums do not vary directly with liability, then the theory would predict no deterrent effect to tort compensation. Thus, we ignore insurance in the rest of this paper. This decision is only questionable if insurance company information problems in the tort area are substantially different from those of manufacturing firms and insurance companies are better able than producers to predict the long-term development of tort doctrine, changes in defense costs, legal culture, propensities to sue and worker demands induced by risk. In the asbestos field, insurance companies discussed surcharges on products liability policies (Brodeur, 1985), but there is no evidence that they even shared claims data to form estimates of incidence or compensation.

context? Since the theory of equalizing differences assumes a substantial amount of information on both sides of the labor market (Rosen, 1986:663), is there reason to believe that we stray farther from this condition when the risk involved is latent rather than apparent? Second, are there alternative theoretical formulations that ought to make us suspicious of the exchange of risk for higher wages? We will discuss these and other caveats later in this paper.

What reservations ought one consider about this economic analysis of discounted compensation, wage rates and safety measures? First, there is the unstable nature of the $100,000 adverse judgment. Maybe it will prove to be $200,000 or $2,000,000 or $50,000. In those cases the reasonable company official ought to spend $12,000 or $120,000 or $3,000 to protect the worker against the risk. The problem is not that the *theory* of deterrence is illogical or that discounting is an inappropriate way to transform future into current values, but that there is no reliable way to determine the future values. Who knows what the legal rules governing the allocation of responsibility or the calculation of damages will be thirty years from now?[12] Asbestos company officials in the U.S. in the 1930s, 40s and 50s were undeterred from putting consumers and workers in jeopardy not because they ignored the legal consequences of their own behavior, but because they did not predict the changes in legal doctrine and pre-trial practice that would facilitate the litigation that eventually erupted.[13]

Are these changes in doctrine and practice of a sort that their effects may be reasonably estimated? Even if they occur over many years, their consequences may be incorporated in rational decision-making if their direction and pace are

---

12. Is this uncertainty like that faced by people who have "no idea" about the height of the Empire State Building? New Yorkers know that the ESB is more than twenty feet and less than a mile high. If asked enough questions they could construct a probability distribution for their best guesses about its height. If the same kind of probability distribution had been calculated by asbestos manufacturers, it would not have been very useful since the actuality proved to be far out in the tail of any manager's likely expectations.

13. Danzon (1987:228) notes that actuarially-fair liability insurance is particularly difficult in the case of latent injuries: "The longer the delay between the triggering event ... and the manifestation of injury and adjudication of claims, the greater the potential for changes in liability rules and damage standards. This sociolegal risk introduces uncertainty as to the mean (the past cannot be used to predict the future) and destroys independence, since trends will similarly affect all policyholders."

reasonably predictable.   But the changes in tort law are neither even nor unidirectional.[14]

The orthodox understanding of the drift of American tort law since World War II is a steady erosion of the fault concept until the 1970's followed by swift and unanticipated changes in so-called superstrict liability, comparative negligence and its connection to joint and several liability, *Sindell* rules, the explosion in large punitive damages awards, changes in the structure of chapter 11 reorganizations under the Bankruptcy Code of 1978, retroactive waivers of statutes of limitation, the formal organization of plaintiffs' lawyers by type of mass tort and the resources that they have been able to generate and deploy, and the willingness of courts to transform insurance contracts into compensation devices.   In the other direction, that is toward limiting tort recoveries, the U.S. Justice Department has given unusual attention to tort reform;[15] and especially to changes at the state level, the growth of a well-financed American Tort Reform Association determined to reverse the doctrinal innovations of the past two decades, the research program of the Rand Corporation's Institute for Civil Justice, founded in 1980, on which much of the tort reform rhetoric is based and the large number of states that have adopted legislative measures to limit the number and level of tort recoveries such as caps on non-economic damages, limitations on contingent fees, mandatory pre-trial arbitration, limitations on punitive damages, facilitating or requiring periodic payment of judgments, prohibiting prejudgment interest, limiting dram shop and municipal liability and modifications to the collateral source rule and of joint and several liability.[16]

---

14.   Nor is the tort law subject to change centralized.   To estimate future recoveries, firms would need to predict the relevant jurisdictions in which their behavior would be evaluated as well as the rules of those jurisdictions.

15.   After years of rebuffs in Congress, proponents of tort reform on the federal level have adopted a new strategy consisting of modest aims (validating the state of the art defense, promulgating a 25 year statute of repose and limiting punitive damages), trying to assure that the business community speaks with one voice and mobilizing more members of Congress not known for a pro-business orientation.

16.   Carroll, 1987:47-72 lists 189 statutes adopted in 1986 in forty-one states that restrict tort recoveries.   These efforts to reduce the number of tort claims and limit recoveries have had limited success in the past (see Adams and Zuckerman, 1984; Sloan, 1985; Danzon, 1985; GAO, 1986).   More recent research on medical malpractice does report a negative effect on claims frequency and award size (see Danzon, 1986).   Since the pace of reform accelerated substantially in 1987 and the effort shows no signs of slackening, its eventual effect may be substantial.   See also Nelson (1988:686-89) which provides a powerful critique

Just as yesterday's managers grievously underestimated the threat of tort compensation, and underinvested in safety measures, how do we know that their contemporary counterparts are not overreacting to what will prove to be short-term trends in tort recoveries and, as a result, now overinvest in safety. In other words, setting the level above or below which it is inefficient and therefore socially "undesirable" to invest in harm reduction by discounting future projections based on current recoveries is a reasonable process only for analysts who are willing to turn their backs on the enduring volatility of American tort law.[17]

Moreover, there are unpredictable changes beyond those in rules that will influence tort compensation of the future. If Friedman's reading of history in *Total Justice* (1985) is at all accurate, then base rate changes in matters such as public attitudes toward risk and compensation can be expected to alter the behavior of juries and the value of tort cases when the relevant time periods are as long as the 20-40 years involved in many occupationally-generated diseases. Whatever the juries of tomorrow may do, it is often not even clear what they are doing today. Firms may and probably do organize and analyze their own recent experience, but the experience of researchers who have studied asbestos litigation suggests that industry, or even multi-firm, data do not exist (see McGovern, 1988:54): in fact such information is considered more a trade secret than a metafirm asset, despite its obvious utility in predicting long-term exposure of single firms. Insurance and capital markets in theory compensate for a firm's inability or disinclination to respond to the signals provided by future tort compensation. For instance, if firms guard information about risk as a trade secret, rational insurers ought to insist on such information before providing insurance. Moreover, insurance ought to mitigate the myopia of managers intent on today's profits by focusing their attention on the extent to which today's premiums reflect exposure over time, even long periods of time. Bondholders in theory behave in like manner, requiring higher interest payments from firms vulnerable to large future liability claims. The problem with this analysis is that the insurance companies and capital markets are no better able to

---

of the data and logic behind the work of the Attorney General's Tort Policy Working Group.

17. Schuck (1986:185-86) and others have pointed out how in toxic tort cases the combination of the rules requiring a plaintiff to establish causation by a preponderance of the evidence and providing that plaintiffs who meet that standard recover 100% of their damages means that often those damages will be greater or less than the risk created by defendants and that defendants will, as a consequence, be over or underdeterred. Of course, given our view of the deterrence problem, this complication simply makes an impossible calculus worse.

predict the rules, science and culture of the future, to assimilate the imperfections of the legal system into their calculations or to correct the flaws in wage differentials than are the producers themselves.[18]

Second, economic theory assumes that firms take into consideration the costs of defending future claims as well as compensation that they will be required to pay. Such costs are also unpredictable. Variation in costs arises from factors such as the number of defendants involved in typical cases (the more defendants, the more complicated are both discovery and negotiations), the level of disputing between defendants, between defendants and their insurers and between insurers, and the extent to which defendants and their insurers can coordinate their defense efforts. The Asbestos Claims Facility claimed to have reduced defense costs substantially, but how could asbestos manufacturers in the 1940s predict either the need for or growth of a private dispute processing system like the ACF, or its collapse, or indeed the innovative trial and settlement techniques adopted by U.S. federal courts in East Texas (see Hensler, et al., 1985:60-63) and Ohio (see McGovern, 1986; see also McGovern, 1988 for the methods adopted by the bankruptcy court in Virginia to process the 300,000 claims filed against A.H. Robins). Since the defense costs in asbestos cases in the U.S. were through 1982 virtually as large as the gross amounts paid to plaintiffs and their lawyers (Kakalik, et al., 1984:76), their economic significance is as formidable as it was unpredictable.

Third, there is the problem embedded in the reality that not all injured workers or users will recognize that their injuries are work-related or exposure-related and that, among those who make the connection, not all will seek to recover damages (see Felstiner, et al., 1981; Felstiner and Dingwall, 1988). One

---

18. "Many of the nation's insurers had known for decades that asbestos workers were dying early, but had kept silent while their underwriters wrote policies for workmen's compensation and comprehensive general liability as fast as they could put pen to paper, and as the premiums from those policies were invested with the full expectation that few, if any, claims for asbestos disease would ever be made" (Brodeur, 1985:200). Where firms predict that no or minimal damages will have to be paid to victims of occupational disease, it would be prudent for profit maximizers to mobilize a large supply of healthy workers to replace sick employees who can no longer work rather than spend resources on care. This analogy to the use of military manpower has been documented in the construction of the Panama Canal (McCullough, 1977) and the Hawk's Nest Tunnel (Cherniack, 1986). Of course, where there is not perfect substitutability of labor, there is an incentive to care for those with skills in short supply. That is why we see greater care for the health of engineers than of laborers in the Panama Canal saga (see McCullough, 1977). In the military context, if the pool of soldiers is sufficient, the functional equivalent of tort damages as an influence over care is public opinion (see Lorell and Kelley, 1985:56, 74, 82).

reason that some injured workers do not sue is the difficulty they may have in exploiting information about firm behavior developed in prior litigation (or on occasion in identifying experienced counsel) because defendants have been able in settlement of earlier suits to insist that the plaintiffs' lawyers bring no more cases nor assist others that do (see Lord, 1987:45 [Dalkon Shield]; Brodeur, 1985:242 [asbestos]; Yates, 1987:17 [Bic lighters]; Cherniack, 1986:71-72 [Hawk's Nest Tunnel]. The economically efficient penalty would be that amount which reflected the injuries of those who do not claim as well as those who do (Cooter & Ulen, 1988:460-61). Multiplying damages as in antitrust might, or liberal jury sympathy in fact may, internalize these consequences within firms to an extent. However, given the system's lack of stability no information can be generated on which to base the correct multiple.

The Dalkon shield litigation is instructive about the extent to which claiming behavior is a settled social phenomenon. Before the worldwide publicity required by the bankruptcy judge some 16,000 claims had been brought against A.H. Robins, the manufacturer of the device. After the public notice, nearly 300,000 claims were filed with the court (McGovern, 1988:26)[19] and even Robins has acknowledged the validity of 33,000 of them (*New York Times*, 11/7/87). Such huge fluctuations in injury identification and propensity to claim underline the difficulty of making decisions about expenditures to prevent harm that are geared to the present value of an unknown number of injuries that produce an unknown number of claims of an unknown size at an unknown time in the future. The signals that managers need to determine how much to spend on harm reduction are epidemiological while the signals that are provided by the tort system, flawed as they are, are about claims rather than victims and there is no known reliable method of back-estimating the universe from which the claiming sample came.[20]

---

19. After checking for duplication, claims made in error and without injury, 200,000 claims remained, 193,000 of which had not even "entered the tort system during the 15 years of Dalkon shield litigation" (McGovern, 1988:26). McGovern (personal communication), the Special Master in the chapter 11 proceeding, believes that 50,000 of these cases are "lawsuit caliber," suggesting that the tort system in the ordinary course had mobilized about 30% of the potential claimants.

20. The limiting case analysis may differ from product to product. When Ford produced defective Pintos, it knew how many were sold and what percentage were likely to be defective. It did not know how many lawsuits might result, but it had a worst case scenario to serve as a benchmark. Manufacturers of intermediate products like asbestos and many dangerous chemicals have no way to predict the number of ultimate users and thus no credible worst case scenario from which to start risk reduction calculations.

Fourth, tort deterrence must come to terms with imperfections in the legal system.[21] For instance, in the asbestos field many injured workers are faced with absolute barriers such as the statute of limitations in their efforts to secure tort compensation. Limitation rules in states such as New York and Wisconsin with large numbers of asbestos victims from World War II and Korean War shipbuilding programs required injured workers to institute suit before they could be expected even to know that they were sick (Mark, 1983:882).[22] The discounted present value of zero is zero, but no economic theory would tolerate a method for estimating the appropriate level of risk-reduction expenditures that ignores the injuries suffered by large numbers of uncompensated workers.[23]

Fifth, there is the evidence of what firms actually do in response to signals that the tort system in fact provides. We know that in the asbestos industry the response frequently was to suppress scientific and medical information rather than improve working conditions or provide warnings about product dangers (see Brodeur, 1974:142, 207; Brodeur, 1985:111-24, 145, 276; Castleman, 1986:61, 88-91, 608). Even more suggestive is Eads and Reuters's (1983:vii, ix) conclusion after studying nine large manufacturing firms "generally recognized as leaders in the safety field" that "although product liability exerts a powerful influence on product design decisions, it sends an extremely vague signal. Because the linkage between good design and a firm's liability exposure remains tenuous, the signal says only: 'Be careful, or you will be sued.' Unfortunately, it does not say . . . *how careful* to be."

Sixth, the sociolegal risk is exacerbated by unpredictable changes in victim vulnerability. For instance, the chances that asbestos exposure will lead to serious illness are strongly related to smoking. Thus the probabilities over the past forty years that people would suffer asbestos-related injuries depended on

---

21. See Hensler, et al. (1985:37-44) for a review of the procedural obstacles to tort claims for asbestos-related injuries. Problems embedded in legal rules are, of course, deficiencies in the legal system, not in economic theory. But they cannot be ignored by economists on that account unless, unlike most lawyers, economists believe in the perfectability of legal rules.

22. The New York statute was changed in 1986 to the discovery rule. New York also created a one-year window for workers barred in the past by the then existing exposure rule. See Chapter 682, Laws of New York, 1986. Between 3000 and 4000 claimants took advantage of the window.

23. See Johnson and Heler (1984) for an analysis of the adequacy and equity of compensation to survivors of 560 asbestos workers who died from workplace exposure between 1967-77. This paper is more a critique of workers' compensation than of tort damages which became an important source of compensation for asbestos workers only in the 1980s.

changes in population smoking patterns undeterminable by asbestos company officials. Furthermore, changes in medical science cannot be ignored. Although it is probably true that the most threatening latent injuries involve various forms of cancer and cures for many forms of cancer, including lung cancer, have been particularly intractable for medicine, nevertheless the economic consequences of current exposure to toxic substances are affected by unpredictable medical advances and the costs of as yet undeveloped medical therapies.

Seventh, fixing the level of risk reduction is in theory affected by the trade-off between wages and safety measures as well as that between discounted compensation costs and safety measures. If the more dangerous a job, the more that workers will demand in wages, there is a point at which it is in the interest of the firm to reduce the danger rather than pay the added labor costs. This homeostasis at which the costs of accident prevention and labor are minimized will be reached, or even approximated, only if the workers have sufficient information about the risks of their jobs to insist that such risks be incorporated in the wage rate. It is, in addition, dependent on the extent to which a reserve of unemployed workers exists locally.

Thus the question: how reasonable is it to impute economic calculations about risk to workers? The threshold issues concern who has the necessary information about risk in fact and who has the superior opportunity to acquire it in theory. In the asbestos context, the manufacturers had the information and aggressively concealed it from exposed workers. "A worker may be denied information essential to an informed decision as to whether to continue working in a contaminated environment, as happened to asbestos workers in the late 1950's" (Locke, 1985:275; see Berman, 1978:1-4). "Available evidence suggests that few firms make a comprehensive effort to inform workers of the risks they face. For example, no firms tell their employees the average annual death risk they face" (Viscusi, 1983:71). Corporations traditionally consider laboratory studies of hazards in their own products to be secret information (see *Dow v. Ryan*, 484 U.S. 953, 1987; *New York Times*, 11/17/87, p. 13; *New York Times*, 1/30/88, p. 9 [Liggett & Myers Tobacco Company's 30 years of secret studies on the dangers of cigarette smoking]).[24] Not only may company officials conceal from workers information that they have developed, but they may organize corporate behavior so as not to produce relevant information, e.g., by restricting research (see Brodeur, 1985: 111-124).

---

24. "Companies . . . camouflage their [products'] faults from the [government] inspectors by such means as using scientists who regularly test their products and can be relied upon not to submit distressing results" (Flood, 1988:813). Firms are even reluctant to grant employees access to their own medical records (Braithwaite and Fisse, 1983:75) and have been known to conceal clinical indications of occupational disease from them (Berman, 1978).

Information is itself a complicated variable in any risk-related calculations. The best signal concerning job-related risks is one's own injury experience (Viscusi, 1983:65). Victims of latent injuries rarely have such experience until it is too late to quit a hazardous job. How many workers know that the history of medicine suggests that the negative health effects of toxic substances are likely to be more numerous and more serious than the first identified risks.[25] Moreover, risks often are stated in ways that are inaccessible to laypeople or mistakenly oversimplified;[26] and recent research indicates that most people systematically misunderstand important probability relationships (e.g., they treat low probability events as having either a zero or excessively high probability) (see Tversky and Kahneman, 1974). In view of these considerations it is not at all surprising that asbestos workers secured only small wage premiums on account of the added risks of their jobs (Barth, 1982; Boden & Jones, 1987:337).

The task of separating economists from their theory is formidable, even in the presence of data that strongly suggest that the theory is inapplicable. Nowhere is this observation more trenchant than in the asbestos case. The *theory* of compensating wage differentials has been a tenet of welfare economics since Adam Smith (Landes and Posner, 1987:309). Paul McAvoy, onetime member of President Ford's Council of Economic Advisers and Frederick William Beinecke Professor of Economics at Yale, now Dean of the Graduate School of Management at the University of Rochester, *really* endorses the theory. Writing in the *New York Times* (2/82 Sunday Business Section) McAvoy criticized workers for failing to demand higher wages on account of the risks they faced in the asbestos insulation industry. The crisis in the insurance industry produced by asbestos claims was theoretically unimaginable by McAvoy and occurred only because the workers let the theory down. A more empirically inclined social scientist might have concluded that the theory let the workers down.

Setting aside information problems, evidence as to the adequacy of compensating differentials for latent injuries is unpersuasive. Empirical tests of the theory of compensating wage differences are inconclusive except for the risk of death (Smith, 1979:349). Moreover, wage differentials based on risk of death provide poor signals about risk reduction since large variation in risk is associated with small variation in wage differentials (Smith, 1979:346). Most

---

25. Asbestos and tobacco products are obvious examples. The first connections of these substances were to pulmonary diseases, but they were followed by links to stomach cancer and heart disease.

26. See, for instance, the *New York Times'* misstatement of the risks of breast cancer at the time of Nancy Reagan's mastectomy (see Altman, 1987). How many people untrained in probability theory could understand the Love correction (see Love, 1987a,b).

importantly, Smith (1979:349) notes that "all the studies on compensating differentials for the risk of death use data on traumatic injuries or known excess death rates--data where the assumption of worker knowledge is plausible." Where such an assumption is implausible, as in the case of latent injuries, employers are not pushed in the direction of safety measures by the threat of increased labor costs if they fail to make risk-reducing adjustments in production methods.

The wage differential theory may have another practical flaw for occupations in which risk and work are inseparable and the work is relatively skilled. The connection between compensating wage differentials and social optimality depends on the availability of safe, but otherwise equivalent, jobs (Boden & Jones, 1987:333) and such employment is not always available. Boden and Jones (id. at 337) illustrate this point by the case of asbestos insulation workers who were paid a "very small" differential (compared to bricklayers) although 44% of the deaths among insulator members of the relevant union were due to asbestos-related diseases. They attribute this small effect to the "lack of comparable job opportunities."[27]

Moreover, the model of people as interest maximizers is limited in the area of employment decisions. Because work is an important expression of their identity, people often work when to do so is economically irrational. For an Appalachian coal miner to leave mining to work in a shop to reduce his employment risk would frequently be an unthinkable mode of calculation; his sense of self-worth is as a coal miner, in this case an identity that allows no place for worrying, or being seen to worry, about the risks of the work. Akerlof and Dickens' (1982) economic model of cognitive dissonance explains how workers may systematically and "rationally" tend to ignore occupational risk. The model starts with the observation that "workers in dangerous jobs are often quite oblivious to the dangers that are involved" (id. at 308). Cognitive dissonance operates because "persons not only have preferences over states of the world [as is typically assumed in economic theory], but also over their beliefs about the state of the world" (ibid.). Dissonance reduction requires that the worker in an unsafe job "choose his beliefs according to whether ... the psychological benefit of suppressing his fear exceeds the cost due to increased chances of accident. [If so] the worker will believe the activity to be safe" (ibid.). The model demonstrates that in the presence of cognitive dissonance, fully-

---

27. The predicament has become more acute in an era of migratory employers who have little hesitation in exporting dangerous jobs to labor markets where the economic value of life is lower than in the U.S. Viewed in this light, Bhopal-like disasters are predictable for if expenditures on safety ought to be a function of compensation paid to injured consumers, bystanders and workers, then more ought to be spent on safety in the U.S. than on a comparable plant in India.

informed, utility-maximizing workers will nevertheless make suboptimal choices about the amount of workplace risk to which they are exposed.

The theory of compensating differentials predicts that in a situation of perfect information, all positive and negative dimensions of jobs would be factored isomorphically into the wage rate. The risk increment would be equal to whatever additional wage qualified workers would demand, assuming no other qualified workers could be found to work for less. Does this theory ignore the existence of tort and other compensation systems?[28] Where the potential of risk is transformed into the actuality of accident or illness, the consequences to the worker are additional expenses, lost wages, pain and suffering, emotional distress, loss of consortium and incidental damages. Some of these items are the ingredients of workers' compensation recoveries and almost all of them are covered by tort damages before attorney's fees are deducted.[29] If the theory ignores compensation systems it would predict worker demands that are greater than actual demands since workers surely know something about their health insurance and rights under workers' compensation and tort. If the theory does not ignore compensation, what does it assume that workers do know about these compensation systems? A worker with as good information and data skills as an economist who is also a tort lawyer ought, we suppose, to take into account the value of any preference for no injury over an injury coupled to compensation, the probabilities that he will secure various forms of compensation, the extent to which compensation is incomplete or duplicated and the transaction costs of securing it. Whatever such a theory might assume that workers know about compensation for traumatic injuries, it must assume that workers have at least the same difficulties in estimating compensation for latent injuries that we have in earlier parts of this paper shown to face managers. The obvious conclusion is that a worker cannot be expected to include in wage demands information that is unavailable even to economists, lawyers and managers; which is to say that the

---

28. Rosen's (1986) review essay in the *Handbook of Labor Economics* never mentions the effect of tort or workers' compensation or first-party insurance on the theory of equalizing differences.

29. We ignore further complications like the existence in the U.S. of contingent fees and the collateral source rule, the effects of which are quite surely unknown by workers. There is, moreover, a way of looking at the accident problem in which workers may secure double recovery from the combination of higher wages and tort damages since the wage ingredient of damages would be inflated for the disability period although the worker would not be at risk in that period.

information on which the theory of wage differentials depends almost certainly will be unavailable to those to whom the theory presumably applies.[30]

Conclusion

We are skeptical of reliance on the deterrent effect of discounted future compensation and risk-induced wage differentials to determine socially optimal levels of safety measures when a substantial portion of the information that is in theory to be relied on is opaque or distorted in practice. Information difficulties are related to difficulties in predicting the rules of the future, the so-called sociolegal risk; the imperfections in claiming behavior and in the legal system; limitations in information that the tort system provides about future recoveries and transaction costs, limitations in worker information and in worker assessments of risks and consequences; knowledge limitations regarding latent injuries in existing studies on compensating wage differentials.

These difficulties do not mean that tort compensation has no deterrent effect. If firms were relieved of responsibility for latent injuries caused by their products and working conditions, the care taken with respect to users and workers would almost surely be diminished. But deterrence claims of laissez-faire economics are much more ambitious than a simple unmeasurable connection between legal responsibility and care. This economic theory asserts that tort compensation and, where workers are concerned, wage rates tell firms how much care to exercise. Our analysis suggests that tort compensation does not and, if the tort system remains in its current form, cannot provide such guidance.[31]

---

30. Unlike the situation of firms and managers, there are absolutely no competitive forces that serve to check worker deviations from utility maximization.

31. We are not first or foremost in this conclusion. "The [deterrent] value of tort liability . . . is thought on the whole to be negligible" (Ison, 1967:89). On the other hand, Landes and Posner (1987:ch. 7) have suggested modifications of the present system which they feel will overcome most of its weaknesses. They argue for awarding probabilistic damages to *all* those who might potentially be affected by a catastrophic or latent tort, regardless of whether they have experienced an actual injury at the time the suit is filed. Thus, suppose a nuclear reactor melts down, exposing 100,000 people to radiation. Twenty-five percent of those exposed will develop cancer thirty years hence, and the monetary damages of those affected will be $200,000. The Landes and Posner proposal calls for the court to award damages of $50,000 to each of the 100,000 potential victims, rather than awarding the full $200,000 to the 25,000 who eventually developed cancer.

To reject tort compensation and compensating wage differentials as the basis for safety-related decisions does not demonstrate the superiority of alternatives. Given the acknowledged difficulties in government supervision of worker and consumer health and safety issues (see, e.g., McCaffrey, 1982; Nobel, 1986; Nelkin & Brown, 1984; Claybrook, 1982; Hill, 1987; Eads and Reuter, 1983:x, xi), especially the instability of such programs from one federal administration to another (see Shapo, 1984:ch. 10 at 87)[32] and the current tendency toward deunionization of American industry (Kochan, 1985; Ginger & Christiano, 1987; Grenier, 1988), the prospect in the U.S. of relying on government and/or union intervention is hardly encouraging.[33] Nevertheless, skepticism about the

---

While this suggestion may offer an improvement over current practice, it is not a complete solution. First, the most troublesome kinds of latent injuries arise from gradual exposure to an ongoing hazard (asbestos) as opposed to a sudden and discrete event (nuclear meltdown). Second, the scientific and epidemiological data needed to assess future harms are often likely to be unavailable at the time that exposure occurs--in fact, the exposure might not even be widely recognized as problematic until its effects begin to be felt, many years in the future. Finally, Landes and Posner underestimate the importance of legal infrastructure to the prosecution of compensation claims for latent torts. Such claims are not only brought on a contingent fee basis, but generally require significant out-of-pocket investment by individual lawyers or small firms to develop the basic case against producers and to prepare individual lawsuits. Any rule change that reduces the recovery per case reduces the incentive for lawyers to hazard such investments unless they are assured of a corresponding increase in the number of clients they represent, a consequence there is no reason to predict. For a description of the problems of organizing class actions in mass tort cases, see Hensler, et al., 1984:52-60. Oi (1984) has raised similar objections to an earlier version of the Landes/Posner proposal.

32. A comparable lack of faith in the stability of regulation of health and safety may not be appropriate for the U.K.. Regulatory arrangements are in Britain derived from tradition more than from formal rule and regulatory agencies are run by civil servants relatively impervious to ministerial direction. Thus, the power of a new national government to alter the course and intensity of regulation is limited because it cannot change the regulators and there are by and large no constitutive rules for it to amend. For econometric evidence that British regulation in the form of notices (but not factory visits and prosecutions) makes a difference in the level of ingested lead in exposed workers, see Fenn, 1988:7.

33. John Braithwaite suggests that the same collective action dilemma that exists with individual corporate actors may apply to individual regulators. To an important extent both corporate and regulatory executives are evaluated by one or a number of "bottom line" measures. If the bottom line disaster does not materialize for thirty years and if the assessment system is (for good reason) unconcerned with second-guessing the executive's assessment of the facts, but

deterrent value of tort is politically important. Serious efforts are underway to replace tort with various forms of workers' compensation and social insurance (see Stewart, 1987; O'Connell, 1985, 1987a, 1987b). It would be a mistake in that corner of the debate that is concerned with latent injuries to prefer tort over alternative compensation systems because of its theoretical advantage in deterrence if that advantage were an illusion, if in this instance the hand of the market has in fact disappeared.

---

only with assessing outcomes, then long latency is an unsolvable performance assessment problem. The assumption that the regulatory executive will strive to be good at achieving the agency's goals is generally not misplaced: performance assessment tends to secure this identity of interest between the individual executive and the interests of his organization. But the longer the latency period, the more likely the executive will have moved on to another agency (or have retired) before the performance assessment system catches up to him and the less plausible the assumption of an identity of interest between the individual and the organization.

6

Shifting Risk in
Business Bankruptcy

Kevin J. Delaney

The popular image of business bankruptcy is sharply at odds with a series of major Chapter 11 bankruptcies. The former sees bankruptcy as something to be avoided at all costs, a last resort, a reluctant managerial reaction to indisputable economic conditions. But recent business cases confound this common-sense notion of bankruptcy. The Chapter 11 filings of the Manville Corporation (formerly the U.S.'s largest asbestos manufacturer), A.H. Robins (manufacturer of the Dalkon Shield), LTV (steel manufacturer), Continental and Eastern Airlines, and Texaco demonstrate that bankruptcy is not always anathema to good business, but can in fact be used as a managerial weapon.

Each of these bankruptcies fall into a category of cases I call "strategic bankruptcies" (Delaney, 1992). The cases are strategic in that managers invoke the bankruptcy process to pursue an organizational objective that they had pursued unsuccessfully outside the legal system. But what exactly is distinctive about these cases? Certainly *all* Chapter 11 reorganizations have some element of strategy if only in the sense that management files for Chapter 11 to gain temporary relief from paying its bills. "Strategic bankruptcies," however, indicate that managers may be using business bankruptcy to achieve much larger organizational objectives, never envisioned by framers of modern bankruptcy

---

I am grateful to Lee Clarke for his suggestions throughout several drafts of this chapter.

law. Specifically, management at each of these firms has been accused of using Chapter 11 to wrest concessions from labor unions (Continental and Eastern Airlines), to reduce punitive damage awards caused by injurious products (Manville, A. H. Robins), to push pension obligations onto the government (LTV), or to frustrate a business rival (Texaco). In these cases, it appears that the firm in question files for bankruptcy *only* to accomplish some limited financial or political goal that it had tried to accomplish outside of bankruptcy. Thus, the management of Manville, A.H. Robins, Continental and Eastern Airlines, LTV, and Texaco have been accused of manipulating the bankruptcy process to gain strategic advantages. Interestingly, these firms were not really bankrupt in the usual sense. Rather, through creative accounting, separating parent company assets from those of a subsidiary, or shifting assets from one corporate entity to another, the claim to bankruptcy was "constructed" or "manufactured" to define the firm as bankrupt to pursue a strategic end under Chapter 11 protection.

In this paper, I demonstrate that these large bankruptcy cases are really about shifting financial risk to more vulnerable parties. I conclude that large organizations have more opportunity to avoid or shift risk than do unorganized individuals. In this way, financial risk shares common characteristics with other types of risks.

The Legal Background

The 1978 Bankruptcy Reform Act broadened the definition of a claim against a company to include, "any right to payment, whether or not reduced to judgement, liquidated, unliquidated, fixed, contingent, matured, unmatured, disputed, undisputed, legal, equitable, secured, or unsecured" (U.S. Code, Cong. & Ad. News, 1978:5807). Congress hoped that by broadening the definition of a claim it would allow firms to enter Chapter 11 earlier, providing a better chance of successful reorganization. While the expanded definition may have indeed increased the flexibility of Chapter 11, it also created an opportunity for more firms to declare bankruptcy based on a claim of "equity insolvency" (future liabilities will outweigh future assets) rather than the traditional "balance-sheet insolvency" (current liabilities outweigh current assets). Equity insolvency is a concept more open to manipulation and interpretation than balance sheet insolvency, since it involves predicting assets, liabilities, and risks far into the future.

Strategic bankruptcies existed before the 1978 Bankruptcy Reform Act. White (1984) cited 30 cases of firms declaring bankruptcy primarily to eliminate labor unions prior to the 1978 Reform Act. But the 1978 law accelerated the number and size of these types of cases. One indicator of this trend is *Business Week's* listing of Chapter 11 bankruptcy as one of the business trends considered

"IN" that year (Byrne, 1986). For their part, legal experts have begun to fashion new ways to use the bankruptcy process for strategic ends.

Strategic bankruptcies challenge not only common-sense notions of bankruptcy but also a host of theories of business bankruptcy; these theories have always neglected the strategic nature of the process.

Conceptions of Bankruptcy

Bankruptcy as Punishment

Bankruptcy was originally conceived as a punishment for individuals who offended the social order by refusing to pay debts. The word bankruptcy comes from the term "banca rupta," or "broken bench," referring to the Italian custom in medieval outdoor markets of smashing the benches of merchants who refused to pay their bills. In the earliest bankruptcy statutes of Europe, bankruptcy was defined as an act committed by an individual, rather than a *state of financial affairs*. Thus, "bankrupt" status had little to do with whether a merchant was insolvent; rather it commenced upon a merchant's action indicating to the community that he or she was going to renege on debt. On the Continent, the most common "act of bankruptcy" was "fleeing to parts unknown" (Tremain, 1927). Other bankruptcy acts included "seeking sanctuary" (entering a designated area that was off limits to debt-collectors) and "keeping house" (based on the common law maxim "a man's house is his castle," debtors in England locked themselves in their houses, refusing to meet creditors and effectively thwarting all legal efforts to collect payment).

This conception of bankruptcy as a morally offensive act against the community explains why the earliest statutes used the term *fugitivi* (fugitive) more often than *banca-rotti* (bankrupt) (Tremain, 1938:192). The law focused on when an individual had committed an "act of bankruptcy" not on the debtor's balance-sheet. Bankruptcy was a social and moral judgement, rather than a purely economic situation.

The specter of bankruptcy carried a heavy social stigma. Those who "made bankrupt" were judged moral scoundrels by the community and were thrown into debtor's prison, sometimes for life. This harsh attitude toward bankrupts can be seen in a 17th century case, *Manby v. Scott*:

> If a man is taken in execution and lie in prison for debt, neither the plaintiff at whose suit he is arrested, nor the sheriff who took him, is bound to find him meat, drink, or clothes; but he must live on his own, or on the charity of others; and if no man will relieve him, let him die in the name of God ... (*Manby v. Scott*, 1 Mod. 124, 132, 86 Eng. Rep. 781, 786 [Ex. 1659]).

Social stigma, backed by state power, helped keep the incidence of bankruptcy down, but the notion of bankruptcy-as-action presented a problem for creditors: how to collect money from debtors who had not committed one of the legally prescribed "acts of bankruptcy." The only method available to creditors in such cases lay outside the bankruptcy system in the realm of common law and involved a time-consuming process of proving claims and obtaining individual writs (court orders) for the debtor's property. The common law remedy was an individual one, meaning that each creditor raced all other creditors to make claims against the debtor's property. This often resulted in a single creditor garnering all assets at the expense of other creditors with equally valid claims against the debtor.

Under pressure from creditors, the scope of bankruptcy law was gradually widened to include the "honest but insolvent" debtor who had not committed an act of bankruptcy (see Warren, 1935; Delaney, 1992). In 1841 voluntary bankruptcy was added to the books for debtors who chose to precipitate their own bankruptcy, an idea that would have been inconceivable to the Italian vendors of the Middle Ages. The Bankruptcy Act of 1867 was the first to include business bankruptcy. An 1898 act incorporated the goal of a "fresh start" for individuals who found themselves unable to pay their debts. Thus, the conception of bankruptcy as punishment for morally reprehensible, individual actions waned in the late 19th and early 20th centuries. In its place arose an economic notion of bankruptcy as a financial state of affairs.

Bankruptcy as a Technical Relation of Assets-to-Debts

As bankruptcy became less a moral offense than a simple economic condition, the relevance of punishment declined in favor of an emphasis on the ratio of debts to assets. Although technically many firms (particularly start-up firms) are in this financial position, bankruptcy commences when creditors or management lose confidence in the firm's ability to retire its debt. Although technically the current bankruptcy law does not require that a firm prove that it is insolvent (i.e., its debts outweigh its assets) in order to file a Chapter 11 petition, a firm's bankruptcy petition can be challenged on the ground that the company is really solvent. If a company is indeed shown in court to be solvent, its petition can be rejected by the court on grounds of "bad faith." Thus, a major part of most Chapter 11 cases today is the argument that the firm's debts outweigh its assets.

This notion of bankruptcy as a financial state of debts overwhelming assets underlies current theories of business bankruptcy. Many economists, for example, have developed bankruptcy prediction models that look to financial ratios such as asset-to-debt, debt-to-cash flow and other such ratios to "predict" firm failure (see Altman, 1968, 1971, 1983; Ang and Chua, 1980; Beaver,

1968; Gordon, 1971; Johnson, 1970). While these models perform relatively well in predicting national bankruptcy rates, they have reinforced what I think is a misleading conception of business bankruptcy: that bankruptcy results from poor company-specific economic factors (e.g., poor cash flow) combined with large-scale market factors that are not conducive to business prosperity (e.g., a high national interest rate).

Because economics typically focuses on the "bottom line" in this way, it adopts a functionalist interpretation of business bankruptcy, concluding that managers file for bankruptcy because they have no other choice. Managers, from this view, simply respond to negative company-specific and national market indicators. Following from this, Dun & Bradstreet concludes that the "causes" of business bankruptcy are mainly "experience factors" (e.g., management incompetence, lack of line experience, unbalanced managerial experience) and "economic factors" (e.g., low profits, high interest rates, loss of market, no consumer spending). These two sets of factors are said to account for approximately 90% of the business failures in 1985 and 1986 (Dun & Bradstreet, 1985, 1986). However, this analysis tends toward the tautological since lack of experience and poor economic factors are only identified in the firms that fail and presumably "lack of managerial experience" might be found in thriving firms as well.

All of these models are based on analyses of balance sheet data provided by companies in their Chapter 11 filings. What they miss is how these numbers are created in the first place. Later I argue that balance sheet data are only one of several legitimate portrayals of a firm's financial state and indeed that such data can be the result of political or strategic decision-making. Indeed, some Chapter 11 filings are more usefully analyzed as organizational *action* rather than *reaction*. This perspective acknowledges that Chapter 11 may be chosen not because of undisputable economic data but because of organizational strategy.

Bankruptcy as a Neutral Debt-Collection Device

Many legal analysts, particularly those in the law and economics tradition, argue that bankruptcy is nothing more than a neutral debt-collection device (see Baird, 1987a, 1987b; Jackson, 1986). In this view, the bankruptcy process avoids the common law problem of one creditor garnering all company assets leaving nothing to remaining creditors, by providing a regulated, collective system for collecting debt.

Two major principles are central to the debt-collection mechanism of bankruptcy law: absolute priority and temporal equality. According to these principles, each party to a bankruptcy case is assigned a priority level. For example, all secured creditors are accorded a top priority level and paid first (after government claims and taxes). This priority level is paid in full before the next level (unsecured creditors) receives anything. If there is not enough money to pay all secured creditors in full, each receives a *pro rata* share of money owed. If money is left after paying all parties on this level in full, the next level, unsecured creditors, are then paid. Only after both secured and unsecured creditors are paid in full do shareholders receive any of the firm's value. Legal rules are said to ensure fair treatment within categories of creditors. In large reorganization cases, however, these rules are rarely followed and instead the amount reimbursed for valid claims is open to extensive negotiation. Since a reorganization plan must be approved by all groups to avoid extensive legal delays, a great deal of bargaining over payoff occurs.

The untested assumption in the law and economics approach is that groups bargain on equal footing. Bargaining strategies are often simply deduced from legal rules rather than empirically studied. Thus, legal theorists have not, by and large, studied how powerful organizations might use power and influence to affect the timing of the bankruptcy filing, their own placement in terms of priority level, and the negotiations that follow.

In fact, large organizations have a variety of powerful tools at their disposal to influence the bargaining process in their interest. For example, commercial creditors' control over loan capital (which is needed by almost all firms after their emergence from Chapter 11) has been largely ignored. How this leverage might be turned into actual gains in bargaining over payoff remains a pressing sociological and legal question. Do asbestos victims and labor unions actually stand on equal footing with a large commercial bank in bankruptcy negotiations? Clearly, they do not. For example, the legal status of "secured" or "unsecured" debt is subject to bargaining between the firm and its lenders. Often, commercial banks include covenants in their loan agreements that prohibit firms from taking on any commitments with priority over the banks' loans. Asbestos victims are assured no such bargaining power and are assigned to unsecured status. Power rather than pure law or economics is clearly crucial to understanding the bankruptcy process.

An Alternative View: Bankruptcy as Strategy

Even in strategic bankruptcies, analysts tend to conclude that the company in question had no choice other than bankruptcy. Evidence from the Manville, Continental, Eastern, and Texaco cases, however, challenges this interpretation and suggests a critical evaluation of how organizations shape balance sheet figures. Contrary to received theory, "the balance sheet" is not an objectively given fact, but rather a social construction of considerable malleability.

The first way the claim to bankruptcy is shaped is in defining assets and liabilities. For example, Manville chose not to record its asbestos liabilities on its balance sheet for several years in the late 1970s and early 1980s (*In re Johns-Manville Corp.*, Bankr. No. 82B, 11,656-11,676 [Bankr. S.D.N.Y. 1982]).

Manville's auditors qualified (footnoted) the firm's annual report, stating that the firm's asbestos-related liabilities were not estimable. Thus, Manville was exempted from the Financial Accounting Standards Board (the governing body for the accounting profession) regulation that requires a firm with an outstanding liability to set aside a reserve to cover a potential liability. If Manville had been required to book such a reserve, it would surely have had a difficult time expanding into new areas such as paper products to take the place of its once-lucrative asbestos business (Delaney, 1989b).

Just weeks before its 1982 Chapter 11 filing, Manville reversed course, claiming its asbestos liabilities were indeed estimable. Thus, the firm was required to record a $2 billion liability on its annual report. Manville was then deemed "bankrupt" and eligible for Chapter 11 relief. But the actual damage that would eventually lead to the asbestos lawsuits had occurred many years prior to the 1982 filing. The firm's liabilities were as real in 1980 (when the firm was judged "not bankrupt") as they were in 1982 (when the firm was "bankrupt"). It seems, then, that we can distinguish *existing liabilities* from *official liabilities*. Manville had an existing liability from the moment damage resulting in cancer was inflicted upon workers and others who came in contact with the firm's asbestos products. The liability only became "official" when it was recognized as real by governing bodies such as courts and financial auditors. In the Manville case, the firm and its auditors were able to control the process whereby their existing liability became recognized as an official liability. Once official, Manville had a legal claim to bankruptcy.

A second way to strategically shape the claim to bankruptcy is in designating the "bankrupt unit." Although Texas Air owned 90% of Continental Airlines and the two firms engaged in numerous business transactions that indicated Continental was often treated as a subsidiary, Continental excluded Texas Air from its Chapter 11 filing. This eliminated consideration of the parent company's substantial assets. If Texas Air had been included, Continental's filing may not have been accepted by the court. The legal test for such exclusion is that the two firms must do business at "arm's length." The law does little more in defining this test other than this vague description.

Like Continental, Texaco also carefully chose what part of the company to put into bankruptcy. The oil giant chose to designate only the holding company and two financial subsidiaries in its Chapter 11 filing. This allowed numerous operating companies to promise suppliers and creditors that they could carry on business as usual outside of the bankruptcy process.

Corporations may move assets from the bankrupt unit to other corporate entities deemed outside the bankruptcy process. In the Continental and Eastern Airlines cases, unions charged that Texas Air purchased assets at discounted prices from the bankrupt units just prior to bankruptcy. This movement of assets from the bankrupt unit both legitimates the claim to bankruptcy and reduces the assets available to those making claims against the bankrupt company. In fact, in the Eastern case, the bankruptcy court declared that approximately $200 million would have to be given back to bankrupt Eastern Airlines by Texas Air because of just such financial maneuvering (*New York Times*, 3/2/90:A1).

A third method for shaping the claim to bankruptcy is provoking a strike by employees. In the Continental and Eastern bankruptcies, management seemed eager to incur a strike by employees. In the Continental case, management employed the unusual bargaining tactic of continually reducing its offer throughout the collective bargaining process, thereby ensuring a strike by its machinists. Once all unionized employee groups were on strike, the firm could claim that bankruptcy was justified to prevent the further destruction of the company. Using the concept of equity insolvency, the firm could show that its future liabilities would soon overwhelm its future assets.

Another mechanism for shaping the claim to bankruptcy is found in the process known as "valuation." Throughout bankruptcy, company valuations are used to measure the current and future value of the firm. If the firm is judged to be worth more kept together than sold, the company is allowed to reorganize and continue in business. But despite its quasi-scientific quality, the valuation process can be easily manipulated. Firm value is generally determined by the equation, $V=I/i$, where $I=$ the typical annual earnings the reorganized entity can be expected to attain in the future and $i=$ an appropriate capitalization rate for determining the present value of that earnings stream in perpetuity. As one legal analyst has aptly commented:

> the inescapable fact remains that the process involves solving an algebraic formula in which all of the elements are unknown. It is hardly surprising, then, that the valuation process...is at best a ballpark guess and at worst a wild figment of some expert's imagination (Rosenberg, 1975:1186).

This quote makes the valuation process sound serendipitous, as if no organizational or individual actors have interests in the outcome. I think it is much more likely that particular valuations will be pursued by different interests in a given case. For example, an unsecured creditor might want a valuation high enough to ensure that his priority layer is paid in full while shareholders want a valuation high enough to give them a share of the firm's assets.

The valuation figure can be drastically altered simply by changing the capitalization rate (figure used to compute the present value of future assets and liabilities). Consider the following example (see Rosenberg, 1975 for further details): If the annual earnings stream of a reorganized firm is predicted to be $100,000 and you capitalize this amount at 10%, the current value of the firm is $1,000,000 ($100,000/.10). However, if you merely change the capitalization rate to 12%, the current value of the firm is reduced to only $833,333

($100,000/.12). This is a dramatic difference in percentage terms (16.67%) and could easily prove decisive in whether the firm is forced to liquidate or is reorganized.

Thus, if management or creditors desire to make the firm appear solvent, they may choose one capitalization rate, if they desire insolvency, they choose another. In all bankruptcy cases, there is a substantial amount of uncertainty in estimating a company's value. This uncertainty is exacerbated in "strategic bankruptcies," which center on arguments over future assets and future debts. In the Manville and A.H. Robins cases, for example, asbestos and Dalkon Shield injuries as well as company profitability had to be estimated for twenty to thirty years into the future. In the Manville case, epidemiological experts admitted their estimates of the incidence of asbestos could be twice their expectations (Epidemiological Resources, Inc., 1982).

Some bankruptcy judges have admitted just how arbitrary the valuation process can be. In a bankruptcy case requiring a valuation of oil that had not yet been found in a large parcel of Arctic land, a judge wrote in his judicial opinion:

> [to say] that you can appraise the values in the Canadian Arctic is to say that you can attend the County Fair with your crystal ball, because that is the only possible way you can come up with a result...My final conclusion...is that it is worth somewhere between $90 million and $100 million as a going concern, and to satisfy the people that want precision on the value, I fix the exact amount at...$96,856,850, which of course is a total absurdity that anybody could fix a value with that degree of precision, but for the lawyers that want me to make that fool estimate, I have just made it (*Citibank v. Baer*, 651 F. 2d 1341, 1347 [10th Cir. 1980] as quoted in Fortgang and Meyer, 1985:1131-2).

Why Choose Bankruptcy as Strategy?

It seems inconceivable to many observers that managers would choose bankruptcy given the costs, in terms of the firm's reputation, legal fees, and constraints on managerial discretion while under court scrutiny. However, in certain cases, I argue that bankruptcy is indeed chosen as strategy. In these cases, Chapter 11 bankruptcy provided companies and creditors with the opportunity to attempt "network surgery"; to transform troublesome ties in a way that might not have been possible outside of the bankruptcy forum (Delaney, 1989a). Thus, bankruptcy is often not a passive reaction to economic imperatives. Rather, institutions "mobilize" or invoke bankruptcy to achieve strategic ends (Zemans, 1982, 1983). In the following section, I provide some examples of strategic objectives that have been pursued through bankruptcy.

To Reduce Labor Costs

A firm may opt for Chapter 11 to transform a troublesome tie with another organization or group of individuals that the firm has been unable to alter outside of the bankruptcy process. After purchasing Continental Airlines, Frank Lorenzo announced his desire to "provide all the frills of flying at discounted fares" (*Fortune*, 1/9/84:66ff). The only way to do this was by drastically reducing costs and Frank Lorenzo chose to focus on reducing labor costs.

Shortly after purchasing Continental, Lorenzo imposed a 15% wage cut on non-union employees. He sought an additional $100 million in labor savings from unionized workers. However, management was unable to wrest labor concessions from its unions through collective bargaining. Management began to contemplate a bankruptcy filing coupled with the abrogation of the firm's labor contracts. Richard Adams, Senior V.P. of Flight Operations, jotted down these notes during a management meeting: (court testimony, *In re Continental Airlines*, 3 Bankr. L. Rep. [CCH] [Bankr. S.D. Tex. 1984]; Murphy, 1984:223):

> I don't believe we can get these concessions on a voluntary, persuasive basis. We must get awfully big stick... Most effective stick might be Chapter 11.

Chapter 11 bankruptcy, in other words, was a tool management could use against its unions. After emerging from Chapter 11, Continental had reduced its cost per seat mile (a common industry measure) from 8.5 cents to 6.3 cents by reducing its labor costs from 36% of total operating costs to 22% (Delaney, 1992). Declaring bankruptcy, apparently, can be very profitable.

To Alter Bargaining Position

Texaco entered Chapter 11 to transform a troublesome tie with a competitor, the Pennzoil Corporation (*Texaco Inc. v. Pennzoil Co.* 784 F.2d 1133 [2d Cir. 1986], rev'd, 107 S. Ct. 1519 [1987]). Texaco hoped to frustrate Pennzoil's effort to collect an $11 billion damage award granted to Pennzoil in the takeover battle for the Getty Oil Company. After the court ruled in Pennzoil's favor, awarding it close to $11 billion, Texaco management argued that paying the award was "financially impractical."[1] By entering Chapter 11, Texaco drastically

---

1. Note that management did not say that it was financially impossible. A series of creative linguistic distinctions were employed in an attempt to explain why Texaco was calling itself "bankrupt" even though it admitted that it had the assets to pay the damage award. One oil analyst at investment firm Tucker,

improved its negotiating stance with Pennzoil. Since all payments were "stayed" during Chapter 11, Texaco did not have to pay the damages to Pennzoil until it emerged from bankruptcy.

The case became so widely viewed as organizational strategy that many observers dubbed it "The Bet Your Company Case" implying that Texaco had in essence said to Pennzoil, "we'll hold our breath and risk Chapter 11 to force you to accept a lower payment." Pennzoil and Texaco eventually negotiated a reduction in the damage award and Texaco emerged from Chapter 11 very much intact.

To Limit Tort Liability

Both the Manville Corporation and A.H. Robins entered Chapter 11 to limit impending liabilities linked to injurious products. Manville, which had been the nation's leading asbestos producer, faced the prospect of decades of lawsuits from customers, workers, and their families exposed to the firm's asbestos products. Robins faced lawsuits from women injured by the medical company's Dalkon Shield intrauterine device.

Both companies successfully invoked the Chapter 11 process and eased their liability problems by replacing individual tort remedies with collective compensation board systems. These systems are supposed to save on lawyers' fees and, therefore, have been hailed as more efficient at paying claims. Compensation boards, however, often bar punitive damages against the companies. Those injured or killed by asbestos will collect an average of only $30,000 to $50,000 per claim through the compensation board system (Delaney, 1989a). A group of victims challenging the Robins settlement claim that there will not be enough money to cover all those injured by the Dalkon Shield (Greenhouse, 1989:D1).

In addition, the bankruptcy settlement spares Manville the continued embarrassment of court testimony that had produced damaging evidence that the firm might have known about the danger of asbestos much earlier than it has publicly stated. In the Robins case, the bankruptcy settlement prohibits women from suing senior Robins officials and Aetna Casualty, Robins' insurance carrier.

To Shift Financial Risk

Another reason for choosing strategic bankruptcy is to shift financial risk from one party to another. In the Manville bankruptcy, commercial creditors

---

Anthony & R.L. Day said at the time, "While Texaco will be in bankruptcy, Texaco won't be a bankrupt company" (*Time*, 4/27/87:52).

pushed for a Chapter 11 filing in hopes of fashioning a collective settlement to the asbestos crisis that reduced the risk of their outstanding loans to Manville (Delaney, 1989b). Just prior to Manville's Chapter 11 filing, creditors refused to lend additional money to the firm until the asbestos litigation was resolved. As Manville's Vice President, G. Earl Parker, told a Senate hearing:

> Our investment banking advisors told us that, until our asbestos-health claims were resolved, there was simply no way for Manville to raise any significant amount of expansion capital anywhere in world markets (U.S. Senate, 1982:22).

Prior to its 1982 bankruptcy filing, Manville's accountants approved several SEC filings that stated that the firm's future asbestos liability was inestimable, exempting Manville from entering the liability on company balance sheets. This kept Manville out of bankruptcy.

But, after Manville failed in its attempt to gain passage of a federal bill that would have mandated a compensation fund, Manville's commercial creditors decided to act. Manville's long-time commercial lender, Morgan Guaranty, had a former Vice President, John Schroeder, strategically situated on Manville's board of directors. Schroeder headed a subcommittee that hired a new auditor who in turn declared the future asbestos liability estimable and thereby paved the way for the claim to bankruptcy (Brodeur, 1985). Manville did indeed declare bankruptcy just weeks after the liabilities were recorded on the firm's balance sheet.

After five years in Chapter 11, the firm emerged with a collective compensation scheme funded by Manville's profits into the 21st century. While commercial creditors received all of the money owed them, plus stocks and bonds in lieu of interest, asbestos victims must count on a fund dependent on the firm's profitability into the distant future.[2] The fund, in fact, has already run into financial trouble, facing a cash crisis that threatens to delay payments to asbestos victims for as long as twenty-five years (Labaton, 1989:D1). In this case Chapter 11 became the vehicle for shifting future financial risk from a more powerful organization (Morgan Guaranty) to a more vulnerable group (future asbestos victims).

In the Manville case, financial risk was also shifted to other asbestos manufacturers that did not declare Chapter 11 bankruptcy. During Manville's

---

2. The reorganization case also failed to resolve the potential lawsuits related to schools, office buildings and homes that contain asbestos insulation. Lawsuits designed to recover the cost of removal of this asbestos may represent damages even larger than asbestos-health cases. Manville could easily return to Chapter 11 bankruptcy in the future.

five years under Chapter 11 protection, asbestos victims continued to sue smaller asbestos manufacturers since they could not pursue Manville in court (many asbestos cases are against numerous manufacturers since many plants used asbestos from several sources). In this way, financial burden was shifted from Manville to other asbestos companies. Several of these smaller asbestos companies have been liquidated (e.g., Nicolet and Forty-Eight Insulations Inc.) (Feder, 1989:Section 3, p.1).

Conclusion: Implications of Strategic Bankruptcy

These cases demonstrate that Chapter 11 bankruptcy can provide companies the opportunity to attempt network surgery; to transform troublesome ties in a way that might not have been possible outside the bankruptcy forum. Organizational actors may "mobilize" bankruptcy law to achieve strategic objectives. Bankruptcy, therefore, may not act primarily as a neutral arbiter of efficiency, nor as a neutral debt-collection device as posited by existing theory, but rather as a political arena in which organizations and individuals use the power at their disposal to gain strategic advantage. In this arena, large organizations work to avoid financial burdens and shift financial risk to weaker parties.

Most theoretical treatments of business bankruptcy, however, continue to cling to the notion that managers have no choice upon entering Chapter 11 and simply respond rationally to indisputable economic data--both company-specific data and national economic data. Thus, as noted, scholars have failed to explore the strategic implications of business bankruptcy.

Existing theories need to address the power of various actors in the bankruptcy forum. Theorists should assess the sources of power exercised by creditors, debtors and other parties involved in bankruptcy cases, not simply by deductive methods but through analysis of actual organizational behavior in bankruptcy. For example, deductive theories of law and economics cannot assume that all organizations will act alike when confronted with similar levels of assets and liabilities. Whether a liability is with a single, powerful commercial creditor or with an amorphous mass of future asbestos victims will almost certainly affect the debtor organization's ability to reduce that liability.

In a sense, bankruptcy is a process of risk-shifting. Often there are losses to be borne by some party or parties. Debtors attempt to shift this burden onto various creditors. Creditors use their power to resist both current financial burden (taking less than 100 cents on the dollar) and future financial risk (creditors prefer current cash to future promises in the form of stock, loans, or future profit-sharing). We need to seriously assess the success of different groups of creditors in the struggle to avoid financial burden and financial risk. In the collection of cases cited here, it appears that large organizational actors have more power than individual actors to shift financial risk away from them and onto other parties. As has been found in a variety of other settings, organizations often have more choices when confronting risk than do individuals.

PART FOUR

Institutional Responses to Uncertainty

7

Genetic Screening in
the Workplace

Dorothy Nelkin

Advances in genetics are providing screening techniques to detect those who may be susceptible to future health risks. The use of genetic tests in the workplace began in the 1970s when several large chemical companies began to use such tests to identify and then exclude employees suspected of being predisposed to illness when exposed to certain chemicals. Such exclusion was a paternalistic measure designed in the first instance to protect workers' health. At the same time, screening can be used as a means to avoid costly structural changes in the workplace by placing responsibility on the individual at risk.

Identifying and excluding "hypersusceptible" workers is a way to decrease the incidence of occupational illness and the associated costs of compensation. Prediction through genetic tests enhances the control of employers by justifying exclusionary practices that might otherwise appear arbitrary or discriminatory and therefore subject to political and legal challenge. From the employer's perspective predictive testing of workers is rational policy.

This paper briefly reviews some economic and regulatory pressures that encourage workplace testing, and suggests its implications in light of the rapid development of genetic tests able to predict the future health status of individuals.

This paper is adapted from Dorothy Nelkin and Laurence Tancredi, *Dangerous Diagnostics: The Social Power of Biological Information*, New York: Basic Books, 1989.

Pressures on the Firm

Corporations in the United States play multiple roles in their relationship to their employees. They act, in the first instance, as employers. But through their benefit packages they also act as insurers and health care providers. Employer concerns, then, begin with occupational hazards and their effect on productivity. But they extend beyond the workplace to the general health of employees and the future cost of their medical care.

The pressures to reduce occupational illness are most obvious in those many industries using commercial chemicals to create products including basic chemicals, pharmaceuticals, plastics, paints and pesticides. Federal laws such as the Occupational Safety and Health Act and the Toxic Substances Control Act require industry to assume responsibility for protecting employees. The Occupational Safety and Health Administration's regulations, enacted "to assure so far as possible every working man and woman in the nation safe and healthful working conditions," require the Secretary of Labor to set standards assuring that employees are protected from threats to their health "to the extent feasible economically and technologically" (OSHA, 1981). Screening individuals and excluding those possibly susceptible to risk is a means of protecting workers while minimizing the costs of meeting regulations.

The litigious nature of the regulatory environment encourages employee testing as industries seek ways to protect their economic interests. Administrative decision-making in the United States is an adversarial process, delegating ultimate responsibility to the courts. The litigation model for resolving regulatory dilemmas emphasizes "finding the facts" and "establishing the truth," a process often ill-suited to dealing with the problem of scientific uncertainty so characteristic of occupational health (Jasanoff, 1985). In this adversarial context, industries look with favor on diagnostic techniques that provide "hard," scientific data.

Competitive pressures for efficiency and productivity reinforce the appeal of scientific tests. Industries view tests for drugs, for AIDS or for genetic information as a means of providing help for workers while reducing medical costs, decreasing absenteeism and increasing productivity. It is also far less costly to control access to the workforce than to change the structure of the workplace. Shifting the locus of responsibility for occupational health from the workplace to the worker reduces the need for costly clean-up programs.

The threat of litigation has further encouraged corporate health screening policies. Traditional tort recovery is precluded under most worker compensation schemes, but workers still have several possible grounds for litigation.[1] These

---

1. See Barth and Hunt, 1980. Compensation laws were developed to substitute predictable administration programs for the more arbitrary decisions of the courts. They do not allow workers to sue their employers directly for

include tort action against third parties such as a chemical manufacturer. In 1981, for example, Johns Mansville faced 16,500 lawsuits from workers harmed by asbestos. Workers can also sue on behalf of a fetus harmed because of exposure to chemicals. And they can also sue corporate physicians.

The very existence of corporate medical services encourages diagnostic screening. As industries increasingly assume the role of health care provider, they also assume a duty to warn. The courts have considered in-house medical programs as a business endeavor intended to fulfill corporate purposes (e.g., cost savings). Thus companies are liable for the professional acts of the physicians they employ (Blum, 1978). In particular corporate physicians can be held liable for injuries resulting from inadequate diagnosis and failure to warn employees against potential harm. If a company has not used an available test to detect a potential problem, it may be considered at fault. In this legal context, if diagnostic tests to identify an individual's susceptibility to chemical exposure are available, the duty to warn encourages their use.

In light of such pressures, corporations have developed four strategic responses to occupational health problems, each of which encourages genetic screening. First is the tendency, even in the absence of definitive scientific evidence, to place responsibility for risk on the individual worker rather than on the conditions of the workplace (McGarrity and Schroeder, 1981). If workers get sick, it is often attributed to personal habits such as smoking or unhealthy life style, or to genetic predisposition to disease. Second is the establishment of in-house medical services responsible for defining the health status of workers. Company doctors welcome scientific tests as an objective means to clarify the ambiguities of their role (Walters, 1982; Walsh, 1987). Third is the effort to predict who may be prone to illness in the future. Companies already use tests to predict potential productivity and to identify those prone to alcoholism or drug abuse. Testing is viewed by employers as an appropriate and defensible way to evaluate job applicants and to minimize future risk (Draper, 1991). Fourth is the current existence of practices and policies--such as fetal protection policies-- to exclude workers or to increase control over their private lives (Williams, 1981; Bertin, 1982).

These strategies meet the institutional needs of companies faced with litigation and regulation, as well as with economic and social pressures. They

---

compensation, but instead provide social insurance against workplace accidents without regard to fault. However, compensation laws were designed for problems of safety, and do not allow proper assessment of the more ambiguous damages associated with occupational disease (see Felstiner and Siegelman, this volume). This has encouraged efforts to get around their limitations through litigation.

set the background for corporate receptivity to new genetic screening techniques that can identify the genetic susceptibility of individual workers.

Genetic Testing Techniques

The field of "ecogenetics," based on the idea that genetic variation should be considered in assessing responses to environmental agents, emerged in the 1960s, and gained increased credibility throughout the 1970s. A National Academy of Sciences Report in 1975 devoted a special section to the role of genetic metabolic errors as predisposing factors in the development of toxicity from occupational or environmental pollutants (Calabrese, 1986). The report listed 92 human genetic disorders thought to predispose affected people to toxic effects. In response, a number of industries began to use such knowledge as a screening tool in their effort to deal with problems of occupational health. They have employed two basic types of genetic tests: chromosomal monitoring and genetic screening.

Chromosomal Monitoring

Chromosomal monitoring is employed to assess whether exposure to workplace chemicals or radiation has caused chromosomal damage. Monitoring programs involve collecting blood and urine samples from workers when they are first hired in order to evaluate them for chromosome breakage and to establish a baseline for the individual. Existing chromosome damage could be due to parental exposure to mutagens, previous exposure of the individual in an occupational or environmental setting, or natural mutation. Once a baseline for the individual is established, later samples are periodically collected and compared. Presumably any change in the amount or type of chromosomal aberration could indicate damage resulting from workplace exposure to toxic substances. Any consistent changes revealed by the monitoring of a working group could alert management to an exposure problem and call for engineering controls in the working environment, greater use of personal protection devices, or the substitution of chemicals in order to reduce exposure levels.

Monitoring presently relies on cytogenic techniques that look for chromosomal aberrations in blood or urine samples as an indication of damage to the DNA. This is an indirect method based on the assumption that abnormalities in blood cells reflect DNA mutations. Non-cytogenic techniques are being developed that directly assess damage to the DNA itself. While the value of chromosomal monitoring has sound theoretical and experimental grounding, epidemiological studies using such monitoring techniques are inconclusive. Some studies have established a dose-response relationship between increased exposure to a chemical agent and increased chromosomal damage, but none definitively show a correlation between chromosomal damage and greater risk of disease. As long as the evidence of their value remains inconclusive, employers are reluctant to undertake costly monitoring programs. They have argued that monitoring may cause unnecessary alarm among workers and lead to stricter regulations and requirements for costly structural changes in equipment. Labor interests, by contrast, favor monitoring as a means to detect chromosomal changes indicating exposure hazards for all workers.[2]

Genetic Screening

Employers have shown greater interest in the use of genetic screening techniques (Ratcliffe, et al., 1986). Genetic screening is a one-time procedure designed to detect those workers who have specific genetic traits or variant alleles that might predispose them to illness when exposed to particular chemical agents. The United States Office of Technology Assessment (OTA) reports advances in genetic diagnostics with the use of DNA techniques, but "possession of the genetic predisposition alone may be insufficient to cause disease. It is likely that for some time modern science will be more successful in identifying the genes...than in identifying the environmental agent(s) necessary for activation of the predisposing genes" (Office of Technology Assessment, 1990:11). Moreover, the current state of knowledge does not explain differential susceptibility, which may be influenced by development and aging processes, nutritional status, and other variables besides genetic traits. According to the OTA, the data on the correlations between given genetic traits and risk for disease are simply not extensive enough to draw predictive conclusions. Nevertheless, the data are suggestive, and some employers are using genetic screening as part of pre-employment medical exams.

Employers favor screening as a cost-effective protection for individual workers--a way to fulfill the duty to inform workers about potential risks to their health. At the same time, it may minimize the risks of future liability, trim insurance and the cost of compensation claims, and avoid costly structural changes in the workplace. An OTA survey of the Fortune 500 companies in 1982 found that 17 of the 366 companies that responded had used genetic screening, and 59 intended to do so. Those corporations using the tests said that they had selected employees for screening on the basis of job category or ethnicity. They had taken a variety of actions on the basis of this screening: informing the employees of a potential health problem, transferring them, or denying employment to potentially susceptible individuals (OTA, 1983).

---

2. For a review of the arguments concerning genetic screening and monitoring, see Draper, 1991.

From the perspective of labor, genetic screening is a discriminatory measure that allows industry to select employees to fit the workplace rather than making the workplace fit for employees (Mazzochi, 1980). Thus labor groups have responded to genetic screening practices with outrage. Negative media coverage of the American Cyanamid case, and then a 1980 *New York Times* series on genetic screening led to political activity among both labor and women's groups, and then to Congressional hearings (U.S. Congress, 1981, 1982). Labor activists in particular called the identification of "hypersusceptible" individuals a form of workplace discrimination.

Following this publicity corporations became cautious about announcing their policies. Only five major companies continued to admit performing any kind of genetic testing. However, corporate interest in diagnostic technologies that would divert compensation claims and financially debilitating lawsuits remained high, especially after the lawsuits filed by asbestos workers against the Johns Manville Corporation. In 1990 OTA reported that the controversial use of screening had not increased, but concerns about health care and compensation expenses, absenteeism and reduced productivity, as well as potential law suits continue to stimulate employer interest in screening programs--not only to detect workers' susceptibility to toxics, but also to assess their likelihood of developing genetically-based disease.

The appeal of genetic screening techniques is consistent with the corporate discourse on occupational health. The chemical industry, for example, embraces the goal of health and safety, but emphasizes that decisions about worker protection must be made in an economic context--that there are necessary constraints on creating a "zero-risk" environment. In effect, health and safety is an economic commodity. Accordingly, the language of efficiency enters the discourse on health. How can society best invest its limited resources in this area? How can money be spent on health and safety in cost-effective ways? How can we balance demands for increased safety against the costs of meeting them? From the perspective of an individual corporation a rational economic approach is to seek predictive measures that would exclude high-risk individuals and therefore avoid costly structural changes in the interests of relatively few employees. Genetic screening fits into this context. Monitoring, with its implications for changing the organization or physical environment of work, is a less attractive alternative.

The principle that a susceptible or vulnerable class of workers can be treated differently, that there are "scientific reasons" for discriminatory exclusion, has taken on political meaning in the context of genetic screening and the association of susceptibility with ethnicity. Susceptibility to toxic chemicals is linked to the genetic conditions associated with particular ethnic groups. Predisposing genetic characteristics may leave individuals susceptible to environmental disease including sickle cell anemia, thalassemia, and a dozen other heritable traits. Susceptibility is most commonly associated with sickle cell anemia, a mono-genetic disorder caused by the substitution of a single amino acid at one locus on the hemoglobin chain. A person with the anemia produces an abnormal hemoglobin molecule (HbS instead of HbA). Anemia is found in one out of 400-600 American blacks, or 0.2% of the American black population. The actual anemia is highly debilitating, and it is therefore unlikely that an individual could reach employment age and remain unaware of the disease. However, about one in every 10 to 12 American blacks is a carrier of the trait. The sickle cell trait is usually asymptomatic, and a carrier will experience sickness only when blood oxygen is greatly reduced. Under most circumstances the health hazards of carrying the trait are minimal or nonexistent, and individuals have no way of knowing whether they are carriers or not (Rothstein, 1983, 1984).

A person with black ancestors might want to be tested for the presence of the sickle cell trait in order to make family planning decisions. But employers have screened job applicants for the trait in order to exclude those at risk from jobs requiring contact with certain chemical compounds. In fact, this practice lacks strong scientific justification. While most screening in the workplace has been for the sickle cell trait, few people in the United States have had occupational health problems associated with this condition. According to the OTA survey, "the attention given to sickle cell anemia has led to a significant number of incidents in which individual blacks have borne the cost of actions based on mistaken judgments by employers and others" (Office of Technology Assessment, 1983:16). Nevertheless, if genetic tests are to be reasonably accurate, they must focus on groups that have predisposing characteristics. The predictive value of such tests is very low when they are used to screen the general population. Indeed, if all employees in a firm were to be screened, a very large number of false positives would occur, and the test would be virtually useless.

If accuracy requires screening a high risk population, namely those already suspected of having the trait, corporations are faced with a dilemma. In order to gain accurate test results in a cost-effective testing program, companies would need to determine who was likely to be susceptible before administering the test. In the case of the sickle cell trait this is possible; those most likely to have the condition are ethnically identifiable. But the ethical problem of singling out blacks for testing and perhaps exclusion are obvious, and critics were given to associate genetic screening with racial discrimination.[3]

Sensitivity to screening for the sickle cell trait had developed during earlier disputes over employment policies in the military. In 1969, four Army recruits

3. See Canter, 1984. Four states -- Florida, Louisiana, New Jersey, and North Carolina -- have laws banning genetic testing by employers. These grew out of the debates over sickle cell tests.

with the trait died while training at relatively high altitude. The Department of the Navy then promulgated a ruling that all recruits must be tested for hemoglobin S. Though studies of naval recruits indicated that those with the sickle cell trait were at no special risk, the Navy's policy disqualified them from a number of occupations. Ten years later, The Air Force Academy expelled several black men with the trait on grounds that their health might be endangered by the rigorous training program. The exclusion was strongly criticized as a means to restrict opportunities for blacks. Subsequent studies have differed considerably about the actual risks. Some have found a causal relationship between the trait and the few incidents of death from exertion; others have denied it. A 1987 study suggests that blacks with the trait are at somewhat higher risk. However, the policy question pervading the 20 years of controversy is whether suspected problems should be met by excluding those with the trait or by adapting their training and the conditions of their service.[4]

The same question emerged in the 1980s in response to the growing use of genetic screening in the workplace. The discussion at Congressional Hearings illustrates the way in which a policy which had first been implemented for the purpose of protecting black workers became viewed as a form of discrimination and a method of social control.

DuPont began its testing program at the request of black employees. The company first intended that the results would be given to the employee for use in family planning decisions. Under the provisions of the program the test results were retained in the employee's medical file on a confidential basis and were not intended for use as the basis for employment decisions. A DuPont physician specializing in occupational medicine testified before a Congressional subcommittee that the test for the sickle cell trait at DuPont was "purely for the education and edification of the individual involved."[5]

This may have been the intent of the original employee request for a screening program, but upon further questioning at the hearing a spokesman from DuPont's public relations department admitted that the company did not have a policy for explaining the test or its results to employees. According to an investigative reporter from the *New York Times*, the screening program had in effect been transformed from a potential information source to help employees make personal decisions into a biased tool to help the company implement exclusionary policies (Severo, 1980).

---

4. For reviews of these disputes, see McKenzie, 1977; Hoiberg, et al., 1981; Holden, 1986.

5. Testimony of Bruce W. Karrh, M.D., Corporate Medical Director of DuPont (U.S. Congress, October 15, 1981).

Further investigation of corporations using genetic screening techniques found that few medical directors had systematic data on the results of genetic tests or on their effectiveness. They had no systematic idea of how the results were used in the workplace, or how many workers had been denied employment or given alternative job placements because of genetic susceptibility. Nor were there coherent policies for maintaining confidentiality.

As predictive tests become more refined, for example, through the development of non-cytogenic screening techniques, they are likely to be more widely used, even though the relation to actual illness or job performance may not be demonstrable. Industry justifies testing and the exclusion of high risk workers in terms of protecting their health. The executive director of the New York Business Group on Health, a corporation of 300 businesses concerned about health and productivity, provides the rationale: "If an employee is an epileptic and subject to fainting spells, does it make any sense to put him to work on a scaffold" (*Industry Week*, 1987)?

Genetic Struggles

The debates over genetic screening in the workplace of the 1980s are likely to accelerate in the 1990s as tests become available to detect not only susceptibility to workplace hazards, but also predisposition to genetic disease. Tests now exist to diagnose single-gene disorders such as Huntingtons. They will eventually detect more common disorders such as some forms of cancer, heart disease and even a predisposition to addiction (Holtzman, 1989). If workers and job applicants were screened for their risk of developing genetically-based disease, many individuals could find themselves on genetic blacklists, classified as unfit for work. While medical records are private, the protection of confidentiality is in some circumstances limited.[6] Thus, some union leaders are concerned that workers will bear a "genetic scarlet letter," that they will become "lepers" or "genetic untouchables"[7] (Nelkin, 1985).

Genetic screening is far from infallible. Moreover, there may be little correlation between positive tests and impaired performance. Yet data from tests are compelling: though a person may have no symptoms, a diagnosed predisposition to risk can itself become perceived as a kind of abnormality, a disability, a disease. A person can be transformed into a patient without actual

---

6. A 1986 case, *Child Protection Group vs. Cline*, 17296 (W. Va. Sup. Ct., November 12, 1986) suggests that while disclosure of medical information about mental competency of employees (in this case a bus driver) would be an invasion of privacy, compelling public need can outweigh issues of confidentiality.

7. Quoted in *Wall Street Journal*, February 24, 1986.

manifestations of disease. Indeed, in the discussions of genetic screening, "hypersusceptibility" is treated as a handicap justifying exclusion, even though proneness to disease has nothing to do with present performance.

Routine negotiation and conflict-resolution methods offer relatively few ways to deal with such issues. Collective bargaining is an unlikely forum. Unions tend to focus on "bread and butter" issues of wages, hours and benefits. Health and safety issues have been traditionally less important. Moreover, collective bargaining agreements do not presently address decisions about the criteria for employment.

Legislative protection available to those subject to exclusion on the basis of genetic testing is also limited. The Civil Rights Act of 1964 prohibits job discrimination, but the U.S. Supreme Court has held that apparently discriminatory practices are permissible if they are based on "business necessity." Similarly, the Rehabilitation Act of 1973 in theory would protect against discrimination based on genetic screening. However, it too is limited if policies can be shown to be "business necessities." The fact that few laws directly address the problem of genetic screening allows corporations considerable independence in interpreting diagnostic information (Rothstein, 1984).

Actions against those employees already working is limited by laws requiring compensation and health benefits for sick and injured workers, such as the Employment Retirement Income Security Act (ERISA). But these protections, applying to employees, not applicants, tend to encourage more rigorous pre-employment screening and the exclusion of those likely to be predisposed to illness.

Industry has tended to deny the adversarial implications of occupational health policies. A rhetoric of consensus pervades the corporate discourse. Health is discussed as a common interest shared by management and labor alike: "All of us are in favor of good health," says Elizabeth Whelan, an epidemiologist and critic of federal regulatory policy (Whelan, 1981). Diagnostic screens are viewed as a humane measure to protect potentially vulnerable workers against unnecessary risk. And, with increased accuracy and reliability, genetic tests are seen as neutral scientific tools providing the means to protect worker health.

More precise information about individual vulnerability would help to define both ethically acceptable and economically rational policies; for there are certainly cases where exclusion would be a reasonable protective measure. However, even with improved techniques, decisions about genetic susceptibility can be linked to existing stratification systems, that is, to race, gender, and social class (Conrad, 1987; Draper, 1991). And they are implemented within an existing structure of power in the workplace. Corporate managers and the medical professionals accountable to them control diagnostic procedures, interpret the data from screening tests for their predictive value, and decide the appropriate course of action. And they are necessarily guided by the need for economy and productivity.

Despite increasing precision, predicting the level of "risky" susceptibility, defining "problematic" exposure levels, and resolving the many uncertain dimensions of diagnostic interpretation still involve many discretionary policy decisions. What are the thresholds of dangerous exposure? How much certainty is necessary before excluding a person from a job? It is left to the company doctor--beholden to the firm-- to translate ambiguous data into unambiguous corporate policy. In this discretionary framework, testing, when used as a criteria for social action, can become a strategy to extend corporate power and control beyond the workplace into the personal life of workers; beyond their manifest fitness into their genetic profile; beyond their present productivity into their future prospects for a productive and healthy life.

8

Libel Lawyers as Risk Counselors: Pre-publication and Pre-broadcast Review and the Social Construction of News

Susan P. Shapiro

The press in our society is beset by profoundly conflicting values about truth and falsity, free expression and restraint. On the one hand, journalists embrace First Amendment guarantees of freedom of expression and share the national commitment that debate on public issues "should be uninhibited, robust, and wide-open" (*New York Times Co. v. Sullivan*, 1964:270). They argue that the role of the press is to shine the light of public scrutiny on society's powerful institutions, acting as a public watchdog, exposing wrongdoing, and providing an unfettered exchange of ideas. Indeed, as argued by the Supreme Court, this commitment to "free and robust expression requires a rule which protects some falsity in order to assure that truth is neither punished nor deterred" (Bezanson, Cranberg, and Soloski, 1987:2). These sentiments reflect a passionate concern for the possibility that news organizations may fail to publish or broadcast something that is true because of fear that it is not.

On the other hand, the First Amendment carries with it obligation as well as protection. The press is a public trust, the argument goes, and that creates an

This research was supported by a fellowship from the Gannett Center for Media Studies, Columbia University. The American Bar Foundation provided funds for the analysis. Special thanks to Mary Corcoran for research assistance, to David Anderson, James Short, and Diane Vaughan for their comments and suggestions, and to the lawyers who generously shared their time and experience with thoughtful reflection, colorful detail, and candor.

obligation of responsibility, objectivity, even-handedness, accuracy, impartiality, fairness, balance, and credibility (Isaacs, 1986). Insiders warn of an implicit quid pro quo between the continuous indulgence of a constitutional protection of free speech and the exercise of responsible journalism (MacNeil, 1985; American Society of Newspaper Editors, 1986; Isaacs, 1986; Oakes, 1986). Moreover, others argue, market pressures demand it as well. In the face of increasingly stiff competition from other forms of entertainment and new information technologies, credibility has become the press' most distinctive feature and valuable asset (MacNeil, 1985). Journalists, therefore, strive to minimize falsity at the same time that they seemingly embrace or, at least, tolerate it.

In short, journalists face a tension between unknowingly printing falsehood in pursuit of free unfettered speech and practicing excessive restraint in the name of objectivity and responsibility (the so-called "chilling effect").[2] Because of the timeliness of the news and various impediments to collecting accurate information about complex social events (S. Shapiro, 1990), this tension is ever present, played out in a high-stakes daily drama.

Nowhere is this conflict more powerfully captured than in contemporary libel law and the intricate balancing act that it requires between the State's interests in compensating private individuals for reputational injury and in fostering free expression and uninhibited public debate (Ashley, 1976:4).

An Overview of the Law of Libel

For much of the history of libel law the balance clearly was tipped in favor of reputational interests. In primitive Iceland, the libel victim was allowed to kill his accuser. In 9th century England, the punishment for defamation was to cut out the offender's tongue. Libel was generally considered a criminal matter; the law was used to punish criticism of the government or the Church and imposed the harshest jail terms and corporal punishments for statements-- whether true or false--which defamed a nobleman or public official (Dill, 1986:8). In American common law, libel was a strict liability tort. As Justice Holmes warned, "whatever a man [sic] publishes, he publishes at his peril" (Smolla, 1988:1-7). "If publication, defamation (reputational disparagement), and injury could be shown, the publisher was strictly liable, even if there was an honest mistake or understandable oversight" (Bezanson, Cranberg, and Soloski, 1987:1), indeed, even if the publisher had exercised every conceivable precaution.

---

2. One might liken this tension to the choice between Type I and Type II errors in statistical inference. For a rather different socio-historical account of this tension, see Tuchman (1978:Chapter 8).

Plaintiffs did not need to prove that the defamatory information was false; rather, truth was a defense for which the defendant had the burden of proof.

Common law privileges modified these strict-liability standards in specialized settings. Somewhat expanded versions of many of these privileges continue to apply in contemporary libel law. An official records privilege, for example, enabled fair and accurate reports of "official charges, findings, recommendations, and official debate to be passed on to readers, free from the usual obligation that the journalist verify the truth before publishing and refrain from publishing unless it is confirmed" (Dill, 1986:79).[3] An opinion or fair comment privilege protected the publication of opinions on matters of public interest--however outrageous--as long as journalists made clear to the reader that they were presenting opinion and that they stated the facts upon which the opinion was based (Smolla, 1988).[4]

Twenty-five years ago, the balance between reputational and free speech interests began to shift in the United States. Beginning with the landmark decision in *New York Times Co. v. Sullivan* (1964), the Supreme Court "constitutionalized" the common law of libel, "holding that the First Amendment places limitations on the defamation rules created by the states" (Smolla, 1988:1). The decision altered the common law tort in two ways: First, actual falsity became a constitutionally required element of the tort, with the burden of proof shifting from the media defendant to the plaintiff. Second, fault--also subject to proof by the plaintiff--was introduced, thereby striking down the common law doctrine of strict liability. These constitutional

---

3. This privilege covers records from executive, legislative, administrative, judicial, or other public proceedings, arrests and other law enforcement activity; motions, exhibits, affidavits, and deposition transcripts that are signed and filed; public audits; regulatory findings; coroner's reports; public minutes of government authorities; etc. (Dill, 1986:79; Smolla, 1988). "The intent of the official records privilege is to insulate reporters from errors in official documents that they would have no reasonable way of recognizing or guarding against" and thereby furthering "the press's vital function of keeping people informed of government and public issues" (Dill, 1986:86, 79).

4. In distinguishing opinion from fact, "the courts assume that facts are indisputable, but...if people realize they are confronting an opinion, they can decide independently whether they agree or not" (Dill, 1986:99) The Supreme Court has argued that "under the First Amendment there is no such thing as a false idea. However pernicious an opinion may seem, we depend on its correction not on the conscience of judges and juries, but on the competition of other ideas. But there is no constitutional value in false statements of fact. Neither the intentional lie nor the careless error materially advances society's interest in 'uninhibited, robust, and wide-open' debate on public issues" (*Gertz v. Welch*, 1974).

privileges were intended to protect the press from the self-censorship that inhibits vigorous expression on issues of public concern. The Court argued that the difficulties of legally proving truth under the common law rules may deter critics of official conduct "from voicing their criticism, even though it is believed to be true and even though it is in fact true, because of doubt whether it can be proved in court or fear of the expense of having to do so" (*New York Times Co. v. Sullivan*, 1964:279).

The law now differentiates between public officials,[5] all-purpose public figures,[6] limited public figures,[7] private figures involved in public controversies, and private figures involved in no matters of public concern, imposing different fault standards and opportunities for recovery on each. Public persons must prove that the defendant exhibited "actual malice" when the material was published, that is, it was published with knowledge that the material was false or with reckless disregard of whether it was false or not. Private persons must at least prove that the material was published with "negligence"--that is, without the exercise of reasonable care--though individual states can ask private persons to prove a greater degree of fault (for instance, gross negligence, gross irresponsibility or even actual malice). In creating this double standard for public and private plaintiffs, the Court argued "that private plaintiffs deserved to be treated differently from those in the public spotlight" because they had not voluntarily taken a position for which public scrutiny and criticism is common, lacked easy access to the press to respond to such criticism, "were more vulnerable to injury, and less able to defend themselves" (Dill, 1986:23). In short, the private person had no recourse but to go to court to win vindication.

In requiring the plaintiff to prove the defendant blameworthy, to have acted with a culpable state of mind, the fault-based privileges actually introduce a new form of "falsity" into the libel--"subjective falsity" or "what the publisher thought about the truth or falsity *at the time of publication*"--which has had the effect of proceduralizing the common law tort (Bezanson, Cranberg, and Soloski, 1987:183, 208).

---

5. Persons who work for government in a position of authority, who have substantial control over the conduct of governmental affairs, and whose position in government invites public scrutiny.

6. Persons who occupy persuasive power and influence in the nation or in a community or who are constantly exposed to media attention.

7. Persons who voluntarily become involved in an important public controversy in order to influence public opinion regarding the resolution of that controversy. Also highly visible persons, for example, those in professional sports.

Using a regulatory metaphor, Martin Shapiro likens strict liability and reckless disregard standards, respectively, to performance and process standards of regulation (1986:885-6). "Under a performance standard," he notes, "the regulated industry is told what its end product must be, not what processes for producing that product it must employ" (885).

> A strict-liability-truth standard...is an output [or performance] standard. The government will not care how you arrive at a good news product, so long as you arrive at one. The *New York Times* reckless-disregard standard is [on the other hand] a process standard. It requires a high degree of government...intervention into the internal processes of news gathering to determine whether there was reckless disregard in a particular instance. ...over time the reckless-disregard cases should generate a set of judicially declared standards for news gathering as courts tell us what journalistic practices are and are not reckless. ...By using a process standard, the Court has created for itself the paradox that the law it invented to protect critics of public figures now makes them subject to a degree of intrusiveness in their news gathering and writing process that they might otherwise have avoided (M. Shapiro, 1986:886).

Bezanson, Cranberg, and Soloski arrive at a similar interpretation:

> the very privileges designed to safeguard editorial freedom, ironically, have required the searching judicial examination of the editorial process.

> It is because of the need to find fault that the editorial process must be disgorged, that the steps leading to publication must be explored, and that the actual frame of mind of the principal parties to the publication must be ascertained (1987:209).

They conclude that the libel tort today "is one for abuse of privilege, or for enforcement of responsibility, rather than for vindication of narrow and private interests in reputation, or for broader public interests in truth" (1987:199). Moreover, as David Anderson observes, the *New York Times* privilege ironically "perpetuates a system of censorship by libel lawyers--a system in which the relevant question is not whether a story is libelous, but whether the subject is likely to sue, and if so, how much it will cost to defend" (1975:424).

The Costs of Libelous Speech[8]

Today the average cost of a libel damage award is roughly $2 million, considerably more than that in a medical malpractice ($650,000) or product liability ($750,000) case where tangible economic injury can be more readily demonstrated (Gannett, 1986:2). Perversely, that is the good news. The vast majority of media defendants (87%) ultimately win[9] --either through summary judgment[10] or other pre-trial case dismissal (74%), at trial (3%), or through the appeal of trial judgments that invariably favor defamation plaintiffs (11%).[11] Therefore, four-fifths of the money spent in libel litigation contributes, not to damage awards, but to attorneys' fees (Garbus, 1986:34; Gannett, 1986:3). Estimates of the average overall cost of defending a libel case vary. The American Society of Newspaper Editors puts it at over $95,000, libel insurers at $150,000 (Weber, 1986:38; Gannett, 1986:3; Ruhga, 1987a:8); others suggest

---

8. The following section presents data on the stages and dispositions of libel litigation and their associated costs for plaintiffs and defendants. Although these data are relatively current, they come from various sources--some based on social science research methodology, some the techniques of journalism, and others bandied about without any documentation of their source or basis. Most figures seem reasonably consistent across several sources. I do not vouch for these data, however, but use them to provide a very general profile of the risk of libel--at least as perceived by representatives of news organizations.

9. Strikingly, while roughly a tenth of libel plaintiffs win their lawsuits, 90% of the plaintiffs in general civil litigation are successful (Bezanson, Cranberg, and Soloski, 1987:70).

10. In a motion for summary judgment, defendants ask the court to dismiss the lawsuit prior to trial, "arguing that the significant facts are not in dispute and that the law mandates a judgment. The plaintiff may contest the motion and argue that a trial is necessary to resolve disputed questions. The judge decides on the basis of the motion papers and both sides' briefs, with the help of oral argument. Summary judgments have been granted in a variety of circumstances, such as where public officials and public figures could not possibly have proved actual malice, or where the statements in issue were nondefamatory terms, privileged opinions, or protected publications of official records or proceedings" (Dill, 1986:200).

11. These data are drawn from a random sample of media libel cases filed between 1980 and 1984 and a survey of 164 libel plaintiffs in these cases conducted by Bezanson, Cranberg, and Soloski (1987:131).

that the sum may be closer to $200,000 (Garbus, 1986:37).[12] Even the price for securing the most expeditious (and common) outcome of a libel suit is not insignificant. By the time a case reaches the filing of a motion of summary judgment, media defendants have already spent $20,000 in legal fees (Garbus, 1986:37)--and 60% of these pre-trial dispositions are subsequently appealed at least once (Bezanson, Cranberg, and Soloski, 1987:133), further escalating pre-trial costs.[13] And the meter continues to run when libel cases go to trial and throughout the inevitable post-trial appellate process (91% of verdicts are appealed--Bezanson, Cranberg, and Soloski, 1987:129).

Defense costs of libel litigation rise because media defendants, championing First Amendment principles and their integrity and reputation, are reluctant to settle. Over two-thirds of all filed claims in general civil litigation are settled, compared to roughly one-tenth of those for libel (Bezanson, Cranberg, and Soloski, 1987:134).

Costs of libelous speech to news organizations do not end with the legal fees that even successful defendants incur. There are the ancillary insurance costs. In the face of escalating damage awards and huge attorneys' fees, insurance companies have been dropping out of the libel field, increasing deductibles and limiting coverage, doubling and tripling rates for low-risk media and refusing to insure altogether those with a history of libel problems or a tradition of aggressive investigative reporting (Gannett, 1986:2; Ruhga, 1987a, 1987b; Baer, 1985; Heavner, 1985).[14]

There are other less calculable costs: to journalistic reputation and integrity and in disruption of journalistic productivity by pre-trial and litigation activities. "...it may take hundreds or thousands of hours of discovery to prove that a publisher did not know the falsity of the statement and was not reckless. In addition to the costs of legal fees for discovery, editors and writers bear the psychological costs of spending many hours answering probing and personal

---

12. Expenditures can well surpass these estimates. Defense costs in the notorious Sharon and Westmoreland cases reportedly exceeded $15 million (Garbus, 1986:34).

13. "In *Herbert v. Lando* (1979), a libel case that never went to trial, the legal fees were estimated at between three and four million dollars"--mostly for discovery (Thomas, 1986:1027). "CBS spent well over $100,000 a month in the pre-trial rounds of Gen. William Westmoreland's suit against the network" (J. Anderson and Spear, 1987:9).

14. Since the *New York Times Co. v. Sullivan* decision in 1964, libel damage awards have risen by 400% and the cost of defending these suits has increased 200-400% (Gannett, 1986:2). During 1986, seven of the ten major insurers stopped selling libel policies altogether (Ruhga, 1987a:6).

questions about their mental processes during publication" (Thomas, 1986:1026). Finally, in extreme cases, small publishers--especially those unable to obtain insurance--may face organizational demise from the costs of defending libel charges and paying for awards.[15] In short, as Malcolm Feeley (1979) has argued in a different legal context, "the process is the punishment."

These onerous costs stand in marked contrast with those borne by libel plaintiffs, 86% of whom engage counsel on some form of contingency fee basis (Bezanson, Cranberg, and Soloski, 1987:69). While media defendants will typically spend $5,000 to $10,000 on legal fees even before an answer to the libel complaint is filed (Garbus, 1986: 37), complaints are "prepared in a couple of hours, at the cost of at most a few hundred dollars" in most cases (Garbus, 1986:36). For those plaintiffs (including those on full or partial contingency arrangements) who pursue their claims through disposition, the average attorneys' fee is $3,468 and total average cost $7,015 (Bezanson, Cranberg, and Soloski, 1987:178). Plaintiffs can protest defamatory charges, proclaim their integrity, attempt to save face or vindicate their reputation, and engineer political advantage by filing libel suits at little personal cost.[16]

Responding to the Risks of Libel

Given the minimal cost of filing even baseless or frivolous libel charges, coupled with the fact that a news organization prints or broadcasts hundreds of millions of words and millions of facts, opinions, or accusations about hundreds of thousands of individuals and organizations every year, accusations of libel are relatively rare. A 1985 survey found that 63% of a random sample of 188

---

15. The Alton, Illinois, *Telegraph*, for example, a small paper with a circulation of 38,000 and an annual profit margin of about $200,000, spent $612,795 in defense costs only to lose a $9.2 million libel judgment, forcing the paper into bankruptcy. The *Telegraph*, unable to afford to bring an appeal, settled for $1.4 million, enabling it to reorganize from bankruptcy; the owners then sold the paper (Dill, 1986: 189; Gannett, 1987: 5; Smolla, 1986:74,113; Curley, 1983).

16. "...the present law and social climate offer undeserving plaintiffs substantial vindication by the mere act of suing the media. By merely filing complaints, undeserving plaintiffs can mislead the public into assuming that their claims have merit and immediately undermine the defendant's credibility. ...Even if the challenged statement is eventually found to be true, that finding will come too long after the publicity to be of consequence. And if, as is far more common, the plaintiff loses not on truth but on a privilege claim, the plaintiff is free to maintain the posture of innocent victim by arguing that the defendant was saved by a technicality" (Barrett, 1986: 862).

domestic newspapers had been sued for libel *at least* once in the previous *ten* years (this figure was 90% of newspapers with circulations over 100,000); about a quarter of the papers had been sued five times or more (Hartman, 1987:691,693). Presumably, broadcasters are no less vulnerable. Though matters could obviously be much worse if every defamatory statement aired gave rise to a libel suit, the risks are real and the financial and reputational costs considerable, if variable, across different news organizations, news formats, and insurance arrangements.

Journalists and their employers respond to the risks of libel in various ways. Many simply engage in self-censorship--what is popularly referred to as the "chilling effect" (Massing, 1985).   Journalists are more cautious, less aggressive, kill high-risk stories or those that require more manpower than the story is worth because of its inherent legal dangers. They shy away from stories about private figures; litigious organizations; business leaders, doctors, and lawyers; bankruptcies; legal affairs; corruption, graft, malfeasance and misfeasance by government officials. They abandon investigative reporting or stories based on the allegations of confidential sources, and muffle feisty editorial pages.[17]

Many media lawyers question a chilling effect, especially for journalists working for the larger newspapers, magazines, and broadcasters. Others concede the specter of libel suits has a pervasive, if subtle effect--"a sort of pursuing demon that has everyone in the news business looking over their shoulder," as one respondent in my study characterized it. The full extent of such self-censorship is, of course, "impossible to determine. Much of it is inherently unmeasurable; it occurs whenever a reporter or editor omits a word, a passage, or an entire story, not for journalistic reasons but because of the possible legal implications" (D. Anderson, 1975:430).

Many news organizations respond to libel risks by offering special seminars to educate journalists and editors about the intricacies of and changes in libel law and how to identify and respond to these risks. Ninety-four percent of the inside counsel and 85%[18] of the outside counsel interviewed in my study indicated that they ran such seminars for their clients, usually at least annually. News

---

17. One hears anecdotes about publishers who have totally changed their editorial format because of the specific deterrence generated by a libel suit. A respondent in this study described a small weekly newspaper run by a "fire and guts kind of guy. He will not print anything controversial anymore. He prints church weddings, social events, and sports--and he's happy. His paper is selling as well and no libel suits!"

18. Another 6% of the outside counsel conducted these seminars in the past, but now delegate responsibility to their clients' inside counsel.

organizations also adopt--sometimes at the behest of insurance carriers--various self-regulatory approaches that indirectly, at least, reduce the risks of libelous speech or of aggravating those defamed by news stories. They include codes of newsroom standards,[19] tighter editorial supervision and control (Breed, 1955), letters to the editor and corrections columns (American Society of Newspaper Editors, 1986; Whitney, 1986), ombudsmen (Mogavero, 1982; Tate, 1984; Glasser and Ettema, 1985), the use of fact checkers (Ridder, 1980; Blow and Posner, 1988; S. Shapiro, 1990), and the use of lawyers to review news stories prior to publication or broadcast in order to advise editors about libel risks (Lincoln, 1972; D. Anderson, 1975; Daniels, 1981; Johnston, 1983; Miller, 1985; Sanford, 1985; Julin, 1988). This process of pre-publication or pre-broadcast review by media lawyers is the focus of this article.

A body of work in the sociology of knowledge in general and the sociology of the news, in particular, makes problematic the ways in which the social organization of the production of an account affects the account itself (Smith, 1974:260; see also Berger and Luckmann, 1966). Herbert Gans' work (1979), for example, examines how organizational, political, commercial, economic, and cultural forces and agents shape the selection of stories by popular national news media. Gaye Tuchman's research exposes how the social organization of newswork defines and constructs social reality, transforming everyday occurrences into news events, simultaneously producing and limiting meaning about these events (1978:180). "[N]ews professionals' claim to produce veridical accounts of social life" (1978:209), notwithstanding, Tuchman demonstrates how the techniques and practices of newswork themselves shape the news. My case study of media lawyers draws on this tradition in the sociology of knowledge, mirroring Tuchman's approach, but applied to a much more narrow slice of newswork. It looks at a minor social role standing outside the journalistic hierarchy in large complex news organizations, faced with the management of diffuse risk, and constrained by a set of idiosyncratic legal norms, and examines their mark on the social construction of news. It exposes the irony that these legal norms, developed to protect free unfettered journalistic expression and to encourage multiple voices and competing versions of the truth in a marketplace of ideas, sometimes achieve quite the opposite result.

---

19. For example, two source rules, policies that forbid the use of an anonymous source without an editor's permission, policies about naming rape victims or juvenile suspects, conflict of interest policies, fair comment or right of reply rules (Hartman, 1987).

The Study

A research assistant and I conducted open-ended interviews in 1987 with a "snowball" sample of 19 in-house and 34 outside counsel who review stories for news organizations.[20] Thirty-eight percent of the interviews (mostly of lawyers working in New York city) were conducted in person, the remaining ones by telephone. Interviews ranged in length from twenty minutes to two hours; the median in-person interview took sixty minutes, the median telephone interview, forty minutes.

The 53 respondents comprise a significant proportion of the population of lawyers nationwide who do this kind of work with any regularity. These lawyers represent a wide range of news media:[21] four television networks or broadcast chains; virtually all of the major newspapers in the country, including a few newspaper chains; a large number of smaller daily newspapers, especially those located in the south, west, and southwest; two newspaper tabloids; three national weekly newsmagazines and many other weekly and monthly special interest or trade magazines; local television and radio stations nationwide; a wire service and

---

20. I began with a list of lawyers across the country (known to be involved in pre-publication or pre-broadcast review) developed by a legal scholar who works in the area. Each interview concluded by asking the respondent to name others to whom we ought to speak. After the same names began reappearing in the interviews, I shifted strategy, indicating to respondents that we had a fairly complete list of counsel for the major national and east coast media and asking for suggestions of lawyers who represent smaller clients in other areas of the country about whom we were less likely to know. Finally, I searched for the names of counsel representing a few of the major media that had somehow never appeared in any of the lists. The response rate was 96%.

21. Although I attempted to include a representation of all kinds of news media that utilize legal review, the sample is not representative. It probably overrepresents large news organizations with national visibility, lawyers who specialize almost exclusively in a media practice, inside over outside counsel (while slightly more than one-third of my sample of lawyers work in-house, a random sample of U.S. newspapers with a daily circulation of 15,000 or more found that only 3% consulted in-house counsel when they encountered potentially libelous stories--Hartman, 1987:688), and New York media clients (although respondents in the sample resided in thirteen different states and the District of Columbia, 36% worked in New York City). Though one must read the data cautiously, they still yield a fascinating profile of this group of legal specialists.

a news service; book publishers; student newspapers; media hotlines; and a press association.[22] For a few of the larger newspapers and broadcasters, I interviewed both inside and outside counsel.

This account of the pre-publication review process is, of course, based on self-reports of professionals known for articulateness, caution, and skillful information control. Their responses must, therefore, be analyzed critically and a bit skeptically.[23] More problematic analytically, because the interview questions telescope a lawyer's experience with many stories of many types produced by many clients, they conceal some of the fascinating variability in the review process. Perhaps for this reason and because the sample was self-selected, concentrating on specialized practitioners who devote a good proportion of their practice to media work, one finds more uniformity than variation in their accounts.

---

22. In drawing the sample, I tried to focus on legal review of news stories. Therefore, nominations of lawyers who exclusively represent book publishers, movie studios, advertisers, non-news-oriented magazines, and the like were not pursued. However, because most of the outside counsel in the sample (82%) have more than one media client and some in-house counsel oversee all of the media properties owned by his or her employer, non-news media inadvertently slipped into the sample of clients. They are greatly outnumbered, though, by daily newspapers, broadcast news, and weekly newsmagazines. Forty-two percent of the inside counsel represented a newspaper, 11% a newspaper chain, 10% a magazine or magazine group, 26% a television network or broadcast chain, 5% a television station, and 5% a combination of print and broadcast media. Eighteen percent of the outside counsel represented one or more newspapers, 3% magazines, 29% a mixture of print media, 0% broadcast media exclusively, and 47% a combination of print and broadcast media.

23. Fortunately, during an unrelated observational study of magazine fact checkers, I enjoyed an occasional glimpse of the legal pre-publication review process. These observations were rare, by no means systematic, generally involved relatively short stories about public figures, and, obviously, reflected only print media. The impression made was not radically dissimilar from that conveyed by the self-reports, except perhaps that the review process observed was a bit more informal, cursory, and haphazard than the one the lawyers describe.

The Process of Pre-publication or Pre-broadcast Review

As noted earlier, about a third of the lawyers in the sample conduct pre-publication or pre-broadcast review in-house;[24] the other two-thirds work as outside counsel, mostly in law firms, and represent several media clients. About three-quarters of the respondents are assisted by one or more colleagues in pre-clearance review.

In rare cases--for a few monthly or weekly magazines or tabloids and a weekly television news show--lawyers review everything published or broadcast (often at the insistence of insurance carriers). For several other news outlets, nearly every story or all stories in a certain category (a particular column, all special series, or all investigative pieces, for example) are sent for legal review. But, for the majority of news organizations, particularly those that issue daily newspapers, lawyers review only selected stories which are usually referred at the discretion of the editors with whom they subsequently work. Because of these differences in the extent of selectivity of review and number of clients, respondents devote variable amounts of time each week reviewing disparate numbers of stories.[25]

The vast majority of the respondents (87%) indicate that they begin their review only after a story has been written or edited, though half concede that they

---

24. In general, the presence of inside counsel is a reflection of the size of the news organization. Only newspaper chains, national or large-city newspapers, magazine groups, or broadcast networks can afford the economies of scale that make in-house legal assistance affordable. Though there are exceptions. A local TV station in a mid-size city employs a part-time lawyer to conduct pre-broadcast review in-house, while a large-circulation national newspaper employs outside counsel for its pre-publication review.

25. There are few regularities in the time required for review. Respondents indicate that they may spend a few minutes reviewing a troublesome sentence in a news story or the good part of one or more weeks advising on a complex piece. Although estimates are difficult, on average, a little more than three-quarters of the outside counsel and one-third of the inside lawyers estimate that they spend no more than five hours each week on pre-publication or pre-broadcast review, whereas 5% and 14%, respectively, spend more than 20 hours a week on these activities. The median amount of time committed by outside lawyers is 1-2 hours/per week and for inside ones, 6-10 hours/week. Roughly two-fifths of the outside and one-fifth of the inside counsel do not even review one story a week, in contrast with 7% and 25%, respectively, who scrutinize more than 20 pieces weekly. The median number of stories reviewed is 1-2/week for outside and 6-10/week for inside counsel.

may occasionally be consulted earlier on newsgathering questions, sensitive stories, long investigative series, or stories for which there are threats of litigation. Counsel for television stations are more likely to be consulted earlier in the process because the time and cost needed to make changes are so high. A few buttons on a word processor can alter a print news story; revising television news generally requires more shooting, more editing, new voice-overs, and the like. As one respondent commented, "it's easier to fix before it's broken." On special investigative series, therefore, broadcast lawyers may set ground rules in advance, advise on newsgathering techniques, clear a script before crews are allowed to start shooting, or just ask to be kept apprised of the status of a complicated story.

Although most respondents admit they have to clear stories over the telephone more often than they prefer, they generally try to review hard copy of a story and ask to be shown headlines, captions, photos, illustrations, "intros" and "outros" (that are read by television anchors to lead in and out of a piece of reportage), teasers, and promotions along with the text. Counsel for television stations try to read the script and then see a videotape of the broadcast (and in some instances may ask to see outtakes and supervise film editing as well); most often, though, they must rely on the script alone.

Lawyers devise all sorts of arrangements with their clients to provide expeditious counsel on breaking stories. Inside counsel often will have computers in their offices hard-wired to those in the newsroom, and may routinely visit newsrooms, studios, and editorial offices; one newspaper counsel keeps his office in the newsroom to facilitate consultation with the journalists. Outside counsel have more impediments. Some also have computer hook-ups in their homes or offices (one boasted that his computer had no keyboard so that he would not be tempted to change anything); others make routine visits to the news organization (especially the tabloids) at least once or twice a week or stop regularly on their way home from work. Some visit only for complicated stories that have a lot of documentation to review or to view the videotape. Perhaps most often, though, messengers deliver hard copies of the stories to their homes or offices. A few inside and outside counsel indicate that they wear beepers on nights and weekends, so that they can be reached in not-so-uncommon emergencies.

Evaluating the Story

Lawyers ask basically two threshold questions as they evaluate news stories. First, is the story potentially defamatory? Does it contain material that is offensive; that would shock, anger, hurt, or outrage the subject of the story's allegations; that accuses a person of being dishonest, incompetent, or unworthy of respect; or that damages a reputation or holds a person up to hatred, ridicule, or scorn? Second, does anything in the story or the newsgathering practices suggest that journalists have invaded the subject's privacy? In most cases, it is the first set of questions and their implications that lawyers wrestle with in pre-publication review. This paper will concentrate on them as well.

Since editors most often refer news articles for legal review because they consider them potentially defamatory, the first threshold question is usually quickly and easily answered by the lawyers--and in the affirmative. The words on their face betray the disparagement of reputation; as one lawyer noted, "you develop a sixth sense; things leap out at you." But reviewers go beyond the obvious defamatory implications contained in the central assertions of the story. One respondent explained:

> Rarely is the problem in the lead. Reporters know how to check that and the central claims of the story exhaustively. It's usually several paragraphs down in the story--a story in a story or a small detail or an ancillary point. For example, you're reporting a fire and mention that an adjacent building, a bankrupt business, was also burned. Turns out the business is not bankrupt.

So reviewers reread the story very closely, highlighting or circling every person, company, entity, organization, or association mentioned, noting whether anything written about them is negative, offensive, or "could even remotely be construed as sensitive." They are on the look-out for the minor issue and the throw-away line and for secondary, ancillary, tangential, peripheral characters, mentioned only in passing, who may be tarred by implication--the inadvertent plaintiffs that no one is focussing on who lawyers believe often are the ones to sue.

Once defamation has been established, reviewers are left to consider the two remaining elements of libel: falsity and fault. Neither are easy to ascertain. Because lawyers are rarely consulted until after the story has been written or produced, they face two severe impediments. First, most stories must be reviewed on deadline with at best a few hours available to evaluate often complex issues. Second, and more problematic, legal review of this sort is necessarily retrospective. Lawyers have not been in the field. They did not observe the events, listen to the press conferences, read the documents, hear the interviews, talk to the sources. They did not see who or what was not consulted in reporting the story. Nor did they see the "edit"--how pieces of data were ordered and assembled into a narrative story and other pieces ultimately cut from that story. In short, reviewers do not know from personal experience either the truth or falsity of the story's assertions or whether they were gathered and presented with due care, with negligence, or with actual malice (i.e., with knowing falsity or reckless disregard). One respondent characterized pre-publication review as a "leap of faith." Another explained:

The ultimate question is one of truth and falsity, and that is one that is not particularly susceptible to any kind of legal review. In the final analysis, only the reporter knows and the source knows if what is being published is true. And you can make stabs at it. You can cross-examine the reporter and look at the notes and examine the documents, but that is no insurance policy that the fundamental facts in the story are true.

Regardless of epistemological debates about the nature of truth or whether sources, documents, or reporters know or are able to convey "truth," legal reviewers indisputably have less access to it than do journalists. Lawyers therefore craft inferential intelligence strategies, subtly shaped by legal conventions about how to arrive at the truth, rules of evidence and standards of proof,[26] in order to guess whether the story as presented bears some relationship to unknowable facts and, more importantly, to reconstruct the process by which the journalists came to believe that the story was true.[27] They do not conduct accuracy checks; most say that is the responsibility of the editor or fact checker. Rather, they undertake a kind of interactive content analysis of the story, the photographs, the videotape, or the script to draw inferences about falsity and

---

26. Examples include cross-examination and rules of evidence concerning hearsay and circumstantial evidence. A television news producer describes the inherent conflict between journalists and lawyers as stemming from these different conventions about truth, evidence, proof, and the like:

Much more frequent are the thrashes that occur in the newsroom en route to a chill because the lawyer must ask the inevitable and nonrhetorical question, "Do you have to say that?" Lawyers will think in terms of admissibility, relevance, pertinence, hearsay, exceptions to the hearsay rule. None of that applies to journalists. So there's this whole body of fact that creates strong cognitive dissonance among lawyers because they're thinking of the standard of proof that would or would not make these events or statements admissible in a court of law; when translated into news stories these points may be absolutely newsworthy, acceptable for publication, and terrific to print or air. And that's where the collision comes (Gannett, 1986:9).

27. Several respondents talk about whether they know the work of the particular reporter and whether he or she has a reputation for thoroughness, care, and balance, or instead a history of libel trouble or of being unreliable. They imply that the rigor and exhaustiveness of their review may be inversely correlated with the degree of trust they have in the reporter.

fault. How do we know that the story is true? How might its truthfulness be proven?

From detailed descriptions provided in the interviews, one can discern nine themes that characterize this inquiry. First the lawyers look for "give-aways"--words, inflections, transitions, and the like that present red flags that something about the story is amiss. They look for words (like "seems that" or "appears that") that suggest the possibility that the reporter is confused or unsure of what he or she is saying. The order or placement of information may convey doubt as well. In commenting on the Sharon libel suit against *Time*, one outside counsel suggested that if he had reviewed that story, he would have asked why the passage about Appendix B[28] was buried in the 65th paragraph of the article. If Sharon really condoned or committed murder, why wasn't it in the lead? Why weren't these serious allegations higher in the story? Could it be that the writer was unsure of their accuracy and therefore buried the charges?

A big jump in the story line, quotes that seem to be cut off, or edits that sound funny provide red flags as well. These indicators are often especially apparent in broadcast journalism. Several television lawyers noted that the transcript may seem perfectly fine but, when viewing the tape, they discover that the inflection of a voice suggests that a statement ends too abruptly and that part of the answer may be clipped and, thereby, distorted or taken out of context. In that case, reviewers will ask about the rest of the statement or to see a transcript of the outtakes. In at least this respect, the marriage of words, audio, and video enhances the opportunities for this kind of inferential analysis and gives broadcast lawyers a distinct advantage over their print counterparts.

A second set of suspicions is triggered by very general allegations, vague or imprecise words, seeming overstatements, passages that appear overwritten, "purple prose," inflammatory language, and strong adjectives or adverbs (such as "only," "all," or "deliberately"). When lawyers encounter instances of verbal excess, they look very carefully for support within the story and check for exaggerated claims.

A third theme in the legal read concerns the plausibility and consistency of the story. Reviewers check that the story is clear and makes sense, that the arguments follow, and that allegations in the lead are supported by the rest of the story. They pause at information that seems confusing; if the lawyer can't understand it, then perhaps the reporter didn't either. And they look for evidence that seems counterintuitive, "fishy," incredible, or inconsistent.

---

28. The secret appendix was to a report of the Israeli commission of inquiry and allegedly disclosed that General Sharon had discussed with the Gemayel family the need for the Phalangists to avenge the assassination of Bashir Gemayel. Two days after this conversation, the Christian Phalangists massacred over 700 Palestinians in the Sabra and Shatilla camps on the outskirts of Beirut.

Concern for the consistency of characterizations or evidence is reflected in a fourth inferential intelligence approach, in which lawyers focus on the juxtaposition of media, ideas, types of information and ways of conveying that information throughout the news story. Reviewers will look at the words, pictures, audio, and video components of the story. Do the pictures match the words? Does the video do what the audio says it does? Does it change the sense of the audio for the viewer?[29] Are the headlines or photo captions in print media, promotions, teasers, and anchorperson's lead-ins in broadcast media, consistent with the central claims of the story? Given the fact that headline-type promotions are not written by those who report the news (coupled with their tendency to hype a story in order to grab attention of viewers furiously switching channels or readers purchasing their newspaper from a line of vending machines), lawyers must be especially wary that these promotions do not distort the news in an inflammatory way or imply conclusions not supported by the story.

Other lawyers look out for instances in which the reporters or editors seem to be using the generic for the specific--a specific quote or specific problem juxtaposed with generic information or generic file photos, street scenes, or "wallpaper" footage. Many respondents used the example of showing a random street scene from New York's Greenwich Village in a story on AIDS. In this case, photographs wrongly associate an individual with objectionable matter implied by the context in which the photo appears. This problem also occurs in print with the juxtaposition of specific claims with generic ones.[30]

Fifth, lawyers analyze the unstated implications of a story. Many indicate that they try to make sure that the story does not imply more or is capable of a broader inference by the reader than is intended or can be supported. They look for unintended innuendo or implications. Have we strung three accurate statements of fact together in a fashion so as to create an inference of a fourth which doesn't exist? They look for transitions or "set-off" words--"buts" and

---

29. A broadcast lawyer explains: "People want pretty pictures, active pictures, moving and telling pictures. And frequently in order to produce attractive video to go with their carefully reviewed audio, they create problems that wouldn't have existed with the audio alone."

30. A broadcast lawyer provided an example he had encountered that morning in a highly-regarded newspaper. The paper is doing a piece on race and indicates that a certain percent of whites don't like blacks. "Then underneath it said 'Marilyn whatever-her-name-was' husband was mugged by six blacks, is in a coma, and so forth and so on.' It doesn't say she doesn't like blacks. Then the article goes on to talk about polarization and so forth...Now she could sue just on the juxtaposition of the general thing, claiming that putting her statement there makes her seem like a racist."

"howevers"--that inadvertently carry hidden meanings or statements of fact or unintended implications.

Sixth, lawyers review the evidence on which the story is based. In scrutinizing the evidentiary claims of the piece, reviewers may consider newsgathering questions and how reporters came into possession of film or documents--the possibility of trespass in getting the film or the use of concealed identities, wiretaps, hidden microphones, or zoom lenses. They will look for corroboration in the story for sensitive allegations and expose and question circumstantial evidence.

But mostly the evidentiary review involves sourcing. Lawyers investigate whether sources are in a position to know whereof they speak. What is their access to information? Have we used these sources before? Have they been reliable in the past? What are their motives for disclosing this information? What kind of personal interest does the source have in the person about whom negative comments are made? Does the source bear a grudge? Might he or she be inclined to give false or defamatory information or extreme perspectives? Those who talk to the press, lawyers believe, frequently have axes to grind, private agendas, or biases; therefore it is essential to insure that these biases are not incorporated into the story inadvertently. Are their assertions confirmed or corroborated by at least two independent sources? Lawyers are especially wary about the use of confidential sources for, if their allegations precipitate a libel suit and the defendant is unable to produce the confidential source at trial, it may be assumed that no source exists and that the allegations were fabricated. Therefore lawyers inquire about the degree to which the story could be defended without reference to the confidential source.

A seventh theme in lawyers' descriptions of how they conduct pre-publication or pre-broadcast review involves "procedural reporting." Earlier in this paper, I cited the work of scholars who have argued that the constitutionalization of the law of libel and the introduction of fault standards bearing on what the publisher thought about truth or falsity at the time of publication has had the effect of proceduralizing the law of libel. This procedural notion of truth or falsity is insinuated in lawyers' efforts to evaluate the evidentiary basis of a news story. They scour the story for inferences of whether (or how) reporters entertained the possibility that their facts or conclusions might be wrong and of whether they sought comment from the other side as one means of entertaining such doubt. They look to see what the story says about the identity and quality of sources of information and about what was done to verify their statements. They check to see whether reporters make clear what they do not know.

Where the story does not convey its procedural history, lawyers will often cross-examine reporters about the factual support for an allegation. One can generally tell from this conversation, they claim, if reporters do not really understand the story or if the evidence is marginal. Indeed, some assert, this conversation is more important than reviewing documents and other evidence. Is there anything reporters know that would indicate that the story is wrong? Has anyone told the journalists that anything they are printing is factually incorrect? Do reporters have serious doubts about the truth? What steps did they take to determine whether they had any doubts? Did journalists talk with or look at the writing of other reporters who have been involved with this person or story in the past to make sure that they are not out in left field? How far did reporters go to check things out? Was the subject of a damaging statement consulted and given a chance to air his or her explanation or denial? Was the target told the full nature, content, and substance of the allegations? To what lengths did reporters go to get comment from the other side?

If scouring the story for defamatory statements, ancillary plaintiffs, and blatant give-aways is the easiest part of pre-publication or pre-broadcast review, certainly the hardest part is assessing what the story doesn't tell, ensuring that material is in proper context, that the story is balanced, and that its reporting or presentation does not betray procedural irregularities, negligence, reckless disregard, and the like. A broadcast lawyer explains this eighth theme:

> I particularly focus on what's not in the story...because what's in there [the reporters] thought about; it's all the other stuff they haven't. ...I want to know all the things that the reporters did not tell me that they could have told me and chose not to include in the story and to make sure that everything in the story is in proper context. So, what do you look for in that connection? Well, you look particularly at quotes that are cut off, statements that are taken out of other things, characterizations of documents or events or interviews. So you have to look not only at what's in front of you, but all of the background information and research that was left out. And I find, for me, that tends to be the greatest potential problem. Because in the sifting through of the hundreds of thousands of facts that go into an investigative story, there is so much left out. And what I consider to be necessary to put back in to balance the story, I'm not going to see in the reviewing of that script. I'm not going to know it even exists. So I look for all the things that I don't know because the script doesn't tell me about them...And it's just really my creativity--or lack thereof--that limits the amount of things I find out.

Another television lawyer indicated that she satisfies discomfort about the unknown by extensively reviewing all the raw footage and outtakes on difficult stories.

Finally, the lawyers evaluate the use of legal privileges in the story. Have the reporters exhausted the possibility of using a public record source to support their claims, so that they are protected even if the allegations are not true? If so, does the source qualify for the legal privilege, have the court documents been filed, has the reporter actually seen the documents, have the story's claims been attributed to the official source, is it a "fair and accurate" report in which reporters have quoted from official documents or taken care in summarizing the gist of the records--as the law requires? Although respondents expressed some reluctance to review the notes and documents amassed by journalists in preparation of a story, many indicated that they do review official documents (especially legal ones like civil complaints, indictments, divorce papers, deeds, politician's statements of economic interest, etc.) when the story is sufficiently complex to ensure that reporters understood and summarized them properly. The lawyers also check to see that the opinion or fair comment privilege is used properly and that it is defensible--that journalists flagged the privileged passage as an opinion and specified the facts upon which the opinion is based.

As the lawyers pursue these nine intelligence themes in their pre-publication or pre-broadcast review, they make overall assessments of the riskiness of the story, the likelihood that it will provoke a libel suit, and the magnitude of defense costs such litigation might incur. Reviewers evaluate who the story is about and try to make a ballpark guess about whether the subjects are likely to be treated by the court as public or private figures.[31] What is the likelihood that the subjects will be offended by the story and how are they likely to react? Have they sued in the past or are they known as particularly sensitive or litigious? What jurisdiction could we be sued in? Will the plaintiff expose him or herself to discovery? What might come out in discovery? Is there anything in the reporter's notes that might prove problematic--for example, lists of investigative leads left to pursue, doodles, carelessness, embarrassing characterizations?[32] What are the chances we'll win a summary judgment motion? If the case goes to trial, will the evidence be preserved? Will we have the documents when we need them? What witnesses would we call? Are possible witnesses around and in good health? What are their motives? Would we be proud to have this witness on the stand for us? Who is going to say what at trial? Have we acted in a responsible manner? How will our conduct look to a jury? In short, what is the risk of losing and the potential damages?

---

31. Most, though, indicate that such guesses are notoriously unreliable and conduct their review as if subjects are private figures and entitled to the weakest standard of fault.

32. Lawyers indicate they will examine the reporter's notes during pre-publication review only to assess problems they might pose for discovery. They sometimes advise reporters to destroy their notes or they will take possession of the notes under the attorney-client relationship, so that they won't be subject to discovery later on.

Fixing the Story

The lawyers are reluctant to advise editors to kill stories in which they have found problems. Indeed, all but two of the fifty-three respondents indicated that they virtually never gave such advice.[33] In an almost unified voice, respondents explain:

> I have never advised that a story be killed. I have, in some instances, pointed out some significant risks; in others, pointed out some minor risks; and in all instances, suggested modifications that will save the story. Most of the people with whom I work are of the view that without taking at least a little bit of risk, you're never going to get the news out. But I always view my job as identifying the risks and trying to find ways to reduce or minimize them.

So the lawyers advise editors about the legal risks posed by the story and then set about the task of finding ways to "enable reporters to say what they want to say...in a form that gives the newspaper [or broadcaster] maximum legal protection."

The irony of some of this country's most devoted First Amendment advocates exercising a backstage censorship role is not lost on these lawyers. Because of their sensitivity to this censorship function and because most seek to maintain a kind of "Chinese Wall" between legal and editorial judgment, the process by which lawyers advise "fixes" sounds a bit like a game of "Twenty Questions." One prominent attorney explained, "I don't want a question of mine to become an answer by the very fact that I've asked it." So lawyers claim they push journalists hard, force them to find their own solutions, reappraise revisions, and send them back, yet again, when necessary.[34] The *most*

---

33. One of the two lawyers, outside counsel for a weekly newspaper tabloid, indicated that "it happens very often." The other, inside counsel for some television stations explained, "I don't believe and I don't think this company believes in pushing our First Amendment rights up to the limit. I think that reporters and journalists have to use some good judgment in what they decide to cover and what they don't decide to cover. And not everything they happen to find out about has to be broadcast on the air because they happened to fall over it."

34. One respondent illustrated this sort of exchange: "I might ask, look, what if you tried this way of expressing it? What would that do? Would that destroy what you are trying to accomplish in the story? Would it water it down too much?" These somewhat elusive strategies sound a bit like those used by the

interventionist respondent in the sample described her, still rather indirect, advisory role:

> Sometimes I will suggest ways of redrafting it so that I will be satisfied with it. Sometimes I will tell them what I think needs to be said--that they need to add a section balancing out what's there or to add further information or to take out certain information and to recharacterize it. And I tell them to redraft it. And I will look at four, five, six scripts sometimes before something is okay.

Though they refuse to kill a story, lawyers will counsel that material be cut, usually by telling editors that the story would have fewer problems if it ran without particular information. They might suggest that the editors take out an irritating statement, a particularly sensitive word, a sequence on film, a random photograph that creates an unfair link, a troublesome paragraph, extraneous information, or a specific charge that cannot be supported. Perhaps the safest thing to do, though--and one respondents invariably mention--is to cut potential plaintiffs out of the story entirely. In an effort to minimize the "unintended plaintiff problem," lawyers frequently advise that editors reconsider a decision to even allude to noncentral, peripheral, second or third-tier individuals or organizations.

Many recommended fixes focus on the writing. Respondents spoke at length about precise writing so that charges are specific and no broader than they should be. They advise that editors avoid words that are difficult to define or to prove in court and to avoid short-hand words (Mafia, scam) or words that have specific definitional needs (fraud, murder). They remind editors to delete the "onlys," "every times," "alls," "deliberatelys," and "knowinglys" and to use synonyms for inflammatory language. If something is ambiguous, they recommend rephrasing. Reword the passage, tone it down, shift emphasis, change the focus of the lead, soften the conclusion. Where necessary, attach a qualification or put in a caveat.

Where lawyers worry that unintended implications or innuendo are suggested by the story, they may advise that editors restructure the story and reorder material, moving some information higher up so that the reader will not draw some conclusion or inference before he or she gets to that information or to redirect some of the factual findings so that they point away from a certain implication. Sometimes it is necessary to change the order of material because the juxtaposition of names and data or generic and specific information creates an

---

white-collar crime defense bar to counsel their clients to withhold evidence from government investigators without directly advising them to obstruct justice (Mann, 1985).

unintended innuendo or inference. When all else fails, lawyers suggest that editors explicitly deny in the text an implication that might otherwise be drawn.

Less frequently, the problem is in the video. This is probably fortunate since, on deadline, there are few alterations that can be made in a television piece other than changing the "studio portion," the verbal lead-ins and lead-outs spoken by the anchors. Where there is more time, it may be necessary to reshoot the video, use a different piece of the outtake or file footage, rewrite the script, retrack the story, read it again on the audio, and reedit the video. For juxtaposition problems in a broadcast story, lawyers will advise that editors change the audio or video, substitute a different visual, or use talking heads (non-action shots of people speaking). If a remark is not in context, they recommend that another piece of the outtake be used in the program.

Respondents spoke often about repackaging the story so that it is protected by legal privileges. They advise that, instead of repeating information from interviews, journalists quote from public proceedings, official documents, depositions, court testimony, indictments, civil complaints, and the like. They recommend that editors try to couch statements in terms of opinion and provide more facts so that they will be able to support the claim that the column is an opinion.

The most sustained theme in lawyers' suggestions pertains to the evidentiary basis of the story, the sources and quality of information reported and disclosure about the newsgathering process. That concern is reflected, for example, in lawyers' advice to rely on privileged documents rather than other kinds of evidence. Respondents express frequent discomfort with news sources. Should you be accepting the word of this source, they ask reporters. You need to talk to somebody else. Can you get the confidential source to go on the record or use his or her allegations as a springboard for developing other leads? Can you find another source, a documentary source, an on-the-record source, a more credible source? If all the sources have the same axe to grind, you need to confirm something in another way, they advise.

Often lawyers suggest that more substantiation or better corroborative evidence is needed.

> There isn't quite enough support for the truth of what you are saying yet and a little more work needs to be done, which will turn up one of two things: either more factual support and enough that you are comfortable that it is probably true, or, alternatively, that there is a real dispute as to where the truth lies, in which case you will want to report both sides of it.

Lawyers may tell reporters to go back and ask specific questions; look at another document; check with people who are more knowledgeable; check a person's bio file to make sure our statement is consistent with reported incidents in his or her past. They recommend that reporters go back and get responses to every allegation, even from secondary figures. If a series of people were referred to, contact everyone on the list. Make sure their views are fairly set forth. Don't be derogatory when stating that someone declined to respond. If their reaction was "no comment," try to quote someone sympathetic to the person being attacked. Try to give the other side in some way. If necessary, hold the story for a day or two.

Finally, lawyers encourage "procedural reporting," that stories explicitly present the newsgathering process, announce the legal privileges taken, expose how journalists came to learn what is reported, doubts that were entertained, and steps taken to resolve these doubts. They counsel editors to identify protected opinion as such or preface a passage with "In x's opinion...." They instruct reporters to make it clear to readers where information comes from. They will suggest ways to phrase things to make it clear that *the reporter* is not saying something, but that he or she is attributing it to someone or something else. Lawyers recommend that reporters carefully record that the subject was given a reasonable opportunity to comment and declined. In cases of great danger, they request that some sort of reliable documentation--a telegram or certified letter written for the benefit of a future jury--be sent seeking comment. Where there is sufficient doubt, they advise that journalists say so and report both sides of a story.

In short, lawyers retrospectively reconstruct and build a record of a newsgathering process in which reporters and editors, if ever challenged, will be able to demonstrate that they exercised reasonable care in ascertaining truth at the time of publication or broadcast. Despite the cleverness and persistence of their inferential intelligence, lawyers still do not know the "truth" of a story's allegations. They may tinker with the language to ensure that is not misconstrued or gratuitously inflammatory or offensive, but such fixes will not make defamatory allegations praiseworthy or false charges true. Though they may try, they cannot cut every potential plaintiff out of the news. And because the costs are low and the reputational benefits of filing a libel suit high, counsel can rarely predict or discourage frivolous lawsuits. But they can minimize their cost. Since questions of fault are often resolved in pre-trial motions for summary judgment--when legal defense costs are still relatively low--it is therefore not surprising that lawyers' advice concentrates on ensuring defensible newsgathering practices. Media lawyers, in pursuit of constitutional protections of free speech, have come to enforce responsible journalism.

Pre-publication Review and the
Social Construction of the News

I asked the lawyers what impact they thought their work had on the journalistic process. One respondent unabashedly argued that pre-publication review, because it is a form of censorship, necessarily makes a story worse (and more vapid and insipid). Most of the others, however, modestly suggested that their impact was rather small and that, although lawyerly advice tends to make stories slightly more boring and convoluted, it also leaves them tighter, more balanced, better corroborated, and less inflammatory. Several mentioned that they could often detect the "hand of a lawyer" in their daily news fare.

One can also discern more systemic effects of legal intervention. For example, lawyers' preoccupation with the inadvertent libel of more marginal figures in a story very often results in advice that reference to secondary characters be excised. The effect is to narrow stories, to conceal the complex social networks and interorganizational relationships that figure in collective action, crime, and deviance. The reluctance to name these ancillary contributors to newsworthy events creates a simplistic (mis)understanding of social behavior by a citizenry whose formal education in the social sciences often comes from its exposure to the press.[35]

Lawyers' advice to couch accounts in legal privileges provides a second example. The impact of this strategy is to homogenize the news by pushing competing news media to rely on the same protected records and official sources in constructing their accounts. Moreover, it gives a kind of spurious authority and facticity to official records and proceedings at the expense of sources closer to the story that might provide competing and very different conceptions of reality. As Theodore Glasser notes in a related critique of the ideology of objectivity in journalism, legal privileges create

a bias in favor of leaders and officials, the prominent and the elite. It is an unfortunate bias because it runs counter to the important democratic assumption that statements made by ordinary citizens are as valuable as statements made by the prominent and the elite. In a democracy, public debate depends on separating individuals from their powers and privileges in the larger society; otherwise debate itself becomes a source of domination. But [the law] reinforces the use of official sources, official records, official channels (1984:15).

So consumers of the news are treated to accounts projected through the distorted lenses of elite and powerful apologists for the system (see also Tuchman, 1978). The role of the press as a Fourth Estate, an adversarial watchdog of those in

---

35. Or, as Herbert Gans notes, "journalists transmit the only nonfiction that most Americans see, hear, or read" (1979:298).

power, is subverted by the vulnerability of those who rely on unofficial, often confidential, sources to debilitating libel suits.

The bias here is more profound than simply protecting powerful voices over weak and marginal ones. It provokes at least two additional questions. First, what are the social conditions under which particular actors, events, or processes become subject to official attention--the circumstances under which private grievances and disputes end up in court, biases by race, class, or organizational size in the likelihood that deviance will lead to arrest or indictment, the predilection of Congressional committees or special commissions of inquiry to focus on particular social problems over others, and so forth? Second, how is information selected, distorted, and transformed once matters become subject to particular kinds of official attention?[36] The first question reminds us that there are important stories, for example, about private business, that are not told in official records and, therefore, not told by a timorous press. As one respondent explained, "...things are not getting the attention from the press that they might have gotten because there's no way to get it out to the public except to use non-public record sources and sometimes off-the-record sources." The second question reminds us that many voices and kinds of discourse are not heard and expressed in official forums and, therefore, not reflected in press accounts crafted to minimize risk.

This tendency to report certain kinds of stories over others also derives from the constitutionalization of the law of libel and the creation of different standards of fault for stories about public and private figures. As Anderson explains:

> From its inception, the *Times* privilege has best served those elements of the press that adhere to the most traditional and narrow journalistic role. The rule best protects those who concentrate on the workings of officialdom. The publisher or broadcaster whose sense of news does not extend beyond the activities of city hall, the courthouse, the statehouse, and Washington usually operates in protected territory. Extension of the privilege's protection to public figures allows for a slightly expanded sense of news: the publisher or broadcaster may go beyond officialdom, but he should not venture past matters relating to "public figures," that is, persons who already have attracted press attention. Thus, the press can be confident of receiving maximum constitutional protection only so long as it concentrates on government and those persons upon whom the rest of the media focus (1975: 453).

---

36. Think, for example, of differences in discourse about a marital problem as it is addressed in a psychotherapist's office and as expressed in a divorce court, or differences in the nature of a crime as described by victims or witnesses and by an indictment.

The constitutional protection not only has the effect of chilling journalists from reporting on the private sector and abuses of private power; it has also created a triple standard with respect to norms of care and, most likely, to the veracity of the news. The law demands highest standards for stories about private figures (who must prove mere negligence), somewhat lower ones for public figures (who must demonstrate actual malice), and lower ones yet for everything else--the dead, inanimate objects, events, or the description of process (none of which can sue for libel under any fault standard). Although the lawyers vehemently deny that these standards make any difference, one can only wonder, in reading about a devastating earthquake across the globe versus a college president charged with sexually molesting undergraduate men or in perusing a supermarket tabloid about a Hollywood divorce versus a story of a two-headed wolf who taught an unnamed baby abandoned in the forest to play chess, which story was reported with greatest care, factual corroboration, skepticism about sourcing, and the like.

Despite some damning evidence contained in their accounts of pre-publication and pre-broadcast review, most of the respondents deny the existence of a chilling effect afflicting their clients. But focussing on "chill" and its implicit reference to stories not told, misses the more subtle effects of libel law on what is said (rather than only on what is not), on how we are told and how the telling varies by subject, in short, on the social construction of the news. I have enumerated above many of these narrative consequences of lawyers' efforts to minimize the risk of libel litigation, for example:

- narrowing of stories, especially those involving networks of secondary private collaborators;
- quoting from official records rather than from observations or interviews with witnesses of and participants in the events (especially those who insist on confidentiality);
- stories that take pains to show both sides of an issue, even if such balance is achieved in form rather than in substance; or
- procedural reporting in which journalists attribute sources, identify privileged opinions, explain how they sought opposing comments, and generally specify in the story the process by which they searched for the truth.

It should come as no surprise that legal norms shape social discourse, how we tell stories and how we tell the truth in various institutional settings. Laws regulate what advertisers are allowed to say about a product, what corporations marketing their securities must disclose and refrain from disclosing in prospectuses, what free exposure broadcasters are allowed to give to political candidates, what accountants must disclose in a certified independent audit, what kinds of sexual behavior the media cannot depict. Legal systems themselves have elaborate normative rules about courtroom speech and truth-telling--rules of civil and criminal procedure, evidence, and hearsay; adversariness as a device to get at the truth; the use of subpoenas to induce speech; fifth amendment protections against self-incrimination; privileged relationships immune from testimony (i.e. attorney/client, doctor/patient); and proscriptions against perjury, contempt, and obstruction of justice--all of which help to create idiosyncratic versions of contested social realities.

The legal regulation of the press is different from that in these other institutions, of course, because of the First Amendment. Ironically in the name of First Amendment protections of robust speech and free expression, speech has been fettered in subtle ways. In choosing a process over a performance standard in regulating the news, jurists saved journalists from the ultimate chill of being legally protected only when stories were, in fact, true. The downside, as critics emphasize, is that fault or process standards invite courts into the newsroom, empower them to disgorge the editorial process, and allow them, over time, to develop and impose judicially-determined newsgathering standards (M. Shapiro, 1986; Bezanson, Cranberg, and Soloski, 1987). More to the point, given the rarity of libel litigation, process standards invite lawyers into the newsroom to socialize journalists and to shape stories that will minimize the risks of judicial scrutiny in the best case, satisfy judicially-constructed newsgathering standards in the worst case, and socially reconstruct the news in any case.

Justice Hugo Black, who joined with the majority in *New York Times Co. v. Sullivan*, wrote a separate opinion in which he argued:

> "Malice," even as defined by the Court, is an elusive, abstract concept, hard to prove and hard to disprove. The requirement that malice be proved provides at best an evanescent protection for the right critically to discuss public affairs and certainly does not measure up to the sturdy safeguard embodied in the First Amendment (1964:293).

In proposing "absolute immunity for criticism of the way public officials do their public duty," Black (1964:295) moved from performance standards implicit in the common law strict liability tort and process standards in the constitutionalized fault criterion to complete deregulation of this sort of speech (and rather different configurations of risk). One can certainly imagine, if Black's view had prevailed, very different strategies of media self-censorship and significant changes in the social construction of the news.

9

Your Baby's Fine, Just Fine: Certification Procedures, Meetings, and the Supply of Information in Neonatal Intensive Care Units

Carol A. Heimer

Much theorizing about risk revolves around the relationship between information shortages and cognitive and emotional responses to the lack of information. This paper discusses three different aspects of this relationship. First, it takes up the question of what families and hospital staff use information for. Sessions in which hospital staff give out information are also situations in which they take in information. Three main uses of information are discussed. Parents can use information to reassess their commitment to a baby; hospital staff need to know how committed parents are when they are making decisions about treatment and planning for discharge. Parents also need information about

This research was supported in a variety of ways by Northwestern University: research funds were provided by the University Research Grants Committee and the Dean of the College of Arts and Sciences, and the Center for Urban Affairs and Policy Research and Dean of the College of Arts and Sciences both provided released time. The American Bar Foundation has provided both time to complete the work on this paper and support for research expenses. Comments provided by Carl Milofsky, Lisa Staffen (who also provided superb research assistance), Arthur Stinchcombe, Kim Scheppele, and James Short improved the paper. I am also grateful to the staff members and patients' families at the hospital where I did the research, and to the unit's social worker who has been my sponsor and critic.

the child's prognosis to rework their lives to accomodate the infant; hospital staff need to be able to prove that parents have received this kind of information and that parents are competent to care for the child. Parents need information to make decisions about whether or not to consent to certain kinds of treatments; hospital staff need to be able to demonstrate that parents have given full and informed consent, especially to procedures that carry high risks, or to withdrawal of support or a decision not to resuscitate an infant. Hospital routines are not always sensitive to the differences between parental and hospital requirements for information. Preliminary information also suggests that families are especially sensitive (often hostile) to others' suggestions about whether or not they should be committed to an infant.

Second, the paper discusses the role of certification procedures as a central occasion for the transmission of information. Consent procedures are one of the main kinds of certifications used in hospitals. They are supposed to make sure that information is passed from medical personnel about the patient and that the hospital staff in turn collects information about whether the patient (or in this case the patient's parents) really understand what is happening and agree to allow the medical procedures. But such consent procedures tend to focus only on a narrow form of consent, and so to arrange for only certain kinds of information to be transferred between the parties. Similar problems plague other certification procedures.

Third, the paper argues that in order to understand information shortages and their effects, we must understand the social requirements for the transmission and reception of bad (and good) news as well as something about the inherent information shortages. The point here is that the social conditions that facilitate the *transmission* of bad news are probably not the same as the social conditions that facilitate the *reception* of bad news. The paper describes the social settings in which news is given, discusses some of the pressures to structure these encounters in particular ways, and examines the reactions of those who transmit and those who receive news to certain features of these situations.

Uses, Occasions, Settings, and the Raw Materials for the Social Construction of Risk

We have learned a lot over the years about how people perceive and think about risk. We know, for instance, that people are inclined to exaggerate the likelihood of events that stick in their minds because they have read vivid newspaper stories about them (the "availability effect"), that people are likely to come to mistaken conclusions about what group an object belongs to when they know something about the characteristics of the object but forget that that class of objects is relatively rare (the "representativeness" heuristic), that people's estimates of numerical values are affected by reference points to which they end up "anchoring" their own estimates, and that people's unwillingness to eliminate "mirage" choices can lead them to think that they have many choices when in fact they may have only one real option (Tversky and Kahneman, 1974; Thaler, 1983; Ainslie, 1985; Heimer, 1988).

But surely these biases and heuristics are partly products of the social processes by which people receive and transmit information as well as of the cognitive processes that occur once people have received the information. In this paper I will be focusing on three aspects of medical settings that affect the flow of information. I will discuss, first, the uses that parents and hospital staff members intend to make of information, and how these affect what they try to find out. I will then argue that a central hospital institution, certification procedures such as informed consent, provides one of the main occasions for the transmission and collection of information, and that the fact that these procedures are designed for the purposes of hospitals rather than of parents crucially shapes the kind of information that is exchanged. Finally, I will discuss meetings as a central setting in which information is transmitted, and how the structure of meetings affects the likelihood that families will make themselves available to receive information and will feel comfortable soliciting additional information.

The Puzzle:
Why Do Families Sometimes
Not Seek Information?

For families who have babies in neonatal intensive care units,[1] knowable information about how their baby is doing is an essential, but scarce resource.

---

1. A newborn is called a "neonate" during the first four weeks of life. Neonatology, the medical specialty dealing with high-risk neonates, first evolved as a separate medical specialty during the 1960s. Hospital nurseries are classified into three levels depending on the complexity of the problems they are equipped to deal with. Neonatal intensive care units, also sometimes called newborn intensive care units or intensive care nurseries, are level three nurseries and are regional facilities. Parents therefore often must travel substantial distances to visit newborns cared for in NICUs, and the mother is reasonably likely to spend the first few days after the birth of her premature or sick child unable to visit the child because she is still recuperating in a different hospital. For discussions of neonatology and NICUs, the reader can consult medical sources (e.g., Rathi, 1989), discussions by social scientists (e.g., Anspach, forthcoming, Frohock, 1986, Guillemin and Holmstrom, 1986), discussions by legal scholars concerned with the "Baby Doe" issue or with what should be done when late abortions result in live births (e.g., Rhoden, 1984, Rhoden and Arras, 1985), and more

Considerable effort goes into management of this resource. Some families want hospital personnel to call them with all of the details about changes in the baby's situation. Others wish not to be called because they want to have some control over the receipt of bad news--they do not want to worry each time the phone rings that the call brings bad news about their baby. Some parents cultivate relations with particular physicians or nurses. Some parents make a point of being present for rounds each day; some families consult physicians not associated with the NICU. Some parents request formal meetings with hospital staff; other parents agree to come to such formal meetings but then fail to appear at the appointed time. Strategies for managing information vary from one family to another (and even within single families), and such strategies can be thwarted or assisted by other people including physicians, nurses, social workers, parents in similar predicaments, and friends and family members. But nearly every parent who has had a baby in a neonatal intensive care unit has something to say about the kind of information he or she got about the baby.

Despite the high level of interest in information about their baby's situation, parents reported receiving quite different kinds of information. Very few reported receiving any information about the range of possible outcomes, and even fewer reported receiving any information about the likelihood of particular outcomes. A typical comment from a physician, according to respondents, would be that "I can't make any promises."

My first reaction when I heard what parents had to say was to wonder how they managed given that they had so little information about what was happening to their children. A few found the shortage of information troubling and did extensive research; a few others read such publications as Harrison's *The Premature Baby Book*; most of the rest read pamphlets distributed by the NICU and repeatedly requested information from physicians and nurses, but did not attempt to collect any information beyond that provided to them orally by professionals. A few parents visited and called only very infrequently and failed to respond to pressure from the hospital staff to get them to visit more often.

If we are to understand why parents sought so little information, we must ask two related questions: (1) what would they have used the information for, and (2) what kinds of costs--especially costs of resistance from hospital staff-- were entailed in the collection of additional information. In answering these two questions, I will discuss, first, the role of information in commitment and in decision making and, second, resistance to the communication of bad news and the discrepancy between social arrangements that support the hearing and the telling of bad news. I will introduce this discussion with brief illustrations of three different uses of information. These are drawn from fieldwork and

---

popular treatments (e.g., Gustaitis and Young, 1986) including some by parents whose infants received treatments in NICUs (e.g., Stinson and Stinson, 1983).

interviews in an ongoing study of the neonatal intensive care units of two major midwestern hospitals where babies receive state-of-the art treatment; the data referred to here come from only one of these units.

Three Babies, Three Families, Three Physicians, and Three Uses of Information

Case 1:   Information and Commitment to the Baby

A couple of years ago, a couple who very much wanted a second child got medical help with their fertility problems and finally conceived. They were excited and happy when their son was born, but soon after the birth they were told that the baby seemed to have some problems. First they were told that it was unclear whether the child was male or female. The mother was furious. They had had amniocentesis, so knew that the baby was genetically male. His external genitalia were small, but she thought there was no ambiguity about the fact that the child was male, and she was angry that the hospital personnel refused to call the baby by the name his parents had chosen and would not display the usual sex markings (blue blanket etc.) that are used for newborns. But this problem, though it enraged her, ended up seeming trivial in comparison with the problems that emerged later. The baby was not doing well, and it turned out that he had congenital heart problems. "His heart was like swiss cheese," the mother told me, "but fortunately they didn't tell me that until later. I knew it had holes in it, but not that it had that many." As the baby's condition worsened, the staff decided to transfer the infant to another hospital that specialized in cardiac problems. The mother was to be discharged around the same time. As she was dressing to leave, Dr. A, the attending neonatologist came to her room and said "If I were you I would forget him." The mother shrieked at the physician "Get out of my face," and slammed the door in his face. In her view,[2] it was not the physician's business to tell her to forget her child. She was committed to the child and would do whatever she could to save him, but whatever her level of commitment, she felt that this decision was not the physician's business.

---

2. I stress that this is her account; the physician's account might be quite different. In general the image of physicians presented in this paper is quite negative. While I believe that I have given an accurate portrayal of what went on, a more complete explanation would include discussion of some of the reasons for physician behavior. Some of the bad temper, abruptness, and arrogance of physicians is undoubtedly related to the stress of neonatal intensive care, which combines high-skill meticulous work with a daunting responsibility for increasing or decreasing the *potential* of a life that is entirely in the future.

Case 2: Information and Competence to Plan for Taking the Baby Home

In the hospital where I had been doing fieldwork for a couple of years, I listened as a family tried to get information about when their baby would be discharged and what to do if he had problems stemming from his surgery. It was late Friday afternoon, and the chief surgery resident was sitting on the desk talking with the charge nurse. A primary care nurse came to the desk and spoke briefly with the chief surgery resident and the charge nurse. She explained that the family of one of her patients had some questions that they would like to discuss with the surgeon. Their infant came to the hospital with a diaphragmatic hernia, a condition in which a hole in the diaphragm allows the intestines to intrude into the space where the lungs would ordinarily be developing, squeezing the lungs so that they do not grow properly. In some cases after the diaphragm is repaired such infants are put on ECMO, a machine that oxygenates the baby's blood while the lung tissue develops. This child was lucky; he did not require ECMO. The family had some questions, for instance about what would happen if the stitches came out of the repair to the diaphragm (these would be internal, so not visible), and they wanted the baby circumcized before they left. Dr. B, the chief surgery resident, grumbled about all this. The nurse said something to the effect that "Well, they have some questions, and they seemed perfectly reasonable to me." Dr. B didn't quite say that she wouldn't be willing to answer their questions, but she also did not suggest a time, say that she would be glad to talk with them, or anything like that. The only direct comment she made was that "The surgeon [she used his name] won't do circs. He doesn't believe in them."

The nurse finally left, since there wasn't much more she could do--it was clear that the chief surgery resident was not going to give a direct answer. After the nurse went back to her patient's room, Dr. B continued with more irritated comments. "What do they think this is--a gas station? They can just tell us what they want done and we'll do it?"

A few minutes later, both of the infant's parents came out. (This family has been very involved. Both parents, who looked to be in their very early 20s, and one set of grandparents, who appeared to be in their late 40s, had been around a lot, and all four had helped to care for the baby.) The mother came up to the desk, stood directly in front of the clerk, and said "We thought we saw the surgeon go by a minute or two ago. Is Dr. B [she stumbled over the name of the chief surgery resident, and that could have been either because of the difficulty of the name or because of the tension in the situation] around and do you think we could talk to her?" Though the parents had both placed themselves very directly in front of the clerk, they did glance furtively in the direction of the charge nurse and Dr. B. This particular unit clerk nearly always has an irritated look, but she did not react much. I wondered whether Dr. B would try to duck this. The clerk said nothing, just tipped her head in the direction of the charge nurse and the chief surgery resident.

The mother took this as her cue to talk to the surgeon. From her confused, flustered look, I gathered that she had never met Dr. B, but it might just have been that she did not recognize her from the back, or was nervous about her breach of norms in coming looking for the surgeon rather than waiting to be sought out. "We just had some questions about what to do if the stitches in the baby's diaphragm come out, and when we will know if he can go home tomorrow." Dr. B turned toward the parents, and talked with them, but she did not *volunteer* much, and made them do the work of raising all the issues. If they were asking the wrong question or worrying about the wrong thing, she did not straighten them out or tell them what they *should* be worried about. She answered only what they asked.

"How would we know if his stitches came out," the mother asked (the mother did all of the talking). "Would he stop breathing?"

"No--he wouldn't stop breathing. You might not know--you probably wouldn't know--that they had come undone."

The mother did not look reassured. "We live quite a distance from a hospital," she said anxiously.

Finally, the charge nurse explained, "If the stitches come out it won't be an emergency. You will have time. He won't just stop breathing."

The mother then turned to the question of when the baby would be able to go home. They had heard that he might be able to go home tomorrow. "We need to make plans--when will we know?" she asked.

Dr. B seemed annoyed. "Who told you that he might go home tomorrow?" she asked. The words were innocuous enough, though they were open to several interpretations--did she just need to know so that she could fill in appropriate details, was she angry because they have been eavesdropping, did she think someone had given them information they were not supposed to have, or what?

"Dr. [the mother stumbled over the name of the surgeon] examined him yesterday, and he said that he might be able to come home Saturday, and we were just wondering whether he will be ready to go then, when someone would tell us if he can go home then or not," the mother explained.

Dr. B seemed a tad mollified, but she still did not give a very helpful response. "It depends on how he does during the night," she answered, not saying when the parents would find out. Her implication was that *of course* the staff could not say now because it depended on the baby's situation during the night. But she could have said that if he continued to do well he would be able to go the next day--there was less uncertainty than she suggested.

"So when will we know?" the mother asked again.

"Call the nurses at around 8 tomorrow morning. They should be able to tell you then." In this case, then, the parents would not be informed officially that their baby was ready for discharge, but would only get the information through an indirect channel, and who knows whether they would get any instruction. Probably they would--probably a nurse would give them some basic information, but they would be left wondering whether there was something they should have heard from the physician about how to tell whether the child was really okay, whether they should watch for any further problems.

Dr. B finally volunteered something. "Dr. [the surgeon] won't do circs. He doesn't believe that they are necessary."

"Oh, okay," the mother responded. "We just thought we would ask. At the hospital where the baby was born they make you sign a form when you go into labor saying whether or not you want a circumcision. I guess we can just have it done later." She thanked Dr. B and she and her husband turned to leave.

Dr. B turned back to the charge nurse. "I'll get her," she said repeatedly with a tone of vengeance mixed with admiration. "She *sent* them out here. I'll get her for that," she said, clearly referring to the baby's nurse.

"I guess she just thinks that there is more than one way to skin a cat," the charge nurse commented, quietly smiling (she smiles in a way that is universalistically friendly--she could have been siding with either the nurse or the chief surgery resident for all you could tell from her face).

Dr. B continued, "Who do they think he is, anyway? Just who do they think [this time she used the surgeon's name] is?" I was not sure what she was talking about--whether she was still irritated at their request that the surgeon do the circumcision (is he too high status? is it not his specialty? or is it that one does not request/order some procedure from a surgeon?), whether she was annoyed at having to stand in for him (and so by the implication that she was his flunky or secretary--this seemed a bit implausible given how respectful the parents were), or what.

Case 3:   Information and Consent for Treatment

Earlier in this same week, I listened in on a late-afternoon phone conversation between Dr. C, a neurosurgeon and the mother of a baby who had just been admitted with MM (myelomeningocele or spina bifida) and an imperforate anus (the rectum does not open all the way to the surface of the body). The baby was a newborn who had just been transported from another hospital; his mother was still recovering in the hospital where he was born. Dr. C asked a nurse (I think one of the people involved in the transport) to witness since the purpose of this conversation was to get the mother's consent to the surgery necessary to correct the spinal defect. The nurse agreed, but Dr. C did not explain what she was supposed to do, and it became clear that she didn't know the (his?) procedure. The other transport nurse (who clearly had worked with Dr. C before), dialed the number at the other hospital and eventually got the mother.

"Is this __?" she asked. She had gotten the mother's first name wrong and corrected herself aloud, but I think the physician never heard that since he referred to the mother by the wrong name when he got on the phone. The nurse explained that Dr. C wanted to talk with her about her son and to get her permission for some parts of his care.

Dr. C got on the other phone. "Hello," he said, and made sure he was speaking with the right person. He then began to explain the nature of the defect and what is usually done to repair it. "Your son has an opening in his back. The spinal cord is not completely covered--it is just covered with a thin layer of skin--and that is a dangerous condition."

Sometime in the first part of this conversation, the nurse who was supposed to function as a witness managed to disconnect Dr. C and the mother. The nurse was trying to get "parked" on the line so that she could listen in on the conversation. Usually consents are given in person, with the witness listening in on the conversation. Since Dr. C had not explained any alternative procedure, the nurse apparently assumed she had to listen in. As she was poking buttons trying to get on the line, Dr. C began to get irritated. "Excuse me. Excuse me, I'm trying to have a conversation here," he said angrily. When the line got disconnected, he said nothing, but just sat and stared angrily in front of him. The nurses arranged between themselves that the first nurse (the one who dialed the number) would witness, and would do it by talking with the mother afterwards. The first nurse redialed the phone, finally got the mother again, and Dr. C got on the phone, apologized for getting disconnected, and resumed the conversation.

He spoke to the mother for a few minutes about damage to the nerves. "We need to repair this. We would like to close the hole in the morning. He is apparently unable to move his legs and feet now, and there is no guarantee that he will be able to after the surgery. We can't guarantee anything. [He repeated that several times.] He also has another defect. He has no anus. That will have to be repaired with a separate surgery. But for now I want to ask your permission to repair the opening on his back. We will have to do some tests first, and we will have to put him to sleep with anaesthesia to do the surgery. The risks are not great, certainly less than if we didn't do the repair. [He talked for a bit about what would happen if they did not do the repair, about the chance of infection and the like.] We don't know if he will be able to move his legs afterwards. It is hard to predict--sometimes they do, sometimes they don't. Would you like us to call you back after the surgery is done? Hello. Hello."

Dr. C hung up the phone in disgust and turned to the first nurse. "She seems to have hung up," he said. They discussed what to do, since their plan had been for the nurse to get on the line and confirm the mother's consent. They decided that the nurse should call back yet again. "The mom's a little slow," Dr. C warned the nurse.

The nurse dialed again, finally got the mother on the phone. She was very patient, unlike Dr. C who seemed both irritable and abrupt (though he controlled himself better with the mother than with the nurse). The nurse reminded the mother who she was, that she was one of the nurses who had come to pick up the baby. She did not say that she had called back because they needed a witness, but she instead said that she had called back to make sure the mother understood what the doctor had said and to see if she had any questions. "Do you understand what the doctor told you," she asked. "You do agree to give permission for the surgery that he told you about? Okay. We will call you back after the surgery to tell you how the baby is doing. I'll let you go now since I am sure you are tired." She hung up and signed the forms.

These three cases were chosen to illustrate three situations in which parents either seek or are given information, and three corresponding uses they make of information. Race, class, age, educational level, marital status, and gender all affect the experience that families have in getting information about their critically ill infants. In general, better educated people, people with more money, white people, older parents (at least beyond the teens and maybe even beyond the early twenties), and married couples (or at least families in which an identified father also visits the child) fare better in interactions with hospital staff. They get more information and have more say about what happens to their child. Mothers tend to get more information and have more influence on the baby's treatment than do fathers, but it is hard to tell how much this is due simply to the fact that fathers are much less likely to be around than mothers are. For a substantial proportion of the patients, no father ever comes to visit.[3] But when fathers are around they almost always do less talking than the mothers do.[4]

---

3. When I wrote the first draft of this paper, 23 infants were in the hospital unit I had been studying. In ten cases no father was involved. That means that no father's name was listed anywhere in the medical record, that none of the father's kin were inovlved, and that at most a father had called once, or in one case visited once, drunk, with the mother. For four of the infants, a father or father-substitute seemed to be marginally inovlved, in some cases only by blaming the mother for producing a defective child or for spending too much time with the child. For nine of the infants, a father or the father's family was actively involved, though typically the father called less frequently, visited less often, and kept a lower profile even when he was present in the hospital.

4. I think this may be partly because in emotionally charged situations, such as meetings in which parents are being told that their child will never be normal, fathers spend more time controlling or masking emotions and so have less capacity to interact with hospital staff. For instance in one meeting attended by both the father and the mother, the father would appear to be about to respond to queries from the staff, but could not get the answer out fast enough. The staff

The three families discussed above vary a good bit in social characteristics. Two of the babies had married, co-residing parents; one baby's mother was unmarried. One family was white, one black, and one mixed-race. One family was poor, one lower-middle class, and one very wealthy. One infant had a teenaged mother, one had parents in their early twenties, and the third had parents in their thirties.

The Uses of Information:
Commitment, Competence, and Consent

When physicians, nurses, discharge planners, social workers, and other hospital staff members give out information they at the same time collect information. In this section I will discuss the three main uses that parents make of information and the three corresponding purposes for which hospital staff collect information. Parents use information to reassess their commitment to a baby; hospital staff need to judge how committed parents are when they are making decisions about treatment and planning for discharge. Parents also need information to improve their competence, broadly defined. Information about the child's prognosis, about the availability and cost of services, about how to care for the child makes it possible for parents to learn the skills they will need to provide "special" care, to rework their lives to accomodate the infant, and to locate appropriate resources. Hospital staff need to be able to prove that they have given parents information and training, and that they have assessed the parents' competence. When there might be some question about parents' competence, hospital staff will try to assess parents' skill in providing day-to-day care and in making realistic plans. Finally, parents need information to make decisions about whether or not to consent to treatments; hospital staff need to be able to demonstrate that parents have given full and informed consent, especially to procedures that carry high risks, to withdrawal of support, or to a decision not to resuscitate an infant.

Parents first have to decide how committed they are to the infant. Of the 23 infants in the intensive care nursery during one week in late winter, three were quite likely to go to some other institution because of long-term medical problems. Of these three, two could have gone home, at least for the time

---

members would look away, turn to the mother, or go on to the next subject, I think to avoid calling attention to the father's emotional distress. Though the mother also was weeping openly during this meeting, this did not prevent her from talking as well.

being, if their parents wished to care for them there.[5] Four other infants might well end up in foster care because their parents were unable or unwilling to take them home.[6]

Level of commitment affects both the parents' decisions about whether or not to take an infant home and some decisions about medical care. For instance, evaluation of the family and its commitment to the child can affect decisions about how to treat an infant who needs a heart transplant. On the one hand, the family may decide, for a variety of reasons, that it does not wish to pursue a transplant. Parents may not wish to watch their child suffer through the wait and the procedure itself given the low odds of a good outcome, or they may not feel that their family could weather such a storm successfully. On the other hand, hospital staff may conclude that a transplant is not a viable option because the family will be unable to carry out its part of the healthcare. Similarly, for medically equivalent cases, the decision to deal with an airway problem by giving the child a tracheostomy will have different consequences for a single parent than for married parents since a child who is dependent on a tracheostomy cannot be sent home without two trained careproviders.

Several processes occur simultaneously here: parents become more or less committed to a child, hospital staff give information that might affect parental commitment, and hospital staff assess that commitment since what they do will sometimes depend on parental commitment. The first story (above) was about information and commitment. Identity, perhaps especially gender identity, and commitment are complexly intertwined. Ordinarily, staff members take it as a very bad sign if a family has not named its child. But this family had named its child, and was angry that the staff refused to treat the child as a *person*, a person with a name (including a last name, and therefore a family claiming the child) and a sex. In the first part of the story, the staff refused to acknowledge that the parents had already made a decision about their commitment to the child. Despite the parents' angry reactions suggesting that it was time to stop giving information relevant to that decision, staff members continued to supply such information. The second part of the story, about the infant's heart defect, shows a physician with admirable sensitivity to the fact that a decision about

---

5. I do not mean to suggest that this is always a desirable outcome when we consider the effect on the entire family. But as long as a child can safely go home, I think it fair to say that a family that chooses not to take such an infant home--perhaps because of the consequences for the rest of the family--is less committed to that infant than a family that would choose to take the child home.

6. For two of these infants, a pair of twins, it was still impossible to judge medical outcome; but the social situation was relatively clear, and even if the infants were completely normal they might well go into foster care.

commitment must be made, but considerable insensitivity (in the mother's version at any rate) to the distinction between giving information and suggesting what level of commitment is appropriate.

In general, physicians are probably too little involved in providing information that helps parents reevaluate their commitment to a child. Parental commitment is typically discussed in three main contexts. First, parental commitment is discussed (though often indirectly) when decisions are being made about such medical procedures as heart transplants, or when the hospital staff believes that a "do not resuscitate" order or withdrawal of support might be appropriate. Parental consent is required for these procedures, and staff members believe that this consent must be fully informed consent. Consent is not treated as a routine matter here, and at least one and perhaps several formal meetings would be held to discuss the infant's situation.

Parental commitment is also assessed when the child will need continuing medical care and a decision is being made about how vigorously to pursue a home discharge. Depending on the circumstances, parents will have to learn to provide some medical care themselves, may have to co-exist with a nursing staff working in their home, and the like. In such situations, information is given by physicians and other staff members, but information is also *actively* sought by parents who are eager to have sick children home rather than in the hospital. How long discharge takes, and whether discharge is to the parental home or to some other facility, depends on whether parents must be prodded to come to meetings and to learn to care for their child, or whether parents request information, press for discharge, look for alternatives, and pressure bureaucrats for timely decisions rather than letting the wheels of the bureaucracy turn at their own pace. Information will always have to be transmitted in these cases, but the amount of information that gets transmitted, and the variety of channels through which it travels will depend on the level of parental involvement.

Finally, hospital staff members will also be interested in providing information that might affect parental commitment and in assessing that commitment when they are worried that parents (or at least mothers) are not very committed to the child. A mother who fails to visit or who visits infrequently and rarely phones will be called in for a meeting. This may not be because there is any bad news to tell, but only because the staff needs to know whether the mother intends to take the baby home or whether her failure to visit is a sign that she wishes to give up custody of the child. At such meetings or, more likely, in separate meetings and phone conversations that follow the formal meeting, a social worker will talk with the mother about what her alternatives are, why she feels unable to take the baby home right now, and the like. This conversation is likely to be less about the baby's medical condition and more about the complications of the mother's life and her pre-existing commitments. Thus the hospital staff is not so much giving information as soliciting information in this third situation.

In the second story recounted above, the family was not asking for information about life and death, about whether to welcome the child into the bosom of the family. Instead, they wanted information that would allow them to plan daily life, to adjust their routines to accomodate the new member. This category would include the following kinds of information: how often the child would need therapy (occupational, speech, physical); the likelihood that the child would need further surgeries; the likelihood of achieving developmental milestones on schedule (e.g., will the child sit up, learn to walk, learn to talk, or learn to read when he or she is supposed to); whether the child will need to go home on an apnea monitor and how long it will be needed; whether the child will need a tracheostomy for only a year or for the rest of his or her life; whether the child will ever be toilet trained; whether the child's hearing and vision are in the normal range; and who will pay for medical care, home nursing, and medical supplies.

These questions about how to reorder the family life to accomodate a sick child are of course only analytically separable from questions about commitment. But information necessary to resolve questions about how to organize a life around a sick child tends to be provided by a wide variety of people on many different occasions. Since most parents do not have an organization chart of the hospital staff, it is difficult for them to sort out which questions are most appropriately addressed to which people. Nurses are probably the recipient of most questions about the baby's medical conditions. Some of these questions nurses answer themselves; others they tell parents to direct to physicians. But as the second story (above) suggests, physicians are not always available to answer questions. Because the intensive care nursery is neonatology's home base, neonatologists, neonatology fellows, and the residents assigned to the NICU spend considerable time in this unit doing hands-on medical care or working at the nursing station writing in the medical records, writing orders, and the like. This means that parents whose infants are neonatology (or "medical") rather than surgery, neurosurgery, or cardiology patients have easier access to physicians. In contrast parents of surgery, neurosurgery, or cardiology patients will often say that they "try to be there at noon because the doctors come through around then" but will also admit that they do not know when they will get information about a test result or how to go about getting it. Parents get clues from the location of the baby (is she in isolation, in the room for feeding and growing babies?), the type of crib that the baby is in (they know that usually an "Ohio bed" is used for the sickest babies, an "isolette" for babies who are a bit less sick, and an open bassinet or regular hospital crib for babies who are nearly ready for discharge), and the numbers of wires and tubes connected to their child. Nevertheless, most parents experience considerable uncertainty about just what is going on with their baby and what that will mean for the future--both their future and their baby's future. Some of this is irreducible uncertainty, of course--even if the physician could tell the parents that 50% of the babies with their child's difficulty would eventually walk, he or she very likely would not be able to tell them whether *their* child would walk. But many parents report that they are not getting anything like a list of the main difficulties that might lie ahead or rough odds of their child encountering those difficulties, let alone information about how they might tell whether they were likely to experience those difficulties or how they might increase the chance of avoiding them.

Only some of this detailed information should properly be given by physicians anyway, though. Some of the information should instead be given by social workers, nurses, or discharge planners. Nurses give information to parents at three main points. They give updates on the patient's status when the parents visit or when they phone to ask how the baby is doing. They also give information when they are teaching the parent to care for the baby in preparation for discharge. This teaching typically involves an oral explanation, a demonstration (or several), instruction as the parent learns to perform the procedure him or herself, and then a more or less formal examination when the parent demonstrates the procedure back to the nurse. Finally, nurses have a check-list that they go through at the point of discharge. Sometimes nurses go through explanations again; sometimes they simply say "someone explained __ to you, didn't they?" Some of this instruction is specialized instruction in how to give medication, how to place and feed through a nasogastric tube, how to do cardiopulmonary resuscitation on an infant, how to change a colostomy bag, how to recognize signs of illness and danger, and the like. But some of it is routine well baby care, including how to bathe a baby, take a temperature, mix formula, and how often and how much to feed the baby.

Discharge planners, who are also RNs, provide parents with information about how to get medical supplies, what programs (including public aid and private insurance) will pay their expenses, and how to hire and orient nurses. A lot of what they do is to make arrangements for the family--they set up supply contracts, help hire nurses through one agency or another, set up the orientation program for the nursing staff, arrange for the delivery of medical equipment, bully insurers into paying for some things they originally did not think they should pay for, and press bureaucrats for timely decisions about public aid. They also help families set up follow-up care through private pediatricians, clinics, "zero to three programs," and the like.

Social workers and discharge planners coordinate closely on some parts of this. The social worker helps assess what the family needs, not so much because of the child's medical problems but because of the competence of the parents and other demands on their time. She or he (typically social workers in this setting are women) will also coordinate with DCFS (Department of Child and Family Services) workers and public aid caseworkers for some services such as homemakers (who instruct mothers in home management and childcare as well as providing household help and some childcare), drug treatment programs or counseling, or placement of a child outside the home if that is necessary. The social worker's job here is not so much to give new information as to make sure that parents have understood the information that they have already received, and have understood the implications of that information for how their lives must change if they are to provide adequate care for the child.

Parents also get information from therapists--physical therapists most importantly, but also speech therapists, occupational therapists, and respiratory therapists. Therapists teach parents how to perform some of the treatments for their child, but also educate them about developmental milestones (parents for instance learn that if the child is unable to do such age-appropriate things as hold up its head or turn over this may tell them something about the likelihood of walking on schedule), about the goals of treatments (for instance to increase the range of movement in a baby's extremities), and about how to evaluate the efficacy of their own and others' interventions.

Detailed information about the child's current condition and anticipated difficulties in the future is given piecemeal all of the time. Although staff members sometimes sit down with families to organize this information into a coherent picture, for the most part parents must make sense of all of this information on their own. I have categorized this information as information related to competence, since the hospital staff needs to assess the competence of the parents before it sends the child home. From the parents' point of view, detailed information about their child's future is the raw material that they use to develop the competences they need to care for the child. But it is also information that allows them to assess the size and nature of the task and of their capacity to do what is needed. What bodies of knowledge are they going to have to master, what technical skills will they have to learn, and how are they going to have to alter their lives to accomodate a "special" child? With this information a parent can answer the second main question: "Am I competent to care for this child in my home?"

The third story illustrates the use of information for decisions about whether to consent to medical treatment. The transmission and collection of information about consent varies a good bit from one case to another. Parents are given relatively little information when they are asked to sign the pre-admission consent forms that give the hospital permission to treat the infant, including permission to give blood transfusions. (Parents fairly commonly cross out that portion of the form, and so require separate consent for blood transfusions. This can be either because they have religious objections to blood transfusions or because they are worried about the transmission of diseases such as AIDS or hepatitis.) Fuller discussion of medical procedures, risks, and benefits occurs when surgery is required, when more risky interventions are proposed, when parental input (for instance in caring for the child prior to and after cardiac surgery) is necessary, and as the success rate of proposed procedures goes down. Though physicians may ask (sometimes quite perfunctorily) whether parents have additional questions, their attention is focused on getting a signature acknowledging consent. Consent forms do not include lines for physicians to fill in information about the conditions under which consent is given or the conditions under which parents would wish to withdraw their consent. Hospital staff thus collect relatively little information about the details of parental consent. The next section discusses how hospital routines shape the nature and quality of information flows.

It is important to remember that these three questions are only analytically distinct, and that the transmission and collection of information for one purpose often coincides with the transmission and collection of information for other purposes. A physician asking a parent to sign a consent form may conceive him or herself to be giving information for a circumscribed purpose. But the parent may ask questions that seem to the physician unrelated to the procedure he or she is proposing to perform, and the parent will very likely use this information in mulling over questions of consent and competence.

Hospital Routines To Assess Commitment, Competence, and Consent

Hospitals are not isolated institutions. Largely in response to the threat of malpractice suits, hospitals have developed routines to get parental consent for dangerous procedures, have given parents information necessary to care for the child safely, and have checked to make sure that a child can safely be released into the care of particular parents. They also have routines to document that they have done these things. But as Goffman (1959) notes, there is often a discrepancy between appearance and reality, and when workers cannot uphold all of the standards, they will be most likely to sacrifice where the lowering of standards is least detectable. Thus in explaining discharge procedures to an orientee, an experienced nurse may tell the orientee to make certain that the parents know how to care for the child but then will stress that the orientee must document her teaching by checking boxes on the discharge form indicating that she has instructed the parents about particular elements of the baby's care. Full documentation gets more emphasis than full explanation; orientees may be instructed to add additional documentation about what exactly was taught so that the parent cannot later sue the hospital.

Routines center around three kinds of certifications (corresponding to the three uses of information): (1) certification that the parent has consented to medical care of a routine sort and certification that the parent has consented to specialized procedures such as spinal taps and surgery, (2) certification that the parent has not lived up to her or (more rarely) his obligations as a parent in a way that makes her or (more rarely) him a good bet as someone to send the child home with,[7] and (3) certification that the parent has or has not mastered the tasks and information necessary to deal with this particular child.

The development of laws and procedures for certifying that parents have been taught crucial medical procedures, have consented to treatment, and have fulfilled basic parental obligations have probably increased the amount of information given to parents. These rules and routines have certainly increased the uniformity of information flows and have put a floor beneath discussions between parents and careproviders so that nearly all parents now get some information. This is no trivial accomplishment given how easy it would be to leave parents completely out of the decision making, especially if they visit and phone infrequently and are difficult to contact. Even these parents are now at least minimally involved in decision making about their children.

But certification procedures tend to focus on legalistic conceptions of consent, competence, and commitment. Consent, for instance, is considerably more complex than hospital procedures imagine. When families are asked to consent to procedures and treatments, they are also implicitly being asked to accept the consequences of these procedures and treatments for their own lives. Because parents are not legally allowed to remove their infants from neonatal intensive care units (there have been instances in which parents have "kidnapped" their child and in some cases they have been prosecuted for this), there is a sense in which they do not have the right to refuse consent. (Parents can refuse consent to some kinds of procedures--e.g., heart transplants--but if they refuse to consent to more routine procedures--e.g., blood transfusions--the hospital takes custody of the child for that limited purpose.)

There are, then, several separate difficulties here: (1) Consent procedures deal only with limited kinds of consent; they do not assess the extent to which parents have agreed to deal with the consequences of a medical procedure (in some cases to commit themselves and their family resources to a child who is quite different than they one they had expected to have). (2) Consent procedures sometimes do not really allow nonconsent. And (3) the institutional developments that surround consent procedures are not sufficiently sensitive to the need for parents (or whoever is being asked to give consent) to be able to talk freely about morally loaded subjects. Similarly legalistic notions of commitment and competence are produced when the requirement for

---

7. No certification is required for the positive case here. Only when there is some question about a parent's commitment to the child and the parent's reliability as a parent will documentation be required. As a result, nursing notes on parental visitation are notoriously unreliable as a source of data for social science analysis. Only when parental visitation becomes an issue--that is, when parents are not visiting regularly or are behaving "inappropriately" when they visit--are parental visits regularly recorded in nursing notes.

documentation provides the main occasion for transmitting information necessary for developing and assessing competence and for making decisions about commitment.

The Social Conditions for the Transmission and Receipt of Bad News

Thus far I have discussed the *occasions* when parents and hospital staff seek information from one another and the uses they make of that information. My argument has been that the fact that parents and hospital staff are motivated by different purposes and will use the information for different ends sometimes makes them work at crosspurposes. Hospital routines for the transmission of information do not always lead to the transmission of the information that parents need at the time when they need it. A second problem is that the social *settings* in which information is transmitted seem to be designed more around the transmission rather than the receipt of information.

The main occasions for the transmission of information are the three discussed above: when the hospital needs to get consent, when the hospital needs to assess commitment, and when the hospital needs to certify competence. Some of this information is transmitted in one-on-one sessions in which a nurse or physical therapist teaches a procedure, a nurse gives an update on a patient over the phone, a physician (and witness, so really two-on-one) explains a medical procedure and asks for parental consent, or a physician phones parents to come in because their baby has taken a turn for the worse. Physicians stress that they try to avoid giving bad news over the phone.

Bad news comes in two forms with two different timetables. Bad news can have an emergency character as when a baby "crashes," "codes," or "tries to die." In these life-threatening situations, information is given by a single individual or by a pair of individuals. But bad news that lacks this emergency character, perhaps because it is more ambiguous, is conveyed by a group in a formal meeting. Such meetings are also used to discuss discharge plans in medically, socially, or financially complicated cases. Since much of the important information is given to parents in meetings, I now turn to the question of why information, especially bad news, is transmitted this way.

No One Tells Bad News Unless They Have To

There are various myths around the NICU I have studied that support not telling parents bad news. "Parents don't want to hear it anyway," people sometimes say, "so there is no reason to keep saying the same thing over and over about the baby's bad prognosis. Just tell them how the baby is doing day to day." In a recent staff meeting (a weekly event called "social service rounds" at this particular hospital, but labelled "interdisciplinary rounds," or "discharge planning rounds" at some other hospitals), the social worker told staff members that they should not "beat the mother over the head" with information about her baby's prognosis. She and the mother had discussed this, and the mother knew perfectly well that the baby would never do well. But it was depressing to her to be reminded of this every day, so people should not keep harping on this subject.[8]

Staff members speculate about what the parents *really* know, *really* believe about how their baby is doing, and also worry sometimes about discrepancies between the stories given them by various personnel. Part of the problem is that there is a division of labor between medical (i.e., physicians) and other personnel, and non-medical staff are not supposed to give medical information. "They have to hear that from medicine" (that is, from a physician) is a common statement. But parents have more contact with "non-medical" people, especially with nurses, and in some cases with social workers or therapists. These people have to be cautious not to mislead parents, not to present overly optimistic pictures when they really mean to be giving no medical information.

Information discrepancies also arise from the dispersion of responsibility across physicians. At any one time, parents typically encounter residents (first and third year in this hospital) and attending physicians, but they may also have contact with an occasional advanced medical student or neonatology fellow. Given the system of staggered rotations and schedules for who is on duty and who has authority in the evenings and on weekends, parents are likely to encounter more than one set of residents and attending physicians. Though these medical people consult extensively, they may not give entirely consistent stories, and parents with precarious understandings of what is happening in the rollercoaster of their child's hospitalization are surely sensitive to small changes in the message and unsure whether these variations mean that the baby's situation has changed, that individual physicians have slightly different perspectives, that some physician has misread a chart, or that the same message is being given in slightly different words. These different possibilities are difficult enough for experts to disentangle; parents who are not native speakers of the medical language and who are intensely concerned with the message they are receiving can be expected to have even more difficulty. One parent complained

---

8. The line between telling bad news frequently enough and clearly enough so that parents are not misled and telling it so often and so clearly that they feel bullied is of course a fine one. My point is that staff members are likely to err on one side rather than the other because telling bad news is an onerous task. Some staff members do go to the opposite extreme, though. For instance, when one mother inquired whether her child's condition would prevent him from growing hair, one physician answered by saying that the child was going to die.

about this problem when nursing grand rounds at a nearby hospital focused on high risk parenting. "It's hard to tell what's really going on with your baby," the father complained, "when one Attending [physician] is more optimistic and upbeat about his sickest baby than another Attending is about his healthiest."

I do not mean to imply that parents are unambivalent consumers of information about their babies. Of course they wish to hear good news rather than bad; of course they sometimes shade or misinterpret what they do hear. But hospital staff perhaps move too rapidly to an interpretation that any unexplained parental behavior shows an unwillingness to hear bad news and therefore justifies not telling the bad news. For instance, when families fail to show up for meetings with staff, this is taken as evidence that they don't want to hear the bad news. But alternative explanations might be equally compatible with these data: the family may not have enough money for public transportation, may live at some distance from public transportation, may be unfamiliar with the route to the hospital and so misestimate travel time, may be unable to arrange childcare for other children, may be unable to get out of work obligations, and the like. Or their culture may be one in which formal appointments and meetings are not the way things are done. Surely long waits in clinics and public aid offices do little to reinforce a patient's sense that a 9:00 A.M. appointment means that people really will assemble at that time.

My point here is that no one likes to tell bad news; telling bad news is unpleasant and it is hard work. It needs to be done well if appropriate use is to be made of the information that is being transmitted. But because it is a hard job, people develop lots of excuses to justify not doing it and to explain why they have done it badly.

Whose Job Is It To Tell Bad News?

In a formal interview, I recently asked one of the three neonatologists on the staff whether there was any task that he did not feel comfortable delegating to the house staff. "Some kinds of catheterizations," he answered, "and talking to parents." If some people, such as physicians and social workers (for non-medical subjects) regard it as their job to tell bad news, other personnel do not. Nurses for instance, may not. They are not the medical experts and as subordinates they do not want to give incorrect information. When a nurse is caring for a baby who is not her "primary" (as often happens), she is less likely to have a thorough grounding in the infant's medical history and a working relationship with and sense of commitment to the parents, and so is especially likely to avoid telling bad news. Since it is not their job to tell the bad news (that is, to say what a baby's prognosis is, to give assessments of what various developments mean), nurses' reluctance to give bad news is not punished.

This tends to create a normative hole--nurses *are* supposed to give reports to parents about how well the child is eating, whether he or she has had any apneic spells, what the ventilator settings are, and the like, but the nurse need not give anything but the "objective" information, and can even shade toward misreporting by interpreting questions about the baby's status to be questions about whether there is any immediate crisis. Thus a nurse reporting on a baby whom she would describe as "just not *normal*" in conversation with other nurses can tell the mother a minute or two later that the infant is "doing fine, just fine." Only rarely does anyone clarify what exactly is being assessed and summed up in the statement that the baby is fine. An important question here is whether one can conceive circumstances under which the same statement would be given to hospital staff. In this case, I think one can--a nurse would tell the person following her on the next shift that a baby was "just fine" meaning that nothing unusual had happened, no special interventions were needed, but the nurse would never end her report with that. She would also say when the baby had been fed, whether he or she had urinated or defecated recently, and would report on a number of other standardized things which would also be written into the record. So "fine, just fine" would not be the sum total of a nurse's report to another nurse even when it might be the start of the report. A nurse *contextualizes* a report of "fine" to peers, but may leave context ambiguous in a report to parents.

Unfortunately, parents are not always fully aware of this assigment of tasks. They may, therefore, ask for information from the wrong people. Sometimes parents are then told that they need to "ask the doctor that," but sometimes they are given innocuous, but perhaps misleading, answers. In still other cases, people who are not the ones designated to give news (or people who *are* supposed to give news but who are unprepared or unwilling to give the news *yet*) will go to elaborate lengths to avoid being asked for such news. In hospital hallways, elevators, cafeterias, patient rooms, and especially nursing stations, hospital personnel develop elaborate rituals to protect their privacy. Status markers (such as color of garb) tell people who they can interrupt and who they cannot, which conversations they have to pretend not to have overheard, and the like. In general, interruptible people (nurses, clerks) *cannot* give the news, and people who can give the news cannot be interrupted.[9]

---

9. In his chapter "On Bad News," Sudnow (1967) writes that surgeons and obstetricians cannot come through the doors that separate backstage from frontstage without being willing to give the news. News about surgery and childbirth has to be given as soon as one encounters the relevant people--it cannot be delayed. A large backstage protects the physicians, who then take some pain to suggest that they have just completed the relevant task when they finally emerge to face the family, perhaps after a coffee break in the staff lounge. Lower-status staff members can pass freely between back- and frontstage because they are not allowed to announce the news.

Why Bad News Is Likely To Be Told in Groups

Bad news is often given in formal meetings in which there are three or more hospital staffers present (and there may be *many* more). A large meeting might, for instance, include the attending neonatologist, a resident, perhaps a neonatology fellow, a primary nurse, a social worker, a discharge planner, one or more physicians from other specialties (e.g., cardiology, neurology) concerned with the particular infant's problems. An interpreter or a nurse clinician might also be present.

Why would so many people be present at such meetings? First, bad news is hard to give, and staff members need support and encouragement if they are to give bad news. "*You* will have to be the one to deliver that news," the social worker often tells the physician. Physicians accept the primary obligation willingly if not cheerfully. But though they have the obligation to tell the core medical facts, others are responsible for giving information about other aspects of the situation or checking to see that the parents have understood. A second reason that meetings are big, then, is that there are several jobs to be done, and different actors have different parts in this drama.

Which parts of the bad news are to be told by whom may be carefully worked out in advance.[10] The physician tells the basic medical facts. Social workers and related specialists (e.g., clinical specialists, discharge planners) monitor the physicians carefully to see that (a) they tell enough but not too much bad news (parents should have a realistic view but should retain enough hope to remain committed to the child), (b) they tell the news in language that parents can understand (this is a big problem, particularly for residents who may

---

10. The exact division of labor between physicians and other staff members varies from one situation to another. As far as I can tell there are three sources of variation: (1) variation between hospitals, with some hospitals having a culture in which there is no rigid line between medicine and other disciplines in who has the monopoly on explaining medical facts (as long as the person who is explaining understands, of course), (2) variations between cases within hospitals, with greater attention to maintaining the distinction between medicine and other disciplines when families seem likely to react angrily if they feel they have been misled into expecting a better outcome than they are actually getting, and (3) variations between individuals, with some physicians (and other workers) being less comfortable with having other workers claim any expertise that might overlap with the physician's. I have talked about this issue with non-physician staff members at four hospitals. In one case my informant insisted that she would never clarify medical information even when she was confident that she understood the matter and that the parent had misunderstood; in the other three cases the line between medicine and other disciplines was considerably more permeable.

expect the attending physician to be judging their competence as native speakers of the medical language), and (c) parents are given a chance to react, to ask questions, and the like. After the main meeting (and sometimes before as well), the social worker may meet with parents to help them process the information they have received, discussing with them whether they have understood the basic message, what this message implies for their lives, what decisions they need to make, and what questions they still have. The primary nurse may attend several of these meetings and may meet with the parents after the social worker is finished, depending on to whom the family is perceived to be closest.

These formal meetings with the family are the subject of considerable discussion by staff members. Notes on the meeting (often quite abbreviated) are incorporated in the infant's medical record. Staff members discuss the parents' reactions, what they and others told the parents, and whether or not various people did a good job in telling the family the bad news, who should follow up on which parts of the message, and the like.

This extensive discussion plays yet another role (in addition to division of labor and social control). Younger staff members, especially interns and residents, have to be included in meetings because they must be taught how to tell news, how to translate their complex medical knowledge into lay terms (and that it is okay, even good, to do this even though they have spent years mastering this arcane and precise language). In addition to such house staff, there are also social work interns, student physical therapists, and the odd sociologist doing field work who may occasionally be included in meetings.

Inclusion issues also affect the size and composition of meetings. Tension between members of different medical professions and turf battles between different specialities (see for comparison Coser, 1958 or Bosk, 1979) make it imperative to include anyone who might feel slighted if he or she had not been invited to the meeting. If nurses are not invited they may feel that physicians do not value their contribution; discharge planners who are invited only to meetings occurring just before discharge may be angry that others see their role as limited to implementing discharge plans drawn up by others. In some cases representatives of different disciplines have such different perspectives that they must all be included, but in other instances, a single individual may represent several co-workers (e.g., a discharge planner might give the views of physicians and nurses).

Finally, there are legal reasons for people to attend meetings. The hospital staff is acutely aware that malpractice suits are possible and that giving full information to parents and having records and witnesses to provide documentation or testimony are important ways of preventing suits and of winning them should they be brought. In a more positive light, the practice of having meetings can also be seen as an institutional commitment to a form of due process.

Why It Is Hard To Hear Bad News in Groups

Ironically, though it may be easier to *tell* bad news in a group, it is probably easier to *hear* bad news without all those observers. This need for privacy when facing grief is recognized by the hospital staff in a number of ways--screens are put up around the beds of babies who are "actively dying" to give families some privacy in their last moments with their child; when the stage of medical intervention is over and a child has died, parents who wish to spend some time alone with their child's body will spend that time in the "parent room" or the "quiet room" near the nursery rather than in the middle of the hustle and bustle of the nursery itself.[11]

Two separate issues get conflated here: whether more social support is needed for telling than hearing bad news, and *who* needs and gets support. It may be that the reason that families appear to prefer small groups for hearing bad news is that these groups are not composed of *their* supporters but instead of supporters of the hospital staff. Composition rather than size may be the key issue. Support is required both for hearing and telling bad news, but the supporters necessary to enable staff members to tell bad news are (not surprisingly) different than the supporters that make it easier for the family to hear bad news. In addition, staff members may be insensitive to how this assemblage feels to the parents because the ideology of primary nursing (used in the five hospitals about which I have information) is that the primary nurse will have become close to the family and will be perceived by them as someone they can lean on. Ideally, then, the group of physicians, nurses, and other staff members assembled to tell bad news will feel as intimate to the parents as to the staff members. In practice, there is no doubt substantial variation in the closeness of ties between the "team" and the parents.

The problem is not simply that of grieving in a group of strangers. In a large group of "experts," it is also hard to deal forthrightly with one's own moral faults, one's feelings of inadequacy, one's ignorance, and the like. A parent may not feel comfortable expressing anger at the birth of a baby with a myelomeningocele. (One parent who did express anger could be overheard in the adjacent nursery as he shouted that either someone had made a big mistake or someone had lied to him and his wife. This family had known that the baby had spina bifida, but had been told that the lesion was a low lesion and unlikely to be serious. As it turned out the lesion was a high one and the baby was in bad shape.) A parent may not feel able to ask how she could possibly earn a living if she had to spend all of her time bringing her child to clinic on public

---

11. In one hospital, parents do not get much privacy when their babies are dying. I was told that this nursery simply does not have screens to shield parents. In four other hospitals screens were used for this purpose.

transportation. Nor would parents be likely to feel comfortable discussing anxieties about how they could manage their other children if they had to care for a vegetable. Parents only rarely manage to tell physicians that they can't understand what all those big medical words mean. Meetings may not work well, then, because what families have to say is not morally neutral.

Why Bad News Is Told in a Group Exactly When It Is Hardest To Hear in a Group

Ironically, those people for whom it is most difficult to hear bad news in a large group may be the very ones who are most likely to receive the news that way. Meetings, especially large meetings, are more likely to be held when an infant has been hospitalized for a long time, when the family has "social problems," when the family has no private health insurance or when that insurance does not cover all expenses, and when the baby's medical situation is so complex that a large number of medical specialists need to be involved. Though medical complexity is probably not much related to parental competence in hospital meetings, the other four factors are.

Meetings solve several problems simultaneously: they enable staff to monitor and enforce the telling of bad news, and they allow staff members to twist parents' arms to make themselves available to receive information. Despite their importance as solutions to these two problems, meetings often are not a good way to *hear* news. Meetings are too large and too much imbued with the authority system of the hospital. Because the larger the group the smaller the proportion of people who speak, and because the likelihood of speaking in such settings depends on social status, parents are less likely to talk in larger meetings than in smaller ones, and lower status parents are especially unlikely to speak. Insofar as the point of meetings is to give parents information, to answer their questions, and to learn something about how they think, this is a disaster. One attending physician confessed that when parents had no questions he was sometimes tempted to respond, "Well, here's a list of things other parents have wanted to ask in similar circumstances," just to get them thinking about what they needed to know.

Meetings are especially difficult for people who are unaccustomed to them either because of youth or because of not having had occupational experiences in which people do business in meetings. But these are the very people for whom the social control aspect of meetings makes it most likely that meetings will be called, and that these meetings will be intimidatingly large. If the family has private health insurance, and there is no need to arrange follow-up care, then the discharge planner need not come to the meeting. If the mother has been visiting regularly, has no history of drug abuse, and shows signs of being ready and able to take the baby home, then the social worker may not need to attend. If the baby has not been hospitalized for very long and the parents have been visiting regularly, the tie to the nursing staff will probably not be so important. Families are likely to have some contact with a physician early in their infant's hospital stay; if the child's hospitalization is brief, then the disproportion between contact with nurses and contact with physicians will not be so great. Parents who visit as well as phoning are also more likely to make contact with physicians since physicians are only put on the line when there is important news to communicate but will sometimes chat with parents at the bedside or greet them in the hall. Parents don't "run into the doctor by accident" if they only phone.

Conclusion--What Kinds of Distortions Occur?

I have argued that the intended uses of information, the certification procedures that provide for the exchange of information, and the meetings that are the setting for discussions of medical and social facts about babies and their families shape risk perception through their effect on what information does and does not get transmitted.

Documentation is fundamentally about risk--the risk of being sued. But it is easier to sue hospitals and their staff members for some things than for others. In particular parents can sue hospitals and their staff members for performing inappropriate procedures, failing to perform appropriate procedures, or performing procedures ineptly. But parents cannot sue hospitals because their infant happened to be born with some dread disease. Because information tends to be given on occasions when documentation is required, information is more likely to be given about medical problems that require hospital staff to act than about ones where no action is required. Most parents can therefore be expected to get more information about surgery than about dread diseases. We would also expect that information about a range of possible outcomes might get transmitted, but that information about the odds of one outcome rather than another would not, especially if there were any possibility that such predictions might be interpretable as a promise. Parents might have a different view than staff members after the fact about how such statistics should be and were interpreted.

Because so much information is given in meetings, the features of this setting have predictable effects on what information gets transmitted, how much gets transmitted, and to whom.[12] For instance, information about which there

---

12. Maynard (1991) makes a related argument that the asymmetry of discourse in medical settings has an interactional foundation (as well as an institutional one), and that we cannot understand what goes on in the telling of bad news (for instance) without investigating the interactional devices developed to manage this difficult task.

is consensus should be more likely to get transmitted than information about which there is disagreement. Meetings as a setting privilege already-privileged parents who are comfortable in meetings and with well-educated professionals. Middle-class, well-educated, and older parents thus get more information in meetings than poorer, less educated, and younger parents do. Risk perception, then, is affected not just by the biases and heuristics of human cognitive processes but by the biases and interests of social organizations whose routines influence what information the human cognitive system will get as raw material.

10

Field-Level Perceptions of Risk in Regulatory Agencies

Bridget M. Hutter and Sally Lloyd-Bostock

Concerns with risk permeate every level of regulatory agencies, from policy making (e.g., Manning, this volume) to enforcement at field level (e.g., Hawkins, this volume). Drawing on our empirical research on health and safety agencies, we concentrate specifically on the perception of risk by field level inspectors and the impact of those perceptions on their everyday enforcement activities. Our discussion is confined to inspectors' perceptions of risks of injury and damage to health, rather than other risks that might influence their enforcement decisions, such as the risks of losing a prosecution case (see Hawkins, this volume). The whole range of inspectors' enforcement activity, from deciding what visits to make through to deciding what action to take and what to accept as compliance, involves implicit or explicit assessments of risks of injury and ill-health. We examine how inspectors' perceptions of these risks are shaped, paying particular attention to the role of accident experience; and how their perceptions in turn shape their approaches to enforcement.

Inspectors in the agencies we studied were occasionally called on to make explicit estimates of risk. However, we use the term "risk" quite broadly to include any consideration of potential harm, whether explicit or implicit. Inspectors continually operated with notions of risk and uncertainty. While risks

Most of the research we draw on in this paper was supported by a grant from the Health and Safety Executive. We are grateful also for the extensive co-operation of staff in the institutions we studied. We would like to thank Keith Hawkins for his helpful comments on an earlier draft. Points of view expressed are those of the authors.

were by definition theoretically calculable, they were not necessarily calculated, nor was it necessarily only explicitly calculated risk that informed inspectors' decision making. We suggest in this paper that inspectors continually operated with implicit notions of risk, and that when they made explicit risk assessments, these were usually hybrid judgments involving factors other than calculable risk.

Our discussion is based on research on the work of the Factory, Agricultural, and Industrial Air Pollution[1] Inspectorates of the Health and Safety Executive (HSE) in Great Britain; and the Railway Inspectorate, which at the time of the research was part of the Department of Transport operating under an agency agreement with the Health and Safety Commission. The research was part of an interdisciplinary programme of research at the Centre for Socio-Legal Studies, Oxford.[2] During the period 1982-1986 we collected data by means of observation of the work of inspectors, interviews with a range of HSE personnel, and analysis of documents and computerised records held by the HSE (see Centre for Socio-Legal Studies, 1983). We refer also to a small comparative study of the Occupational Safety and Health Administration (OSHA) in the U.S. (Lloyd-Bostock, 1988). We thus include inspectors working in a range of circumstances and in varying industrial, legal and cultural traditions, with differing enforcement approaches.

Inspectors' notions of risk contribute differently to their enforcement activities depending on the legislative framework defining their role, and the enforcement style traditionally adopted in a particular agency. The nature of the risks inspectors encounter range from those that are obvious and tangible to health risks that may be invisible and difficult to detect. There were notable differences amongst the agencies we studied. The extent to which our comments might apply beyond these agencies is a matter of speculation.

Risk and Compliance

In this section we consider how those at the sharp end of regulatory enforcement were influenced by consideration of risk at three main stages in the

---

1. At the time of our research, the Industrial Air Pollution Inspectorate was part of the Health and Safety Inspectorate. In 1987 it returned to the Department of the Environment.

2. Other projects within the same programme of research on the regulation of health and safety at the Oxford Centre for Socio-Legal Studies have focused on a variety of other levels of the organisation. Keith Hawkins and Peter Manning, for example, studied policy-making levels of the HSE (see their papers in this volume).

enforcement process, namely the definition of compliance; the assessment of compliance; and the way in which compliance was achieved.

At the most basic level compliance can be taken to mean a desired state of affairs. Its *definition* is the decision as to what constitutes an acceptable act or state of affairs. The scope of interpretation in implementing the law may be structured by a variety of factors such as the way in which the law is framed and worded; agency directives about legal interpretation; and the application of these interpretations by individual enforcement officials. The *assessment* of compliance is the process of determining whether or not a particular act or state of affairs meets the requirements of the definition. Compliance is *achieved* by techniques ranging from formal-legal techniques, such as prosecution, to informal enforcement methods such as persuasion, advice and education.

The Definition of Compliance

In Britain, generality and flexibility characterise legal and administrative definitions of compliance in the spheres of health and safety and the environment. The legislation is broadly framed. For example, Sections 2 and 3 of the Health and Safety at Work etc. Act, 1974, place upon employers a general duty "to ensure so far as is *reasonably practicable*" the health and safety of their employees and the general public (our emphasis) whereas employees are obliged to take "reasonable care" of their own health and safety and that of others (Section 7). The concept of "best practicable means" is similarly central to environmental legislation. Because the legislation is so general and flexible, it is important to focus on the working definition of compliance, i.e., the definition employed by enforcement officials during the course of their routine work.

Risk is often juxtaposed with cost as the central dilemma of regulatory enforcement. Some have argued that health and safety and environmental legislation is a compromise between the conflicting interests of humanitarian reformers and high status manufacturers and businesses (Carson, 1974; Gunningham, 1974). Others see the legislation as a practical response to the problems that could be associated with stringent legislation, namely the closure of businesses and unemployment (Kagan, 1978). Whatever the reasons for the broad legislative framework, the fact is that in Britain the precise balance between the factors defining compliance is a matter largely left to the discretion of the enforcement agency or official, the main message of the legislation is that officials should be "reasonable." Rather than asking for a totally risk-free workplace or environment, the law requires that risks be considered alongside other factors. The legal tools available to inspectors acknowledge differences in risk. Prohibition notices forbid the use of machinery or activities that are an immediate danger to health. Improvement notices pertain to less "dangerous" activity and accordingly require improvement within a specified period of time, that is, sanction a temporary definition of compliance which is less than full compliance.

Across all areas of enforcement researched risk was a core principle to which inspectors adhered in constructing a definition of compliance. They considered the dangers associated with a given substance, machine or activity and the probability of something going wrong. Generally inspectors offered no relaxation in their definitions of compliance in cases where they believed that there was a significant risk of something going wrong and harm being caused. Similarly close surveillance was accorded those works which engaged in high risk activities. In these cases proactive strategies of inspection and monitoring were accorded high priority. For example, the Chief Industrial Air Pollution Inspector explained the need to register di-isocyanate works as follows:

> This class is scheduled because of the toxic nature of these chemicals. They can induce asthmatic response in some individuals at very low concentrations, and also have the potential to sensitise some people who then react to very much lower concentrations on subsequent occasions. (HSE, 1986a:20.)

The Report continued to explain that for these reasons such works were accorded a higher inspection priority. Industrial Air Pollution Inspectors, like others researched, kept a close eye on all such works. Hence all inspectors regularly monitored the coke ovens at steel works because of their carcinogenic emissions. Asbestos removal demanded similar attention as did large chemical works. Non-compliance with requirements pertaining to high risk activities was most likely to increase the probability of legal action. In the most extreme cases a prohibition notice was served and a prosecution also brought. This was especially likely where non-compliance had resulted in a high level of publicity and public concern.

Situations where inspectors encountered an imminent or significant risk of injury were the exception rather than the rule. When the risks appeared less immediate, inspectors did not overlook matters which needed attention, but they might be prepared to relax the time period within which full compliance was sought. An example of this arose during a Railway Employment Inspector's inspection of a mainline station. The inspector was shown plans for improvements to the station, the station manager was keen to emphasise that there would be a lot of reorganisation over the following three to four years. This was in order to forestall the inspector's requests for improvements in areas where refurbishment was planned in the foreseeable future. It transpired that those areas that the inspector wanted to improve did not involve matters of high risk. For example, a mess room which the inspector wanted refurbished was scheduled to be used for another purpose and a new mess room provided. The inspector was satisfied with this and prepared to wait for full compliance until the reorganisation was completed. In such cases inspectors operated with definitions of temporary compliance--a state that was less than full compliance but which inspectors were prepared to tolerate for a fixed period until full compliance had been achieved.

The Assessment of Compliance

The assessments of risks inspectors constructed--including whether or not a temporary definition of compliance could be tolerated and if so how long for-- took account of what was being regulated and why. The legislation enforced by the inspectors related to a wide range of activities, some directly concerned with health and safety, and others with less risky matters such as welfare and amenity. It was invariably the case that inspectors accorded higher priority to health and safety matters than they did to welfare and amenity shortcomings. They did not ignore less risky problems, rather they were prepared to tolerate non-compliance until more pressing matters were attended to, that is those that were perceived to involve greater dangers to health and safety.

Inspectors' perceptions of risk were also influenced by the visibility and tangibility of the various problems they encountered. Safety matters were often more visible and tangible than those concerning health (Felstiner and Siegelman, this volume; Hawkins, this volume). While it might be fairly straightforward to understand and explain that an unguarded machine could lead to the possibility of a finger being chopped off, it could be more difficult to explain and understand that exposure to sustained high levels of noise could in the long term, cause deafness. Not only might this affect the ease with which compliance could be sought, it might--albeit on an unconscious level--influence inspectors' daily routines. At the level of the Inspectorate these factors were also relevant. Generally the Industrial Air Pollution Inspectorate regulated a greater proportion of intangible and invisible matters than did the Factory Inspectorate and Railway Inspectorate. Moreover, the harm that could be caused by noncompliance with the Industrial Air Pollution Inspectorate demands were often health related. As noted below, this affected not just the ways in which compliance was assessed but the way in which it was achieved.

Inspectors could employ several methods to assess whether or not compliance was being achieved. Proactive enforcement is essentially law enforcement through agency initiative and mainly refers to inspection and sampling. Reactive enforcement refers to agency action prompted by an outside person or event, typically through lodging a complaint or reporting an accident (see Black, 1973). Risk figured prominently in each of these categories.

Much of the proactive work undertaken by inspectors was structured in the form of a monitoring programme (Hutter, 1986). In the case of Factory Inspectors this programme was both formalised and computerised. Industrial Air Pollution Inspectors and Railway Employment Inspectors operated according to similar principles but the decision of where and when to inspect was explicitly left to the discretion of local inspectors. Essentially all inspectors and inspectorates categorised premises according to their potential risk and from this deduced how frequently they should be inspected and/or sampled. Risk was assessed in a variety of ways. Not surprisingly, account was taken of the type of materials handled and processes used. Activities, machines and substances which were known to be a high risk were visited regularly. Inspectors also took into account a range of other criteria as indicative of risk, including their confidence in management and the workforce. Here inspectors considered commitment to health and safety or environmental control. They also assessed ability to regulate these areas, both in terms of financial back-up, technical expertise and the co-operation of all levels of management and the workforce. These assessments were, of course, in part the result of previous visits to a site. As the Chief Inspector of Factories wrote in the Inspectorate's 1985 Annual Report:

> Certainly the inspector is .... looking to see that there is compliance with the law .... he will wish to satisfy himself that overall standards of health, safety and welfare are acceptable, that adequate resources in terms of money are made available to ensure that those standards are maintained and that the management of health and safety within the firm or organisations is under control. (HSE, 1986b:35.)

Another important criterion in determining the level of proactive enforcement was any reactive work associated with the premises. Particular attention would be paid to the firm's accident record and in the case of the Industrial Air Pollution Inspectorate to a high level of complaints about air pollution. Only a minority of accidents reported are investigated by the inspectorates. However, records of all accidents, whether investigated or not, were regarded by inspectors as informative about the general level of awareness and concern with safety issues. Reports of accidents coming into Area Offices were regularly scanned by inspectors so that decisions might be made as to which merited investigation. A run of accidents at an establishment over weeks or months might be taken as a signal that compliance could be falling below acceptable standards. Eventually an accident would be selected for investigation, not so much to investigate the accident itself, but in order to make a more general assessment of compliance at the establishment.

The emphasis placed upon accidents as a way of assessing compliance varied between Inspectorates, as did the emphasis placed upon investigating complaints. The Railway Inspectorate placed most reliance upon accidents and their investigation. In part this was because of the high visibility and high profile of railway accidents, especially when the public was involved. The importance of public involvement was also significant in relation to Industrial Air Pollution Inspectorate complaints. These were always taken very seriously and investigated, in part because it was politically expedient to do so but also because the public could act as the "eyes and ears" of the Inspectorate (see Hutter, 1986:118). However, complaints were not always about the most risky problems, some of which related to substances such as asbestos fibres that were neither visible nor tangible to the public or workforce. In these cases assessment had to rely upon sampling.

Achieving Compliance

Achieving compliance was the main objective of all British inspectors in the research. The bulk of inspectors' time was devoted to educating, advising and persuading the regulated to attain the highest possible standards, rather than seeking out and punishing offenders. (The working mode of OSHA inspectors was, as many commentators have indicated, rather different -- Bardach and Kagan, 1982; Kelman, 1981; Lloyd-Bostock, 1988; Vogel, 1986). Some of the factors British inspectors took into account when deciding how, and in particular, how strongly, to seek compliance were the same as those they used in defining and assessing compliance. Risk was hence an important consideration in the decision of what action to take. As noted earlier, risk was central in the decision to serve a prohibition notice, its explicit purpose being to counter immediate risks to health. It was partly for this reason that prohibition notices were seldom used by Industrial Air Pollution Inspectors, that is, because the risks posed by non-compliance with air pollution legislation could not often be proved to be an *imminent* risk to health. It is partly because the risks to health and safety were more long term, difficult to evidence and in some respects less visible and tangible that Industrial Air Pollution Inspectors were less inclined to legal action than Factory Inspectors (Hutter, 1989). Conversely, legal action was more likely on those occasions when non-compliance could be clearly demonstrated as a risk to health and safety and when a clear-cut legal case could be constructed (Hawkins, this volume). The most obvious examples of this arose when accidents occurred (see Lloyd-Bostock, 1988). Moreover, complaints and accidents were much more likely than proactive enforcement methods to bring inspectors and the workplace to visible attention. Both inspectors and agencies were aware that complaints and accidents increased the likelihood of public attention to their work. Accidents and complaints therefore increased the pressure upon and within the agency to pursue legal action (Black, 1971; McCabe and Sutcliffe, 1978).

Achieving compliance was not simply a matter of theoretical risks associated with non-compliance, nor the risks of winning or losing legal action. Many other factors were taken into consideration, some only indirectly related to risk. Again, whose compliance was being sought emerged as important, including a multiplicity of issues such as the size and complexity of the business concerned. Inspectors typically took size as an indicator of likely standards of compliance. Small businesses would usually be characterised as not having many resources to devote to such matters as health and safety at work and environmental pollution. Generally they were not expected to adhere to such high standards as their larger, especially multinational, counterparts. By implication, larger businesses were regarded as having the resources and the specialist know-how to comply. So, while advice and education might be seen as an essential and integral part of achieving the compliance of smaller firms, they would not be accorded such priority for large organisations. But these very broad characterisations were cross-cut by other considerations such as the stability of the business involved. Transitory businesses, such as construction firms, were regarded with suspicion. When such firms were found not complying with the law, inspectors were markedly more severe in their responses, often demanding that, where possible, matters be improved or remedied before the inspector left the site. Indeed the speed with which anyone complied with inspectors' demands was taken as an indication of their intention to comply. It was no coincidence that many of the prosecutions initiated by Industrial Air Pollution Inspectors pre-1984 were against Metal Recovery Works, especially illegal cable burners. These were often transitory operations. Likewise, Factory Inspectors working in the Construction Industry Groups tended to be more sanctioning than many of their colleagues (see Hutter, 1989:170). The greater inclination to legal action in the these areas of industry did not just relate to the dangers associated with the activities involved: it was also a reflection of the inspectors' inability to form a long term relationship with the regulated. This had a number of implications. It meant for example, that because of the short term nature of, for instance, construction sites inspectors were unlikely to have the opportunity to return and check that improvements had been effected, hence the demand for immediate compliance. It also meant that they had less particularistic knowledge upon which to base assessments.

How much inspectors relied on broad characteristics and stereotypes depended upon how well they actually knew those they regulated, which in turn was related to how frequently they were able to visit the workplace concerned. In this research the Factory Inspectorate was responsible for regulating the greatest number of different businesses. The Railway Inspectorate dealt with the fewest employers, with British Railways being the main company subject to their control. This does not mean that they dealt with few workplaces, however, for the whole of the operational railway was subject to their control. Indeed, any part of the railway could become a transient worksite whenever temporary repairs were necessitated. Nevertheless, the line of control in the industry to which inspectors would refer problems of non-compliance was a well-known one to inspectors. Factory Inspectors, in contrast, had to familiarise themselves with the information networks and sources of power and influence within each organisation. In cases involving regular contact with a company well placed to know what was possible and how best to achieve the possible, negotiation was likely to be a central method of achieving compliance. Long-standing relationships enabled inspectors to raise the possibilities of improvements and to persuade businesses that they were advantageous long before they actually requested them. Their demands were more likely to be finely tuned to the capabilities of the business.

In short, where inspectors could visit works frequently and had detailed knowledge of the site and personnel they were more able to assess risks rather than uncertainties. This affected their ability to accurately define, assess and achieve compliance.

Perceptions of Risk and Experience of Accidents

Inspectors' perceptions of risk of injury or harm to health were clearly the product of many different influences, including training and experience. We expected that experience of accidents would play a special part in forming inspectors' perceptions of risk of injury. It is generally accepted that concrete instances of harm have greater psychological impact than abstract information about risks (cf. Hutter and Lloyd-Bostock, 1990). Risks of injury tend to be more immediate and tangible than risks to health, and as noted above, inspectors often responded to them more readily. An inspector was more likely to attend to a risk of a finger being caught in a machine than to a risk of gradual hearing loss. Recognising the importance of direct experience as opposed to abstract theory, the British Factory Inspectorate explicitly considers accident investigation an important part of factory inspector training. Accidents were regularly selected for investigation expressly in order to give a trainee inspector experience of taking a close look at a particular machine and seeing for him/herself the kinds of accident that could occur whilst it is operated. Since experience of accidents brings risks to life, inspectors' perceptions of risk are very likely to be influenced by accidents they have seen. Moreover, if accident experience is biased toward certain types of accident, then inspectors' awareness of risk will tend similarly to be biased.

There were two levels at which we found that accidents influenced inspectors' perceptions of risk. At one level, individual accidents could have lasting effects on inspectors' subsequent enforcement practices. Inspectors in all the organisations concerned with safety that we studied talked much about nasty accidents they had seen. While this talk was sometimes jocular and often appeared callous, it was clear that inspectors were sometimes deeply affected by accidents they investigated, particularly those resulting in horrific injury. Factory inspectors were aware that, following such accidents, they or their colleagues might change their criteria for tolerance of specific risks. Accidents thus had a direct impact on their working definitions of compliance. The result of some accidents was that inspectors developed "hobby-horses" -- paying special attention to the particular hazard in future, perhaps at the expense of other hazards. One OSHA inspector was an ex-construction worker who joined OSHA as a consequence of accidents he had seen. He carried with him a photograph of a fatal accident victim impaled on spikes after falling from an unfenced area at a construction site. The accident had clearly had a powerful effect on him, and he described how he could not tolerate seeing construction workers exposed to the same risk, and how he brought out the photograph at inspections to hammer home his message to employers. Some British inspectors said they were aware of the tendency in themselves or their colleagues to be sensitised to certain hazards as a result of accidents.

A second, more subtle impact of accident experience was the cumulative effect of exposure to accident information. The cumulative effects of accidents on perceptions of risk were particularly marked in the Factory and Railway Inspectorates, because their inspectors gained wide experience of accidents. Area Offices of the Factory Inspectorate in the U.K. received reports of accidents across a wide range of injury and accident types, and investigations were conducted into a varied sub-set of these at inspectors' discretion. Any work accident resulting in over three days off work was reportable to an Area Office of the Factory Inspectorate. While investigation activity tended to concentrate on certain types of accident within the three-day criterion, the range investigated was nonetheless varied, and by no means confined to serious injuries. Fewer than half of the accidents investigated were defined as fatal or major (see Lloyd-Bostock, 1990 for a fuller account of how the selection of accidents for investigation was made). Factory inspectors therefore acquired quite extensive accident experience. The processes of scanning accident reports and investigating accidents built and continually updated British factory inspectors' knowledge of accidents occurring (Lloyd-Bostock, 1990).

That knowledge visibly influenced inspection practices. During accompanied visits to premises, British factory inspectors frequently mentioned accidents they had experienced at the type of site being visited, not only to us but also to management and workforce. Accidents may have been mentioned in order to make certain points more vividly, or to see how we would react. Whatever the reason, inspectors drew readily on memories of an extensive range of possible accidents that might happen. Their comparatively extensive experience of accidents resulted in a valuable "feel" for accidents that contrasted markedly with the sense that OSHA inspectors, with their much more restricted experience of accidents, tended to display: in the U.S. only fatalities and catastrophes (FATCATs) had to be reported to an Area Office of OSHA.

Although the range of reported accidents was very wide in the British Factory Inspectorate, the selection for investigation tended to follow well worn grooves. By far the majority of accidents investigated involved machinery trapping fingers or a hand. Other types of machinery accidents and falls from heights were also frequently investigated. Other rarer types of accident that attracted attention were electrocutions, burns, explosions and poisonings. On the other hand, sprains and strains, often back injuries, occurred in comparatively very large numbers but were rarely investigated (see Lloyd-Bostock, 1990). Inspectors' knowledge of certain categories of accident--notably machinery accidents caused by failure to guard--was thus being continually updated through investigation, while other categories--notably back injuries--were rarely investigated. Their awareness of risks associated with frequently investigated accident types was fuller and more vivid to them, while risks associated with types of accident that are rarely investigated remained more vague and abstract. Similarly, when OSHA inspectors were asked to give examples of hazards giving rise to frequent accidents in the industries they dealt with, they were most likely to cite hazards associated with fatal accidents--that is, the accidents they usually investigated.

Perceptions of Risk and Opportunities for Enforcement

If the cumulative impact of accident information affects perceptions of risk, what determines the patterns of accident knowledge that inspectors acquire? What types of accident were selected for investigation and were thus likely to contribute to inspectors' repertoire of accident knowledge? Lloyd-Bostock (1990) found that inspectors' responses to accidents were embedded in the particular regulatory context in which they worked. Attention was paid to those accidents where it appeared most likely that inspectors would be able "do something."

The possibility of being able to "do something" was in turn largely a function of existing safety regulations. Decisions as to which accidents would be investigated and what action would be taken following investigation were largely at the discretion of field level inspectors. Their use of this discretion was very much structured by existing regulations and the enforcement opportunities these created. It is generally accepted that field level inspectors find specific and clear regulations more enforceable than vaguer standards (Dawson, et al., 1988). In Britain, Section 14 of the Factories Act (1961) states that "Every dangerous part of any machinery shall be securely fenced." Accidents possibly resulting from a breach of this requirement are comparatively easy to identify as such, and they were routinely selected for investigation. The phrase "a Section 14" was commonly used as a shorthand way of referring to accidents caused by failure to guard a machine. In 29% out of 381 accident investigation reports studied, the inspector specified a possible breach of this one Section of the Act; and in 15% an actual breach was found at investigation. Also frequently cited were the 1974 Woodworking Regulations (relevant to 17% of accidents investigated) and the 1966 Construction Regulations (relevant to 12%). A circularity thus develops. Inspectors learn more and more about certain types of accident, and their perceptions of risk are moulded by that knowledge.

Since inspectors became familiar with hazards through enforcement of existing regulations, it was largely the existing regulations, indirectly as well as directly, that gave focus to their perceptions of risk and their routine enforcement action. But enforcement opportunities were not the only factor considered. A second major reason for investigating accidents was to display to management, the workforce and the public that the inspectorate took such accidents seriously. Considerations of risk now entered inspectors' decision making much less directly. Their enforcement activities were to an extent an exercise in managing public perceptions of risk--perhaps performing what Reiss (this volume) refers to as a latent function of regulatory agencies, namely to assure the public that corrective actions will be taken; or more broadly, to reconstruct public perceptions of risk and uncertainty. Detailed consideration of indirect considerations of risk of this kind is beyond the scope of the present paper. What remains central to the present theme, however, is that inspectors' accident experience was partly determined by concerns with managing public perceptions. Indeed, it appeared that for OSHA, those concerns had become overriding in accident investigation policy: inspectors' accident experience was virtually confined to FATCATS (see above). To the extent that accident experience played a role in forming perceptions of risk, any biases in accident investigation policy of risk would be reproduced as biases in inspectors' perceptions of risk and might inform their enforcement activities.

Explicit Use of Estimates of Risk by Field Inspectors

In certain circumstances field inspectors were specifically required to make estimates of the risk attached to processes, establishments, and situations they encountered. Sometimes there was simply a requirement that inspectors should have risk concepts in mind as a consideration. For example, the guidelines to inspectors on selection of accidents to investigate indicated that inspectors should consider the potential severity of injury that might have occurred as well as the severity of injury that actually occurred. On other occasions, the action inspectors took had to be backed by an explicit estimate of risk. But in all of these instances, it was open to question whether the action *resulted from* an estimate or perception of a certain level of risk; or whether the inspector wished to take the action, for whatever reasons, and had to justify the action with reference to risk. It became clear that explicit assessments of risk were not purely assessments of the likelihood of certain levels of harm, but were mediated by broader, implicit assessments of the risks associated with the process or establishment; and by and what, given the total regulatory context, the inspector wished to achieve.

Two occasions that arose for the British Factory Inspectorate illustrate the point. Firstly, the selection of premises to be the subject of a basic inspection involved the application of a formula, part of which was the "inspector's rating." After a basic inspection, the inspector assigned numerical values to a range of factors that would contribute to determining when the establishment next received a basic inspection. The components of the rating included explicit estimates of risk--the extent of safety hazards at the establishment, health hazards, hazards to the public, and hazards to employees, together with a rating for the inspector's confidence in the safety and health awareness of management. While it was designed as a composite scale with specific components, inspectors treated it as a more general opportunity to influence how soon the establishment would be re-visited (Hutter, 1986:117). Their overall judgment as to how soon the next general inspection should come around presumably draws implicitly on assessments of risk, but the numbers they assigned to components of the ratings may or may not directly reflect those assessments.

A second decision involving explicit estimates of the risk of harm or damage was the choice of formal enforcement tool. A prohibition notice was a powerful enforcement tool, but, as discussed above, its use had to be justified with reference to imminent risk. Again, the question arises, which came first, the desire to impose a prohibition notice, or the estimate of risk? One of us witnessed a prohibition notice being imposed on a machine at which an accident had occurred while it was operated unguarded. It was certainly the case that further serious injury could have occurred if the machine was operated in the same unguarded state. There was therefore imminent risk of serious injury. However, the decision to impose a prohibition notice involved many further considerations, in particular the inspector's belief, formed as the investigation visit progressed, that the employer would not be stirred into action unless deprived of the use of the machine in its present state.

Explicit estimates of risk formed a more routine part of OSHA inspectors' work. The calculation of fines to be imposed for citations involved what amount to estimates of the risk of serious injury resulting from the violation in question. Again, explicit estimates of risk were influenced by broader implicit notions of risk. An elaborate formula was set out in OSHA's Field Operations Manual, which produced a starting figure based on the gravity of the offence. Gravity was to be decided on the basis of the severity of the injury or illness that could result from the violation. That figure could then be modified according to a "probability" quotient, derived from estimates of the number of workers exposed, the duration of exposure, personal protective equipment available, and possibly other factors. The resulting "gravity based penalty" might be reduced by up to 80% for size of the firm, previous history of the firm, and "good faith".

Instructions in use of the formula occupied sixteen pages of the OSHA manual. Nevertheless, there was a considerable margin within which estimates could in practice vary without departing from the letter of the instructions. Indeed, leeway was explicitly built into the instructions on how to use the apparently restrictive formula. Several qualifications called for the use of discretion--for example: "Since many employers will not fit exactly these general criteria ...professional judgment will be required to balance the important factors in determining the appropriate rate for a particular employer " (VI-11). Despite the appearance of defining closely the basis of penalties, the method thus explicitly relies at least partly on "professional judgment" as to what would be a reasonable penalty for the offence. Further opportunities for using discretion arose in the grouping and combining of citations, which could have the effect of either multiplying or reducing fines by considerable amounts. If a violation could be classified as "other than serious," no fine at all was imposed. One of us witnessed a fine of several hundred dollars being wiped out over the telephone by a "mistake" being discovered in its classification as a "serious" rather than "other than serious" violation. In these various ways, the basis of the fine in an *explicit* risk assessment becomes somewhat diluted. On the other hand, *implicit* judgments of risk evidently permeated the calculation of penalties, in the same way as they permeated British inspectors inspection ratings. The figure put on elements in OSHA's penalty formula, or on elements in the inspectors' ratings, were not simply estimates of calculable risk, but were hybrid judgments. They might incorporate such factors as inspectors' impressions of an employer's safety consciousness, the co-operativeness of the employer, and other types of risk, such as the risk to the inspector of awarding (or failing to award) a high penalty (see Hawkins, this volume).

Conclusion

Where the stated function of an agency is to regulate health and safety, its credibility partly depends on how it overtly manages risk. Concepts of risk must at some level be dealt with explicitly. How explicitly depends on the framework of rules or regulations enforced. Thus, in Britain health and safety legislation dictates that risk should be considered alongside other factors, such as the economic consequences of expenditure on health and safety measures. While implicit estimates of risk are reflected in the more precise regulations, the Health and Safety at Work etc. Act, 1974, is so framed as to accord the field inspector a significant role in both calculating risk and acting on those calculations--that is, in the definition, assessment and achievement of compliance. In the U.S., by way of contrast, the task of defining risk lies to a much greater extent with the legislation and the detailed General Industry Standards promulgated under the Occupational Safety and Health Act of 1970. Inspectors operate with much less discretion over the three stages of compliance, from definition to achievement, and their own perceptions of risk are accorded a much less prominent role in enforcement.

We have looked at how, in practice, notions of risk informed the work of field level inspectors within different organisational and legislative contexts.

Where inspectors exercised discretion in enforcement, as in the British inspectorates, we have described how they constantly explained and justified their actions with reference to concepts of risk. While inspectors may have been influenced by more personal risks such as risks to their own credibility (Hawkins, this volume), there was little evidence that these concerns diverted them from the goal of maximising health and safety. Though they had discretion, where the calculable risks were perceived to be high we found no relaxation in definition, assessment nor achievement of compliance. In taking account of risks to health and safety British inspectors considered not only the theoretical risks associated with a given machine, substance, process or activity, but also the risks associated with particular industries and firms. Inspectors' experience in the field thus shaped their perceptions of the risks associated with particular firms as well as particular processes. Here again, contrasts were found between Britain and the U.S.. In Britain an important source of inspectors' information on risk was accidents reported to them and investigated by them. In the U.S. inspectors acquired a much more limited range of accident knowledge: OSHA inspectors rarely investigated accidents other than FATCATS (fatalities and catastrophes). OSHA policy for responding to accidents appeared to be dominated by concern with public perceptions and the need to display a response to serious accidents.

The agencies we studied differed not only in the extent of discretion exercised by field level inspectors, but also in the nature of the activities regulated and the nature of the agency's relationship with the regulated. The role of risk assessments differed in these varying settings, particularly in the extent to which risks were related to immediate and readily understandable harm through accidents as opposed to more remote longer term damage to health.

While agencies concerned with health and safety are bound to display concern with risk, assessments of risk are implicit. Implicit risk assessments were inferred from the actions taken by inspectors and from their preoccupations. They directly affected action rather than only justifying it. Explicit assessments of risk by inspectors were clearly a compound of various concerns. When they volunteered accounts of their actions in terms of risk, it is important not to assume on that basis alone that concerns with risk were in fact influencing their actions. A multi-method approach, including observation, is necessary. The influences of risk assessments on field level enforcement activity are pervasive, but they are often subtle, indirect, and implicit rather than explicit.

PART FIVE

Choosing Technologies, Managing, and Regulating Risks

11

Expert Advice and Formal Public Involvement on Public Policies Involving Risk

Anthony Barker

Governments of advanced western countries have established various official "decision advice processes" (inquiry commissions, expert panels, and the like) to generate expert recommendations on projects involving potential public hazards.[1] These decision advice processes furnish responsible political executives with information and argument, often including political and social data on how affected local populations and the nation at large view such projects and attendant risks.

If the amount and quality of this political material is more than merely nominal, a second function may be performed by these processes: politically legitimating a decision to proceed with a project on the grounds that all voices will have been heard and considered. The people will have had their say. This is the world of "public hearings" (possibly "rule-making" hearings) as known in the United States; "public inquiries" (possibly "major" or "big" public inquiries) with a single "inspector" or (in Scotland) "reporter," as known in Britain; or group efforts by commissions or committees (possibly, but not often,

---

1. The distinction between "risk" and "hazard" as used here will follow that of the Beijer Institute volume (Kasperson and Kasperson, 1987, p. viii). "Hazard" is a potentially harmful state of affairs which could cause damage or injury to life and property or social amenity. "Risk" is the possibility of this harmful condition coming about. The term includes both the possibility or chances of the hazard occurring and its likely consequences (Griffiths, 1982).

committees of the legislature) in various other Western European countries such as Germany, Italy, or in Scandinavia (Barker and Peters, 1992).[2]

Governments are often nervous about imposing additional risk on local populations, even when major economic benefits to the local area may seem assured--and even when most local people share that view. Three broad areas are of concern: people's legal (property) rights; their prospective loss of what the British call amenity (environmental quality of various types, but normally excluding specific risks from hazards); and the extra risk that will be added to their lives by a major project and its likely consequences (including such elements as extra urbanization, road traffic danger, and the personal stresses that can flow from such changes; see Barker and Couper, 1984).

The root of the risk problem reviewed here is thus *additional* hazard. All local populations are exposed to risks associated with natural and man-made hazards. These "revealed risks" (Douglas and Wildavsky, 1982) may be assessed and judged to be those which the local population has revealed itself as "willing" to accept. If this existing level is unusually high, promoters of a new hazardous project may be tempted to claim that it will make little difference. An already dangerous place will become only slightly more so. This extra risk will be offset by benefits such as additional jobs (short-term construction or continuing jobs) which the project will bring.

More objective analysts should pause, however. "Revealed risk" is a genuine sign of an "acceptable level" only if, firstly, every local person knows what that risk is. This is a very tall order when even the experts among both operators and official regulators of a project may not know just how dangerous it is in certain conditions. This applies particularly to the very dangerous consequences of mixed or "cocktail" accidents such as occur in or around petro-chemical plants with dangerous substances which could set one another off in an unpredictable but catastrophic sequence. Such an accident may never have happened anywhere and its consequences may not have been assayed in computer simulation. Secondly, there is the much more subtle and elaborate problem of assessing how willing the different local socio-economic classes are to "accept" a high risk when they would like to move away if only equally cheap housing or an equally lucrative job could be found elsewhere. The extensive trailer home parks that stand next to some of the world's most hazardous petro-chemical sites on Britain's Canvey Island (in the Thames estuary) for example, are not located to take advantage of the view, smells, or the risks of either poison gas or a fireball holocaust. They remain as cheap housing and cheap holiday accommodation for poorer people.

---

2. The glaring exception is France's government, some of whose environmental enthusiasms are mentioned later in this and in the following chapter, by James Jasper.

An extreme case of this economic imperative which draws people into apparent acceptance of severe risks emerged in the inquest of the Bhopal disaster. Several thousand people were living on low ground adjacent to the plant that Union Carbide's American managers had warned their Indian successors in the plant--and local government and political party leaders--must not be built on, particularly for housing, because an escape of cyanide gas would lie in this spot until the wind dispersed it. Hundreds died from cyanide in their sleep because they or their relatives had demanded of political and municipal leaders that they be allowed to live in tenements on this land conveniently close to their work. These leaders and, perhaps also, the new plant management, had acquiesced in a grievously irresponsible course of action. The environmental or risk preferences of residents with jobs in the plant were "revealed" by political lobbying to allow housing to be built on that fatal spot.

When new plants replace old ones with superior machinery and materials, safety as well as efficiency may be improved. But often a new plant will work alongside the old--or parts of it--so that hazards and risks are exacerbated. Moreover, if the new plant is dealing with new and different dangerous substances, the overall risk may be greatly increased by the cocktail effect. An escape or explosion of one or more chemicals may interact with the plant next door or down wind, thus threatening a type of disaster which the designers of both plants failed to consider. Having two petro-chemical works making a range of dangerous products or two liquified natural gas (LNG) tank farms side-by-side, for example, is more hazardous than only one of each type. A mixed pair or foursome offers much more than double risk because the range of dangerous substances on the joint site could set off a multiple interaction of fire, poisonous fumes, or explosion (Davis, 1979).

Promoters of new, potentially, hazardous plants, if they cannot claim risk reduction, have traditionally tried to ignore the concept of interactive or multiple risk. On this simple view, one nasty new chemical works placed beside a nasty old LNG depot simply makes two undesirable neighbors when, in fact, the joint risk may be much greater, depending on the specific substances involved. One of the achievements of a good "decision advice process" (hearings, inquiries, commissions) is to expose and avoid such oversimplification.

Once the nature of a new plant's additional hazards is thus clarified, spokesmen may then try to individualize and trivialize the extra hazard. The risk of death or serious injury from the plant will be no more for each local resident than crossing the local main traffic route on foot twice a year, for example: an act performed daily by residents on their way to work or to the shops. Radiation leakages from a nuclear plant will be no more than a dose from a chest x-ray, or a day watching TV, or from keeping a luminous clock on the wall. If the country is a granite area, such as England's Cornwall or Scotland's Grampian Mountains, then the natural and unavoidable radiation from these rocks equals or exceeds the new plant's ambient level. As everyone accepts these very small risks for convenience's sake (and as everyone in Cornwall or the Grampians is not ill or dying) there can be no problem.

Just as promoters may not encourage local populations, regulators, or government decision-makers to think about multiple interactive risks, they may also assess the prospect of major disasters only in terms of individual deaths. Opponents must distinguish between deaths of mainly unrelated individuals (such as the roughly one hundred car and truck drivers caught in the LNG explosion and fireball on 24 September, 1990 beside Bangkok harbour) and those of whole families (such as at Bhopal; at the holiday camping ground in Spain when a passing LNG truck exploded in a fireball; or those who live next to the LNG and other hazards on Canvey Island in England). The notion that deaths of whole families is more damaging to the general "gene pool" than even very numerous individual deaths, deriving from massive genetic losses to Jewish, gypsy, and some Slav populations at the hands of the Nazis, has been introduced into public hearings on hazardous plants, including those at Canvey Island. By introducing such considerations, decision advice processes may question evidence of risks local people are willing to accept as the price of daily existence--their revealed risk.

Hearings or inquiries are also highly likely to focus attention on people's "expressed preferences" (Douglas and Wildavsky, 1982; Gould, et al., 1988) in the form of opinion survey responses or as evidence presented at hearings. Expressed preferences may include fear of or hostility towards a dangerous, noisy, dirty, or smelly industrial plant, notwithstanding one's decision to remain living nearby for economic (housing costs or job opportunities), or family reasons (relatives are also nearby, this locale being the family's base). Such views may be very strong, despite their never having been placed explicitly on a personal agenda for reasons of impracticality. The "decision" to remain is, in fact, a nondecision (Bachrach and Baratz, 1970).

It bears repeating that the objective of government in such matters is both to investigate and (thus) to legitimate decision-making by the one process. In a reasonably liberal and open government system, approval should, if at all possible, follow only from an investigation or review of some kind: but that exercise can greatly assist the government if the approval (and, even more, the practical purpose of getting the plant built and running) can be achieved without public protest and disruption. This elementary but fundamental point means that the rationalist (investigative) and subjective or symbolic political (legitimating) functions of any commission or hearings are bound tightly together. Each critical question that an objector is allowed to put to one of the promoter's managers or hired experts is a blow to the political acceptability of a project, with or without conditions or limitations based on public examination. Only if criticism is so damaging that the government can no longer support a project (or promoters decide to postpone or cancel it) does this ironic process of objectors helping to legitimate a project not apply. It is for this reason that some smaller and more radical anti-nuclear power groups in Britain do not appear at public inquiries into nuclear power plants. In the absence of financial support for objectors at British public inquiries, these groups have chosen to avoid a great deal of work and expense in waging a wholly unequal battle with the (then) state electricity monopoly in England and Wales (the Central Electricity Generating Board). Of equal importance, they have viewed their participation as giving the appearance of "fairness" to what they perceive as an inevitably favorable government decision to build nuclear plants.

Some measure of legitimacy may be obtained for a major hazardous development by the simple process of having it described and justified at some kind of public hearing, even if objectors have either absented themselves or seem not even to exist in significant numbers. In earlier years, Britain has had nuclear power stations approved by the national government either after a public inquiry lasting only two or three days or after no inquiry at all. By contrast, the most recent case--Britain's second proposed pressurized water reactor (PWR)--had an inquiry lasting 182 days over an 11 month period. The first (Sizewell, Suffolk) occupied 340 sitting days within a total inquiry period of over four years. To have a brief hearing with no more than a few minutes of stated opposition from local folk gives the project's promoter and the government some claim to having presented the scheme to the public for critical review. In Britain, the central government must hold a public inquiry into an electricity generating project (whether or not nuclear) if the relevant local government, in this field the county council, enters and maintains a formal objection. Ministers may also hold an inquiry if they otherwise so decide, perhaps to accommodate a vocal public opposition even though the county council (perhaps thinking about local job opportunities) does not object. This latter case applied at Sizewell and produced Britain's largest and most elaborate public inquiry (O'Riordan, et al., 1988).

If some political legitimacy can still be obtained by the government even if public objection at a very brief hearing is very minor, can it also be had if the hearing or commission is not seen to be in truly independent hands? This is very much a question of the *political or civic* culture of the country in question. Probably no government of a major industrial nation would allow a decision on a major industrial project investment to be taken away from its own departments or agencies. A strongly judicialized system such as the United States may allow judges in various levels of courts to rule out particular sites for hazardous projects such as nuclear stations, but few other countries would contemplate such powers for such inexpert and unelected (in most cases) figures; nor would the judges. But these are project-specific and site-specific decisions which an American court may take. They are not policy decisions against classes of hazardous plants, whether nuclear, petro-chemical, or other types. Decisions barring broad classes of plants belong with legislatures, or perhaps with voters on a popular proposition or referendum.

A formal investigation and advice exercise necessarily gives considerable political resources to persons who are invited to perform it. Even if they are not empowered to make a formal recommendation, their mode of inquiry and the tone of their report may strengthen or weaken the political standing of a project. Where, more usually, the investigator or commission is required to make an overall recommendation, there is great scope for political behavior and various forms of finesse on all sides: investigators, governments, promoters, and interested publics at both local and national levels.

In thinking about this subtle and delicate field, a first distinction should be made between hazardous developments which are, directly or indirectly, the national government's own projects and those that are the responsibility of private commercial firms or other unofficial bodies. Note that responsible central government departments do not necessarily support every state project; nor are they always disinterested towards every private project. A government may, for example, have a policy to locate psychiatric offenders in only semi-secure prisons or centres and another policy to promote importing of LNG as a cheaper and highly flexible energy source. When both the offenders' centre and the LNG terminal and tank farm provoke hot local opposition, the government may well not court local unpopularity by forcing through the centre while doing exactly that for the terminal on the grounds that one is more important and urgent than the other. In such a case, the government's project for the psychiatric centre (perhaps the direct responsibility of a different government department from the one issuing the formal consents) might be withdrawn or relocated while the private enterprise LNG project might be pushed through, perhaps on an urgent basis as part of national energy policy.

It is unusual for the investigator or commission conducting a decision advice process to recommend flatly against a government or quasi-government scheme. However, a positive recommendation may be so set about with limitations and conditions, or damned with faint praise, that it may be judged as quite negative. Despite this fact, even the most diluted positive recommendation is still positive, and a government that wishes to proceed often can rely on only small attentive public notice of the weakness of a recommendation. Even weak support following a hearing or commission has useful legitimating authority among the wider inattentive public and nonspecialist circles such as the mass media and government party legislators and other supporters.

Formally negative recommendations from a commission or inquiry often occur with respect to commercial, nongovernment projects, particularly if the government has not signified its support during hearings or other types of investigation. When government policy favors such projects, however, a plainly negative judgment from the decision advice process presents a problem. Once a hearing or inquiry has been held, hostile ranks of the public may be outraged (genuinely or affectedly) by a decision to proceed with a project against adverse advice of investigators. The fact that an investigator has only recommended and lacks power to stop a project often is not firmly grasped, if local newspaper stories, readers' letters, and editorial comments are any guide. As a result, the government may be reported as having overruled an investigation's decision when it has simply rejected its recommendation. Alternatively, the government may be accused of having ignored the recommendation. Critics of a project speak of having "won the inquiry" (to use British terms) but lost the decision. Unfairness and irrationality are charged or implied. Did not the investigators rather than the government ministers or senior officials spend the effort to study the project and weigh the evidence? How can such well-informed sources that were specifically asked to investigate and report, have their considered judgments thrust aside?

A central issue is whether any advisory process, however conscientious and detailed, ought to be in the business of recommending for or against a hazardous project which embodies national policy. One line of thought maintains that, if it is not constitutionally possible or politically legitimate for the government to delegate decision-making authority to an appointed commission or investigator, it is wrong to request an overall recommendation. Instead, only a factual inquiry should be held (including no doubt, the political facts of what local residents or other elements of public opinion think) and only straight description of a project and such surrounding facts should be reported. This is indeed the traditional stance of the retired official who spends a day or two in the local town hall and around the proposed site collecting views on development projects--including hazardous ones--to form the *enquête publique* stage of the French land-use planning system. This listening but noninvestigative role is so much weaker than, for example, the British form of adversarial public inquiry usually conducted by an expert official ("the Inspector") that it is best not to translate the French term from that language and to avoid any wholly inappropriate conflation of these two quite different forms of "public inquiry."

On this more limited view of what a decision advice process on a major hazardous development ought to undertake, the policy decision must rest wholly with the government. Even a merely advisory recommendation which went against the policy grain would be an unnecessary embarrassment: policy-making cannot be shared, certainly not with an unelected individual or commission which ought only to act as the government's eyes and ears at the local scene. This view can be applied in two ways to the problem of the government's need to know more about specific projects. Either government policy can be propounded prior to a decision advice process--probably written into its terms of reference--or the process can be commissioned first and its results considered together with a policy announcement when a decision is ready to be published.

Of these two courses, the latter is greatly preferable because it largely avoids a very awkward conundrum. That is, if the government presumes to announce its "policy" on a particular class of projects, such as nuclear reactors, before a major example has been examined in detail, it cannot rationally know that its policy is well-based. It ought, therefore, to keep quiet until it has the benefit of a good quality decision advice process. This is particularly the case in fields where the need for additional capacity is contested. It also very much applies to cost-benefit considerations--whether in financial value-for-money terms or on a wider canvas, including social cost elements running to issues such as the cost and quality of mass evacuation or major fire brigade services if a serious accident or terrorist attack were to occur. The government may well have a general policy of advancing nuclear PWR stations (as in France, or Britain during 1979-1990) as the "best buy" in electricity generation, or of encouraging lucrative imports of spent nuclear fuel rods or pcb chemicals for reprocessing and treatment, as in Britain. But it cannot know whether this policy is well-rounded in present investment terms until particular schemes have been costed and investigated, preferably adversarially. Only if it is demonstrated that weaknesses, hidden subsidies, and unstated assumptions have been looked into is legitimacy likely to be conferred. Only when the commission of inquiry has reported after a thorough study can the government be confirmed in its general policy, at least so far as the particular scheme may take it: other schemes on other sites to be built in the future may turn out from their own detailed investigation to be different matters. Only when a government can afford, both politically and financially, to ignore the cost-effectiveness of arguments and to rush ahead does it make sense to declare a policy of promoting any major projects before studying the fine print costs and returns. The French government has followed this "snowblower" technique on various occasions (notably on the Concorde aircraft and the building of Charles de Gaulle Airport [Feldman, 1985]). In more recent years it has been applied to the policy of the national state electricity monopoly, Electicité de France, of building PWR reactors on a factory production line and erecting them in groups (nuclear parks) around the country. As a result of this huge expenditure campaign, France now gets 70% of its electricity by nuclear methods and is grossly over-supplied with power. It sells all it can at whatever price it can get to its neighbors, including Britain. Because a national policy of particular force, even by the robust standards of the French, was behind this bonanza, there was even less official interest in expert decision advice processes than characterizes other major projects, or land-use planning as a whole, in France. Local opposition has been reduced by giving bribes to local populations who are now at risk from this huge array of inherently dangerous PWRs. These inducements take the form of local community facilities, such as sports and social centres (a practice also followed in Britain) but also, unlike any other European country, of reduced electricity bills for a certain local area's residents. This has proved quite popular. Local legitimacy and acceptance seem to have been achieved by these and other means, including prospects of new local employment at and around these stations.

Differences Among Western Developed Countries

How may differences between Western developed countries in treatment of hazard and risk issues be characterized? In her comparative review of scientific risk assessment in the U.S.A. and some Western European states, Sheila Jasanoff points to considerable differences between political and administrative contexts (Jasanoff, 1986). Based on study of the carcinogenic properties of formaldehyde, her general statement about the powerful effects of political and general social context on what actually happens on scientific controversies of this type runs as follows:

> The efforts of modern governments to regulate chemical carcinogens reveal deep-seated differences in national attitudes about the characterization and control of risk ... In dealing with uncertainty and expert conflicts, national regulatory systems take into account a host of interests besides the scientific community's views about risk ... Different societies also respond differently to questions of political process and institutional design: who should participate, how much should they know, and how should disputes be resolved and by what ultimate authority? The answers to these questions (lead) in the end to widely divergent policies for managing the same technological hazards (Jasanoff, 1986:79).

Jasanoff identified West Germany as a political system which accepted the advice and scientific justification of officially appointed expert scientific groups, free of nonscientific issues. Britain and Canada were both dealing with the same issues (alleged carcinogens) in a more mixed mode of scientists and administrators so that "public policy" or "national interest" considerations played a part--but secretly, within government departments and their expert advisory committees. This method reduces public controversy and (possibly also) interest group activity, leaving the government to take action without the need for full scientific validation of its policy position (as a scientist-dominated mode would require). Thus, the Canadian government banned urea-formaldehyde as unhealthy without extensive scientific debate as to its carcinogenicity. The British government introduced control on the product, also without publishing a full scientific critique. In the U.S., procedures requiring more extensive public review and quasi-judicialized adversarial principles were adopted. Extensive publicity and participation, particularly by well-organized and powerful commercial interests, attended these procedures. Perhaps for this reason, decisive regulatory action was not taken. As Jasanoff sums up, the dilemma lies between trusting the scientists to act against a hazardous substance (but never knowing quite what they are doing or which policy interests may be partly interfering with them) and trusting in open and democratic debate (which may produce stalemate between purely political forces rather than between reasonable scientific judgments).

Both rigid, adversarial methods and private negotiations (with their potential for powerful groups to dominate or incorporate others) have their weaknesses. Open, formal adversarial methods may offer more expressive satisfactions and more symbolic rewards to nonexpert participants who have their day in court even though nothing much happens afterwards. This may be particularly attractive in a political culture based upon principles of open participation and freedom of speech as in the U.S. case. But quiet progress behind closed doors (if any progress is actually achieved) may appeal to more distanced publics (for example, labor union members) who may be more deferential towards how things are done and who simply want "redress of grievance," to use an old English phrase. The ideal, Jasanoff suggests, is the intervenor culture where nonexpert and non-elite interests can intervene, participate, see some progress made, and then revert to their normal private concerns if they are broadly satisfied. This notion is very similar to Almond and Verba's sequence of citizen "disinterest-involvement-influence-withdrawal" (Almond and Verba, 1963).

Jasanoff comes down rather on the side of negotiation as against adversarial presentation, at least on the question of the balance of advantage. She is skeptical of claims, sometimes emanating from West European systems, that multi-interest negotiations (for example, labor and employers, or labor, employers, and consumers committees) can often achieve a true concensus. The result, she notes, often is standing, institutionalized conflict which has to be managed year by year as different issues arise. The more European style of private or semi-public negotiation does have real strength. A major condition for its success, however, is that values and preferences rather than facts should be the main subject for negotiation. An example from the U.S. is the informal talks involving the industry, environmental groups, unions, and customers in 1985 on reforms to U.S. pesticide laws (see Bosso, 1987).

Success requires that some common ground on policy exists. It must be recognized all around that negotiations are not a zero sum game but may result in shared benefits beyond what each party could achieve from their own stated position alone. The official regulators should probably signal certain "limits to the game," to keep negotiations more focused by ruling out marginal options. If they also offer the prize of desired progress if agreement is reached and the threat of a long stony road lying ahead if it is not, then negotiation may succeed. Finally, if they have power to impose a decision, official regulators should be sure that negotiating parties fully understand this as it will help to concentrate their minds. This is virtually impossible in the U.S.: ". . . unilateral action is circumscribed by legal requirements that all viewpoints be considered and that explanations be provided for selecting a particular course of action" (Jasanoff, 1986:67).

Interaction and Negotiation Among Government Agencies

When two or more different legal consents are required for construction and operation of a new and hazardous plant , the interested public may benefit from public interaction between the official and formal processes by which such consents are obtained. One process may overlay the other or rub against it to produce official friction and thus some public enlightenment. The public officials responsible will try to negotiate these legal procedures without any threat of bumps or ungainly manoeuvres but they do not always succeed. A degree of chaos may result. A case in point is nuclear power siting in the U.S., which appears to outsiders to be endlessly tossed between and among utilities, public interest groups, state and federal regulators, and various levels of courts. But even much simpler versions of plural "licensing" for a major hazardous project--such as may be found in Britain's procedures--can quite dramatically open up previously secretive and wholly unpublicized procedures.

This is very much the case if even a touch of high politics from the national level is brought to bear. This was well illustrated in Britain in 1977 and in 1983-85, involving two unprecedented and highly controversial nuclear power projects: the fuel rod reprocessing plant at Windscale (now renamed Sellafield) and the first British PWR station (of the Westinghouse type as modified for greater safety) at Sizewell. Both projects' nature and design were new to the Nuclear Installation's Inspectorate and both underwent long public inquiries before gaining their land-use planning consents. The Windscale inquiry lasted for 100 days and the Sizewell inquiry for 340. At the time, the Windscale inquiry seemed very long and elaborate, perhaps because the strain on the volunteers attempting to mount an adequate objection to the reprocessing project was great. And 100 days was then a record length. But the parallel and secret process by which the NII agreed to license the reprocessing plant did not obtrude into the public inquiry. The *ad hoc*-appointed inspector conducting the inquiry (a High Court judge) heard the safety evidence of the scheme's promoter, British Nuclear Fuels, Ltd. (a government-owned company) and declared that he preferred to accept it rather than the objectors' safety evidence. The judge was uninterested in the quality of either NII's analysis of BNFL's safety case or in that of NII's proposed methods of monitoring and improving safety once their site and operating licenses were issued and the plant was working. As these matters were provided for under a different Act from his inquiry's basis (the Town and Country Planning Act) he no doubt considered them to be beyond his remit (Parker, 1978; Wynne, 1982).

When another *ad hoc* inspector (a distinguished planning lawyer) approached the same matters in 1983-8 at Sizewell, he took a bolder view. He reasoned that he needed to know how NII would do its work on issuing licenses and how it would relate to the operation once the PWR station was working. If he did not discover this he could not report that he was satisfied on the safety issue, as required by his formal remit for his inquiry on behalf of the Department of Energy. He did not seek to second-guess the NII's technical judgments but he did insist on learning, at a public hearing, exactly how they were preparing to address them. Their standards, guidelines, preferences, criteria for coming to a positive judgment on the PWR's safety must therefore be laid out in public. The touch of "high politics" on Sizewell, which was lacking at the time of Windscale (although it was very politically controversial) came from the Government who made it clear that safety was to be a major feature of the Sizewell inquiry. In asking the NII to give extensive evidence to his inquiry and generally to invest thousands of staff hours of effort on matters which lie under a different Act, the inspector, Sir Frank Layfield, QC, carried a good deal of political weight as the Government's emissary. One unprecedented touch was a promise in the Conservative Government's manifesto of policies and pledges for the 1983 general election that a re-elected Conservative administration would not give legal consent to the PWR at Sizewell unless the inspector (not merely the government) had found it to be safe (Layfield, 1987).

In this dramatic case, the political publicity surrounding the Layfield inquiry and the political authority which Layfield was seen to carry (on the safety issue in particular) did not merely flood the NII licensing process with unaccustomed light. It ploughed it up and left the NII to replant it under the scrutiny of the Department of Energy, interested professional and specialist groups in the nuclear industry and among the public, as well as that of the Layfield inquiry.

The NII's safety licensing is done in secret without right of appeal to any other authority, such as the government. For many years the licensee operators were the Central Electricity Generating Board (in England and Wales) and the South of Scotland Electricity Board plus British Nuclear Fuels Limited with respect to nuclear reprocessing; they are now two government-owned companies, Nuclear Electric and Scottish Nuclear, plus BNFL. An appeal procedure could open up the process, even possibly involving public hearings of some kind. Neither the NII, the licensees, nor the government want such an outcome, although that is close to what they got at the hands of the Layfield inquiry into Sizewell's PWR. The result is that private bargaining between professional experts is the preferred style--very much in line with many other professionalized exchanges in British public affairs when they can manage it without public "interference" (Vogel, 1986; Friedson, 1986; Manning, this volume). The Sizewell public inquiry constituted massive interference in the private processes these professionals had developed over the years. For the first time, as O'Riordan puts it, "it had to be opened up to public scrutiny. This put the NII on its toes and forced it to justify its whole approach to safety assessment" (O'Riordan, 1987:208).

The scale of this work is worth noting. The CEGB was obliged to spend some 20 m pounds on design work and 200m pounds on computing effort (at around 1986 prices) merely to produce the Preconstruction Safety Report in order to gain NII consent in time to benefit from a government decision to go ahead with Sizewell. This document encompassed the whole safety case for the reactor, and much other work was done outside its own confines in order to bring it forward as the principal source.

Sizewell had a novel type of witness, invited by the inspector rather than retained by any of the adversarial inquiry parties (CEGB and its various critics such as Friends of the Earth). These official witnesses gave evidence on subjects that the inspector wished to explore further; for example, Sir Alastair Frame on the management problems of constructing the nuclear station efficiently.

O'Riordan summarizes his view of the U.K. system for nuclear licensing as being professionalized, self-regulating, technically grounded, and divided into four camps: the manufacturers of equipment; its operators; the license authority; and the nuclear engineering, etc., academic community. It is a crucial feature of the British system that the operator is responsible in law for safety. The operator is not merely required to meet standards laid down by an outside regulator but also to consider the constant task of promoting safety on a daily basis. Thirdly, there is continual monitoring of plant and of ways of improving safety standards by the regulator, the NII. The industry provides independent lines of communication between safety experts inside the stations and the regulators, without passing through the main lines of management. This further helps to maintain the standing of safety without becoming dominated by production values (as is the general British perception of the U.S. industry, not to mention other nuclear industries elsewhere).

The drawbacks of the British system centre on the familiar British disease of too much secrecy. Until recently, there has been a lack of third party independent expert review. There is, secondly, a lack of civil service checks on interpretations of technical material before ministers are briefed and policy positions decided upon, despite the dearth of technical expertise within the ranks of the senior officials or of ministers themselves. Thirdly, senior officials in the government's Department of Energy have withheld independent technical advice from outside experts, including academics, from the CEGB and SSB as operators (and certainly have withheld it from the public) when the processes of peer discussion would have benefited from sharing such material.

Public Involvement in Advice Processes

I have argued that public attitudes rest on perceptions of risks from hazardous projects and from judgments of personal costs and benefits in participating formally in the official proceedings to investigate and recommend (or simply report) upon it. Only a small proportion of the public goes so far as to register as objectors at such inquiries. However, participation in demonstrations may reach several thousand. This occurred, for example, with respect to Britain's nuclear stations at Sizewell (now building) and Hinkley (officially consented to by the British government in September, 1990). Most objectors simply filled in a printed postcard with their "grounds for objection" preprinted by one of the local or national anti-nuclear groups fighting the project: virtually a petition. This activity, carried out in local pubs, churches, or other social organizations in the rural areas where nuclear stations are located, serves to spread the word against the project and to make propaganda from the appearance of thousands of formal objections. Public opinion poll evidence often adds to this picture.

Of the thousands of objectors to a major project such as a nuclear station, only a few dozen will appear personally at the hearings stage of a public inquiry. Some of these will formally represent members of protest groups which have formed specifically to fight the project (the fire brigade groups) or an established association which opposes a project as just one of its current concerns. Often these two groups are run by the same people locally and they combine their input into the inquiry by putting up a single witness. They may well also combine financially to hire a lawyer or other professional to be their advocate or expert adviser and, in particular, their skilled cross-examiner of at least some of the promoter's technical witnesses.

For the few local objectors who speak at public hearings, this novel and often intimidating experience is only a part of their political campaign. Raising consciousness and raising funds--the two being often synonymous: "I give, therefore I agree"--is the main work which goes on prior to and after a public inquiry.

Valuable data on participation in public hearings and other protest activities have been reported recently from the U.S. In a major, innovative public attitude survey, Gould and his colleagues compared both the general public and environmental activists in the states of Connecticut and Arizona (Gould, et al., 1988). This sophisticated survey studied "expressed preferences" (as opposed to people's "revealed preferences;" see above) toward nuclear power and the transport and disposal of industrial chemicals, the handling of nuclear weapons, policy on handgun ownership, automobile use, and commercial air travel. Respondents' perceptions of the benefits of these aspects of modern life and notions of acceptable risk and personal risk-management strategies were also studied.

The general public--and even the much smaller attentive public on environmental and risk issues--are ill-informed on actual death rates from different types of risk activity such as operating nuclear stations, coal mines, or the mass use of cars. People tend to ascribe risk to things such as nuclear power accidents that almost never happen because of their potentially disastrous or even cataclysmic effects if they ever did happen. Coal miners and road users, by contrast, die every day but in a large number of mainly individual accidents.

Because the more horrendous type of potential accident is a remote prospect and because daily deaths from more familiar kinds of accidents are spread thinly over the country and are routinized, the general public accords low saliency to different types and levels of risk. Gould, et al., also surveyed samples of people who had spoken at public hearings in Connecticut or Arizona for or against proposed hazardous projects (principally nuclear power in Connecticut, where half the electricity is nuclear). These small minorities know more and hold stronger beliefs than does the mass public. Connecticut and Arizona are compared, as are their two general and two special publics and the two camps within each of these special publics--the broadly "pro-safety" group and the "pro-benefits" group speaking at the public hearings.

The study selected its active or special public on risk issues from those who had given testimony at a public hearing into such matters. This highly specific and novel activity is only one among many aspects of political behavior on public issues and is not necessarily seen as the most important. Both the general public respondents and these public hearing intervenors were asked whether they had taken some nine other specified actions apart from giving testimony on each of six risk-related subjects (nuclear power, handguns, etc.): letter-writing (or telephone or telegram) to an editor, a company, or an elected or appointed public official; petition signing; petition circulating; voting for or against a candidate partly, at least, on the basis of this issue; attending a hearing or group meeting; boycotting a company's products; joining or giving money to an organization; attending a public demonstration; or joining in a lawsuit.

Within this elaborate context of activities, giving testimony at an official public hearing or equivalent forum proved to be a very unusual action. In nearly all six policy fields in both states, the experience of having spoken at a public hearing is the second most rare. Lawsuit experience was rarest, although circulating a petition was, overall, hardly more common than speaking at hearings. Sending a letter, telegram, or phone call on an issue was relatively common but, except for one Connecticut figure concerning car travel, nowhere exceeded 4.4%.

Conclusion

There will probably never be a bridging of the divide between expert and general citizen perceptions of risk, or of the merits of hazardous projects. Douglas and Wildavsky's (1982) approach may be, as some critics have suggested, unhelpfully tautologous in emphasizing how different social contexts "select" different types and levels of perceived risk (see, also, Hargreaves-Heap, 1986). To the extent that more hierarchical and formal social contexts promote optimistic and insensitive perceptions of potential risk (while more diffused, open ones do the opposite), however, little consensus between the many publics and the pro-development technology elite camps is likely to occur. Only favourably disposed publics are candidates for agreement, and Western society--perhaps all the world--appears to be moving steadily away from hierarchy and authority towards a more questioning and critical stance concerning many risks.

The more socially critical and risk-perceiving members of the public will continue to see the forces promoting new hazards (whether they are state agencies or private sector firms) as aggressive, unfeeling and dangerous. Efforts by promoters to express abstruse estimates of risk in less opaque forms than, say 10^{-6}, as recommended by the British government in a broad environmental policy statement of September, 1990 (DOE, 1990) will probably make little difference to anyone. Such coming together between elite hazard promoters and hazard resistors as there may be is likely to rest on shared decision advice processes. Between these rival camps there is a gulf: available knowledge on hazards is inadequate and consensus is lacking (Douglas and Wildavsky, 1982, Chart A). Being both contested and uncertain in form, the issue is insoluble. No extra information will, by itself, stimulate agreement on the values involved in the issue. The assumption, by scientists and technologists, that "more information" to the public on contested issues such as nuclear power will ensure conflict reduction is, alas, incorrect (see Nelkin and Pollack, 1979).

Decision advice processes will also not bring consensus where conflict reigns--that is where both "the facts" and the values embedded in an issue of hazard and risk are contested. Perhaps, modestly or symbolically, these processes can serve as mediating devices (Bingham, 1986). They usually serve, at least, to establish what facts and analytical methods are agreed upon or accepted by both sides to a conflict, and thus to identify more precisely the bases of continuing disagreement. They are informative and legitimating for governments and expressively satisfying for many local objectors and other testifying citizens. For more policy-oriented objector groups, hearings and other investigations are of central importance in illuminating the scene. With luck, they may also seriously jeopardize the chances of government and investor approval and even project construction.

12

Rational Reconstructions of
Energy Choices in France

James M. Jasper

Making sense of history is one of the most important things humans do. Out of the chaos of individual and collective experiences, all societies must decide what to forget and what to remember, what to imitate and what to avoid, what (and whom) to blame and what to honor. This work--part mythmaking, part history writing, part individual choices--shapes our own identities, society's distribution of resources, and our sense of the possible and the desirable. All human projects depend on an image of the past, even in societies that are said-- usually by Western historians--to lack history. As Milan Kundera wrote in *The Book of Laughter and Forgetting*: "The struggle of man against power is the struggle of memory against forgetting...The only reason people want to be masters of the future is to change the past. They are fighting for access to the laboratories where photographs are retouched and biographies and histories rewritten."

Choices between technologies rarely have mythic dimensions, yet they are subject to the same retrospective reworking into coherence that all other experience is. When created by groups and individuals sympathetic to the original actors, this work most often takes the form of "rational reconstructions." I mean to imply both that there is a retrospective effort to make sense of what happened, and that this effort portrays the decision making process to be calculated and rational. Most often, these reconstructions have direct political implications: what is said to have succeeded in the past should be used in the future.

The immense power brought to bear on the interpretation of past experiences challenges the student of technological choice: how to separate the rational reconstruction of the actors from the actual--usually messy--processes by which one technology replaced others? Because power in one sphere of social life can usually be transferred to other spheres, the same actors who were responsible for the choice of a technology typically also influence the rational reconstruction of their own choice. In recent years historians have learned to listen to the voices of the losers in history, in order to see how winners have written history to their own advantage. Similar trends in philosophy and literary criticism have discovered how language itself contains traces of alternatives, of dissent, of suppressed perspectives. Social scientists, alas, especially those who study technology, have yet to perfect these skills.

In the struggle over the meanings of history, political, economic, and administrative elites have immense advantages over the rest of us. Greater wealth and power, the long memory of bureaucracies, personal ties to intellectual elites, and various controls over cultural institutions: all these help them spread their own version of events. In contrast to rulers of the past and many celebrities of the present, contemporary economic and political elites--that combination of public and private experts and bureaucrats often dubbed technocrats--typically rewrite history to hide their own role. They normally shun publicity, hidden in their skyscrapers, boardrooms, and government office buildings. We watch the antics of elected officials while we ignore the administrative bureaucrats behind them. Elites' greatest strength is the ability to cover their own tracks, to hide their own influence, to set the terms of a debate before the rest of us know there is a debate. Everyone knows the truism that history is written by the winners, but how do they pull this off?

French energy policy is one case of extremely effective rational reconstruction.[1] In fifteen years, the dramatic battles and intense dilemmas of the 1970s have disappeared into the abyss, replaced--in official policy statements, the news media, and even much scholarly work--by a straightforward, rational account of why France (elites love to speak of their country as a unitary whole) had to embrace nuclear energy. Dissenters, lacking funds and a forum, have been almost powerless to tell an alternative tale. The French energy elite--in both state bureaucracies and private companies--has not only persuaded the French population, which now heartily favors nuclear energy, but has neatly packaged the story for export in the form of "lessons" from the French nuclear experience.

Constructing the Myth

The narrative they have constructed begins with poor little France, lacking energy resources of its own, buffeted by the winds of international oil markets.

---

1. This story is documented more fully in Jasper, 1990.

Before OPEC quadrupled oil prices at the end of 1973, France had experimented cautiously with several nuclear reactor designs, found the most economical one (the American light water design), and begun a commercial line based on it. When the oil crisis struck, top politicians realized that the only way to avoid economic disaster was a maximal industrial effort to deploy nuclear plants. The Messmer Plan of 1974 settled on one standardized design for both the reactor and the plant surrounding it, and redirected capital to attain a program of several dozen reactors in a decade or two. Although some soft heads were suspicious of a risky technology, the "hard facts"--both economic and technical--were so clear that no major politicians opposed the plan. In this reconstruction of events, elites may be congratulated for their accurate foresight, but they were really just responding in the only rational way to the available data.

French politicians, executives, and bureaucrats have assiduously spread this legend. Jean Guilhamon, Director of France's national electric utility *Electricité de France* (EDF), gave a speech to the American Nuclear Society in 1983. "Indeed, for us, there were few choices: France had no oil or gas, and the coal from its own fields was too expensive and insufficient in quantity. New forms of energy (solar, wind, tidal, etc.) would, then and now, require many years of research and development, with no certainty as to the result. Only nuclear power, with the mastery acquired by the French Atomic Energy Commission at the end of the 1950s, held out any promise of a dependable supply of adequate quantities of energy sheltered from the fluctuations of the international market." Elites often hide their tracks by claiming they have no discretion, but merely respond to the unalterable givens of the situation: resource availability, the state of technology, markets. When elites write history, they often deny there is such a thing as technological choice.

Tensions Within the State

But in the mid 1970s France's nuclear future was still up for grabs, highly contested, not only between factions of French political and economic elites, but between these elites and a variety of external opponents. Even before the oil crisis there had been conflicts and choices. One in the late 1960s was over reactor designs. The American light water reactor, based on highly enriched uranium, was not definitively cheaper than the indigenous French line based on natural uranium; rather, the battle between them pitted the organizational interests of EDF against those of the nuclear regulator, the *Commissariat à l'Energie Atomique* (CEA). De Gaulle had favored the French line, as his image of national independence involved technological autonomy; Pompidou reversed the policy when he became President in 1969, as his image involved the ability to compete on international markets with the most fashionable product. The choices of both Presidents were based on personal inclinations, ideologies, and images of France's role in the world, not--as policymakers have since reworked it--on technical comparisons of costs, benefits, and risks.

In the early 1970s another conflict occurred within the political elite, pitting the "nucleocrats"--EDF, its regulator (and this time its ally), and the Ministry of Industry--against the Finance Ministry. EDF and its allies wanted to build as many nuclear reactors as possible, while the Finance Ministry saw little or no economic justification for such a program. The result was stalemate: a modest program to gain industrial and commercial experience. These conflicts within the elite were largely hidden to public view, and, again, were driven by organizational interests and contrasting beliefs, not a unified rationality shared by all French policymakers.

The oil crisis brought energy issues to public attention in the months following October 1973, as oil prices skyrocketed. Desiring a bold move when presidential elections were probably only months away (Pompidou was already gravely ill), Prime Minister Pierre Messmer announced his nuclear plan in March 1974. Thirteen reactors would be ordered immediately, more would follow, and by the year 2000 nuclear power would meet half of France's total energy needs. This rate of deployment was Messmer's assessment of the maximum effort French industry could make. One large manufacturer was assigned to produce steam turbines for the nuclear plants, and the subsidiary of another to build the reactors. Because speed was the overriding consideration, most elements of plant design were to be standardized. By December potential sites had been chosen for most of the planned reactors.

The tension between the economic perspective at the Finance Ministry (wait for energy prices to rise and demand to fall) and the engineering perspective of the nucleocrats (build as much physical generating capacity as possible) had to be settled by the country's top politicians. The policy bureaucrats themselves were too divided over the issue. Messmer consulted few people in formulating his final plan, and certainly few economists. To a large extent he merely unleashed EDF's ambitions for a huge nuclear commitment. As nuclear power replaced fossil fuels, EDF's electricity would penetrate hitherto forbidden markets--especially space heating, not a terribly efficient use of electricity--of its sister company Gaz de France. Once again, energy policy was driven by organizational interests rather than what was rational for French society.

Public Controversy

Before the oil crisis the French antinuclear movement consisted largely of local opponents fighting specific proposed sites, but the Messmer Plan inspired something that almost no other country had: the antinuclear movement developed a moderate, technically sophisticated wing that was not unalterably opposed to nuclear technology, only to its present shape. One cluster of opponents, centered around the *Confédération Française Démocratique du Travail* (CFDT) trade union, consisted of researchers from universities, the electric utility, and state nuclear research laboratories. They felt too little was known about the new American reactor design for such extensive deployment. Another strand in the moderate opposition consisted of economists who continued to find a diverse mix of energy options--especially conservation--preferable to single-minded concentration on one source and one technical design. They also recognized that cost calculations were based on too many arbitrary assumptions to clinch the case for nuclear, and worried about the domestic and external effects of borrowing for such a large capital investment. These economists were not marginal people: many were at the Institute for Economic and Juridical Studies of Energy, one of France's most respected think tanks on the economics of energy; another was head (although not for long) of economic forecasting at EDF itself; a third was director of the econometrics laboratory at the prestigious *Ecole Polytechnique* (from which most of the top nuclear engineers had graduated). Even administrative--and especially intellectual--elites contributed members to the antinuclear movement.

The less technical but more visible segment of the antinuclear movement, favoring large demonstrations, site occupations, and ecology candidates, was larger than its counterpart in the United States or most other European countries in the 1970s. It also grew steadily after the Messmer announcement. 10,000 attended a Paris bicycle rally in March 1974; 26,000 submitted written comments to oppose the Blayais reactor in December; by July 1977, 60,000 protestors were ready to occupy the site of the new breeder reactor at Creys-Malville, despite heavy rains. Power lines, construction buildings, the reactor itself at Fessenheim, EDF offices, and even the apartment of EDF's director were all bombed. When EDF Assistant Director Remy Carle said, in a *New York Times* (8 May 1989) interview, "The nuclear issue in France was never a political one," he was distorting the truth. Until 1979, according to virtually all surveys conducted, public opinion in France was more antinuclear than in the United States.[2] Contrary to later revisions, the controversy was hot in the mid 1970s.

Rather than trying to use the moderate wing of the antinuclear movement to defuse public protest, the French state did its best to marginalize both segments. The riot police were sent in to break up site occupations, killing one and injuring one hundred at Creys-Malville in July 1977. At this event the "forces of order" systematically pursued protestors through the countryside and into neighboring villages, beating them and smashing the windshields of many cars with foreign license plates. The movement quickly abandoned such protests.

---

2. I compare French, Swedish, and American attitudes toward nuclear energy in Jasper, 1988.

The moderates were treated similarly, if not violently. They were accused of being traitors and, along with the more radical protestors, were labeled "les marginaux." State elites closed ranks against all criticism, rejecting any calls for developing a safer reactor design, moderating the size of the program, or slowing the pace of deployment. Even so, some policymakers admitted in interviews in the late 1970s that they feared the extensive protest would probably curtail EDF's nuclear goals.

Opposition political parties also had reservations about the government program. While few politicians questioned nuclear energy in general (few did in any country, including the United States), the Left lambasted the Messmer Plan as a profitable boondoggle for private industry. In the presidential elections of 1981, three antinuclear candidates (two of them from small leftist parties) won enough votes in the first round--7.2%--to affect the outcome of the second round, which Mitterand won by 3.5%. Even the Socialists signed a petition against the Messmer Plan after the Three Mile Island accident in 1979. A sizable minority of Socialist Party deputies were against nuclear energy, but they were abruptly silenced after the party came to power in 1981. Party leaders such as François Mitterrand and Jean-Pierre Chevènement threatened the collapse of the government if members of their own party proposed antinuclear policies and reports. The antinuclear movement Right collapsed into oblivion, so that there was no one to resist the revising of history by state bureaucrats and industry representatives.

When the Three Mile Island accident occurred in March 1979, French politicians were quick to go on television and assure citizens that "It could not happen here." This claim was false. A virtually identical accident could certainly happen in France. The French, indeed, did not believe what their leaders told them. In a poll, only 20 percent believed they had been told the whole truth about the accident, and only 13 percent believed a similar accident could *not* happen in France. Nevertheless, polls show that nuclear power became more popular in France after TMI and has continued to gain support since then. Invidious comparisons with American inadequacy appealed to French national pride; nuclear energy began to be seen as a French success story.

Fateful Choices

In several French government agencies, arguments in favor of conservation as an alternative to a large nuclear commitment continued to surface and be suppressed. An agency was established in 1974 to develop and promote energy-saving practices and new technologies. Even though it was supported by the Ministry of Finance (still not convinced of the economic sense of such a large nuclear program), EDF managed to block all its efforts. When the Socialists came to power in 1981, a new agency made some headway with conservation and efficiency, but France never invested the research funds in renewables and efficiency that other countries did. They invested even less than the United States. At every step, French policymakers faced choices--and were divided-- between more than one rational option, always taking the pronuclear path. Yet today they insist they had no choice.

Policymakers chose pronuclear energy paths because EDF managed to outmaneuver other bureaucracies, imposing its own agenda on the rest of the state. Top decisionmakers at the Ministry of Industry were enchanted by nuclear energy for reasons having to do with their common training at the *Ecole Polytechnique*, in mathematics, in broad problem-solving, in large technical systems. Top politicians jumped on the bandwagon as national pride and state power became associated with the nuclear program. Could the French handle a complex technology that the Americans could not? Did the French state have the power to impose its energy policy on society, or did "the marginals" have the power to stop it?

The nuclear elite became so obsessed with nuclear expansion that it built more reactors than were economically efficient. Nuclear-generated electricity had to be used more and more for space heating, a policy that fit with EDF's expansion but was not altogether efficient. Excess electricity had to be exported to surrounding countries; exports are now around ten percent of total production. The industrial capacity for reprocessing spent nuclear fuel has been put in place, even though it is widely thought to be uneconomical. The economists who suggested waiting, on the grounds that electric demand growth would slow, turn out to have been right. Surprisingly, however, economic efficiency continues to be a central tenet in the current rationale for nuclear power.

Public policies, especially concerning new technologies, often have to be chosen before all the information is in. No one knew how expensive nuclear energy would turn out to be when the Messmer decision was made in 1974.[3] EDF and reactor manufacturers predicted costs would fall rapidly due to the economies of scale from a large commitment; as in the United States, French costs have risen steadily (though not as much as in the U.S.). The economics of reprocessing were uncertain; now they are almost certainly unfavorable. Most of all, future electric demand was uncertain. This alone might have been reason to pause, reason to maintain flexibility. Huge, expensive nuclear plants provide little flexibility. Yet decisions were made on the basis of nucleocrats' and

---

3. Much of the French enthusiasm for nuclear power was based, not on American experience with the light water reactor, but on inflated expectations of American manufacturers and utilities. For example, the French were given an estimate of 146 dollars per kwe for the Diablo Canyon nuclear power plant; when the plant came on line, its costs were almost 3,000 dollars per kwe. See Bupp and Derian, 1978.

politicians' assumptions about the way the world works. The top French elite, heavily influenced by the engineers from the prestigious *Corps des Mines* and *Corps des Ponts et Chausées* who populate the management of the Industry Ministry and nuclear agencies, believed that large-scale technology would inevitably have good consequences.

One surprising outcome is the extent to which the choices made by the French elite in 1974 have reshaped French political and economic contexts so as to make those choices look more reasonable. Public opinion has become more favorable. The costs of nuclear plants have not risen as fast as in other countries. Financial structures have been created to provide the necessary capital. Political elites and the news media can now portray the antinuclear movement as a case of mistaken idealism, for there are few antinuclear organizations to dispute the revised history. Today nuclear energy is probably France's cheapest option for producing electricity. One reason is that the nuclear commitment has prevented full recognition of the energy resources available through conservation, as EDF and the nuclear industry have silenced the policy recommendations from agencies charged with promoting energy efficiency. (In all cases, the opposite has happened in the United States, as our nuclear industry has collapsed under its own mistakes, souring public opinion and suggesting the need for conservation and other energy sources.) Because the current nuclear commitment in France appears uncontroversial and rational, it is easy for elites to claim it has always been this way. By the 1990s, economic, political, and technological structures-- which elites themselves had constructed--have hardened, taking away some of the earlier flexibility. This rigidity makes it easier for the same elites to deny having ever had choices to make.

French energy decisions of the 1970s were never simply a rational response to "exogenous" factors such as the state of technology, available resources, and market prices of oil. They have always been, and always will be, driven by bureaucratic interests and conflicting belief systems, even within political and economic elites. Yet, because nuclear energy today looks like a reasonable choice for France (if one can accept the daunting idea that occasional catastrophes are worth the regular benefits, and the rising popularity of nuclear power seems to show that most French citizens do), the elites get away with saying that is *why* those decisions were made. They project far too much rationality back fifteen years.

Exporting the Myth

Members of the French elite are not shy about packaging and presenting their experience with nuclear energy as a model for others to follow. Here pride in their own skills--and a desire to show that they are more clever than American managers and politicians--conflicts with the strategy of hiding their own discretion behind a cloud of facts that, they claim, determined their actions.

One set of lessons deals with political conflict.[4] The boldest revision of history is to deny that France had political conflict over nuclear energy. Nuclear energy may be hopeless with a public as ignorant as the American. Remy Carle of EDF says, "The public has to say what it thinks, and you cannot impose nuclear power" (although this is precisely what the French did). Others admit there was resistance, but point to French legal frameworks that kept protest from interfering with "economic rationality." The unfortunate implication is that regulation should provide less opportunity for public participation, that delays should not be allowed because they increase costs, and that policymakers must be free to respond flexibly and rationally to price changes such as those from the oil crisis in 1973. In their advice, the French misunderstand the American experience, for it was not antinuclear protestors that hurt nuclear power, but managerial incompetence and high costs.[5]

Another "lesson" is that American regulators should cooperate with nuclear utilities rather than (so the claim goes) harassing and punishing them. A cooperative system has worked well in France, more because of EDF's high management standards than because of cooperation per se. American regulators and utilities have often cooperated, usually to circumvent stringent safety regulations or to license a plant, not to improve performance and safety. American utility management must be improved directly, and utilities that cannot be improved must be excluded from nuclear energy. Giving more flexibility to bad managers is hardly the policy the United States needs.

French spokespersons most often point to the high level of standardization of reactors and plants as the reason nuclear plants are cheaper and safer in France than the United States. (French plants probably are cheaper and safer, although the evidence on safety is far from decisive.) In this way they can tell a story of rational choices based on apparently incontrovertible physical evidence. They forget that American reactors were ordered in the 1960s and very early 1970s, while most French reactors were ordered after 1974. Reactor designs were more refined by 1974, so that standardization seemed a more reasonable option for the French. Even so, their reason for extreme standardization was speed of deployment more than costs or safety. And standardization on one design was very risky even after 1974, for a hidden flaw could--even today--disable the whole system. Technical and economic rationality did not absolutely demand standardization in either country; in the United States in the 1960s it may even have precluded standardization.

---

4. All the following lessons can be found in their least refined form in an NBC documentary, "Nuclear Power: In France It Works," broadcast March 11, 1987.

5. Even *Forbes* Magazine points the finger at bad management in Cook, 1985.

Few of these lessons are appropriate for the United States. The best American utilities have recently completed nuclear plants as cheaply as EDF, so there is nothing in our system that prevents success. It is managerial problems within individual utilities that raise costs and cause accidents. The danger is that our nuclear industry will use the French "lessons" to reduce regulation--a step sure to increase management problems in American utilities, not solve them. The rewriting of history in another country may have unfortunate fallout in our own, for American manufacturers and many policymakers are anxious to listen to the revisions.

Conclusion: How Reconstructions Succeed

Why have French elites succeeded in their efforts to rewrite nuclear history? If any country has a technocracy--an elite of capitalists and state officials who rule through the use of educational credentials and technical knowledge and rhetoric--it is France. This elite is perhaps more arrogant, more confident in its decisions, and more insulated from public pressures than in most countries. Other elites also attempt to rewrite history, but the French elite may be better situated to succeed. The timing was also right for this revision. Mitterrand has blurred the old ideological divide between the French Left and Right, so both were open to a rewriting of history that portrayed objective, technical factors-- rather than ideology--as the driving force behind policy decisions. Administrators of both Left and Right like to claim they are responding rationally to "hard facts." This revised history has also worked because so many French take pride in their country's technical accomplishments; nuclear energy may be a better national symbol than the expensive, inefficient *Concorde*. Then there is the rationalization that occurs once a decision seems irreversible. People learn to live with it. It is hard to live downwind from a nuclear reactor you believe is dangerous; life is more comfortable if you reduce cognitive dissonance by deciding the reactor is safe.

American news media have bought the new French story for familiar reasons. The reporters covering the topic today are not those who were on it during the controversy fifteen years ago; they know little about nuclear energy; when they bother to travel to France they rely on interviews with utility executives and state bureaucrats. So they have never heard the other side. There are no longer antinuclear organizations that reporters can ask for comment, in traditional journalistic fashion of "on the one hand..." But American coverage of French nuclear energy has never been good. Political coverage has never been a strong suit in American news reporting from abroad. With French and American nuclear energy, the theme of a stark black and white contrast is too tempting a frame for an otherwise complex story. The French did what they had to, while the Americans mangled the job.

More puzzling is the acquiescence of scholars, not pressed by a deadline, in the elite reconstruction. The villain in this case may be the latest fashion in political analysis, structuralism. Serious students of politics do not doubt the importance of political and economic structures in shaping policies, positions, and decisions. However, driven by the desire to seem rigorous, analysts often puff these structures into the beginning and end of all explanations of politics: structures are said to determine who the contenders are, their abilities to push their goals, and the outcomes. Most contemporaries are not as explicit as the Marxist Louis Althusser, who proudly proclaimed that individuals are simply the "bearers" of structures, but individuals and their discretion, elites and their interests, nevertheless disappear under the weight of the structures. Scholars thus collaborate in the efforts of elites to hide their own tracks across history. Political and economic structures are certainly influential; but elites operate within them, and alter them, to attain their goals.

I end with a pair of conclusions, one academic and the other political. Scholars of technological choice must pay careful attention to the reconstructions given them by others, and they must create their own reconstructions--rarely portraits of a rational process--from a variety of sources. But they can fall into their own kind of trap, which consists of confusing descriptive and prescriptive analyses of technological choice. This has happened, I feel, in much risk analysis. A careful weighing of costs, benefits, and risks is a reasonable ideal for choosing between technologies, depending on how each of these is measured. But this prescription comes very close to the rational reconstructions offered by policymakers, who argue that this weighing was precisely what they did. Scholars should be concerned to show the divergence between real processes and rational ones.

My political conclusion is similar. Elites forever shape the world around us, imposing technologies and products and constraints that are hard to resist. But they are not all-powerful, and it is important to monitor what they do--and often to resist. To do this we must study how they usually win. It is also important, as writers and analysts, not to take away the reason for resisting. Once a technology appears inevitable, resistance seems pointless. But technologies are never inevitable. They are developed and deployed by groups and individuals for a variety of reasons. It is important to point to these people, and blame them when things go wrong. Blame allows moral outrage, and such outrage is often the proper response. In nuclear energy, things inevitably go wrong, devastating accidents happen. As Charles Perrow (1984) has shown, accidents are "normal" in such complex technologies. Let us not forget who deployed such a dangerous technology. Let us not allow elites to rewrite history altogether.

13

Regulating Risk: Implications of the Challenger Accident

Diane Vaughan

As the January 28, 1986 Challenger accident recedes into history, it is remembered as a technical failure. The fault lay in the O-rings. The primary O-ring and its back-up, the secondary O-ring, were designed to seal a tiny gap created by pressure at ignition in the aft field joint of the Solid Rocket Booster. The O-rings' resiliency was impaired by the unprecedented cold temperature that prevailed the morning of the launch. Upon ignition, hot propellant gases impinged upon the O-rings, creating a flame that penetrated first, the field joint, then the External Tank containing liquid hydrogen and oxygen (Report of the Presidential Commission, 1986; Report of the Committee on Science and Technology, House of Representatives, 1986).

The image retained in the collective American eye is that of a billowing cloud of smoke, from which emerged two white fingers tracing the diverging paths of the Solid Rocket Boosters across the sky. While that image has remained clear, the image of what happened on the ground in the months and years before the accident has begun to blur. Post-accident accounts by the Presidential Commission (1986), the House Committee on Science and Technology (1986), whistle-blowers (Boisjoly, 1987), and journalists (e.g., Broad, 1986; Bell and Esch, 1987) revealed the O-ring problems had a well-

I gratefully acknowledge a 1988-1989 fellowship from the American Bar Foundation, which provided a stimulating yet peaceful environment and the time necessary to do this work.

documented history within NASA. Earliest documentation appeared in 1977, nearly four years before the first shuttle flight in 1981 (Commission, 1986:122). Moreover, on the eve of the Challenger accident, concerned engineers argued against the launch on the grounds that the O-rings were a threat to flight safety.

Given this history, why did NASA officials proceed with the launch? The Presidential Commission identified a flawed decision making process at the space agency (1986:82-119). The Commission's report did not single out individual NASA managers; nonetheless, the report's implication was that both individuals and the NASA organization were to blame. Data on decision making in organizations prior to a technical system accident are rare. The Challenger accident provides a unique opportunity to explore the decision to launch and the structural factors that influenced that decision. The Commission's investigation produced a five volume report containing the entire verbatim testimony from the official hearings. In addition, these volumes contain Tables of Organization, documents generated by NASA and its contractors for internal purposes for years prior to the Challenger launch, and other information crucial for an organizational analysis. This information, along with other government documents, interviews with participants in the event, and written accounts of scientists, journalists, and whistle-blowers, permits analysis of the NASA organization's contribution to the technical failure.

Exploring the organizational contribution to technical failure has implications for regulating risky technologies. Policy designed to control some phenomenon is most successful when the cause of that phenomenon is known and understood, for the policy then can target the specific causes. The NASA/Challenger analysis suggests how strategies aimed at organizations might reduce technical system accidents.

NASA's Contribution to the Technical Failure

Analyzing decision making by focussing on the individual as unit of analysis fails to take into sufficient account the fact that individuals work in organizations. An individual's position in an organization affects the behavior of that person (Kanter, 1976; Zey-Ferrell and Ferrell, 1982). In turn, an organization's position in its environment affects organizational behavior. The connection between these structural factors and individual choice is, therefore, essential to an understanding of both. However, the complexity of environmental and organizational influences must be narrowed for research purposes to those bearing on specific individual choices.

The decision to launch the Challenger was influenced by:
1. the *competitive environment*;
2. *organizational characteristics*; and
3. the *regulatory environment*.

While each of these three factors is related to the decision to launch, each is necessary but not sufficient for understanding the roots of the accident. They are interrelated, in that the decision resulted from the three in combination.[1]

The Competitive Environment

All organizations require resources in order to survive. Essential resources are not limited to those ordinarily associated with economic success (profits, donations, government funding and other forms of revenue), but may include the means necessary to achieve economic goals:[2] for example, physical space for operations, customers and clients, members, sales territory, prestige, market entry, and/or raw materials for product development. An organization's ability to obtain necessary resources, however, may be constrained by the source, nature, and abundance of resources, by the behavior of other organizations in the environment, and by the resources already possessed by the organization and pre-existing demands on those resources (Pfeffer and Salancik, 1978:39-59; Hirschman, 1970:21-54). Because scarcity tends to be endemic, organizations are forced to compete in order to survive.

Moreover, competitive pressures seldom are reduced should an organization succeed in attaining its goals. Organizations are subject to rising expectations. Once a goal is achieved, a new one usually is established. Because scarcity and competition continue to raise the possibility that access to desired resources will be blocked (even for organizations apparently succeeding), tensions to attain them are continually generated (Vaughan, 1983:54-62).

Scarce resources plagued NASA's shuttle program from its inception (Congressional Quarterly, 1967; McConnell, 1987). NASA called in a think

---

1. These three factors constitute the major building blocks of an integrated theory of organizational misconduct (see Vaughan, 1983:54-104). The application of that theory to the NASA/Challenger case and other examples of misconduct in organizations that vary in size, complexity, and function is guided by the principles of Theory Elaboration. For the logic and rationale of Theory Elaboration, see Vaughan, 1992a; 1992b.

2. This conceptualization is a revision of Merton's "Social Structure and Anomie" schema (1968:185-214). Reconceptualizing both "means" and "ends" (whatever their material referent) as scarce resources for which organizations must compete has two advantages: 1) it escapes the troublesome theoretical and methodological confusions between means and ends for which Merton's theory repeatedly has been criticized (Cole, 1975; Lemert, 1964), and 2) it widens potential theoretical application to the behavior of diverse organizations, rather than only corporate profit-seekers. For details, see Vaughan, 1983:55-66; 84-87.

tank, Mathematica, Inc., to analyze these difficulties (Roland, 1985). Using data supplied by prospective shuttle contractors, Mathematica reported that the payload capacity would allow the vehicle to pay for itself, provided it had a launch rate of more than 30 flights a year, which was considered a conservative estimate in 1971. NASA was expecting 60 by 1985. Congress appropriated funds, but the program's achievement of military and scientific goals depended upon its success as a business.

But the shuttle never paid its own way. Cost estimates were off in the beginning, rose in unpredictable ways, and inflation had its effect. Add to these difficulties the development of new commercial satellite services in other countries (Overbye, 1985). NASA had to keep payload cost per pound down in order to compete. If the price were raised, NASA ultimately lost business, increasing the cost of each flight.

Like any organization confronting a similar business problem, NASA management responded to these environmental pressures with a concerted effort to attain the resources essential for survival. From the beginning, the shuttle program had been depicted as the space vehicle to make space operations "routine and economical" (Commission, 1986:164). Matching this image was a key to resources. Consequently, NASA emphasized a flight schedule that would attract both continued commercial payloads and continued Congressional approval. The greater the number of flights, the greater the degree of routinization and economy. The greater the routinization and economy, the greater the commercial appeal-- thus, the emphasis on schedule.

The effort to maintain the positive image that would continue to secure resources necessary for operation put further stress on the system. NASA was required to make system changes in order to support a re-useable fleet, and it was slow to develop these capabilities (Commission, 1986:165). Human and material resources devoted to any single flight were diluted. Inadequate replacements existed for parts that were damaged in flight, resulting in the "cannibalization of spare parts" from one vehicle to another in order to launch (Commission, 1986:173-174). Not only was this costly in terms of manpower, but it was disruptive and created opportunities for component damage during the transfers.

Furthermore, production pressures resulted in skimping on launch safety (*Time*, 9 June 1986:17; Diamond, 1986). The expensive redundancies that were built into the Apollo program were missing, for the shuttle had no room for luxuries. The crew escape system was scrapped (Roland, 1985:29); NASA trimmed 71% of its safety and quality control staff in the several years preceding the accident (*Time*, 9 June 1986:17). Yet management continued to rise to the challenge of an accelerated flight schedule, despite the fact that safety had been compromised and resources devoted to any single flight diluted. Threatened by scarcity and by competition for resources, NASA was a system under stress prior to the Challenger launch (Haas and Drabek, 1973:120; House Committee,

1986:116-119). The organization was experiencing environmentally produced production pressures with a limited capacity to meet those demands (Commission, 1986:176). Understanding how these factors affected internal decision making, ultimately culminating in the tragedy of January 28, 1986, calls for closer examination of the NASA organization.

Organization Characteristics: Structure, Processes, and Transactions

The Challenger mission (as all shuttle missions) was the product of an organizational structure that merged government and private enterprise. In addition to Morton Thiokol, Inc., the contractor for the Solid Rocket Booster, other contractors were responsible for the main engine, external tank, orbiter, system integration, and shuttle processing. Add to this picture NASA's own decentralized structure, which included NASA headquarters, the Office of Space Flight, Johnson Space Center, Kennedy Space Center, and Marshall Space Flight Center (Commission, 1986:226-231). These organizations combined in a loosely coupled system characterized by unique domains, technology, expertise, language, and geographic location.

The structure of organizations limits members' access to information. The components of specialization--division of labor between and within subunits, hierarchy, geographic dispersion, for example--segregate knowledge about tasks and goals. When organizations are large, no one individual or group can command all the knowledge pertaining to particular operations, materials, or technology. Efforts at coordination and control result: rules and procedures designed to handle the various internal problems that accompany complexity by specifying how, when, and by whom tasks are to be performed. Although directed toward integrating the separate parts of the organization, the potential for rules and procedures to achieve internal control varies considerably.

Structure interferes with the efforts of those at the top to "know" the behavior of others in the organization--and vice-versa (Tullock, 1964; Wilensky, 1967). The rules and procedures intended to facilitate systematic exchange of information seldom achieve perfect control. Decision making necessarily occurs in a world of incomplete information (Spence, 1974). Within an organization, transactions between subunits in a given day are many. This abundance results in information being *systematically censored* when relayed from subunit to subunit: that is, hierarchy, specialization, and technological developments systematically inhibit information exchange in the following ways.

In the interest of efficiency, complex issues are summarized for transmittal, causing some information to be dropped, never to be known to people in some parts of the organization. Rapidly changing technological developments also contribute, for news of such changes frequently lags behind the changes. Specialization and the technical language that accompanies it also interfere with the ability to know, for unless the receiver of information can recognize and interpret it, communication is not complete. Finally, the volume and diversity of daily internal transactions result in overwhelming paper accumulation on individual desks. Some transmittals never get read. Thus, some information, though transmitted, remains uncommunicated.

In the attempt to coordinate and control NASA's unwieldy system, rules and procedures routinized exchange between component parts. The overall effect was a "blizzard of paperwork" (*Time*, 9 June 1986:14): multiple transactions between units, on a daily basis, in highly technical language. Some NASA decision makers were inhibited from accurate assessment of the O-ring problem by virtue of systematic censorship of information resulting from hierarchy, specialization, and technological developments. Early in the O-ring problem history, some important information about the frequency and extensiveness of the problem and management actions taken in response was not passed on to upper level NASA administrators (Commission, 1986:134-138; 159).

Some information that *was* conveyed up the hierarchy was confounded by a changed technical status for the field joint. Documents bearing a Criticality designation indicating that the O-ring problem was not a threat to flight safety were in circulation along with documents bearing a designation it *was* a threat. As a result, some upper level administrators wrongly believed the O-rings were not a serious problem (Commission, 1986:128; 156-157).

Specialization sometimes interfered with communication because the recipient of information did not have the relevant expertise or the historic context with which to assess it. Consider the following quote from the Associate Administrator of Space Flight at NASA, reporting to the Commission about the pre-launch review for a July 1985 mission (1986:159):

> And then we had a Flight Readiness Review, I guess, in July, getting ready for a mid-July, a late July flight, and the action had come back from the project office. I guess the Level III had reported to the Level II Flight Readiness Review, and then they reported up to me that--they reported the two erosions on the primary (O-ring) and some 10 or 12 percent erosion on the secondary (O-ring) on that flight in April, and the corrective actions, I guess, that had been put in place was to increase the test pressure, I think, from 50 psi (pounds per square inch) to 200 psi or 100 psi--I guess it was 200 psi is the number--and they felt that they had run a bunch of laboratory tests and analyses that showed that by increasing the pressure up to 200 psi, this would minimize or eliminate erosion, and that there would be a fairly good degree of safety factor margin on the erosion as a result of increasing this pressure and ensuring that the secondary seal had been seated. And so we left the FRR (Flight Readiness Review) with that particular action closed by the project.

The Administrator concluded it was safe to fly. His frequent use of "I guess" and "I think" indicate a fair amount of uncertainty, however. More seriously, this quote reveals that his conclusion was based on misunderstanding. First, he believed the problem was fixed because of a "new" procedure (increasing the test pressure to 200 psi). In fact, this "new" procedure had been in use since the O-ring problems had become frequent (Commission, 1986:155; 159). Moreover, this pressure level, although essential for testing the joint, was suspected of weakening the putty used to seal the joint, *contributing* to the erosion problem.

The tendency for structure to affect knowledge and its distribution gives some insight into the launch decision. But structural exclusion does not completely explain the incident, for it does not account for the actions of those who had all the technical information and the expertise necessary to interpret and understand the consequences: those NASA middle managers who participated in the sequence of events in the 24 hours preceding the launch in which engineers energetically raised serious objections to launching.

Organizational processes are critical to understanding these managers' decision making. Processes are the dynamics of organizational life affecting individual members. While the notion of organizations as actors is legitimate and effectively accounts for certain actions, organizations must rely on individuals to act as their agents. To describe accurately the behavior of organizations, we need an explanation that connects the goals of the organization with the actions of its members (Vaughan, 1983:68-73). Organizational processes (recruitment, selection, socialization, promotion, rewards and punishments, informal associations, fostered dependencies) are designed to create a situation in which the individual identifies with the organization and its goals. The survival of one becomes linked to the survival of the other. Given competitive pressures and resource scarcity, individuals become motivated to attain resources on the organization's behalf.

Individual response to competitive pressures is shaped by other factors, both internal and external to the organization, however. Among them are (1) subunit membership, (2) position in the information system, and (3) rewards and punishments from a variety of sources both inside and outside the workplace. Organizational position figures importantly in internal decision making because vulnerability to competitive pressures, responsibility for and opportunity to act on them, sanctions, and access to information vary by position (Vaughan, 1983:68-73; 84-87).

Concern about cold temperatures at the Cape began at 2:00 p.m. January 27, 1986. Two teleconferences were set up on the evening of the 27th to discuss temperature. The principal actors in the subsequent decision making were Thiokol managers and engineers in Utah, NASA's Marshall Space Flight Center managers and engineers in Huntsville, and Marshall managers and Thiokol's

Director of the Solid Rocket Motor project, who were together at Kennedy Space Center. No upper level NASA administrators participated (Commission, 1986:87-88, 111). In the first teleconference, Thiokol engineers expressed the opinion that the launch should be delayed (Commission, 1986:106). A second teleconference was set up to transmit data to all parties and to involve more personnel.

In the second teleconference, Thiokol engineers presented charts chronicling the history of O-ring erosion. They argued that O-ring ability to fill the gap created in the SRB joint at ignition would be slower at predicted temperatures (low twenties) than in the worst case to date: January 1985, when the calculated O-ring temperature was 53 degrees F. In that flight, O-ring erosion occurred in joints on both Solid Rocket Boosters. Thiokol engineer Roger Boisjoly testified:

> that was the first time we had actually penetrated a primary O-ring on a field joint with hot gas, and we had a witness of that event because the grease between the O-rings was blackened just like coal...and that was so much more significant than had ever been seen before on any blow-by on any joint...the fact was that now you introduced another phenomenon. You have impingement erosion and bypass erosion, and the O-ring material gets removed from the cross section of the O-ring much, much faster when you have bypass erosion or blow-by (Commission, 1986:135).

Based on this history, Thiokol recommended the Challenger not fly. NASA personnel--Marshall managers at Kennedy and in Huntsville--challenged Thiokol engineers' conclusion (Commission, 1986:90; 94; 107). Thiokol managers and engineers in Utah then held an off-line caucus. After some discussion, Thiokol engineers were excluded from the decision making. Included were 4 senior Thiokol managers, one of whom was vice president of engineering. He was asked to "take off his engineering hat and put on his management hat" (Commission, 1986:93). The four assessed the data, concluding that:

1. There is a substantial margin to erode the primary O-ring by a factor of three times the previous worst case.
2. Even if the primary O-ring does not seal, the secondary is in position and will (Commission, 1986:108).

The second teleconference resumed, and the people at Kennedy and Marshall came back on-line. The Thiokol managers indicated that they had reassessed, saying temperature effects were a concern, but data were inconclusive. They reversed their first position, recommending launch. Marshall managers at

Kennedy then proceeded with the launch, neglecting to pass news of this midnight-hour controversy up the NASA hierarchy (Commission, 1986:101).

The distinction between "engineering hat" and "management hat" is a key to understanding this decision in the face of what in retrospect seems clear evidence of danger. Managers and engineers occupy distinctly different cultural niches in organizations. While both managers and engineers pursue production goals and safety goals (along with many others) they are differentially rewarded in their pursuit of these goals--first in the professional training that necessarily precedes such occupations, and later in the organizations in which they practice their respective professions (Becker and Carper, 1956). The rewards for managers come primarily through the achievement of production goals; for engineers, rewards are primarily for technical achievements. Through socialization into two separate specializations, managers and engineers develop very different frames of reference, or world views, which affect the interpretation of information (Dubinskas, 1988; Goffman, 1974; Heimer, 1988:499-501; Janis, 1982:174-175; Marris, 1974:5-22; Short, 1984; Zaltman, 1982).[3]

NASA managers were the direct recipients of the environmental pressures and the consequent emphasis on commercial goals (Commission, 1986:165). The nine missions in 1985 were the background against which an announcement for 24 missions a year by 1990 had been made. The Challenger was the first launch of 1986, and already had been postponed three times and scrubbed once (Commission, 1986:17). The competitive pressures to stick to the flight schedule were exacerbated by publicity for the launch's Teacher in Space program and the subsequent vicarious inclusion of school children across the country in the flight, in addition to the usual waiting media (Boot, 1986:25; Van Allen, 1986). Moreover, the President's State of the Union message was to be the night of the launch, which some sources reported was to include a mention of the first teacher in space (*Boston Globe*, 10 June 1986; *Time*, 9 June 1986).

The Commission's investigation questioned individuals who were involved to a greater or lesser extent in the decision to launch concerning the report that NASA management was subjected to outside pressures to launch (1986:176). The major figures testified that there had been no outside intervention or pressure of any kind leading up to the launch. Twenty-eight affidavits, making similar statements, were submitted to the Commission (1986: 176-177). The fact that evidence of outside intervention was not uncovered does not mean that intervention did not occur. The ambiguity remaining about this issue does not

---

3. We cannot assume that people who are grouped together by a shared characteristic share a culture. Because of paper length restrictions, the analysis here is necessarily brief. Extensive arguments concerning the influence of culture on decision making at NASA will appear in Vaughan, *The Social Construction of Risk: NASA and the Space Shuttle Challenger* (forthcoming).

discount the existence of "pressure to launch", however. The focus of investigation was on pressure directly or indirectly exerted by *individuals*. But environmental pressures can filter through organizational structure, affecting individuals in key positions, without explicit articulation (cf. Feynman, 1988:217). Pressures did exist, and affected the decision making of NASA managers by *affecting the interpretation of information*.

The predicted low temperatures would have an unknown effect, thus a condition of uncertainty existed (Commission, 1986:94; 96). Although Thiokol engineers were stating that the O-ring temperature must be 53 degrees F. at launch, *no rule* existed describing what action to take under these circumstances (Commission, 1986:89-90; 92; Wynne, 1988). Consider Marshall's Solid Rocket Booster Project Manager Mulloy's explanation of his widely quoted comment, "My God, Thiokol, when do you want me to launch, next April?":

> The total context I think in which those words may have been used is, there are currently no Launch Commit Criteria (LCC) for joint temperature. What you are proposing to do is to generate a new Launch Commit Criteria on the eve of a launch, after we have successfully flown with the existing Launch Commit Criteria 24 previous times. With this LCC, i.e., do not launch with a temperature greater (sic) than 53 degrees, we may not be able to launch until next April. We need to consider this carefully before we jump to any conclusions. It is all in the context, again, with challenging your interpretation of the data, what does it mean and is it logical, is it truly logical that we really have a system that has to be 53 degrees to fly? (Commission, 1986:96)

In trying to assess the uncertain consequences of the cold, Marshall management asked for evidence of certainty that the O-rings would not work. Engineer Roger Boisjoly of Morton Thiokol testified:

> I was asked, yes, at that point in time I was asked to quantify my concerns, and I said I couldn't. I couldn't quantify it. I had no data to quantify it, but I did say I know that it (the predicted cold temperature) was away from goodness in the current data base (1986:89; 93-94).

In the absence of Thiokol engineers' ability to "prove" that they should not launch, Marshall management assessed the engineers' warnings within a context of another factor supporting a decision to launch: a history of successful launches. The past became a strategic factor which was read as a part of the present (Barnard, 1938: 208-209; Commission, 1986:93; Feynman, Vol. II:F-1; Feynman, 1988:220-237). Success had become the normative standard within that NASA managerial culture, which has variously been described as "success-oriented," (in that the absence of failure is success) and "can-do" (the idea of accepting an exciting challenge) (Commission, 1986:171; Roland, 1985:38). The responsibility for meeting the flight schedule and a history of successful flights became a part of the frame of reference within which Marshall management weighed the evidence. Encouraged by Thiokol managers' recommendation to launch and *uninformed that Thiokol engineers in Utah did not concur* (Commission, 1986:96; 100; House Committee, 1986:228; Interview, Thiokol engineer, 26 June 1988), Marshall managers proceeded with launch preparation, concluding that the evidence indicated it was safe to do so.

Why did they not pass the information about this midnight-hour controversy up the hierarchy? Lawrence Mulloy, Level III Manager, SRM Project, Marshall Space Flight Center indicated in testimony that it was because of task segregation and standardized reporting channels and procedures (Commission, 1986:97-98; 102):

> At that time, and I still consider today, that was a Level III issue, Level III being an SRB element or an external tank element or Space Shuttle main engine element or an orbiter (1986: 98).

This statement is correct, in that the responsibility for these components did belong to the Level III Marshall managers in question. Since all the evidence on this issue (and others) may never surface, however, we might speculate about another possible explanation for Marshall managements' failure to pass this information up the NASA hierarchy and similar failures earlier in the O-ring problem history. Since all individuals (and organizations) manipulate the image of themselves they present to others (Goffman, 1960), the incentive to create an impression of managing well in order to reap rewards and avoid negative sanctions would tend to lead to damage control: suppression of information about internal problems and controversy--especially when those difficulties are believed to be resolved (cf. Feynman, 1988:215; Wilsnack, 1980).

The Commission's Report expressed concern at "what appears to be the propensity of management at Marshall to contain potentially serious problems and to attempt to resolve them internally rather than communicate them forward" (1986:104). This position assumes that, had NASA's upper level administrators known about the controversy that night, they would have delayed the launch. Given that 1) these upper level administrators' definition of the situation would be shaped by the middle managers reporting to them, and 2) these upper administrators were also subject to professional and organizational socialization and norms that positively sanction the attainment of organizational goals (thus sharing a similar frame of reference, or world view), the fascinating question is: if they had known, what would they have done?

The Regulatory Environment

Regulatory agents also influence decision making in organizations. By rewards, by punishments, and/or by interjecting information into the decision making process, regulators can alter management definitions of a situation. The opportunity to intervene would seem to be greater when the behavior in question occurs over a long period, as did the O-ring problem history. In the NASA system, however, the regulatory mechanisms that were set up to assure safety were insufficient for this task.

Research on agencies regulating business firms indicates that the ability to regulate is frequently undercut by the autonomy and interdependence of regulators and those they regulate (Vaughan, 1983:88-109). Because agencies and business firms are physically separate, independent organizations, business organizations retain elements of autonomy that mask organizational behavior from outsiders. Structure insulates one organization from another, inhibiting discovery of violations or potential violations. Organizational size, complexity, numerous daily transactions (often in difficult to monitor forms), specialization (and the language that accompanies it) further reinforce autonomy, creating barriers to effective regulation.

Paradoxically, regulatory organizations and the organizations they regulate have the capacity to be "joined," although they are physically separate. Interdependence--the fact that shared interests and resource exchange link regulators and regulatees so that outcomes for each are, in part, determined by the activities of the other--also influences the ability to regulate (Pfeffer and Salancik, 1978:40-54). What is known about the effects of autonomy and interdependence on the social control of organizations has grown primarily from analysis of interorganizational relationships between legally-empowered agents of social control and business firms. These same factors characterized both inter- and intra-organizational relationships between the space agency and its regulators. Autonomy and interdependence limited the ability of safety regulatory units to monitor and investigate the O-ring problem and bring it to the attention of NASA decision makers (for details, see Vaughan, 1990).

Monitoring safety at NASA was primarily the responsibility of three organizations. Two were NASA's own internal safety subunits. NASA and these two subunits were interdependent. Although NASA was dependent upon them for close surveillance, they were dependent upon NASA in ways that affected their ability to monitor and intervene in behalf of safety. The first, NASA's Safety, Reliability, and Quality Assurance Program, was dependent upon NASA for resources. Those resources had been cut (Commission, 1986:159-161; Diamond, 1986). Several internal Safety, Reliability, and Quality Assurance offices scattered throughout the NASA system were either reorganized around other responsibilities or continued with reduced personnel. Regulatory capacity was further impeded by the placement of Safety, Reliability and Quality

Assurance offices at Kennedy and Marshall under the supervision of the very organizations and activities they were to check--a situation hardly conducive to altering decisions by management (Commission, 1986:160). In addition, these special offices were dependent upon the NASA management structure for transferring information and recommendations about safety problems throughout the organization, and for implementing suggested changes.

The second internal regulatory subunit was the Space Shuttle Crew Safety Panel. Established in 1974, its purpose was to identify possible hazards to shuttle crews and to advise management about the resolution of such hazards (Commission, 1986:161). Dependent upon NASA administration for its existence, the Crew Safety Panel was eliminated in 1981 when, after 4 successful flights, the shuttle officially was declared operational.

In addition to these internal safety regulators, Congress enacted legislation after the January 1967 Apollo spacecraft fire establishing an external body, the Aerospace Safety Advisory Panel, as a senior advisory committee to NASA (Commission, 1986:160). Comprised of aerospace experts, the panel's duties primarily were oversight: adequacy of proposed or existing safety standards, review of safety studies and operation plans, and examination of NASA's various programs and their management. Although this panel actively investigated a wide variety of specific subjects, the Commission found no indication that the Solid Rocket Booster joint design or in-flight O-ring problems ever were assessed by them (1986:161). The Commission praised the panel, citing its accomplishments and attributing this omission to its many oversight responsibilities.

Just as the physical separation of government regulatory agencies and business organizations inhibits regulatory activities, this panel's externality limited its ability to deal effectively with its wide scope of safety responsibilities. Panel members did not participate in NASA's daily activities, and thus were forced to rely upon insiders for information. Technology and specialized language were barriers, despite the aerospace background of most panel members. Furthermore, members belonged to other organizations, and these commitments reduced the time these nine panel members spent on safety at NASA to, on average, thirty days a year (Interview, ASAP Staff Director, 2 March 1988). As a consequence, NASA retained elements of autonomy, reducing the possibility that the panel could identify the O-ring problem and alter the actions of NASA decision makers.

Although all three safety organizations were designed to assure the safety of the space program by influencing management decisions about both technical and procedural matters, the autonomy and interdependence that resulted from inter- and intra-organizational relations between NASA and these regulators inhibited the realization of this mandate.

Implications:
The Connection Between Cause and Control

Although the NASA/Challenger accident is a unique event, limiting the conclusions that can justifiably be drawn from its analysis, other research confirms that organizations contribute to their own technical failures (see, e.g., Kemeny, et al., 1979; Perrow, 1984; Shrivastava, 1987). Turner, investigating "man-made disasters" (1976; 1978), pioneered in discovering organizational patterns that systematically contributed to the disasters he studied: norms and culturally accepted beliefs about hazards, poor communication, inadequate information handling in complex situations, and failure to comply with existing regulations instituted to assure safety (1976:391). He concluded that these factors created an absence of some kind of knowledge at some point. Crucial to understanding such accidents, then, is discovering how knowledge and information relating to events provoking a disaster were distributed in an organization before the incident (1978:3).

Analysis of the Challenger accident not only confirms Turner's findings about the relevance of knowledge and information in organizations, but also identifies structural factors that systematically affected the *distribution of information and its interpretation* at NASA: the competitive environment, the organization's structure, processes, and transactions, and the regulatory environment. These factors combined to affect the decision to launch.

Identification of these factors has implications for the social control of risky technologies. Perrow (1984) found that certain accidents in high risk technological systems were unavoidable, or "normal," resulting from the tightly-coupled interactional complexity of the technical system itself. But the probability of other accidents, resulting from systematic organizational patterns that contribute to technical failures, may be reduced. To be effective, strategies to control, change, or eliminate undesirable behavior should address the cause of that behavior. Consequently, attempting to correct the technical cause of accidents is not enough. The organizations that produce high risk technological systems also must be assessed and, when appropriate, altered. Most often, post-accident strategies to prevent a recurrence of technical failures first (and correctly) are directed toward the technical problem. This strategy is usually accompanied by regulatory efforts to strengthen discovery, monitoring, and sanctioning capabilities, and (perhaps) to punish the organizations and/or the individuals responsible. The organization in question may respond by transfering, retiring, or firing individuals who, because of position and either by action or inaction, had some responsibility for the outcome. Although these latter strategies are directed toward the organization (human actors do act in an organization's behalf; strengthening surveillance and sanctioning capability of the regulatory environment can influence individual choice), they are insufficient.

Targeting the structural determinants of individual behavior is paramount in designing strategies for social control. Strengthening the regulatory environment and sanctioning individuals may conform to this broader strategy by altering normative standards in the competitive environment and within organizations to affect individual choice in more desireable ways. Despite these possible structural effects on internal and external normative environments, such strategies do not go far enough. In the NASA case, the competitive environment, organizational structure, processes, and transactions, and the regulatory environment *combined* to affect decision making. This finding, plus other research confirming the importance of these factors in organizational deviance, indicates that strengthening the regulatory apparatus is less effective than going back farther in the causal chain and *in addition* altering the influences of the competitive environment and relevant organizational characteristics that affect individual choice.

Some scholars, acknowledging the role of the competitive environment, argue that a capitalist economic system is causally related to organizational misconduct. Implicitly if not explicitly connecting their notion of cause with strategies for control, they suggest that replacing capitalism with an alternative economic system would control or reduce the importance of profits and production goals in organizations (see, e.g., Pepinsky, 1974; Quinney, 1979: 141-215). Leaving aside the possibility of this change occurring, the suggested strategy holds little promise for reducing competitive pressures in the space program, or for that matter, in organizations in general.

First, NASA was not a corporate profit-seeker, but was subject to competitive pressures and experienced resource scarcity nonetheless. Resource scarcity is a fact of organizational life; consequently, all organizations, not just profit-seeking corporations, must compete in order to survive (Vaughan, 1983:54-62). Government agencies compete for budget allocations; the police require equipment and personnel; colleges and universities compete for funding, students, and athletes; the Girl Scouts seek to win members away from the Blue Birds and to sell cookies; research institutions must secure funding; churches need members, space, and annual fund drives. With the exception of organizations designed to fail, competition for scarce resources is essential to organizational survival (Vaughan, 1983:62-66). Thus, competitive pressures are likely to continue influencing management decisions, regardless of the nature of the economic system (Berliner, 1957; Gross, 1978: 72; Lampert, 1984).

Second, changing the economic system in this country (or other arrangements altering the competitive structure within the existing system, such as assuring abundant resources for certain products or industries) does not eliminate the influence of the international competitive environment. In this country, the space agency was competing with other agencies for government funding. Internationally, NASA was competing with other countries, not only for commercial payload customers, but for U.S. supremacy in space science and military power. Many U.S. organizations compete in the international arena. Thus, despite altering institutional arrangements at home, international competitive pressures would still figure importantly in decision making in many organizations--especially those with products considered essential to national interests.

The uncertainties of armchair theorizing aside, the threat of accidents in high-risk technological systems suggests a short-run, pragmatic approach: rather than altering the competitive environment, focus upon altering its influences on the organization. To be most effective in reducing the probability of organizational-technical system accidents, however, social control strategies should address all three: the influences of the competitive environment, relevant organizational characteristics, and the regulatory environment. In order to alter the full complement of contributing structural factors, a crucial role must be assumed by organizations producing high risk technologies. Only they can address the crucial nexus between competitive pressures and the many aspects of organizational structure, processes, and transactions that are relevant to organizational-technical system accidents.

This approach calls for organizational analysis that prospectively identifies points of vulnerability in a specific organization. Inquiry could address the following questions. Historically, which subunits or divisions of an organization are most likely to experience competitive pressures? Does this vulnerability vary over time? Can the variations be predicted? Of those subunits experiencing competitive pressures, which, if any, in the past have been identified with deviant events? What are the differences and similarities between these units and others not identified with deviant events? Can positions in these subunits be pinpointed whose occupants are more responsible for responding to pressures to attain organization goals? What are the characteristics of structure, processes, transactions, and information exchange associated with these positions and how have they affected individual choice? Analysis of this sort would give some clues about organizational patterns that potentially contribute to technical system accidents. Once identified, they can become targets for change (see, e.g., Stone, 1975).

Consider the recommendations of the Presidential Commission following the Challenger investigation. In its report, the Commission recommended that the faulty Solid Rocket Booster joint and seal be changed. Moreover, although guided by retrospective rather than prospective analysis, the report unerringly addressed the NASA organization's contribution to the technical failure (1986:198-201). The influence of the competitive environment was acknowledged by the Commission's recommendation that NASA establish a flight rate consistent with its resources, thus realigning goals to reduce environmentally-produced internal strain. The internal safety regulating system also was a target. The Commission recommended re-establishing a Space Shuttle Crew Safety Panel, similar in responsibility to the discontinued panel. In addition, they recommended an adequately staffed Office of Safety, Reliability, Maintainability, and Quality Assurance with direct authority, *independent* of other NASA program responsibilities.

The Commission recommended additional intra-organizational changes. They suggested improving the flow of information by expanding reporting channels, clarifying the authority structure, instituting more oral inquiry, and recording discussion of issues. They suggested greater participation of astronauts in management, safety regulation, and pre-launch decision making--thus integrating another world view into the decision making process: one with a very personal interest in safety and human life. They called for a review of all Criticality designations, more rules to govern information exchange, and rules against removing parts from one shuttle to supply another. Moreover, they decried Marshall management's failure to provide information to upper-level administrators, and recommended elimination of this problem, "whether by changes of personnel, organization, indoctrination or all three" (1986:200).

Replacing a "technical fix" with an "organizational-technical fix" such as the Commission recommended reduces the probability that organizational-technical system accidents will occur. But they will still occur, for the following reasons. First, determining precisely how organizations contribute to technical failure tends to get sorted out only after a technical failure occurs. What was an "ill-structured problem" before an accident becomes a "well-structured problem" when evidence is aggregated afterwards (Turner, 1976:106). Hence, identifying actions necessary to prevent an accident becomes most clear after one has happened. Even when successful, fixing the organizational problems associated with one technical system accident does not preclude the occurrence of others that may arise from a unique confluence of organizational factors.

Second, the fix itself changes the system, making it less predictable. One of the problems with the shuttle program was that each vehicle that was launched was different than the rest, for the science of shuttle development was constantly changing. Thus each launch was a unique event: a flying technical system non-comparable to the others, although parts remained the same from launch to launch. Changes instituted to correct a particular deficiency may result in a complex system (organizational or technical) failing in new ways. A troubling possibility is that a factor identified as contributing to a particular organizational-technical system accident may have contributed to successes in the past. For example, NASA's competitive pressures (for funding, for international military and space science supremacy) may have contributed to design innovations and organizational arrangements at NASA that enhanced safety. What, then, are the ramifications of change?

Another complication is that since the influences of the competitive environment, organizational characteristics, and the regulatory environment combine to affect individual choice, altering one factor may have unintended consequences for another. For example: changing organization structure, processes, and transactions requires funds and personnel time and effort, for people implement changes. The immediate impact of a technical system accident is to drain organizational resources. In the Challenger accident, NASA lost crew, vehicle, and payload. In addition, the agency lost $200 million in fees it would have collected from commercial launch contracts it was forced to cancel after the accident, plus further losses from crew family lawsuits (*Time*, 6 June 1986:17). The official investigations and publicity put additional strain on existing resources. When an organization is already operating under a condition of scarcity, the diversion of resources from existing goals to accomplish mandated internal change can create additional stress on a system already struggling --ironically exacerbating and reinforcing competitive pressures while trying to alter the contributing organizational characteristics.

Furthermore, the dynamics of organizational behavior often are subtle, and although it remains to be proved, we may be better at identifying, understanding, and fixing technical problems than organizational problems. Both preventive strategies and after-the-fact attempts to fix things are handicapped by the rudimentary state of knowledge on the causes of organizational deviance as well as by unsophisticated capabilities of converting theory and research into diagnostic skills in specific cases. Finally and fundamentally, any system that involves human actors has a risk of failure, no matter how well it is designed (Perrow, 1984; Short, 1984).

What conclusions can be drawn concerning the regulation of high risk technological products, given these uncertainties? First, controlling the organizational contribution to technical system accidents can reduce the probability of these accidents, but can not prevent them. Second, policy recommendations that rest upon categorizing some technical systems as having a higher or lower probability of accidents than others should be weighed with great skepticism and caution (see, e.g., Morone and Woodhouse, 1986; Perrow, 1984). Risk assessment based upon the characteristics of a particular technical system and its failure consequences leaves something crucial out of the calculus: the tendency for organizations to increase the probability of their own technical system accidents.

Those technical systems that are less complex and interactive and thus thought to have a reduced propensity for accidents are produced by organizations that themselves are complex interactive systems with structural propensities to fail in unpredictable ways. System complexity is positively related to deviant events (Perrow, 1984; Vaughan, 1983:105-112). Predicting the behavior of either a complex technical system or a complex organization in order to prevent accidents in either is a challenge; predicting and forestalling accidents based on the interaction of the two systems is more difficult still. The policy implication is that when technical systems are assigned low, moderate, or high risk potential without considering the organizations that produce and run them, the risk is always greater than we think.

14

Managing Risk: Managing Uncertainty in the British Nuclear Installations Inspectorate

Peter K. Manning

The study of risk is now emergent, and new critical essays succinctly criticize the psychological, individualistic, and rationalistic biases of current research and programmatic statements. According to one eminent and quite sensible study of modern risk-reduction, "risk" can be defined as the existence of a threat to life or health amongst the consequences of alternative courses of action (Fischhoff, et al., 1981:2). This definition of risk is unfortunately narrow, and does not entirely suit our present purposes. Risks may be positive or negative, known or merely affecting, and are always, in part, collective and structural as well as individual or a result of individual choices. Risk is a component feature of social structures. It can be coercive in nature such as when governments draft individuals to fight in wars or place fuel reprocessing plants in their back yards. Risk may be a product of a life style such as IV drug use. The virtually exclusive focus on calculating assorted negative consequences of risks based on individual-level data (rates of morbidity and mortality for example)

Revision of a paper delivered to the Annual Meeting of the Law and Society Association, Vail, Colorado, June, 1988. Some aspects of this argument have been rehearsed in seminars at The Management Centre of the University of Aston, Birmingham, Lancaster University, Bailrigg, Lancs, the Sloan School of Management at M.I.T. and the Centre of Criminology, University of Toronto, Toronto, Canada. Unfortunately, the incisive comments of my colleagues in these diverse locations did little to correct the errors for which I am responsible. Jim Short provided editorial guidance. I am also grateful for the facilities and assistance of the School of Criminal Justice, Michigan State, and Robert Trojanowicz, Director.

severely limits the applicability   and scope of conventional   risk-analyses (Short, 1984; Clarke, 1988; Douglas, 1987; Douglas and Wildavsky, 1982). A broad conception of risk and risk analysis is required if social scientists are to participate in the debate about the nature and consequences of risk.

Uncertainty is a feature of social structure, and abundant risky choices and outcomes are characteristic of complex social structure. Furthermore, many decisions take place in collective and organizational contexts that involve inter-organizational relationships. The consequences of decisions do not exclusively affect individual decision-makers, but may affect others who have no voice in the decisions, as in siting a reactor, military base or toxic waste dump. If additional social facets of risk are to be discovered, studies must address the social organization within which risks are defined as well as the perceptions and choices of individual actors who make decisions. The social construction of and tacit grounds for risk assessment are as central to the study of risk as are studies of rates of exposure to radioactivity, risk trees and algorithms of choices in disasters.

A sociological analysis of risk should entail the analysis of modes of enstructuration (Giddens, 1964, 1981, 1984) of risk, especially collective risks that affect social groups, and as a feature of organizations mandated to regulate risks. Ethnographic sociological analysis of collective risk is required. Close description of *how* organizations negotiate and bargain with other organizations, and the "role of organizations in making choices among risks..." (Clarke, 1988:24) is a first task for serious fieldwork. A logical corollary is careful study of the internal processes by which such definitions of risks are formed, and how patterns of responsibility for assessing and deciding about risk are distributed within the organization and linked to its mandate, or political mission, strategies and tactics (Hughes, 1971).

Organizational decisions create and maintain the political economy of risks. Selection and maintenance of a risk-focus reflects the implicit structure of interests and power in a society as well as the hierarchical ordering of authority within the organization. Ultimately, organizational decisions concerning the existence, level, kind and location of risks and the consequences for target populations are political decisions. The values by which decisions are rationalized, and the grounds presented to publicly account for these decisions, are in the first instance neither "legal" nor based entirely on scientific reasoning. They do not rest solely on probabilistic calculations of likely outcomes. This is true even if the rendered accounts for the decisions are cast in the language of "risk analysis" (Kahneman, Slovic and Tversky, 1982), scientific evaluation (Lindblom and Cohen, 1979) or in the legal rhetoric of contracts and liability (Calabresi and Bobbitt, 1978).

Central to the study of the regulation of risk is the social construction, or perception, definition and typification, of modes of risks and the sanctioned means by which control of risks and accidents is carried out. "Believing is seeing," the social psychologist Karl Weick (1979), following Blake, has argued. It follows that organizations bracket and selectively process or enact portions of the available stimulii in the environment. The socially constructed or enacted environment is a partial version of the "raw data" that an organization "senses" and gathers (Weick, 1979). Culture and the organizational culture are ways of restricting the range of relevant events and processes, pinning them down to routines. Events in the external world have meaning conferred upon them, and do not have intrinsic features and intervention points. The study of risk is as much a study of the social organization of "cultural biases" (Douglas, 1987) concerning "risk" (or tacit assumptions about the nature, location and character of risk) as it is about the events or processes at issue seen within the primary framework of natural or physical causation (Goffman, 1974: 22).

Regulatory agencies and agents in complex societies serve as the "first-line" apparatus for scanning and monitoring the environment. They act to not only socially construct or define the nature of the risk, placing it within the framework of social causation, or "guided doings." They are structured through political decisions and historical events to respond, contain, or anticipate such risks. Regulatory agencies do not see or "read off" (Goffman, 1959) unexpected events entirely as "accidents," or naturally occurring events. The process of social construction of risk and the editing of social reality suggests that as much attention should be given to readings of organizational readings as to the analysis of the complexity and coupling of subsystems within complex and risky technological systems (Perrow, 1984). Although rather awkward efforts have been made to distinguish the "task environment" from the "organization," and to see the organizational structure as caused by an "environment" (Wilson, 1978), especially by naive ecological-evolutionary theories of organization (Hannan and Freeman, 1977; Young, 1988), it is difficult to determine the direction of the causal flow. The nature of risk can not easily, and perhaps never can be, distinguished from the perceptions, organizational routines, decision-practices and structure of organizations. Risk is represented within organizations as well as in the environment on which they act.

Regulatory bodies' definitions of risk are internally embedded in organizational structure and practice, but they emerge in part as a product of intra-organizational relations, especially repeated and patterned transactions with the organizations that are regulated (Clarke, 1988). The organizational/ industrial structure that operates with a characteristic technology and regulation agencies, also bureaucratically structured, are locked in a dance of control responding to each other as well as to the publics in whose name regulation notionally occurs (Manning, 1989b). The concept of "regulatory culture" provides an insight into these nuanced connections between regulators and regulated in the context of public opinion (Meidinger, 1987). The collectively shared representations of risks, vocabularies, names, routines and explanations, represent risk to the regulators and the regulatees.

Collective representations, biological and material constraints, all feature in a close analysis of the regulation of risk. The basic question addressed here is how complex and collectively represented social objects, such as industries, power plants, and reactors, and abstract concepts like safety, license and risks, are frozen and fixed and how, on the other hand, organizations are enstructured around these collective representations and symbolically encoded systems of signs. In the case of nuclear reactors, the technology is exceedingly complex and it conveys abundant expressive symbolism of fear, anxiety and even dread. Both aspects are of public and regulatory concern.

The paper, based on data gathered during the course of a fieldwork-based study of the British NII,[1] describes the bases on which HM Nuclear Installations

---

1. The data on which this analysis is based were collected as a part of a large program of research on health and safety undertaken at the Centre for Socio-Legal Studies, Wolfson College, Oxford and supported by funding from the Health and Safety Executive. While a Senior Scientific Officer at the Centre and a Fellow of Wolfson College, I carried out a fieldwork study of H.M. Nuclear Installations Inspectorate (NII) in England, primarily between 1983 and 1986. The research involved gathering lengthy interviews and other forms of fieldwork done in the NII between March 1984 and March 1986. The aim of the research was to integrate notions of safety with the social organization of the Inspectorate. Several types of data were gathered for this purpose.

The research included bibliographic historical research on the origins of nuclear power and the shape that that quest took in Britain specifically just before, during and after World War Two. These developments, spawned by war, and then falsely touted as the road to peace, or "Atoms for Peace," as the program was known in America, patterned the growth of the regulatory structures for the production of nuclear-generated energy. The war and related events shaped the development of nuclear energy and regulation in European industrialized nations rather differently than they did in America, and this was a background for the English research (see also Campbell, 1984). Clippings from newspapers published in Britain and America on nuclear power and related issues such as waste disposal, fuel reprocessing, the economics of power production, and international developments in nuclear power have been collected and filed since 1982. Documents and records produced by the Sizewell Inquiry (1983-85) and the *Layfield Report* (1987) summarizing these hearings and recommending the development and building of a pressurized water reactor (PWR) on the site of a current reactor at Sizewell on the far southeast coast of England, were consulted.

Fieldwork included observations, interviews, attending meetings, joint conferences between NII and the Central Electricity Generating Board and plant management, a site visit to a power station on an inspection, and records analysis. Three of the then four branches of the Inspectorate were studied.

Inspectorate (NII) in Britain defines and manages a particular kind of risk, contamination by radioactivity resulting from either long-term exposure, abrupt release, or catastrophic accident attendant to the operation of electricity generating plants powered by nuclear reactors. These installations produce electrical power, but occupy a central role in national defense since they are the primary source of the plutonium essential for producing atomic weapons. Three sections follow, the first of which discusses concepts of uncertainty and the associated term, risk. The second describes the institutional mechanisms developed by the NII to control uncertainty: organizational structure, ideology and a strategy of licensing. The conclusion speculates about relationships between regulation and collective risks.

The NII Described

The stated or official purpose of the NII is to insure that the licensees who operate nuclear installations do so within the principles of safety assessment developed by NII, and that they do so using "reasonably practicable means." This means in practice that some balance should be struck between costs and safety. In many ways, the Inspectorate is devoted to negotiating a mutually acceptable state of compliance with the licensees. Producing an agreement upon conditions of operation and management to be stated in the license could be considered a central mission of the organization. This mission-focus has emerged from a series of decisions and historic developments that shaped organizational structure, mandate and practices.

History

The NII came into being in April, 1960, following the passage of the Nuclear Installations (licensing and insurance) Act of 1959. The organization was created in part as a response to the serious fire and radioactivity release at the Windscale (now Sellefield) fuel reprocessing plant in 1957 and the resultant Fleck Commission Report published in December, 1957 (Patterson, 1983). A number of topical issues or crises have shaped the Inspectorate from the beginning, including the Windscale explosion: crises continue to shape the organization, to reshape priorities and the allocation of resources (Hutter and Manning, 1991).

Branch three, fuel reprocessing located at Bootle, was omitted from the study. In total, 21 lengthy interviews were gathered with NII members including the Chief Inspector, Mr. Anthony, Deputy Chief Inspectors, section heads, and inspectors. Fieldnotes were gathered during two periods of intensive fieldwork.

With the passage of the Health and Safety at Work Act in 1974 establishing the Health and Safety Commission and consolidating the several inspectorates under one umbrella, the NII was shifted from the Department of Energy to the Ministry of Employment, Trade and Industry. It was placed under the Health and Safety Executive (HSE) (with the Factory, Mines and Quarries, Agriculture, Industrial Air Pollution and Railway Inspectorates), and as a result became a part of an organization dominated and controlled by the numerically superior Factory Inspectorate. In its initial guise, it was more closely aligned with the Department of Energy, and the guidance of energy production, but with the transfer to the HSE, it was organizationally and symbolically placed closer to health and safety concerns (cf. Carson, 1982). Presently, its considerable energies are divided between maintaining power production and a viable electrical industry and ensuring cooperative environments in which safety is the mutual concern of workers and management. Many matters, those issuing from the wider political ambit outside the Inspectorate, also shape ministerial action.

Structure

The NII is headed by a Chief Inspector and his deputy, and is composed of some 103 persons allocated into five branches. The first branch is devoted to operating plants; the second monitors the planning and building of plants approved and in process; the third regulates fuel reprocessing, and the fourth has responsibilities for future plants. A fifth (policy) branch, created at the end of the study period, is charged with policy development. Each is headed by a branch head, and contains 3 or 4 sections each with a head. There are around 25 people in each section, save the policy branch that contains about six members. During the period of the study, all the branches but the fuel processing branch located at Bootle, near Liverpool, were located in a large office building in central London. In May 1986, after the end of the study period, the majority of the NII moved 100 miles from London to Bootle. The Chief Inspector and his staff and the policy branch remain in London.

These branches are divided functionally between "field inspectors" and "specialists," although this is not a rigid distinction, since many of the specialist experts have served as field inspectors and most of the field inspectors are also specialists. Their specialities range from mathematics and physics to various kinds of engineering training, in and out of university programs. They are uniformally white scientists and engineers, all but one of whom is male.

The organization processes requests from the industry (composed of two electricity-producing organizations, licensees who can be granted licenses to generate power in the U.K.: South of Scotland Electricity Generating Board [SSEGB], and the Central Electricity Generating Board [CEGB], and one fuel-reprocessing/waste disposal corporation, British Nuclear Fuels [BNFL]). These Boards and the industries they represent are semi-governmental bodies. The

American pattern of regulation in which the law places responsibility with the licensee, but charges and ultimately makes the Nuclear Regulatory Commission responsible for implementing safety, differs from the British. Ministerial responsibility shapes choices more than administrative or criminal law (Vogel, 1986), and a case-by-case framework is used to build up conventions and licensing precedents (Reiss, 1983a). Although the responsibility for the safety of the operating plant lies with the licensee, NII judges the adequacy of the industry's arguments for the safety of facets of the operation (called the "safety case"). The work is a series of on going bargaining and negotiation sessions concerning the nature, quality, and indicia of "safety." One of the dominant themes in self-description of the mandate of the NII is that they serve as the neutral, objective and fair "conscience" of industry. The question remains, however, what the nature of the safety sought is, and how it is to be located and "ensured."

Some Aspects of Uncertainty

"Uncertainty" is defined by *Webster's* as "... indeterminate, not certain to occur, indefinite, problematical." These definitions suggest a lack of sureness or confidence about someone or something. Other synonyms are such words as "doubt" (uncertainty and inability to make a decision); "dubiosity" (vagueness and mental confusion) and "dubeity" (wavering between conclusions). These definitions and synonyms connote psychological properties of the human mind, or individuals, especially as regard their degree of confidence in an outcome, person or process. Uncertainty in outcomes that appear to be consequential may entail a degree of risk or threat. Uncertainty is not exclusively a property of individual psyches, however, or of responsible persons taking decisions based on facts *or* values. Facts and values become elided in interpretation of safety cases and in inspection practice. Patterns of uncertainty are subtly interwoven with daily work and are assumed to be the underlying bases for mobilizing resources, and the rationale for organizational action.

Social life is organized in some fundamental fashion as a means to distribute risks and to produce mechanisms for their alleviation. Risk can be institutionalized in wars, gambling, sport, or lotteries, or can be the basis for attempts to reduce the consequences of negatively defined risks as is the case in insurance, medicine, or law. Even social regulation designed to increase the quality of economic life is an attempt to distribute or redistribute known costs and risks.

In pre-literate societies, magic is used, often on false premises, to project a sense of control over threatening external risks. Unlike preliterate societies, modern societies appear to place their trust in the hands of industrialists, scientists and governmental agents rather than Shamans, curers and holy men.

Science and law become sources of sacred texts, and governmental bureaux their instrumentalities. Regulatory agencies, based on science and administrative procedures, *secularize fear and dread*. Unlike the Shaman, who can mobilize a broad ambit of cures and causes, including the supernatural as well as the social and natural (See Fabrega and Silver, 1973), these agencies, over time, seek to narrow and define both the palliatives and the risks of concern. Modern regulatory agencies are mostly concerned with negative individual risks, such as those associated with the growth of high technology and related industry, and with the single catastrophic accident that puts the lie to global assurances of safety. There are, however, as suggested above, alternative definitions of risk.

Risks may be assessed by a variety of means, some of which have been refined into techniques. Some of these are "bootstrapping" using past precedents and experience; others rely on professional judgment (expert systems and the like); or on formal techniques of risk analysis drawn from operations research and statistics (Kahneman, Slovic and Teversky, 1982). Statistical risk analysis has achieved some acceptance in modern government as a means of identifying problems, specifying a range of outcomes, listing objectives, defining possible options and their consequences, and specifying the desirability of these consequences. Given these data, one can analyze and choose among the given options (Fischhoff, et al., 1981: Ch. 3).

Characteristics of statistical risk analysis, most popular in the United States and only recently being adopted in the U.K. (see Jasanoff, 1986), are quite relevant to NII's current definitions of its operational concerns. (These have been shaped considerably by the hearings of the Layfield Commission and public debate about the PWR.) NII are concerned with avoiding the negative consequences of a meltdown or catastrophic accident, failure of a safety system, or release of radioactive material. They are focused on a narrow range of risks; and although they prefer reasoned dialogue based on past precedents and principles rather than absolute fixed levels and rules, recent tendencies suggest that NII is opting for objective figures and tables (e.g., the risk of cancer, given an exposure of 5.5. microcuries is 1 in 5,000) and might favor narrowing their future concern to the prevention of risks with known and calculable outcomes.

Such approaches to risk are limited in several rather important ways. These limitations speak to the organization of NII and how it has chosen to approach the daunting problem of insuring the safety of nuclear installations in England, Scotland and Wales. Such approaches ignore the *background level of risk*, the rising level of radioactivity in the air and the depletion of the ozone layer that changes the chemical composition of the higher atmosphere. They also ignore *social and psychological aspects of risks*, especially collective risks that affect members of groups regardless of individual decisions. Whether positive or negatively evaluated, individualistic risks exclude from consideration the broader collective risks to the "social fabric of the society," the communal ties that link individuals in a comforting tissue of relations and provide them with the support, nurturance and emotional sustenance that sustains them as individual beings (Short, 1984). Collective risks, are of course, quite diverse: they vary in channel, source, cause, duration, scope, intensity and ecological effects. The most worrying are irreversible, invisible, and chronic. They are certainly not easily predicted, prevented or reduced in frequency. They are haunting, very difficult to measure or even name. It seems likely that a single large scale disaster that rents a community asunder is more destructive than individual risks, even when they are arguably fatal (such as smoking or drunken driving). Finally, this type of risk assessment cannot deal with the very low probability/high risk *"unforseen event(s)"* that are of most concern in modern industrialized societies, e.g., the Bhopal, Chernobyl, or Three Mile Island accidents. These types of events emerging as "accidents," commonly feature both iterative and interactive sequences of technological failure, human error and misjudgment, and political and managerial decisions concerning not only the event, but their sequelae (see Clarke, 1988). The work of Erikson (1976) and Clarke (1988), and organizational and political responses to the Three Mile Island, Chernobyl and Bhopal incidents, suggests that inter and intraorganizational decisions taken after the event are as central, or more central, to maintaining the social fabric as preventative regulatory surveillance.

For a variety of reasons, the NII presently confines its conceptions of and risk-reduction efforts to monitoring technological hazards surrounding the reactor and its safety systems, with secondary and tertiary interests in plant management and operations, civil defense and evacuations planning. Selection of these conceptions and efforts from among others and changes in foci over time are a result of complex developments unyielding to brief exposition (see Manning, 1989b). Let us explore, however, selected relationships between conceptions of risk and organizational structure, beliefs and strategy.

Uncertainty in the NII

One may distinguish two types of uncertainties that affect or shape NII's concern with regulating safety: *background* factors that shape and pattern NII's mandate, but which are beyond their direct control, and *foreground* factors, some of which they claim responsibility for managing.

Background

The most important and pressing set of background uncertainties that faced the NII in 1984-86, have changed as a result of the release of the 1987 Layfield Report based on the 1983-85 planning Inquiry. The Report recommended planning permission to enable building a pressurized water reactor (PWR) on the Sizewell "B' site in Essex, where two reactors were already present. The conservative Thatcher government publicly fully supported the policy of nuclear development, and the decision marked again a wish to resuscitate the ever-ailing British nuclear industry, and did much, one assumes, to restore morale in NII. The British people, according to attitude surveys, are the most "anti-nuclear" of any country with nuclear energy; nevertheless, the Thatcher government has set out upon a very optimistic program for nuclear development.[2] The 1987 decision to grant planning permission to design and build a PWR, now being implemented, is the forerunner of a program planned by the CEGB to sustain concerted nuclear power development well into the next century. The decision also asserted by implication the safety of nuclear power.

Several other notable background factors continue to pattern and shadow NII's operational focus. Aside from domestic political questions of policy, governmental support and budgetary resources, the world political economy has important consequences for British nuclear industry and the NII. The changing place of British technology in the world market, and the international markets in fuel generally shape the relative cost of nuclear power in Britain (this is because the price of electricity from nuclear power stations is compared nominally to the cost of coal and oil). The costs of building reactors is linked to the mythical and notoriously inaccurate extrapolations of consumer demand and future costs of electrical power produced by the electricity boards. These predictions, it has been repeatedly shown in Britain, are colored by the CEGB's wish to present the strongest possible case for building additional reactors (Patterson, 1983:177, 216). The present balance of sources of electricity is coal 74%, oil 10%, and nuclear 16%, but this balance shifts seasonally and is also affected by recent agreements with France to buy electrical power transmitted across the channel by cable. The balance among these sources can also be altered by a change in the ruling party. (The Labour Party is "anti-nuclear" and, if elected, would shift greater emphasis to developing coal resources.) Trades union policies and other governmental decisions can pattern the place of the nuclear industry, as can changes in civil and criminal law. It should be emphasized, however, that law in Britain does not occupy the central political and moral role it does in the United States.[3] Ministerial conventions and traditions shape decision-realms more than law. CEGB's plans for future building and development such as remodelling, decommissioning, or replacing aging reactors clearly affect the future of the NII and their plans for regulating safety. World class media events resulting from massive accidents, e.g., the Three Mile Island and Chernobyl incidents, shape the

---

2. This is the third or fourth such new beginning in the drifting and vacillating history of British nuclear programs--see Williams, 1980.

3. See Reiss, 1983a; Vogel, 1986; Hawkins, 1987 and for a counter argument, see Friedman, 1985.

uncertainties, partially at least produced by public opinion, confronting the NII in Britain. The NII, for these reasons, among others, is placed in a responsive or reactive stance.

Foreground

Not surprisingly, foreground factors, so named because they are the more visible and manageable manifestations of uncertainty, are the focus of the NII. They fall within NII's sense of its own broad socio-moral mandate. Respondents were asked in interviews to name and comment upon issues of most concern to the Inspectorate. The uncertainties of interest to NII can be grouped as ranked by respondents: *technological questions* associated with the complexity and risks of nuclear technology; *individual risks* of exposure to radioactivity and accidents amongst employees and members of communities near reactors (governmental policy directs siting reactors in rural areas; they are usually located near rather small villages rather than towns of size); *collective threats and risks*, public fears and perceptions of danger: the risk of invisible, uncertain, irreversible and ominous, dreaded, involuntary, pernicious and potentially fatal radioactivity/accidental release. The level of public collective concern about the risks of nuclear power are considerably less than they are in the United States, and "public opinion" is less a factor in governmental decisions in this realm. Given this range of risks within the general ambit of safety, which are chosen and how are they made manageable by NII?

Managing Uncertainty: The Safety Focus of NII

Uncertainty is routinized in NII. NII has shaped uncertainty in the context of regulation of electrical power production by "nuclear reactors" or more broadly, "nuclear installations." The nature of selection and shaping can be seen in the form of several institutional adjustments or accommodations. Tradition, and to a lesser extent, science and law, are arenas within which the Inspectorate must work out its rather broad and powerful mandate. Often as much by chance as by design, Parliament will provide a vague mandate for Ministries. Mandates are never fully and permanently won or lost: details of operations, strategies and tactics must be carved out, negotiated, shaped and defined.

Given the potentially broad range of uncertainties originating in either back- or foreground domains to which organized attention might be given, it is useful to note that historical and field data demonstrate a narrowing and refining of the workings of the NII. These can be discussed within the context of three developments: enstructuring an organization, through which a pattern of roles, rules and resources are allocated to identified objectives, goals or overall aims; evolving a set of beliefs or ideologies which, to a lesser or greater degree for given problems, spell out the political and moral obligations of the NII and those of the industry; and working out a licensing approach to regulating safety. These are addressed in order.

Inspectorates as an Organizational Type

NII resembles the other inspectorates lodged within the broad umbrella of the Health and Safety Commission of HM government. The structure of HSC (Hutter and Manning, 1991) and other British inspectorates (Reiss, 1983b, 1984) is discussed in detail elsewhere (on NII, see Manning, 1987). Several general points about inspectorates as types of organization should be noted, bearing in mind that, even for inspectorates, the aims of regulation, the sanctioning strategies or modes of governmental control, and the level of market intervention varies.

1. They can be seen as having been established to monitor and regulate phenomena that are infrequent in occurrence, are relatively important when they do occur, and where the society has a commitment to the encouragement and protection of the market in which such goods, services or activities are exchanged. This means that in the event of the establishment of the Inspectorate, some political decision has been made about the relative value of the *activity*, regardless of the regulatory costs associated with the governmental intervention.

2. The purpose of agency efforts is to produce *compliance*. In regulatory structures in which compliance is sought, the aim is to produce an outcome or state of affairs, prevent harm, or restore the *status quo ante*. The process of producing compliance on a case-by-case basis, even when combined with the concern for meeting absolute international standards, and insuring that safety planning, civil defense and evacuation drills have been carried out, is conducive to a flexible approach. The operational aim is to achieve the purposes of the legislation. Monitoring and inspection are used, and administrative definitions of acceptable compliance are paramount (Hawkins, 1984a).

3. The structure of inspectorates is based on the assumption of the need to *monitor events*. Hence, the "bottom-heavy" nature of the distribution of personnel, the concentration of discretion and judgement among the lower participants, and the widely held belief that the work is, at its most effective, personal, interactive, and "hands-on" (see Hutter, 1986; Hawkins, 1984a).

4. Inspectorates allocate substantial resources to the bottom of the organization. They are quite decentralized in authority, and

coordination of collective action comes about through generalized rules and procedures, guided principally by wisdom accumulated and distilled from experience (Reiss, 1983a).

5. Inspectorial work is *case-based*, and seeks solution to individual problems seen in context. A form of "situational logic" (Manning, 1980) that takes into account the context within which decisions are made is employed: this contrasts with long term rationality which emphasizes the achievement of distant goals even at the cost of working out explicit solutions to short-term problems. Incidents or events are seen within the context of current matters at hand while long-term plans and policies serve as "background" for such considerations. As relevant facts are gathered, patterned, and fitted within the decision field, they become the basis for decisions.

6. The enforcement mode adopted by Inspectorates in general is shaped by notions about policies as well as the familiar and routine relationships between the organizations regulated and the inspectors, branch, and section heads. An abiding concern is shown for the particular persons, situations and constraints that reduce or enhance opportunities to comply. In this sense, the working principles that guide regulation in Britain, application of non-numerical "reasonable practical means" and "best practicable means" tests, are short-hand ways of balancing costs to the industry or plant with broad safety considerations. Licenses are in effect glosses on detailed understandings of given plants, reactors, managers and the licensees' representatives (see O'Riordian, Kemp and Purdue, 1985).

7. Inspectorates use a *conciliatory style* of implementing governmental social control (Black, 1976:5). Concern in Britain is with fairness or equity rather than fitting legal definitions to cases as in America. These practices produce what Reiss (1983b:815) calls "... a body of standards virtually unique to a given situation-- standards that the agency more or less holds to enforcing its mandate." The NII, especially in licensing, maintains flexibility to decide matters in each case without being bound by strict rule, provided only that its decisions are consistent with its mandate to encourage safety (paraphrase of Reiss 1983:815. See also Hawkins, 1984a; Hutter, 1988).

These features of inspectorates are found in the NII, but several key *differences* should be pointed out, insofar as they bear on the question of enstructuration of the organization around the key notions of "uncertainty." These tend to support the position that NII is different. The differences are significant with respect to understanding the patterning of the perceptions of relevant risks as well as the extant regulatory culture. Let us consider the three most important of these differences. For a variety of reasons, the NII is in a reactive, or at very least a dependent, position vis-a-vis the regulated industry (Heimer, 1985). When transacting with the governmentally created bodies who seek licenses, NII is engaged in intragovernmental bargaining. The NII are, in effect, engaged in a form of regulating another governmental agency. This occurs in part because the "by-product" of nuclear production of electrical power is plutonium, an essential for the manufacture of nuclear weapons. The NII, because it is both information-dependent and obligated to encourage and protect production, must shape its policies and practices to those of the industry as represented by the applicant for a license.[4]

The NII controls or at least shapes the distribution of a collective goods (i.e. defense and electrical power) to which all are entitled and for which governmental resources are committed. The government of the day seeks to ensure production and relatively fair distribution. Government, working through Ministries, less controls electricity production than the production of automobiles, and focus rests as a result on combining or balancing safety concerns with production. Perhaps because of its position vis-a-vis the industry and national defense and its obligations to safety and the inherent risks of nuclear technology, all NII rulings are final and no structures judicial or otherwise exist within which to appeal a ruling. The NII can close an installation by signing a document, with "the stroke of a pen." Shutting down or reducing the heat in a reactor can be very expensive not only with respect to loss of power generation income, but because the mandated start-up procedures, once a reactor has been shut down, are very elaborate and require written NII approval and consultation at several points. In fact, an installation has been fully closed down only twice. This authority, it is believed, serves to direct attention and shift energies of the parties toward working out in advance mutually acceptable operating agreements.

Beliefs as Ideologies and Operating Tenets

Beliefs, or organized thoughts about the nature of reality that justify and make coherent social life, play an important, albeit unrecognized role, in making sensible the strikingly complex and abstract job facing the NII and its inspectors.[5] These beliefs might be called metaphorically the ways in which

---

4. This dependence upon industry has been discussed elsewhere as the "'irony of compliance;" see Manning, 1987.

5. The importance of beliefs in resolving some apparent paradoxes between beliefs and practice are reported in Manning, 1989a.

people speak to themselves about their work and its parameters. The central beliefs of the inspectors can be noted in outline form and then briefly discussed.

1. The NII belief is that nuclear reactors and nuclear power production are fundamentally and essentially safe. Although there are at least four distinctive designs of reactors in Britain, and the first PWR is now scheduled to be built, they consider the range of current designs licensable in principle.

2. The NII belief is that time produces refinement in reactor design and operation (some have claimed that reactors become more productive in time, that they show a "learning curve"), and that precedents sedimented in licenses are amalgamated into more general principles of safety assessment.

3. The NII belief is that there is an overall growth toward a manageable formalization of procedures and practices of building, designing and operating nuclear installations. As the Chief of NII said, "[these represent a] codification of the collective judgments of experts... a set of standards for the next generation."

4. The NII belief, supported by law, is that the licensee has the primary responsibility for safety, for preparing the argument stating the safety of various components and operational procedures of the installation (the "safety cases"), and for managing, operating and maintaining the reactor once licensed. In addition, the licensee is responsible for protecting the employees working in the plant, the environment and nearby citizens.

5. NII, with respect to accidents of various types, define safety in probability terms with respect to the safety and cooling systems preventing an identified accident, judgments (human factors), e.g., 10^{-4} on redundancy, $+ 10^{-4}$ on diversity (two separate ways to cool an overheating reactor: insert graphite rods or blow in CO_2 gas) and fail-safe measures. These statements of probability, in turn, are based upon fault trees, simulations and individual problem-focus (simulation of real life situations without real-life data).

6. NII view the probability of any sort of accident as low. Nevertheless, when pressed, they can provide detailed simulations of movements of radioactivity (with adjustments for the speed and direction of the wind, the location of the release, the 30 minute lag prior to intervention required on the older graphite and magnox reactors).

These beliefs cohere and guide the complex and iterative licensing process, and are the underlying basis, the tacit assumptions, or knowledgeability

(Giddens, 1984), that patterns organizational routines and decisions. Note that although not stated explicitly, the NII define and restrict their operational role to judgments about technical issues around the safety of the reactor and associated issues of employee and citizen safety, waste storage and disposal and emergency planning.   Discretion at all levels is assumed, even though, from the administrators' standpoint, it is distressingly concentrated at the bottom. The day to day operations of the NII reveal the pattern of their beliefs. The strategy of licensing is perhaps the clearest example of this operational focus.

The Strategy of Licensing

The NII is focused and organized around licensing and inspecting nuclear installations.[6] It is assumed by the NII that at some point a license will be granted, but that relevant variables are time and resources. The outcome, in the final analysis, is known and anticipated by the parties involved. Negotiations are required to ensure that it will be granted through routine procedures and that the necessary context of agreement is established among the relevant parties. The natural history of the licensing process, especially the key turning points, crises, and stages in this process, provides a revealing framework for examining the work of the NII. This is the framework within which the social construction of licensing takes place. Clearly, in this process, the NII views itself as holding final judgment, as well as the ultimate sanction.   However, they remain dependent upon the licensees not only for information, scientific research and candor, but for maintaining a basic level of decency and mutual trust in their encounters. This is clearly the case because the level, kind, quality and amount of information is overwhelming, beyond the comprehension of any person or group of persons, and embedded in past trustworthy interactions and exchanges (see Manning, 1989b). Needless to say, this context is not captured entirely in written records or past agreements.

A series of well recognized stages frame negotiations concerning a variety of issues, taking many forms such as letters, phone calls, memoranda, conferences, small meetings, and site visits, between NII and the licensee. These include: (1) consideration of site and planning permission; (2) review of emergency planning and liaison with county council and regional planning boards; (3) assessing

---

6. The economic literature states some conditions under which licensing is used to regulate markets.   These include a monopoly market, nationalized industries where a level of performance for market entry is required, and the case in which consumers cannot judge the quality of the good (either because of lack of information, or complexity of the good).   Licenses will be granted because the good or service is needed; the concern is with the quality and relative availability of the product.

building and reactor design specification; (4) working out managerial and staff training components; (5) setting out acceptable steps toward the commissioning of the reactor and its components (pressure circuit, safety systems, instrumentation, waste storage, disposal and removal), including testing with and without nuclear rods inserted into the reactor; (6) formulating the specific clauses or conditions to be stated in the license (each reactor has a different set, and licenses vary in length and detail); (7) agreeing on the status of operating approval; (8) once a license has been granted, inspecting to assure performance as well as routine maintenance. Finally, (9) although no civilian reactor as yet has been decommissioned in Great Britain, managing and supervising this process would be an NII responsibility. Decommissioning produces a conclusion to the licensing-planning drama. Revoking a license for a given period of time, or considering any part of a safety case until satisfaction is reached, even if delays ensue, is done and is well within the authority of the Inspectorate. The licensing process involves gradual sanctioning to induce change, and is the focus of the work. Licensing is not viewed as adversarial in character, as it might be in the U.S..

Other rules are enforced and other activities performed. Observation of international rules on exposure to radiation are monitored, as are management procedures and staffing. Yet another set of rules governs plant operation. These may be written into the license, but they vary in breadth and scope, and in the kind of notification required by the NII. Plant operation and modification rules are site-specific, complex and have a flexible bearing on operations.[7] The rules governing plant and reactor operations can be quite specific, but are broadly stated in many cases, and little attention is given to "violations" (not a word used in the NII) or rule-breaking. Enforcement of these rules usually involves a series of carefully nuanced and sequenced decisions. Inspectors may argue for a level of compliance, given other factors such as time, costs, and whether the request is considered to be reasonable.

Other issues of mutual concern are accident/incident reporting, providing scientific data on experimentation, testing and operating conditions; discretion revealing future plans and operations and in communication around shared problems of mutual concern. This bargaining context and shared sense of "openness to argument," whether in regard to licensing, rule-enforcement or

---

7. Rules which guide the operation of nuclear power stations take several forms and arise from quite different sources. Some derive from international bodies, such as the rules about exposure to radiation; some are stated in the conditions of the license; some are developed by the licensee to govern plan procedures, operations and management arrangements. Still other rules are created by the National Radiation Safety Board and a group composed of heads of power stations and research reactors.

monitoring, plant operations, or management, is thematic at NII, and members of NII feel, perhaps correctly, that this view is shared by their counterparts at the CEGB, BNFL and SSEGB.

Conclusion

The theme of this paper has been the social construction and management of risk and uncertainty within HM Nuclear Installations Inspectorate. It has focused on the development of an organizational structure, a set of beliefs and a strategy, licensing, that manage the defined uncertainty.[8] The nature of the posited uncertainty emerged from historical decisions arising from national defense needs, publicly acknowledged accidents and related Royal Commissions and planning inquiries, and parliamentary decisions that served to locate the NII within the Health and Safety Commission. The risks that became salient were those that threatened public consensus on nuclear power, especially releases and accidental spills and dumps of radioactive materials. Policy, as argued elsewhere (Manning, forthcoming), is not directed to creating prospective guidance, but to maintaining flexible discretion in bargaining, and facilitating damage control in the event of an accident. The enstructuration of the Inspectorate reveals a selective concern with types of risk, and focuses attention upon the technical requirements of reactor safety without concern about relative or absolute levels of safety or risk virtually inherent in the technology. From this complex of concerns were forged the everyday practices of working through the safety case and inspecting to ensure compliance. These practices, it would appear, do much to reify the very uncertainty posited as central to the mandate of the organization.

Perhaps this warrants a reflective pause. Consider this lovely quote from Kai Erikson, surely one of the most poetic of sociologists, concerning the relationship between "culture" and "reality."

> one of the crucial jobs of a culture is to edit reality in such a way that its perils are at least partly masked. It *is* a precarious world, and those who must make their way through it without the capacity to forget those perils from time to time are doomed to a good deal of anxiety (Erikson, 1976: 240).

---

8. It is not possible in this paper to explore *why* the NII chooses this view of uncertainty as opposed to others, or focuses on these features of the environment. Also insufficiently explored are national modes of nuclear safety regulation. This is the agenda for comparative research, and will be partially accomplished in my larger work tentatively titled, *Secularized Dread*.

Erikson attributes to "culture" the task of somehow "editing" reality, but perhaps this "editing" is less a task than a premise. The work of editing reality is in part based on enstructured blindness, assumptions, beliefs and strategies. The "editing" or bracketing of cues and events for socially constructing reality and representing it to the organization, and, in turn, rerepresenting this reality to various publics, may be a characteristic of organizations and regulatory agencies, because of their monitoring and surveillance functions, in particular. If so, investigating how this takes place and, if proven, why this is the case, is a worthy scholarly task now before us.

15

"FATCATS" and Prosecution in a Regulatory Agency: A Footnote on the Social Construction of Risk

Keith Hawkins

Risk, sb. 1661. [-Fr. *risque*--It. *risco, rischio*, f. *rischiare* run into danger.] **1.** Hazard, danger; exposure to mischance or peril. Freq. const. *of.* **2.** The chance or hazard of commercial loss, *spec.* in the case of insured property or goods 1719. **3.** *Risk-money*, an allowance made to a cashier to cover accidental deficits 1849.

1. To cut my Elder Brother's Throat, without the Risque of being hanged for him 1696. Phr. *To run a* or *the r.* 2. An Insurance made on Risks in Foreign Ships 1755. Hence **Riskful** *a* hazardous, uncertain. (The Shorter Oxford English Dictionary)

The purpose of this paper is to explore in a preliminary way what the idea of risk means to legal actors. In particular, I am concerned with those who are professionally involved in sighting, assessing, and controlling risks to the health, safety, and welfare of people at work. The focus of the analysis is on the decision-making of English Factory Inspectors. Like all regulatory officials, Factory Inspectors are actors who work with a legal and organisational mandate;

The research on which this paper is based was partly funded by a grant from the Health and Safety Executive, which I acknowledge with thanks. The views expressed are mine, and not necessarily those of the HSE. An earlier version of this paper was presented at the Annual Meeting of the Law and Society Association, Vail, Colorado in June 1988. For helpful comments I thank Bridget Hutter, Diane Vaughan, and, in particular, Albert J. Reiss.

they implement and enforce the law by resort to a variety of informal means (Baldwin, 1987; Hutter, 1987); and from time to time they have to decide whether resort to formal legal action is an appropriate response to the hazards they encounter. How is risk understood by these people, and what especially does it mean when we look at action to implement or to enforce law ostensibly framed to control risk?

The main argument of the paper is that the primary conception of risk held by Factory Inspectors changes significantly in the course of decision-making about action. To contemplate the use of formal legal processes in regulatory work creates an array of very different risks of its own for the legal decision-maker. These latter become crucial in determining whether a risk in the workplace is to become a formal legal problem. Risks associated with losing a prosecution, if calculated to be too great, may lead to an abandonment of the idea of using the formal law to combat the original risk and a substitution of other means of control. One of the defining characteristics of risk, of course, is that it involves a pre-occupation with a possible future. As soon as a case or problem presents the signs of being potential prosecution material, Factory Inspectors behave rather like lawyers (Hosticka, 1979), and become more interested in what is likely to happen, than in what has happened. When the prospect of formal legal action becomes a realistic option, the future contemplated by the legal actor shifts dramatically so that decision behaviour is directed instead towards minimising the risks to that person inherent in the legal process.

The first, and obvious, conception of risk with which Factory Inspectors are concerned is the apparent hazard to the worker and sometimes the public: the *occupational risk*. Indeed, this notion of immediate or long-term risk to physical well-being arising from work is usually the pre-eminent concern prompting a decision by an inspector to take some sort of official remedial action, that is, to create a case (Hawkins, 1984). Once, however, a case has been created and is being handled in some way, it becomes a piece of organisational property, and one in the last resort potentially open to prosecution. As soon as a case is designated, however tentatively, as a potential prosecution, the conception of risk is transformed, for the legal actor is now much more preoccupied with the *legal risk*. The occupational risk to the worker, the precipitating concern, tends to occupy a secondary position, becoming overlaid (often substantially) by the risks to the inspector's sense of competence and the agency's sense of credibility, posed by the nature of law itself, and the vagaries of the legal process. The legal risk is itself a kind of occupational risk to the inspector.

The use of the law seems to be regarded by regulatory officials in Britain as a rather hazardous enterprise, posing risks of failure to both the individual and his or her organisation.[1] Risk is inherent in the nature of law and the processes

---

1.   This theme is pursued in Hawkins, 1984a; see also Cranston, 1979; Richardson, et al., 1983; Hutter, 1988.

of law. Factory Inspectors, indeed, seem to be particularly conscious of the uncertainties of law, which is due in part to the fact that they, in contrast with the practice in many other regulatory inspectorates in Britain, are part of a decentralised structure of decision-making about prosecution. Factory Inspectors in routine cases actually make the decision whether or not to prosecute (subject only to approval by their principal inspector), and then, in contrast with the police, prepare and prosecute those cases in the magistrates' courts.[2] Since the same individual manages a prosecution case from beginning to end, the implication of the importance attached to legal risks is that in the decision whether or not to prosecute, a predominant concern is not so much a preoccupation with the substantive issue of whether a prosecution is deserved, or in some sense needed, as a coldly pragmatic assessment of whether the prosecution will be successful (Hawkins, 1987; see also Hawkins, 1984a). To make the point another way, the first conception of risk organising decisions and actions is one which emerges from the regulatory inspector's legal and occupational mandate. This is broadly construed as the protection of workers and others from the hazards of the workplace. The second organising conception of risk, however, is derived from the nature of regulatory work, an inspector's membership in a regulatory agency, and his or her conception of competence in the job, allied also with some conception of the agency's interest (or not) in displaying activity, effectiveness, and "success" to its interested publics.

The analysis is based on a series of interviews conducted with a carefully-drawn sample of Factory Inspectors. The research was part of a larger inquiry into prosecution policy and practice in the various occupational health and safety inspectorates in Britain conducted at the Oxford Centre for Socio-Legal Studies as part of its programme of research into occupational health and safety regulation (Hawkins, 1987; see also Centre for Socio-Legal Studies, 1983). The particular sample was organised around four administrative areas of the Factory Inspectorate (FI) chosen for the inspectors' apparent propensity to use, or to avoid using, the ultimate sanction of prosecution. Two areas were selected which appeared to make above average use of prosecution, two below average use.[3] The data were collected by means of lengthy, loosely-structured

---

2. Potentially newsworthy or otherwise troublesome cases may be referred to the area director or headquarters for final decision. Arrangements are different in Scotland, of course, where prosecution is the responsibility of the Procurator Fiscal (see Jamieson, 1985).

3. In the absence of data on rates of prosecution, the selection of areas was based partly on statistics of prosecution by area, partly on the reputation within the inspectorate of the willingness to prosecute among staff in certain areas, and partly to align the choice of areas with other colleagues who were also conducting field research on related matters.

conversations (all but four tape-recorded) with subsamples of inspectors drawn according to the nature of their regulatory work, to permit valid comparisons across areas. In total, 52 individuals were interviewed,[4] drawn from the ranks of the 1B grade (i.e., trained field inspectors), together with their supervisors (the principal inspectors) and each of the four area directors. Quotations which follow are verbatim remarks by staff in these grades.

The Factory Inspectorate is the largest of a number of inspectorates charged with the task of protecting and advancing the health, safety, and welfare of people in the workplace in Britain.[5] There are also inspectorates to monitor the health and safety of people at work in agriculture, mines and quarries, nuclear installations, and railways, among other things (such as explosives, and off-shore installations).[6] These inspectorates are directed by a further organisation--the Health and Safety Executive (HSE)--which generally manages their work and formulates broad health and safety policy. The HSE is itself responsible to the Health and Safety Commission (HSC), which represents the major interest groups. FI is divided into 14 administrative areas, each managed by an area director, assisted by a number of principal inspectors, each of whom in turn manages the work on an "industry group" comprised of two or three field (1B grade) inspectors, and possibly one or more trainee inspectors. Each industry group is responsible for regulatory work in distinctive types of industry, such as construction, chemicals, general manufacturing, and so on. Each area is also home to a distinctive National Industry Group (NIG) whose task is to formulate and coordinate national policy on the regulation of particular groups of industries which share common problems.

---

4. This sample represents almost 10% of the complement of 538 field inspectors in FI at the time of research, or almost 13%, if trainees are omitted.

5. Note that historically the early Factory Acts in Britain were more concerned with restricting hours of labour for women and children than with the promotion of occupational safety and health. Enforcement seems to have reflected this pattern; in 1879-80, for instance, fewer than 5% of prosecutions were for breaches of safety regulations (Bartrip, 1987).

6. The Industrial Air Pollution Inspectorate (formerly the Alkali Inspectorate), was also a constituent inspectorate. It has, however, recently been transferred to a newly-formed Inspectorate of Pollution.

Conceptions of Risk

How Factory Inspectors conceive of risk has a number of very important implications for the ways in which they go about their work and the way in which they make decisions. In particular, risk has a composite character which reflects a concern both with the *likelihood* that something untoward may happen and with the *gravity* of a possible undesired event. Factory Inspectors are preoccupied with both actual and potential fatalities and catastrophe (or "FATCATS" as they are engagingly known in the U.S. Occupational Safety and Health Administration; Lloyd-Bostock, 1988). The way in which risk is conceived of by field inspectors also suggests to them what degree of compliance may be expected from their attempts to implement the health and safety legislation, with correspondingly profound implications for the particular enforcement strategy they adopt. This conception of risk may vary greatly depending on an inspector's precise regulatory job and also on characteristics of the regulated firms. Factory Inspectors monitor health and safety matters in a variety of contrasting settings. Since in the organisation they are grouped according to the nature of the particular industries which they handle (with inspectors who deal exclusively with the construction industry, for example, or those who regulate chemicals plants), each field inspector tends to have a more homogeneous conception of risk than might otherwise be expected from the hugely varied nature of work in health and safety regulation. (Inspectors do, however, have their experience broadened by the occasional transfer between industry groups.)

Each type of industry tends to be associated with different kind of risk which confront their workforces. A brief comparison between construction work and the chemicals industry should illustrate the point. The construction industry presents a large number of immediate and sometimes quite obvious risks to individual workers, as compared with the chemicals industry. Construction work is characterised by a high degree of transience. The site and work on it have no permanence at all: building work often starts from virgin ground, developing and changing rapidly, thereby preventing the installation of safety features with any enduring quality about them. Building is an ephemeral activity, moving in a series of phases--excavation, construction, roofing, and so on--with methods of work generally regarded as inherently dangerous, and with constantly changing risks which often involve different kinds of workpeople. The lack of a stable and coordinated social organisation leads to mistakes, and mistakes lead to accidents (Reimer, 1976). As a result, it is generally accepted in FI that the number and kind of risks routinely encountered by construction inspectors are larger and more serious, so far as the individual worker is concerned, then in other types of industry. The occupational risks of the building industry are exacerbated by its current economic context. There is at present considerable competition in the construction industry in Britain and many firms are under extreme pressure to keep costs to the bare minimum. Safety measures can be both costly and time-consuming, profit margins are small, and clients usually demand the speedy completion of the work. In such circumstances, safety precautions are often among the first things dispensed with. Many construction firms are accordingly regarded by Factory Inspectors as having a substantial incentive to save on safety. Allied with this is a general view of management in construction as ill-informed about safety matters, as often disorganized and sometimes disreputable. In the nature of things, inspectors often encounter construction firms only when a risk has been realised and there is a serious injury or a fatality (or, as FI parlance has it, more prosaically, if more graphically, "a body on the floor").

The dangers of collapsed excavations, falls from scaffolding or roofs, or being struck by machinery or falling objects may be more or less apparent to those at risk. So far as the regulatory inspector is concerned, however, transience means that decisions about what action to take have to be made on the spur of the moment, since the chances of a quick return to the site for a follow-up visit to monitor progress with remedial measures, or to continue negotiating for compliance (part of the typical moves in compliance strategy; Hawkins, 1984a) are very remote, given the other typical demands on an inspector's time. This may encourage a tendency to err on the side of severity in approach to enforcement, with (relatively speaking) greater emphasis being given to a sanctioning than a compliance strategy the more serious and immediate the risk.

The risks of the construction industry can be contrasted with the very different risks of the chemicals industry. In chemicals work (and factories in general) the transience of construction work is not a problem for the Factory Inspector:

> If you have a factory, you have a stable situation. You can go to a factory, see a problem, say an unguarded machine, that machine will be there in three months time, twelve months time. You can go to a building site, you're seeing a dynamic situation. It'll be totally different tomorrow, and the day after. Therefore, if you say "Do this, and I'll come back tomorrow, that particular job could be over by tomorrow . . . . With construction, you may never see the company again, so you've really got to decide, when you see the situation, "Well, do I serve a notice and stop the job? Do I prosecute? Or do I merely advise?" But you have to decide there and then. And if you're going to prosecute you get the evidence there and then. There is far more prosecution without prior warning [in construction inspection] because prior warning is impracticable, because if you've never seen the firm before, you may never see them again.

Many chemical firms are big businesses. Plants represent major investments, and manufacturing processes are large scale, and generally prosperous and highly organised. Risks here extend beyond individuals, in contrast to construction. They may involve major hazards arising from events such as leak or explosions which threaten an entire plant, all who work in it, and quite possibly, members of the public. This conception of risk demands that the inspector concentrate more on preventive work, on the identification and assessment of large-scale hazard, to foreclose the possibility--however remote--of a catastrophe. It also suggests to the regulatory inspector that some chemicals firms have a high degree of self-interest in compliance (some would even say over-compliance in some circumstances) with health and safety regulation (see also Genn, 1987). Apart from the risk of catastrophe, the chemicals industry may have a substantial interest in avoiding the loss of skilled workers through injury. As a result, such firms are regarded as very cooperative and very willing to spend money in the cause of safety.[7]

Conceptions of risk held by field inspectors therefore exercise an important influence over their working theories of compliance and noncompliance, and in turn over their monitoring and enforcement behaviour. Even plants with strong self-interest in compliance (due to the remote possibility of catastrophe associated with inherently risky manufacturing processes) will nevertheless attract close attention from the Factory Inspectorate. Those with pronounced incentives to comply are treated in turn as potentially more compliant. If, on the other hand, the risk of catastrophe to plant and self-preservation are low, it will be assumed that the company has correspondingly less incentive to comply, leading to a greater tendency to ascribe to the regulated firm a potentially less compliant character in general. This imagery is important not only because it serves as the basis on which an agency organises its monitoring systems, but also because it leads to differences in the way in which inspectors exercise their discretion: the "compliant" and the "cooperative" are likely to have their rulebreaking framed differently from those who are not viewed so favourably. Accidents are more likely to be defined as excusable when they take place on the premises of compliant or cooperative companies (see generally Hawkins 1984a; Hawkins and Manning, forthcoming). The irony of all of this, as Genn's (1987) findings suggest, is that the possibility for self-regulation are likely to be greater in precisely those risky enterprises which in fact attract more official monitoring and enforcement attention.

What risk means to regulators also varies at different points in the organisation. Inspectors in the field are often confronted with the vivid reality of bodies on floors, blood, pain and so on. Risks confronting work-people are here

---

7. Whether this attitude signals a cultural difference is hard to say, though British regulatory officials do seem to be less cynical about the motivation of their regulated industries than their American counterparts; see generally Vogel, 1986.

made concrete and tangible. This reality is sometimes enough to prompt immediate initiation of legal action. As a result, the field inspector can more readily decide to take action when faced with an unguarded dangerous machine, an unsupported trench, or an improperly erected scaffold (even if there is no body on the floor) because he or she has personally seen (Lloyd-Bostock, 1987; Hutter and Lloyd-Bostock, this volume), or has learned directly from colleagues, what such risks can lead to. Past experience sensitises the regulatory inspector in a very direct way to particular kinds of risk, possibly leading to decision-making of an ad hoc, fragmented, particularistic kind.

Risk also, of course, penetrates the centre of the regulatory organisation where preventive or remedial policies must be devised for classes of problem. The world here is also real, but the nature of that reality is very different. Risks are viewed through the lens of natural scientific rationality in the abstract, as concepts, or as aggregated statistics of actual or potential numbers of corpses, cancers, and catastrophes. A particular risk is not an immediate and precise problem demanding action, as it often is in the field. It is an exemplar of a general threat compelling a strategic response in the form of modification or innovation of policy. Risk here is in a sense speculative, general, and concerned with trends, patterns, and large forces, rather than ad hoc and particular, as it is in the field.

Prosecution

Prosecution is a very important move in the enforcement of health and safety regulation in Britain, even though the power is used very sparingly indeed by some of the HSE inspectorates. In the Mines and Quarries Inspectorate (MQI), for example, there may be no more than one or two prosecutions a year; in the Nuclear Installations Inspectorate (NII), none at all (prosecution being made virtually redundant by extensive licensing powers; Manning, this volume).[8] The Agricultural Inspectorate (AgI) and FI both make greater use of the power, however, with around 300 and over 1500 cases a year, respectively.[9] In both FI and AgI decision-making about prosecution is decentralised, whereas

---

8. The only prosecution in which NII has been involved was of the nuclear reprocessing plant at Sellafield a few years ago. This was for the discharge of radioactive waste into the Irish Sea, a matter, predictably, which prompted considerable publicity.

9. Provisional figures for FI prosecution work in 1984 show 1855 "informations laid," 1649 convictions, 79 "informations withdrawn," and 54 "informations dismissed." The results in 54 cases were not known (from HSE, 1985).

in MQI (as well as in the Industrial Air Pollution Inspectorate (see Weait, 1989), which used to be part of HSE) final decisions about prosecution are made at the very top of the organisation, at the level of Chief Inspector. In FI and AgI, the decision to prosecute is effectively made by the field inspector concerned, in conjunction with, and with the approval of, the appropriate principal officer. FI differs from AgI in an important way, however, since Factory Inspectors actually appear in court to conduct the prosecution proceedings themselves, whereas AgI recruits local solicitors for the purpose. The importance accorded to prosecution by all the HSE inspectorates is suggested by the care with which they make prosecution decisions (Hawkins, 1987), whether they are organised on a centralised or decentralised basis, and by the amount of resources devoted to it.[10] Indeed, prosecution is often treated (inside and outside the agency) as synonymous with "enforcement."

Factory Inspectors may also make other formal legal moves: they may issue improvement or prohibition notices. The former require that certain remedial work be carried out within a period of time, the latter prohibit risky conduct or a hazardous state of affairs with immediate effect on pain of prosecution for failure to comply. Notices are generally regarded as remedial in character, prosecutions as punitive. A notice requires careful drafting to deal with future methods of working, use of the plant or substances, and so on, whereas a prosecution has to be managed extremely carefully not only to prevent wasting a great deal of past work but also to avoid jeopardising future efforts. While the notice tends to act in a practical way at shop-floor level, the prosecution tends to focus on the board room and may prompt an organisational solution to a problem. This is because it has a much more public character.

The risks to the regulatory inspector and to the regulatory organisation posed by a potential prosecution case--the risks inherent in using the law, in other words--shape both *whether* the law is used, and *how* it is used. Prosecution work is not normally a common feature of a Factory Inspector's everyday activities (the mean number of cases per inspector per year is two or three, though some construction inspectors may mount a dozen or more), yet it is treated as work of a substantively different and important kind: "one of the most difficult decisions of the job." There are a number of reasons why this is so. To prosecute health and safety violations is to use the law formally and explicitly. It is to bring a problem or an event to public attention through the medium of the criminal law, with all its implications of stigma, blame, and the like. Use of courts, however, surrenders control over the ultimate disposal of the case to a third party--the magistracy or judiciary--and renders the inspector especially accountable to the regulatory organisation. To prosecute is visibly to

---

10. Legal work, of which prosecution is a major part, consumes about 9% of the total HSE resources.

take sides in the fundamental dilemma of regulatory control about the extent to which the law, with its costs and constraints, can justifiably intervene in the conduct of productive industry. Inevitably, prosecution tends to be used only in those cases which have something special about them.

The character of risk confronting the regulatory actor changes as soon as a case crosses the organisational threshold and is treated as potential prosecution material with the possibility of formal law use coming into play. The shift is the consequence of two broad features: the nature of the work as it affects organisation and individual in regulating business behaviour, and features inherent in character of law, legal standards, and legal processes.

The Nature of Regulatory Work

The regulatory agency, as a law enforcement authority (among other things), is in a difficult and vulnerable position, caught between publics with competing interests as to the degree and kind of legal regulation necessary to control the undesirable side-effects of industrialised life (Hawkins, 1984b). Compared with the other strategies and tactics deployed in the enforcement of regulation by inspectors which are characterised by informality and low visibility, prosecution is dramatic and public. By its use, (or nonuse, in cases receiving widespread publicity) a regulatory agency makes powerful statements about its position on the issues. By its choice of cases for prosecution, or decisions to rule out prosecution, and through its general level of prosecution activity, an agency seeks to balance competing demands for enforcement activity (to those who wish to see it), while at the same time avoiding the appearance of being oppressive, or a burden on productive industry (to those who adopt laissez-faire values). Prosecutorial decisions thus require flexibility. Positions on issues may shift with the political climate. Britain under the current Conservative government is seen by inspectors as generally hostile to regulatory activism, a sentiment which is reflected in the approach of many Factory Inspectors in their decision-making: "I think there's a political climate," said one, "that suggests that the Civil Service ought to be seen as assisting industry, and not acting as a purely prosecution-minded policeman . . . ."[11]

As this remark suggests, the individual regulatory inspector is by no means immune to the broader political and economic pressures and constraints affecting regulatory agencies in general. The fact that prosecution is a very public enforcement move has its advantages, but it also creates certain risks for both the regulatory organisation and the field inspector. So far as inspectors are concerned, prosecution is a means of conveying messages to particular audiences

---

11. Though note that there may be certain special cases where the Government may strongly support prosecution.

which exist both within and beyond their agency. The internal audience is comprised most significantly of the 1B inspector's principal officer (who is the source of reports and evaluations of the inspector's work), and ultimately the area director. Prosecution is an important symbol of organisational work in inspectorates like FI since it provides a concrete index of activity and output which is more salient than advice, education, bargaining, and the other moves of compliance strategy. "It's something they can measure," said one field inspector. "It's something which, frankly, gets you a good reputation." Another reported that he had deliberately prosecuted more cases in his early years as a Factory Inspector because, as he put it, "I wanted to impress my PI [principal inspector] that I was a go-getter." Prosecution creates a paper record within the organisation, one which in FI goes to agency headquarters: "Prosecution does tend to stand out because it means that there are papers floating around when the case is heard . . . . [One] is seen by others to be doing something." Senior staff, for their part, may treat the way in which a prosecution is conducted as a good indicator of the extent to which an inspector possesses some of the most important qualities required in the job: "The way an inspector carries out a prosecution can demonstrate abilities over somebody else. If it's a hard case to take, and he takes it and acquits himself well, this indicates quite a lot of things: his ability to prepare, to think on his feet in court [in] a very public arena."

While the importance attached to prosecution within the agency ensures that the inspector's work is noticed, it is also a risky strategy for the same reason: there is always a chance of losing. A lost case is conspicuous within the organisation, and risks being interpreted as failure, especially at headquarters: "Nobody likes to lose a case, and our system here is that if you do you have to have a report in London the next day [which] is a big encouragement not to lose." As another officer said, ". . . I don't want perhaps something I've made a bit of a balls-up [about] being seen by all and sundry in HQ: 'How the hell did young [so-and-so] lose this case? It's open and shut!'" "I'm certain it's a black mark," said another. There are fewer hazards for the inspector who tries wherever possible to implement the legal mandate by bargaining in private (Hawkins, 1984b). Factory Inspectors inevitably see a prosecution as "their case," as personal property. Such possessiveness is not surprising since they make all the crucial decisions about whether or not to pursue a prosecution in the first place (normally subject only to approval by their principal officer), and then conduct the case for the prosecution in the magistrates' court. To lose a case, then, risks impugning an inspector's competence and credibility within the organisation, and outside as well as among segments of the regulated population.

The risk of losing is, therefore, a primary concern among regulatory inspectors, a concern that increases the less frequently a regulatory agency takes cases to court.[12] Many of the Factory Inspectors interviewed had never lost a case, and of the others who had, about half had only lost one. The ease with which many of them were able to recall and describe the details of their failed cases suggests the salience of the event for them. Nevertheless, although inspectors may devote considerable time and trouble in preparing cases to make sure they win, the decision to prosecute always presents them with a risk of losing. The defendant may plead not guilty and produce new evidence; witnesses' memories may let them down; they may be intimidated by the drama of the proceedings; or the magistrates may simply interpret a rule in an unexpected way. Some inspectors acknowledged that the risks--and in some cases the actual experience--of losing had led them to review their approach, to become more cautious because "If you don't take them, you don't lose them," as one put it. As a result, to quote another, "I tend to go for certainties. It's foolish to put in too much time and effort if you're not too sure." It is interesting to note in this connection that 1B inspectors report that they normally only ask for the advice of senior colleagues about prosecution on technical matters bearing on evidence--not on substantive issues such as whether prosecution is the right course of action in a particular case.

Failure has other implications as well. An individual inspector may discover his or her credibility has been damaged, and it is now correspondingly more difficult to persuade employers to comply, or that the standing of the inspectorate as a whole has been impaired: "It tends to reduce the standing of FI towards industry if they prosecute a bum case." A lost case may also create an unfortunate precedent for the inspectorate. Indeed, it is thought that the risks of legal action are such that even a successful prosecution may prove counterproductive if the resultant fine is so small that it trivialises the original offence.

These constraints all help to support the balance necessary between the display of formal legal activity, on the one hand, and a measure of restraint, on the other. Some cases almost always demand prosecution: very serious incidents; newsworthy cases prompting a great deal of public concern; multiple fatalities; an especially vulnerable victim, such as a young person, and so on. Note that these examples are all of accidents or other untoward events, where the risk has been realised. As one field inspector put it: "If something goes 'Bang' there is an expectation that somebody will be brought to justice as a result. A scapegoat is required."

---

12. In the Regional Water Authorities, for example, where only a few water pollution cases find their way into court each year, inspectors sometimes complain that senior officials have to be 110% sure that they will win before going ahead; see Hawkins, 1984b.

Pre-emptive prosecutions, brought in response to an intolerable risk, are a more difficult matter, and are by no means compelled to the same degree. A hazard is much more difficult to act on by formal means, especially where it is one not readily apparent to those at risk. Action for regulatory inspectors is much more secure when there is already a body on the floor, and people are sufficiently chastened by the experience that they respond readily to demands for remedial measures. In such circumstances, prosecution often comes as no surprise. It is largely for these reasons that there is a marked tendency in FI to prosecute after an accident, in spite of the existence of an agency policy which encourages inspectors to implement a preventive approach and act on risks, rather than accidents. In fact, nearly 40% of prosecutions in FI follow accidents (Lloyd-Bostock, 1987). So far as the 1B inspector sees it: "If there's been a fatal accident, it's very difficult not to take action if the evidence is there and there's a breach there . . . although we are told it's the seriousness of the breach we should consider, rather than the accident resulting from it." Hazards are much less public and are not accompanied by the same expectations.

The Character of the Law

The character of health and safety legislation also poses significant risks for regulatory inspectors. The nature and form of legal rules act upon the individual legal official's exercise of discretion in a very profound way. The demands of the criminal law for a particular standard of proof add to the awareness of inspectors of the dangers in prosecuting certain kinds of offence framed in the statutes in certain ways.

An inspector who has come to the conclusion that substantively a case is worth prosecuting is then faced with the crucially important issue of whether the evidence that can be marshalled in support of the prosecution case can meet legal standards of proof and stand up in court. If so, another important question concerns the number and type of charges: which sections of which legislation are to be employed? Inspectors often have a real choice. Here, again, risks present themselves and again, the choices inspectors make are profoundly affected by the way in which a law or regulation is drafted. How a rule is crystallised and formulated reaches down, as it were, to shape the discretion of the legal actor in choosing whether and how to act. Factory Inspectors respond in patterned ways.

First, a general effect depresses the number of prosecutions. The use of prosecution tends to be restrained because a decision to lay an information usually involves an inspector in a commitment which demands many hours of work, and considerable care and trouble to be taken over the collection of evidence and the other preparatory work before trial. Part of the problem again stems from uncertainty surrounding the prosecution process as viewed by the field inspector. This prompts a defensive strategy. Incidents which look like potential prosecution cases have to be treated at the outset as if they will be prosecuted, for the purposes of taking statements and collecting other potential evidence. Once it is decided that the case should be prosecuted, the case has to be prepared on the assumption that it will be defended, even though few are. Furthermore, the case has to be prepared sufficiently thoroughly in the event that it is tried in the Crown Court, even though few are. All these contingencies must be guarded against, and the more serious the case, the more carefully it must be prepared. Defended cases are a particular burden and an anxiety. Where resources do not permit the preparation of a case to a satisfactory level, a notice or some other enforcement move may have to be adopted instead.

The process is a continual weighing-up of the costs and benefits of prosecuting, and is dependent upon other demands on an inspector's time: "If you've got too much work on at the time, then obviously you'll say 'Do I prosecute or don't I prosecute? I haven't got time to prosecute. I haven't got time to take the statements.' And therefore prosecution falls by the wayside." Or, as a construction inspector put it: "You don't want to have five or six cases lined up on your desk at the same time . . . They certainly need to be staged at reasonable intervals of time. To have two or three complicated cases in the same month would be far too much. [So if another case comes up?] Your reaction threshold is inevitably going to be moved up."

The amount of time needed to prepare a case varies widely: estimates ranged from a few hours to a month, depending on how straightforward it proves to be from the point of view of collecting evidence and fulfilling the other requirements for prosecution. Witnesses may be distant, and an inspector will often weigh the time and trouble involved in travelling some way from the office to gather evidence. This banal fact may serve to skew the distribution of prosecutions taken in favour of locations not too distant from the inspector's area office or usual "patch": "If something happens down there [pointing to a town on the map a considerable distance from the office] it would receive less attention than something happening [here]." For those who have no great taste for the theatre of prosecution (as one of the inspectors called it) the other things they could be doing with their time seem especially attractive: "While you're not prosecuting you're visiting more premises and perhaps achieving an impact by use of less punitive methods, than if you were out there taking all those flaming statements and coming back to the office and spending days preparing a prosecution and worrying yourself sick why they're defending it when it looked to you straightforward."

The risks inherent in the use and nature of the legal process play a major part in determining enforcement strategy in a second sense. Systematic preferences for certain kinds of prosecution case are observable in the decision-making behaviour of Factory Inspectors. Often it is not obvious which piece of legislation should be used for court proceedings. The choice is intimately affected by the way in which a law or regulation is actually drafted, the precise form of a rule again shaping the way in which discretion is exercised. To take two kinds of example, difficulties of proof increasing the risks of losing the case lead to a marked preference by Factory Inspectors for the prosecution of breaches of absolute, rather than general, legal requirements, and for the prosecution of breaches of safety, rather than long-term health, regulations.

Factory Inspectors often enjoy a choice of possibilities in determining how to proceed. The great majority look for a breach of an absolute requirement for prosecution, rather than a failure to observe a general duty, though the latter may have more far-reaching implications for remedial measures taken as a consequence of the legal action. "You go for section 14 of the Factories Act," said a principal inspector in a general manufacturing group, "because it's absolute and there are hundreds of decided cases. You can't lose." Subsection (1) of section 14 states:

> Every dangerous part of any machinery, other than prime movers and transmission machinery, shall be securely fenced unless it is in such a position or of such construction as to be safe to every person employed or working on the premises as it would be if securely fenced.[13]

The popularity of this section--which is taken by inspectors for all practical purposes as imposing an absolute duty on an employer to guard a dangerous machine (notwithstanding the judicial test)--and the success with which it is used is evident in FI prosecution statistics for 1985: of 255 informations laid under s.14, 248 (97.8%) resulted in convictions. Similarly, Lloyd-Bostock (1987) found that the largest single category of prosecution in FI comprised guarding offences, and that the majority of those prosecutions followed accidents. Though absolute requirements are generally regarded as "the easy option, the dead certainty," as one inspector put it, they also possess other virtues. They are quicker to prepare and their unproblematic quality represents the law to people, both employers and workforce, in a straightforward fashion: "They're clear, cast-iron cases, which the company can see, or their lawyers can see." The simplicity of the absolute breach makes it easier for an employer to acknowledge the failure to comply, and, from there, the justice of the prosecution.

That is a more simple matter than a breach of a general duty. The Health and Safety at Work Act, 1974, has changed the conception of enforcement in the law. Whereas earlier legislation tended to rely heavily on absolute requirements,

---

13. The problematic test of dangerousness was addressed by the House of Lords in *Close v. Steel company of Wales Ltd* (1962) AC 367, (1961) 2All ER 953, where it was held that a part of a machine might be dangerous if it might be a reasonably foreseeable cause of injury to anybody acting in a way a human being might be reasonably expected to act in circumstances which might be reasonably expected to occur (per Lord Morris of Borth-Y-Gest): 967.

suggesting a view of enforcement as inherent in the punishing of a breach of a rule, the introduction of general duties in the 1974 Act shifted the emphasis to the more vague purpose of remedying general problems. As a 1B inspector said, its reach is such that "Nearly any offence could also be covered by section 2 of the Health and Safety at Work Act." While in theory general duties, if successfully enforced, may be more effective because they have a wider impact upon the compliance of employers, the risks inherent in prosecuting for failing in a general duty make it a more difficult and cumbersome proposition for many inspectors. Some, indeed, acknowledged that they were deterred from prosecuting under s.2 of the 1974 Act, subsection (1) of which states:

> It shall be the duty of every employer to ensure, so far as is reasonably practicable, the health, safety and welfare at work of all his employees.

Subsection (2) goes on to embellish the general principle:

> Without prejudice to the generality of an employer's duty under the preceding subsection, the matters to which that duty extends include in particular--(a) the provision and maintenance of plant and systems of work that are, so far as is reasonably practicable, safe and without risks to health.

This clause is followed by four others, all requiring, "so far as is reasonably practicable," attention to related matters. The reaction of many inspectors is well summed up in the words of a principal inspector: "It's nice to be able to get a case where there's an absolute duty. There's no doubt about that . . . At one time the words "reasonably practicable" filled me with dread." As a result, most inspectors seem to use this important piece of legislation as a fall-back, for want of something safer, easier, and quicker.

The indeterminacy of the different form of words creates further risks should a case be taken to trial. A prosecution under s.2, in the words of an HSE lawyer, "is a somewhat unusual animal, because it looks to the court much more like a civil case, with experts arguing on either side, rather than an ordinary criminal trial." The problematic standard of the "reasonably practicable" is more contentious, more likely to invite a defence, thereby making real the possibility of losing. From the inspector's point of view, the concept is particularly risky because it is hard to be satisfied as to what is "reasonably practicable," and the test gives ultimate discretion to the court to decide the issue in a system of law which requires proof beyond reasonable doubt. What is regarded as "reasonably practicable" is also, of course, contingent upon the kind and degree of risk to the worker involved. The difficulties of proof (which are said not to be excessive where the occupational risk is clear and the remedies simple and cheap) mount as risks lessen or become more nebulous, adding to the inspector's uncertainties and sense of legal risk. In practice, the courts take the view that for a matter to be reasonably practicable the occupational risks must be easy to quantify, and the costs of compliance must not be great. "You've got to weigh up the seriousness of the risk against the costs of compliance, and so on," said a 1B inspector," so you've got this doubt, and it's up to the court to decide." Some inspectors complained that magistrates sometimes failed to grasp the meaning of "reasonable practicability," since they find the task of proof easier where the test is digital in character (was there a guard or not?), rather than analogic. Indeed, the court's position as arbiter of what is "reasonable" places the central issue into the realm of value rather than fact and adds to its contentiousness, from both prosecution and defence points of view. Similarly, general duties make demands of magistrates' scientific and engineering sense, as they are the ones who have, for example, to make the ultimate judgment as to what is "safe" behaviour. This again makes more demands upon an inspector than a proof that requires essentially that the existence or nonexistence of guarding be established.

As a result of the relationship between form of words and the strategic decisions of legal actors easily-identifiable, specific, discrete forms of rule-breaking seem to be more frequently prosecuted than a general and vague malaise in a company. The ease with which evidence can be obtained and presented in support of a prosecution also influences the use of formal enforcement action which tends to concentrate more heavily on certain industries. In the nature of things it may be easier to obtain suitable evidence in general manufacturing and engineering industries, for example, than in the chemicals industry. Construction cases are relatively straightforward compared with the difficulties which often face field inspectors who are dissatisfied with the performance of chemicals works with their complex and often invisible processes. The pre-occupation of the chemicals inspector--who may be involved in no more than one or two prosecutions a year (if that)--when faced with a possible prosecution case becomes "Are we able to allocate the time it's going to take?" This is ironical in light of the fact that the average construction inspector is involved in many more prosecutions annually.

The second pattern mentioned was the marked preference among Factory Inspectors for the prosecution of safety rather than health problems. This is despite the fact that a substantial number of inspectors believed that more people (possibly ten times as many) die as a result of occupationally-induced disease than as a result of accidents at work.[14] Interesting corroboration of this comes from a study of Trades Unions safety representatives which found that Factory Inspectors were believed to lay too much emphasis on accident work, and not enough on problems of occupational ill-health (Freedman, 1987). The problem

---

14. A recent estimate puts the number of deaths from occupational disease at between 8,000 and 20,000 a year; Meacher, 1988.

is that people are in some circumstances prepared to live with serious risks. They respond to the clarity and immediacy with which risks present themselves, not to the degree of threat the risk poses. This is the case whether we look at the behaviour of employers, employees, or regulatory inspectors. Safety cases come to light more readily. They are more visible and prompt more complaints. They tend to involve more immediate risks and more instantly dramatic consequences. "There's something, to my mind, more immediate about a man having his fingers chopped off," said a field inspector, "than in 20 or 30 years time getting asbestosis, or whatever." Similar patterns are evident where occupational health problems are concerned. Familiar, clearly toxic substances pose less of a problem for inspectors since most people will comply in accordance with the received wisdom about their dangers. Difficulties arise where cause-and-effect or toxicity are disputed, and people are correspondingly less willing to comply. At the same time it becomes increasingly difficult for an inspector in such circumstances to contemplate proving a case beyond reasonable doubt. Safety cases, on the other hand, are thought to be easier. Not only can they usually be handled as breaches of absolute requirements, there also is considerable case law to assist the inspector and the court in establishing what is to be regarded as "safe" or "unsafe." There are fewer authorities to help recognise what is or is not "healthy."

The extra risk faced by the inspector who wishes to prosecute for a violation likely to lead to long-term health problems is inherent in the evidentiary demands of the law. The result is much lower levels of prosecution. Preparing the case to meet the standards of evidence required in an occupational health case will inevitably involve expert medical evidence and can be extremely time-consuming, serving to deter inspectors from prosecuting:

> The medics are the last in the chain. And if they say "no," you've spent days--days!--on the case, to no avail because the final link in the chain says "No." So that's a deterrent . . . We will not now be taking cases like that, even though we might think they are gross breaches. We might chance our arm with a prohibition notice, but we might go down on appeal if the medics won't support us.

Sometimes it is possible for inspectors to adapt by substituting a safety violation as the cause of legal action, in the hope that a conviction will persuade the company, as a result, to effect more widespread remedial measures: "One might let go by . . . an alleged offence under health and wait for an easier prosecution under section 14 to come along, where we can with less resources, less problems, have the same effect." But it remains the case that impediments in the law are responsible for the comparatively low level of formal action concerning occupational health problems. Indeed the same impediments act in civil cases to make it difficult to sustain a claim for compensation for ill-health, serving to reduce the incentive for employers to cut exposure to potentially harmful substances (Baldwin, 1987).

Conclusion

A few general observations are possible on the basis of the argument and analysis presented above. At least three different systems of understanding can be discerned in which conceptions of risk operate in the occupational health and safety field. The *natural scientific* conception calculates risk in a quantitative fashion, transforming risks into bloodless, dispassionate probabilities which are sometimes so remote as to defy lay comprehension. Those who think in terms of the logic of natural scientific rationality do not find risks difficult to apprehend, because they are reducible to numbers which indicate how likely or unlikely it is that something untoward may happen. Policymakers in HSE operate with a natural scientific logic for the most part. Second, the *legal* conception of risk regards systems and standards of proof as central. Criminal law demands that causal relationships be established and then proved beyond reasonable doubt. The legal actors who must fulfill the demands of the legal system are concerned as a result with the evidence a court will accept. As has been argued above, the legal conception introduces its own patterns and distortions in the numbers and kinds of cases handled by formal legal means. Finally, the *lay* conception of risk employs at least two notable dimensions of logic: a preoccupation with what may happen when something untoward occurs (rather than how likely it is that something untoward will occur) and a difficulty in apprehending risk when cause and effect are attenuated by the passage of time (Schrager and Short, 1978). In practical terms the risk of immediate injury seems to be easier to grasp than the risk to health which may only be manifest many years later. This poses a real problem for enforcement: how to persuade employers and employees that certain activities or states of affairs are risky. This can be a particular problem if workpeople's familiarity with occupational hazards is such as to encourage, if not contempt, then at least complacency (what one Factory Inspector described as the "My father did that for forty years and he's alright" problem). This lay conception may operate in complete contradiction to the tenets of scientific rationality. Indeed it was for this reason that a very senior regulatory official expressed impatience with the strong public sentiment in Britain which is opposed to the permanent deep burial of radioactive waste, preferring instead for it to be kept on the surface, where it can be seen and if necessary moved, but where it is, in his view, much more at risk.[15] Nevertheless, scientists, lawyers, and lay people (not to mention regulatory

---

15. From a private conversation; these views have been recently echoed by Ginniff, 1988.

officials) may all in differing degrees find it hard to appreciate certain risks, since it is much easier to know a risk from past experience. Increasingly, however, technological developments threaten to outstrip the legal capacity for their control.

Law finds it difficult to address certain kinds of social problems, such as long-term risks to health arising from occupational exposure, because of the demands it makes for its own kind of certainty--in the case of the criminal law, beyond reasonable doubt. Indeed Factory Inspectors often spoke as if there were many instances where they had wished to act when faced with a threat to workers' health, but could not, because provable scientific knowledge about cause and effect was lacking. The character of the law tends to encourage reactive rather than pre-emptive behaviour. Law operates more comfortably in retrospect, when a risk has been realised, where it can react to the certitudes of things past rather than seek to anticipate what might happen in future. To the extent, however, that regulatory control is concerned to act pre-emptively--in response to risks-- difficulties arise to the extent that knowledge and ability to predict are problematic. These problems often are expressed in differences of opinion among those who lay claim to medical and scientific expertise. The limits of knowledge about occupational risks to health help to depress the level of prosecutions, especially in occupational health cases. While some risks are familiar, such as those associated with lead or asbestos, aetiological knowledge elsewhere is much less secure. Medical evidence in support of a prosecution is often difficult to find, and may be readily opposed by other expert evidence in a defended case. "It's very difficult to convince a court that the activity that's gone on has actually been sufficient to cause ill-health," said an area director, "unless you can produce a person whose health has been affected and a doctor who will say so." In a safety case, in contrast, the inspector can usually conduct the prosecution without having to rely on expert witnesses, thereby maintaining more control over matters. Magistrates, for their part, find issues simpler and more comprehensible; a guard missing from a dangerous machine is a more visible and self-evidently risky matter. The result leads to more ready legal control of certain kinds of cases. That is to say, some problems may not be dealt with as people think they need or deserve, while others receive the attentions of the formal legal process because they are more easily brought to it. This suggests that from a policy point of view it may be more viable to attain the better control of certain kinds of risk by altering techniques of regulation to make them more easily enforceable, rather than by seeking to alter the decision-making behaviour of legal actors. Licensing, for example, may be a more appropriate mode of getting to grips with some problems than are traditional command-and-control methods. Licences can be withheld or withdrawn, and operators can be prosecuted simply for acting without a licence.

The ambivalence with which many inspectors regard prosecution as an enforcement tactic means that its use is rather elastic. Though it is a drastic and public move it seems, ironically, to be regarded as a form of enforcement whose use can be adjusted in light of other demands upon an inspector's time. The constraints inherent in the law allied with a need to conserve resources serve not simply to depress the level of prosecution, but rather to divert its use into certain kinds of case. The very big or very bad case (a relatively rare phenomenon) usually demands prosecution whatever the risk of losing, but otherwise the risks to the inspector and the agency of pursuing cases that are not entirely secure in law--whatever their substantive merits--tend to lead to a preference for quicker, easier problems as subjects of formal legal action. That is, cases that are straightforward as to proof, quick to prepare, and unlikely to be defended are more attractive as prosecution material, and take precedence over other kinds of cases which, although more deserving or appropriate, are dealt with by other enforcement means, if at all. It should not be surprising that Factory Inspectors are inevitably more concerned with problems for which they have ready legal remedies, and remedies that are quick and easy to apply.

Allied with the preference for responding to past events rather than future possibilities, the law seems also better able to respond to the particular rather than the general. It has been shown, for example, that Factory Inspectors find it easier to deal with actual accidents, rather than risks of accidents, and that they prefer to enforce the law formally where they can employ a breach of an absolute rather than a general duty. To require (as in the air pollution legislation) that an industrialist use the "best practicable means" of controlling emissions opens up an array of interpretative problems which tend to deter legal actors from enforcing legislation in court. Inspectors often adapt their enforcement strategy by opting for an absolute standard that will be easier to prove as an alternative, where possible, or by choosing a notice or, in some cases, dropping the idea of formal legal action altogether. Absolute standards are less likely to be defended and they demand less of the magistrates: the case is essentially "open and shut" (as Factory Inspectors are fond of saying) and magistrates simply have to decide whether a guard (for example) was or was not present on a dangerous machine, not whether something was or was not reasonably practicable. The result again is that the complex, the costly, and the defensible are less likely to become legal cases. The behaviour is patterned, the biases are systematic.

Concern for the particular seems to pervade occupational safety and health regulation. Factory Inspectors were criticised by trade union officials for being too preoccupied with individual faults and not with general systems of working, nor with general hazards, not the organisation as a whole, nor the character of the company (Freedman, 1987). Yet trade union officials also were said by some regulatory agents to be too concerned with winning compensation for injuries suffered, rather than with a more activist stance and more broadly-based preventive work. Furthermore, employers may also comply with the particular, rather than the general, since risks that cause accidents tend for the most part to be cheaper and easier to remedy, as compared with those that threaten ill-health.

Indeed Genn (1987) found that long-term hazards to health tended to receive less remedial attention from employers because the costs implied were so substantial. This was true even of companies thought of as "good" because they were prepared to take an active interest in safety matters.

To sum up, ironically prosecution is more readily-used where there is already a body on the floor--where the risk has been realised. When a risk is identified and it is thought that something ought to be done about it, however, a different set of considerations come into play. The nature of the demands imposed by the legal system and legal rules operating upon organisations and organisational actors create their own kind of risks. The Factory Inspector has to handle occupational risks *on the terms laid down by the law's construction of risk*. These legal risks operate to deflect handling and investigation resources away from troublesome cases and into those which can readily be prosecuted, in much the same way that doctors sometimes prescribe treatments that they know for diseases about which they may be uncertain.

PART SIX

Institutionalizing Risk

16

The Institutionalization of Risk

Albert J. Reiss, Jr.

On Risk Making and Risk Taking

A growing body of literature documents the institutionalization of risk and risk analysis--both risk assessment and risk management,its organizational manifestations. Correlatively, a spate of research concerns perception of risk and uncertainty and risk-related behavior by individuals and organizations.

Chapters in this volume amply illustrate confusion that surrounds attempts to define the concepts related to these concerns. It may be helpful, therefore, to remind readers of economist Frank H. Knight's seminal *Risk, Uncertainty and Profit* (1916, 1921), his now classic doctoral dissertation. As Knight's biographer, James M. Buchanan (IESS 8: 424) reminds: "The motivation of this work, as with so much of Knight's writing, was the desire for clarification." Knight sought to clarify ambiguities in the formal neoclassical theory of economic organization, particularly concerning the role and meaning of pure profit and its connection with predictive power. In order to construct an ideal type model of perfect competition, Knight explained profit as the result of uncertainty. Profits are residual returns to an entrepreneur earned as a result of correct decisions taken in the present for a return in the uncertain future. Uncertainty was clearly distinguishable from risk. Risk exists for the entrepreneur when knowledge about a future event is calculable, i.e., when there is adequate information to make a probability calculation. In Knight's theory of economic organization risks can always be insured against; uncertainty cannot. Uncertainty exists in the absence of a probability calculus. The decision maker

---

I am grateful to Jim Short for critical review and suggestions concerning earlier drafts of this chapter.

therefore must rely upon his or her judgment, or upon such information as may be available and deemed relevant to the decision. The entrepreneur attempts to reduce uncertainty to the fullest extent possible, but decisions always must be made under conditions of uncertainty. If on balance events prove decisions correct, profit ensues; if not, loss. In either case the results of decisions affect the entrepreneur's future decisions and decision making.

Since Knight formulated his theory, developments in statistical theory of probability cast formal doubt upon the sharpness of the distinction between risk and uncertainty, and, as James Short observes in Chapter 1, the distinction often is blurred in both risk assessment and management. Yet, Knight's distinction retains substantive validity. Knightian uncertainty must exist in a world where decisions must be made and where some will be erroneous: "As Knight quite explicitly stated...there is no genuine uncertainty where there are no decisions" (Buchanan, 1968:425).

Many of the essays in this volume thus are about how decision makers struggle with uncertainty rather than risk, even when many risks (as in the case of the space shuttle) appear to be calculable. Decisions under conditions of both uncertainty and risk are, of course, subject to error. What is at stake is the acceptability of error (put somewhat mistakenly in these terms by Lowrance, 1976, as the acceptability of risk).

The conceptualization of risk and uncertainty depends in part upon whether one is focusing upon decision makers and decision making, or upon decisions and their outcomes. Focusing upon the decision makers rivets attention upon risk management whereas a concern with the decision and its outcomes draws attention to risk assessment. The chapters in this volume focus primarily upon decision makers, decision making, and risk management. Important differences among risk managers are evident, however. The chapters by Sanders, Felstiner and Siegelman, Delaney, Nelkin, and Shapiro deal principally with decision makers in large profit-making organizations, whereas those by Hutter and Lloyd-Bostock, Manning, and Hawkins focus on decision making in governmental regulatory agencies. Barker and Vaughan treat more complex cases in which large profit and not-for-profit organizations and governmental agencies are linked in complex decision networks, and in which experts and the public have important claims and stakes. Important consequences for understanding both risk management and risk assessment follow from these different organizational foci. The following examples are intended only to sensitize us to the ways these differences affect propositions about organizational risk and uncertainty.

The role of legal rules and lawyers in risk assessment and management seems to depend upon which decision makers one focuses upon, their primacy within the organization, and special qualities of the relevant body of law and the hazards that are at issue. Sanders, for example, concludes that organizational complexity increases uncertainty in the application of legal rules regarding products liability. As a consequence, manufacturers of products often make decisions about product safety that are aimed at avoidance, rather than compliance. Felstiner and Siegelman's modeling of tort litigation in cases of latent injury leads them to the conclusion that other managerial goals about an uncertain future dominate decisions that vitiate the deterrent effect of tort law.

The role of law in risk assessment and management thus varies considerably among organizations, partly as a function of what law is critical to the organization. News media manage risks of libel by employing lawyers to assess possibly libelous material, whereas tort liability rules dominate manufacturers' decisions about product safety. The role of lawyers in risk management seems to vary considerably quite apart from the impact of a particular body of law such as tort or libel law, however. How is one to account for this variation? Lawyers appear to influence social constructions of risk far more in news organizations--where their influence seems to be subtle and indirect--than among product manufacturers. Is this a function of organizational or occupational differences? Shapiro nicely documents how lawyerly skills in inferential intelligence enter into their assessment of the likelihood of a libel suit. Nonetheless, they are reluctant to formalize a decision upon which editors may act. In this context the influence of lawyers is constraining on low level decision makers in the organization. The paramount role of lawyers in risk management for product manufacturers is, it appears, in shaping legal rules-- either by administrative regulation or case law. This, as Sanders notes, may lead the corporation to deal with rules uncertainty by typifying the legal meaning of situations.

The Social Construction of Risk

Central to the study of risk, as noted in all of these chapters, is the social construction of risks and strategies for their control. These researchers focus on the social structural and organizational sources of those constructions, how they are embedded in perceptual processes, and in particular rules (see, also, Tversky and Kahneman, 1973). It seems clear that the social construction of risk is continual or perennial: a continual, sometimes formally repetitive, process within organizational roles and perennial for most any organizational behavior that comes to be defined as risky.

Risk is not a simple construction which decision makers use to guide decisions. Rather, given the uncertainty of outcome and organizational contingencies for review, decision makers engage in a continual process of social construction of risk. Hawkins' work (1984a and b, and in this volume) is illustrative. Social construction takes two distinctive forms, sometimes parallel and sometimes succeeding, which converge in a decision. One form reconstructs risks associated with the behavior being regulated. This is the process that Hawkins' Factory Inspectors go through in deciding to create a case. It involves an intelligence gathering and winnowing process which may be quite simple, as when an actual injury is being examined, or it may be protracted when it involves the health and safety status of a particular site.

The other form of reconstruction relates to the *future* status of a case. It arises from concern both for the possible consequences of any actions that may be taken, and for the possible transformation of the case as a result of subsequent decision making. This latter concern is particularly likely to arise when decisions as organizational outputs are systematically processed in an hierarchical network or system of organizations, e.g., the processing of cases in a criminal justice system (Reiss, 1974).

Several chapters examine particularly what they term the *legal risks* of a case--consequences that may ensue if the case becomes a legal matter. As Hutter and Lloyd Bostock, as well as Hawkins, note, this places both the individual decision maker and the organization in jeopardy if their particular social construction of the case is not sustained. Vaughan (1990 and in this volume) presents an interesting example of this difficulty in decision making when there are both organizational and role conflicts in social construction of risk and uncertainty. Conflicting engineering and managerial constructions about the risk in the Challenger launch existed not only within and between organizations but within particular individuals who occupied both engineering and managerial roles. Similarly, Heimer's analysis of neonatal intensive care units (NICUs) reveals conflicting constructions between and among hospital staff and parents, and on the part of individuals in each of these groups.

Some, but not all risk decisions are subject to multiple social constructions. A risk assessment or management decision often becomes subject to several reconstructions, e.g., scientific, legal, and lay as demonstrated by several of the contributors to this volume. The problem for any decision maker then is how to choose among alternative constructions when making a decision. This is a matter of uncertainty and a matter of weighing or balancing constructions in order to resolve uncertainty.

Intelligence Gathering and Processing in Risk Analysis

Contributors to this volume address the role of intelligence gathering and processing in risk analysis in a variety of ways. Much of the literature of risk analysis makes assumptions about intelligence gathering and processing that are embedded in more general organizational theories of intelligence (Wilensky, 1967). Yet the risk analysis model based on these organizational theories can lead to a flawed explanatory model, especially when it is based on a retrospective or reconstructed account of the "failure" of intelligence gathering and processing in organizations.

The pitfalls in this model are most evident when one reconstructs the intelligence available within an organization in contrast to what is available to decision makers who made decisions that are causally linked to a catastrophe that is to be explained or understood. Typically, as in Vaughan's brilliant reconstruction of intelligence problems after the Challenger disaster, one moves backwards in chains of information, seeking out information that, had it been available to decision makers, might have prevented actions that resulted in catastrophe. The argument is indeed always plausible, whether one is trying to account for such diverse events as Pearl Harbor, the Bay of Pigs, the Three-Mile Island melt-down or the Challenger disaster. In such disasters the intelligence problem typically is carefully reconstructed so as to explain how it happened and to place responsibility on decisions that, retrospectively considered, need not have been made.[1] More careful analysis reveals that such reconstructions do not deal with several major problems in organizational collection and processing of information (see Vaughan, 1990 and in this volume; also Clarke, 1988).

All organizations, no matter what their size, have a surfeit of information. Inevitably, far more information than the organization is capable of processing for transmission to decision makers is available in some form within organizational files and in the heads of managers and other employees. Much information within any organization is unavailable to decision makers as a result of the internal structure of the organization and the positions of decision makers within that structure. Almost all such organizations structure decision making in an hierarchical pyramid of positions with the final authority to make decisions located closer to the top than the bottom. This means that because much intelligence gathering is located at the lower levels of the organization, it must be substantially reduced in quantity as it is passed on for decision making. Moreover, each level of the hierarchy may participate in that reduction. Much hinges then, not only upon what information is processed and how it is reduced, but upon decision rules about what is to be passed on and to whom. Additionally, technical intelligence is generated in specialized units or levels of the organization; yet it must be made intelligible to non-specialists who have the authority to decide. All of the problems of intelligence reduction apply as well to technical units and they may make decisions with insufficient or even erroneous information (Perrow, 1984).

Increasingly, decisions must be made on the basis of information about risks and uncertainties. There can be considerable error in risk formulations, however, and potentially even greater error in evaluations of uncertainties or contingencies. Often, as well, means for validating critical information before a

---

1. To be sure, analysts like Perrow (1984) and Vaughan (1990 and in this volume) are skeptical about whether such reconstructions can deal adequately with the reduction of uncertainty.

decision is made are lacking. Moreover, information which is pertinent--even critical--for a decision often is not passed on at the same time that seemingly extraneous information is provided to a decision maker. Indeed, critical information often is embedded within an information exchange so that its importance is obscured. It should surprise no one then that investigators reprocessing information available in a network to pinpoint failures after a disaster invariably discover information regarded as critical to a fateful decision that was either not passed on or was misinterpreted--invariably because investigators work with a retrospective information processing model.

Despite the excellence of her description and analysis of intelligence failures in the Challenger disaster, Vaughan's formulation might attend more fully to the pitfalls of the retrospective risk management model of intelligence gathering and processing followed by investigating agencies. The model too often substitutes systematic censorship in the organizations for the necessity to reduce information and attend to the fact that the same information can and will be constructed and reconstructed in various ways. Focusing on "a tendency for structure to inhibit information exchange" scants the fact that structure and information flows are *consequences* as well as causes of the manner in which decision-making is organized in complex organizations. A genuine Catch-22 is created in such reconstructions. One calls attention to evidence that too much information was passed on (the mound of seemingly extraneous or undigested paper on one's desk--a chronic condition for this writer!) and that critical information was disregarded. Additionally, Vaughan contends that specialization and technical language accompanying technological development "interfere" with the ability to know and concludes that "rules and procedures intended to facilitate systematic exchange of information seldom achieve perfect control" and assumes that complex issues are summarized for transmittal in the interest of efficiency. As scientists know, complex issues *must* be summarized if they are to be exchanged, given highly technical information and overload. Risk statements, as these chapters make clear, are one form of summary rule but they do not cover much that one wants to communicate about uncertainty. Hence, legal and other rules affect the form that information takes. The problem is exacerbated when decisions must involve exchange of information among linked organizations in a network. Each link may read the information differently, as might occur in reconstructed explanations of intelligence following, for example--if such were possible--a nuclear winter. Indeed, conflicting scenarios of nuclear winter and other global hazards occur for just such reasons.

The point then is that much of what goes into the reconstruction of decision making fails to take into account how information that is collected must *inevitably* take a reduced form and how such reduced forms for passing on information are constructed for decision making. Hawkins' work on decision making on health and safety provides an interesting example of how information collection and processing reflects data-reduction-according-to-rules in an hierarchical organization when most decisions are concentrated at the lower echelons of a pyramidal organization. English Factory Inspectors, while largely in control of both the decisions about violations and responsible for any prosecutions they decide to make, nonetheless are very mindful of doing so in the context of what information may have to be passed upwards in the organization. This means, among other things, that they deal with overload and information reduction problems by taking on very few such cases at any one time (they simply cannot handle very many) and they selectively process information in ways that favor cases where information can be formulated in terms of decisions that minimize error and second-guessing. Factory inspectors are guided by what may have to be passed upwards in the agency and, one suspects, they tend to ignore intelligence that either might be relevant to the decision but does not conform to the rules, or simply not pass upon cases involving intelligence problems. While it might be possible to reconstruct failures arising from such decisions, the absence of a record constrains and limits such reconstructions.

A basic tenet of organizational theory is that all organizations face uncertainty in their environments (Thompson, 1967) and attempt to reduce that uncertainty by links to other organizations (Pfeffer and Salancik, 1978:145). One of the organizational dilemmas of a regulatory agency is how to avoid losing control of the case, which happens most clearly when decisions about a case move both within and between organizations. Within organizations any decision maker stands to be overruled or reversed by higher authority of a branch review and in any hierarchically organized organizational input and output system--such as a criminal justice system for example (Reiss, 1974)--one loses control of the case when it passes to another organization's jurisdiction. Transfer of a case enhances the possibility that one will be found in error. The organizational dilemma is that review is inevitable if one makes the wrong decision within the organization. Thus the uncertainty faced in surrendering control of the outcome of a case to a third party must often be balanced with the uncertainty faced when error is reviewed and one is held accountable for decisions.

What Hawkins regards as risks perhaps might better be regarded as uncertainties found by inspectors in making decisions. (Hawkins tends to use the two terms interchangeably.) It is, as he notes, the uncertainty surrounding the outcome of a prosecution that prompts a defense strategy on the part of the Factory Inspector. Hawkins' research is especially illuminating on the types of uncertainties faced by Factory Inspectors in bringing a prosecution. There is first of all the uncertainty of the outcome of the prosecution, necessitating a defensive strategy to guard one against a host of prosecutorial contingencies. Secondly, there is the formulation of legal rules that shape discretion. This leads to prosecution of breaches of absolute rather than general legal requirements and to the prosecution of breaches of safety which are immediately apparent, rather than to long-term health-threatening violations.

One must be careful not to equate uncertainty with risk-taking or with a particular outcome or set of outcomes. Taken in the sense we set forth then, one does not, as Manning argues, manage risk and uncertainty. One manages, i.e., makes decisions based on information that is organizationally collected and processed. There are calculable and noncalculable risks, but there is an important third ingredient as well--those things that affect outcomes and give rise to errors (accidents) that we do not perceive and which make the outcomes predictable in only a limited sense under conditions of uncertainty.

Hawkins draws our attention to the ways that inspectors create cases and to the idea that once a case has been created it becomes organizational property. One might rather say that the construction of a matter that comes to the attention of an inspector as a *case* is what makes it organizational property. This transformation of observations or matters into cases and, in the hands of Hawkins' Factory Inspectors, into legal cases is what is of interest. What may begin as a classification of the risk of harm from what is observed is transformed into what Hawkins calls a legal risk--an occupational and organizational hazard so to speak. It is unclear, however, whether the law poses risk in the sense of calculable outcomes or rather that it poses uncertainties for successful prosecution. Factory Inspectors seemingly do not operate in terms of calculable probabilities of classes of events; rather they are particularly concerned with the less probable events, and especially those that are deemed serious--not accidents, but fatalities and catastrophes. Factory Inspectors' constructions of risk (shared to be sure) dominate their enforcement behavior. As Hawkins notes, the Factory inspector seems concerned with the risks (and uncertainties) to *him* and for the *regulatory agency* that is posed by a particular case.

For the decision maker this seems to add up less to considerations of the odds of something harmful or hazardous occurring than to concern for the chances that *I* take when *I* call the wrong shot in making a particular decision. In Hawkins' term, the Factory Inspector is geared to the risks *inherent in using the law*--whether and how it is used.

Several of the contributors to this volume draw our attention to the ways in which social life is organized as a means for the distribution of risks and mechanisms for their alleviation. One might restate this to say that social organization fundamentally *creates* and *distributes* risk and uncertainty and that among the greatest of social inventions are those involving the collectivization of calculable risk. Hence *insurance is one of the great social inventions.*[2]

---

2. So also is the concept of accident which is a social construction of the consequences of risk and uncertainty. Note how insurance to cover accidents deals only with accidents as calculable risks.

Manning, for example, contends that modern regulatory agencies are mostly concerned with negative individual risks, such as those associated with the growth of high technology and related industry and with the single catastrophic accident. If, by negative individual risk, he means harm to the individual person, a correction is necessary. Individual risk may be the paramount concern of some, but by no means all regulatory agencies. The FDIC, the SEC, and a host of economic regulatory agencies make no attempt to protect the individual investor against loss but are geared to protecting the integrity of organizations and systems. Depositors are insured primarily to protect the integrity of the banking system and trust in it. The primary goal is to protect the collective system against individual runs on banks, etc.

One of the many insights we owe to the important case studies in this volume (see, also, Perrow, 1984) is the sense that although substantial uncertainties attached to the decisions made on the basis of calculating risks or, in Knight's terms, that the consequences of any decision involve both risk and uncertainty, regulatory and operating agencies increasingly pay attention only to calculable risks. Thus, Vaughan reports that reexamination of what went wrong in the Challenger disaster focused on the calculable risks of the o-ring, while elements that would have added uncertainty in the decision were ignored. There is, additionally, a concern for the fact that decision making is organized and that in the nature of social organization, decisions involve organizational as well as individual error. Moreover, as I have argued, uncertainty is inherent in the very structure of organization for decision-making. One must always selectively organize and process intelligence. Intelligence to be collected is socially organized and carried out by socially organized means. As Biderman and Reiss (1967) demonstrate, there are only socially organized means of knowing. The conceptualization, collection, processing and dissemination of information *is* socially organized. The social understanding of "what went wrong" will lie in understanding the social organization of decision making.

Conclusion: Latent Functions of Risk Regulation

Manifestly, regulation of risk functions to reduce the likelihood of harmful consequences of individual and organizational behavior and to redress harms when they occur. But the regulation of risk performs latent functions, as well.

Peter Manning draws our attention to two of the important latent functions of regulatory agencies. One of these is to obscure risks; another is to make us feel sanguine about the risks that are obscured. Put in simple terms, the FAA must assure us that air travel is very safe and that we need have no fear of accidental injury or death when traveling by air.

Both a manifest and a latent function of regulatory agencies when an accident does occur is to provide assurance that the cause of an accident will be discovered and that it will not happen again. Manifestly, agencies should investigate to search for a causal explanation of the accident (a seeming contradiction) or conduct research on harms that gain operating intelligence for those who may be thought responsible for the harm. Latently, such investigation protects the interests of organizations that are liable for harms and may indeed absolve a particular organization from liability. The terms of such investigations, as Perrow (1984) notes, are to protect organizational interests by holding individuals responsible for particular decisions. Latently, also, such investigations and actions based upon them are intended to give assurance that corrective actions will be taken. Perhaps in some sense then, the latent function of regulation is to reconstruct *perceptions* of risk and uncertainty.

17

Social Organization and Risk

James F. Short, Jr. and Lee Clarke

What difference do organizational and institutional contexts make for explaining decision making under conditions of risk and uncertainty? Stated so simply, this question--though certainly not the answer--seems an obvious one to ask. Until recently, however, it has rarely been asked, perhaps because it permits no easy or simple answers. Organizations differ in the numbers and types of hazards, risks, and uncertainties they confront; they must also weigh conflicting risk estimates, social values, and other uncertainties. Moreover, parties at risk in any given situation often face different risks or they may experience the same risks in quite different ways. Answers to the question, thus, are complex indeed.

Part of the difficulty lies in the advent of new social dilemmas, the result of new forms of social organization, scientific advance, and technological complexity. Hazards associated with space exploration or advances in neonatal medicine, to cite two examples from this volume, or the possibility of gene therapy and other genetic interventions into "natural" processes, now pose risks and uncertainties--even as they yield valuable knowledge, save lives, and improve health. Other examples quickly spring to mind. Nuclear technology and toxic chemicals enrich and save lives even as they create new hazards. Despite, and at times because of, advances in science and technology, work places, homes, and communities--even the biosphere--are exposed to a multitude of threats. Increasingly, scientists and risk analysts recognize the inevitability of uncertainties associated with these dilemmas (see, e.g., Ashford and Miller, 1991; Weinberg, 1972). Calls for new ways of employing and evaluating expert judgments and for increasing and legitimating public involvement in risk management have followed in the wake of such recognition (see Otway and von Winterfeldt, 1992; Funtowicz and Ravetz, 1992). Organizational capabilities and decision making processes are thus challenged on a scale previously unknown.

Scholarship devoted to the connections between rapid social change and risk/uncertainty is also relatively new. This is one reason for the somewhat varied definitions of risk and uncertainty found in foregoing chapters (another, more important, reason is explicated below). The newness of the field also helps explain some of the redundancy in material covered in a few of the chapters. In part, we are seeking common ground in concepts and definitions that are not yet clear or fully understood. As features of the terrain come into sharper relief, such confusion should abate.

Several common themes emerge from the chapters in this book. These themes cohere in their concern with connections between uncertainty and risk, on one hand, and organizations and institutions, on the other. The essays cover a broad range of organizations and institutions, and set forth a variety of risk-related issues. Nevertheless, they are but a sampling of the many issues demanding our practical and intellectual attention. Here, we acknowledge some important issues the book neglects, and then point out some of the book's implications for social theory.

Neglected Issues

First, the book neglects issues of the distribution of risk along lines of class, sex, race, ethnicity, or position in the world political economy. The popular press and a few reports from regulatory agencies have recently focused on the possibility that poor people--among whom African-Americans are disproportionately represented--disproportionately bear the consequences of risk-decisions concerning toxic waste, chemical plants, garbage incinerators, and so on. The extent to which this is so is an exceedingly important question, one with which social scientists and others are likely to become increasingly concerned. Distributional issues are important not only for policy (and political) reasons, but also for how we theorize power, decision making, and institutional analyses of risk in general.

Stratification issues are noted in a few chapters, notably in Short's concerns with fairness in the distribution of risks, Nelkin's observations regarding genetic screening for such race-related conditions as sickle cell anemia, and Heimer's conclusion that affluent, better educated, white, and married parents interact more successfully with hospital staff than do poor, less well educated, minority, and unmarried parents.

When stratification of hazard exposure is relevant to risk-related decisions and decision making, critiques of power clearly need to be further disaggregated accordingly. Several authors here develop the crucial point that organizations and elites, rather than "the public" make the key decisions regarding the development of some technologies, processes, and substances, rather than others. To the extent that there are systematic class and racial differences in exposure, further differentiation is required not only of "the public," but of the impact of stratification on elite and organizational decision making.

Second, several sociologists have recently theorized explicitly organizational--rather than individual--risk perception (e.g., Sabatier, 1978; Feldman and March, 1981; Starbuck and Milliken, 1988; Heimer, 1985; Weick, 1987; Stinchcombe, 1990; Clarke, 1992). Though most of the chapters touch on this topic--Sanders on the theory of the firm, legal rationality, and risk management strategies, and Heimer's report of the very different, often sharply conflicting, perspectives on neonatal care risk perception on the part of parents and hospitals, to cite two examples--none develops an explicit theory of organizational risk perception. This omission is important, especially given the massive emphasis on information in this book. Fundamentally, a theory of organizational risk perception will be a theory of how and why organizations collect, transform, and use information. Key concepts in such theories are likely to be concerned with how organizational interests influence information classification and interpretation, how information is used by responsible organizational elites and by contending elites within organizations, the degree to which technical elites and managerial elites are autonomous or interdependent, and the symbolic roles of technical information.

Third, we lack a sustained argument concerning "high reliability organizations" (HROs), i.e., organizations that are able to structure their decision making processes so that risks, in some cases risks with catastrophic potential, are minimized (see LaPorte, 1991, and Pfeiffer, 1989). Most work in the field of risk, we think appropriately, concentrates on things that go wrong: accidents, exposure to toxins, communication distortions or breakdowns, mistakes on the part of decision makers, etc. But the emerging literature focussing on how organizational structures and cultures can be configured to avoid system breakdown and major mistakes surely has lessons for risk analysis, as well as for organizational theory. Once the evidence and arguments in the HRO literature have been assimilated into the mainstream of sociological thinking, it will be easier to specify the conditions under which theories--of decision making, of power, of information, of institutions--are valid. One such set of conditions is noted, below, in our discussion of the significance of information for decision making under conditions of risk and uncertainty.

Another important area this book neglects are so-called lifestyle risks. Policy elites and some prominent social scientists have been developing the argument that it is politically and intellectually wrong-headed to focus on nuclear power, toxic chemicals, etc., when smoking, diet, and other apparently controllable, individual behaviors kill and maim thousands of people every year (see, for example, *Science* editor Daniel E. Koshland's sometimes humorous editorials, and the more serious "Letters" that occasionally appear in *Science* on the topic). The larger sociological issue here has to do with the sociology of lifestyles and consumption, certainly a neglected area of research and theory.

Sociological study of social movements and social movement organizations, network analysis, interest group formation and activity, are relevant to risk management and often to risk assessment, though most such studies have not been made in risk-related terms. Clearly, however, to the extent that lifestyles, and hence lifestyle risks, are culturally embedded and socially organized--as many certainly are--it is the emphasis on individual control of danger that is wrong-headed.

Finally, although several of the chapters here draw on material from Britain and France, none are systematically comparative. More comparative work is needed to assess the bounds of theories. Culture is an important part of decision process contexts, as legal and organizational scholarship demonstrate (see, e.g., Jasanoff, 1986; Ouchi, 1980). We need to know what happens when similar organizations face similar problems in different cultures. By the same logic, we also need to know how different types of decision processes work in similar cultures. Cross-national research will also yield better understandings of the influences on risky decision making of the many factors stressed in this book: legal institutions, different types and degrees of power legitimation, rationalities, technical information, regulatory strategies, hands-on experience, and organizational interdependencies.

Implications for Social Theory

The value of this book is in its diversity. The authors are not as a group committed to a common theory or model; the empirical problems they are interested in vary widely. Though several common conceptual concerns recur in the chapters, these concerns do not cohere as a theory of decision making, or an institutional theory of risk. Considered together, however, the ideas, arguments, and evidence examined refocus risk-thinking on several common, and important, concepts.

Decision Processes and Rationality

Our contributors show the utility of focusing analytic attention on decision making processes, rather than decision outcomes. While we are all concerned with outcomes, our critical stance toward established theories of decision making leads to a simple question: how are decisions made regarding risk and uncertainty in different contexts? Posing the question this way holds in abeyance issues that economic theory, and rational theory more generally, tend to take for granted. Chief among such issues is the notion that, once exogenous constraints are taken into account, people make decisions in similar ways. Such a view simplifies far beyond the limits of what is intellectually useful. All theories must make simplifying assumptions; the explanatory power of a theory that fully reflected the complexities of reality would be idiosyncratic and trivial. But there comes a point in the theorizing enterprise when simplifications obscure more than they enlighten, when a theory's conceptual apparatus so overdetermines the explanandum as to render the theory phantasmic. The arguments and findings regarding decision making in this book suggest that institutional contexts are so important in explaining decision processes that the search for an overarching rationality inheres in any decision situation should be suspended, at least for the time being.

Emphasis on contexts and local contingencies affords a wider perspective on rationality than is typical of economic and psychological theories. Where those theories locate rationality as something within individuals, the broader view sees rationality as embedded in institutionalized decision-procedures or as an emergent reality that results from interaction and conflict. This view, amply demonstrated in this book, suggests the meaning of rationality itself is context dependent. Rationality is often best conceived as local in nature, highly contingent on situational exigencies. Thus we need better theories of the social structures and cultures in which decision processes take place, rather than "decision makers" or "decisions" per se.

Power

Concern with problems of power is another obvious commonality among the chapters. Authors are mainly concerned with how organizational and institutional elites influence technological choice and the creation of risk objects--decisions that shape the distribution of risks and set the terms of debate concerning control strategies to reduce or to compensate for risks. The power of organizations (hospitals and NICUs), and of elites within them (surgeons and other trained personnel), vis a vis families, is clear in the highly technical, emotionally charged situation of NICUs. Organizational power and power among contending elements of organizational systems are also concerns in several other chapters, such as Delaney's analysis of Chapter 11 business bankruptcies, Nelkin's analysis of biological testing and the management of workplace risks, and Vaughan's study of NASA and its contractors.

The concern with power is not an ideological commitment. It flows rather from the overarching concern with inevitable disparities in the distribution of resources among social actors. Here, also, economics and psychology have failed to explain decision making processes, psychology because psychologists tend to neglect situational exigencies to highlight what happens within individuals, economics because economists similarly neglect situational exigencies to highlight the operation of preferences. Both theoretic approaches thereby have difficulty seeing the influences of culture and social structure; once those influences become theoretically salient, recognition of differential command of resources is unavoidable. Concern with power is critical not only (or even primarily) for political reasons, but because social life is replete with resource disparities between groups and organizations--the basis of power. The scope of a theory that does not have some conception of power and authority is, therefore, extremely limited.

Concern with power is simultaneously a concern with constraints on power. Just as social structure bestows power on certain positions, it also limits power, as the chapters concerned with differential power between and within organizations indicate. Institutional elites often clash over power and other resources, as Vaughan's investigation of decision making by NASA and NASA contractors demonstrates. Production pressures on NASA to launch, information problems, interdependence between regulators and the regulated, and a management decision to overrule the recommendations of scientists and engineers resulted in the fateful decision to launch Challenger.

Limits on the power of even extremely wealthy corporations is found in the strategic uses of bankruptcy law, which is used not so much against individuals as against other businesses, and in some instances against labor unions, as they contest for control of markets and other resources. Further, as several chapters note, organizational theory and research demonstrate the bounded nature of organizational rationality, and suggest that organizations do not always act in the most rational, self-interested manner. They are at times "systematically stupid."

Despite inter-elite, inter-organizational conflict, however, the power of wealth, combined with large-scale organization, is an important aspect of decision making and of decisions that have equally large social impacts. This combination increasingly occurs within the context of governmental involvement in major decisions. Social scientists note that corporations sometimes avoid public opposition by limiting public participation through the creation of subgovernments that limit public participation. This strategy has been especially effective when problems are defined as technical, rather than social, as was the case with the creation of the Atomic Energy Commission (Baumgartner and Jones, 1991; Clarke, 1985). Likewise, chairs of congressional committees, and other congressional leaders, have great power to delay or prevent legislation, or to change policy by influencing legislation. Executive branch agencies also possess considerable power to alter social policy by allocating funds and other means. As an example, a dramatic case of both legislative and executive agency policy change occurred with passage of amendments to the Nuclear Waste Policy Act of 1982. Unlike that act, which was passed only after protracted and highly public debate, the 1987 amendments, which fundamentally altered the process of site selection for a nuclear waste repository by restricting the search to a single site in Nevada, received little legislative or public debate (see Freudenburg, 1991b). These and other actions at the federal level have met with unified opposition from the Nevada congressional delegation and from the state government, as well as opposition from large majorities of Nevada residents. The resulting impasse has led to a "crisis of confidence" that threatens the ability of government institutions to deal effectively or democratically with the disposal of large and growing quantities of nuclear waste (see Slovic, et al., 1991, and accompanying references).

Systems and processes such as these permit only "limited participation" and often resist change. Yet they do change, at times rapidly, as with the breakdown of policy subsystems relating to air and water quality, and other environmental issues, commercial air traffic, trucking, telecommunications, *and* nuclear power-- all of which have changed dramatically over the past two decades (Baumgartner and Jones, 1991). Disposal of nuclear waste has thus far resisted a solution by systems and processes of limited participation, yet policy in this area remains subject to such systems and processes. The issue has many dimensions, not least of which is public confidence and trust in the agencies responsible for nuclear policy in the U.S.[1]

Information

The importance of information is stressed in all the chapters. This makes sense, since all are deeply concerned with uncertainty as well as risk. To analyze uncertainty is to analyze ambiguity, and the key resource necessary to order ambiguity and thereby reduce uncertainty is information. Several issues are important in this connection. First, even knowing what "information" is is not always a simple task. Social constructionists have long insisted on the fundamentally arbitrary nature of social life. The modern world, with its wonderfully terrifying technologies, is a world awash in raw data--about o-rings and nuclear designs and occupational hazards and sick infants, for example. The processes through which data are massaged and made sense of determine whether they become relevant information or are dismissed (or simply tolerated) as background noise. Second, the significance of information goes far beyond its enabling properties. Information also has enormous symbolic utility, making it in turn a crucial connection to power. Thus, information becomes a tool in NICUs and other situations in which unequal participants in interaction must make decisions regarding health, safety, and other matters. Moreover, information reduction becomes critical to its transformation into knowledge and understanding (or to confusion and ignorance). This may, indeed, be one of

---

1. Surveys of Nevada residents in 1990 and 1991 "suggest that opposition and distrust have risen. . . In response to a request to indicate 'how much you trust each of the following to do what is right with regard to a nuclear waste repository at Yucca Mountain,' . . DOE, the Nuclear Regulatory Commission (NRC), and the U.S. Congress were the least trusted entities" (Slovic, et al., 1991:1604). In the spring of 1990 the DOE established a Task Force on Radioactive Waste Management under the Secretary of Energy's Advisory Board, with the specific task of studying and enhancing trust and confidence in the Department's nuclear waste disposal program.

several critical features contributing to the success of HROs, in which information is sharply focused on agreed-upon tasks that require decisions regarding agreed-upon actions. Were any of these features absent (focused information, agreed-upon tasks, and agreed-upon actions)--as is the case with many risk situations--HROs would be much less reliable.

Since Weber, we have known about the importance of legitimation of power (the standard definition of authority). In the present context, legitimation of power is important for at least two reasons. One is that organizations and elites always legitimate their decisions with appeals to the rational use of information. The data suggest, however, that such rationalistic representations of decision making processes are often mystifications; i.e., that information doesn't so much drive as justify positions already adopted. The other is that the institutional fabric of society is fundamentally dependent on the degree to which those without access to centers of decision making trust those who must make decisions on their behalf, and who are charged with making decisions in the best interests of those without such access. William Freudenburg (1991a) has proposed a powerful argument for so-called biases and misunderstandings in public risk perceptions that draws attention away from individuals' cognitive technical errors. He argues, instead, that what people worry about most is whether elites make decisions in a responsible way. To get at this problem, Freudenburg proposes the concept of recreancy, that is the degree to which elites honor their commitment to suppress their own interests, or those of their organizations, in favor of a broader (more socially legitimated) conception of the public good. If Freudenburg is right, and much evidence suggests that he is (see the discussion of public trust, above, and in Chapter 1), studies of risk perception must focus on questions of institutional trust and trustworthiness quite as much as on technical aspects of risks and uncertainties associated with hazards. Freudenburg's argument has the potential to completely reorient thinking about the connections between individual risk perception and the institutional contexts in which those perceptions are formed.

Social Constructionism

A major point that emerges from this book is that work on risk is moving into the mainstream of social science. Along with this movement, as one might expect, we increasingly draw on social constructionist arguments. Among the authors, Hilgartner is most explicit in arguing we not assume the most obvious manifestations of reality are functionally necessary (also highly relevant in this regard are the chapters by Nelkin, Jasper, and Heimer). By drawing attention to how technologies, risks, and social organizations are created, social theory must take account of different interests and forces that shape the conceptualization of raw materials into something recognizably real. More importantly, by insisting that things do not present themselves in a necessarily straightforward manner we are forced to realize that some things are not constructed. As analysts, we are often overwhelmed with social facts, so much so that we usually fail to consider forgone possibilities.

This is not ghost chasing, but an injunction that we remember, and build into our theories, that things could have been different. As Abbott (1990:142) says in another context, "most possible events don't happen." Accepting such a claim has profound implications for theory. For if one accepts the idea that events and sequences of events did not have to happen the way they did, explicit consideration of alternative possible realities that fell away, were defeated, or never arose in the first place becomes a conceptual duty. Such conceptual and empirical exercises will save us from teleological reasoning, and should lead us to consider carefully the causal assumptions that attend any theory. Social constructionist arguments always stress or imply that things could have been different, that there is nothing inherent or natural about the way "risk objects" are defined. Too often, however, the intellectual exercise stops with the demonstration that something is in fact socially constructed; the other half of the story--why it's constructed one way rather than another--requires explicit theories of social actors and mechanisms that defeat other possibilities (Royce, 1985).

The chapters also show that much of the time construction is actually reconstruction, for the social construction of risk is a continuous process, as Reiss notes in his chapter. Reconstruction can serve many purposes and interests. For example, Jasper shows how ideological and political interests were served when technical and political elites in France argued the economic necessity of nuclear power. Some reconstructions are strategic, for immediate, short-term goals, as Delaney argues is the case with firms' reorganizations and reconstructions of their financial condition to fit within the legal requirements of bankruptcy. Others, such as governmental commissions and inquiries (see Barker and Vaughan), and national policy making bodies (see Jasper and Manning) may be both strategic and short run, but with long-run objectives, as well. Commissions and inquiries seek both to explain what has happened (or to anticipate what might happen) and to prevent the ill effects of hazards in the future.

Risk and Uncertainty

A number of authors here draw on the classic distinction between risk and uncertainty, although as Reiss points out, these ideas are not used consistently throughout the book. Social scientists often use terms such as "sociology of risk" or "technological risk" or "organizations and risk" without defining "risk" in the technical sense of the word. Technically, risk is when probability estimates of an event are known, or at least knowable; uncertainty is when those probabilities are inestimable or unknown. When social scientists use the less technical, more expansive, notion they are using "risk" as shorthand for forms of technology and social organization that have the potential to deliver substantial harm to people. Thus the frequent focus on nuclear power, toxic chemicals, occupational hazards, and so on. Still, precision is valuable and where authors mean risk in the technical or the expansive sense they should be clear about the definition.

The technical difference between risk and uncertainty that Frank Knight clarified 70 years ago is useful, because it categorizes the nature of information in decision making processes. But as with all ideal types, this typology may restrict our scope of conceptual vision to only those categories with names. Variation in how chapters use ideas of risk and uncertainty suggests two broad implications for theory and research. First, in the real world--where professionals, elites, and organizations cooperate, conflict, and collude--risk and uncertainty are poles of a continuum. Decision making processes in general, and information in particular, have several aspects or dimensions, which may or may not vary together. One difference between low-tech, mundane hazards and those that are high-tech and morally charged is that political and cultural meanings are more uncertain in the latter. Control of some of our most complex, resource intensive technologies may prove to be impossible--a deep irony indeed for cultures that highly value rational, or at least rational-looking, decision making processes.

Since cultural prescriptions for rationality are strong, uncertainty may prompt institutional actors to search for ways to effect "uncertainty to risk transformations" (see Clarke, forthcoming) in which actors confront and either reshape, assimilate, or shun uncertainties. That is, whether the uncertainty characterizes the state of scientific knowledge, or the degree of organizational competence (e.g., nuclear waste) or technical safety (e.g., breeder reactors), political control (e.g., nuclear weapons), or whatever, something must be done with the uncertainty so that the remaining risk can, at least in principle, be calculated and dealt with. One such mechanism for this is to ignore the uncertainties, as when physicians don't offer information about infant diseases unless prompted (Heimer). Another is to filter out enough uncertainty so that risk can be calculated (or at least presented as such), as when British nuclear inspectors focus on reactor safety rather than possibilities for disaster (Manning). This is also what happens when hard-to-quantify social impacts are neglected in cost-benefit algorithms. Another mechanism is primarily rhetorical, as when workplace risks are redefined as problems of individuals rather than social organization. Yet another mechanism is to offload the key uncertainties to the unorganized and the less powerful, as when apparently healthy corporations claim they are bankrupt. This is also evident with "latent injuries," as when studies indicate danger, but regulators and those who might be harmed are not informed (Felstiner and Siegelman). This brief, unsystematic listing of mechanisms is hardly exhaustive, but does suggest that the sometimes contradictory ways in which "risk" and "uncertainty" are used in this book reflect different points along the risk-uncertainty continuum. Note, also, that whatever mechanism is used to effect the transformation, the potential danger that most worries decision makers is the danger to organizations (e.g., hospitals, newspapers, NASA) or elites (e.g., French or British nuclear technical, administrative, and political decision makers) rather than to individuals.

Socio-Legal Contexts

Founded in probability theory, economic cost/benefit models, and engineering conceptions of social systems, mainstream risk theory portrays risk analysis as mainly a scientific procedure that clarifies choices and alternatives, thus facilitating rational decision making. Several chapters in this volume suggest this view is deficient as an account of risk-related behavior by either individuals or organizations and institutions. In this section we review some of the reasons for these inadequacies, and explore the nature of the concerns and the underlying processes that better characterize and account for such behavior.

Legal concerns are often preeminent in organizational decision making under conditions of risk and uncertainty, and of individuals functioning in an organizational capacity. Among the several dimensions of these socio-legal contexts the following are especially important.

Laws and legal rules define conditions and behavior; they often proscribe and prescribe what is legally permissible or required. In the process, the limits of discretion by both law enforcers and those under legal jurisdiction are implied, and in some cases detailed. Discretion is inevitable, as many studies have demonstrated. A dilemma is thereby created, for laws create legal risks. In some cases these, rather than the intended purposes of the law (e.g., to protect health and safety), become paramount, as Hawkins' study of English Factory Inspectors suggests. Even when they do not assume such importance, the result of discretionary enforcement may be more subtle, but insidious, as in the focus on short-run, immediate dangers (injury rather than health hazards in inspectorates studied by Hawkins and by Hutter and Lloyd-Bostock, for example). Legal risks extend to others, as well as to regulators and other law enforcers, with equally serious consequences. Professionals are subject to malpractice suits (Heimer), journalists and their publications to suits for libel (Shapiro), and businesses to product liability litigation (Sanders; Felstiner and Siegelman). Each of these classes of legal risks has consequences that distort the putative intention of legal controls, often by creating new risks.

This is the down side of discretion. When discretion is severely limited, however, enforcement may become rigid, impersonal, unresponsive and uncaring, thus contributing to the perception of unfairness in legal regulation and enforcement and thereby to the lack of trust that emerges as a primary problem in public understanding and acceptance of risk analysis and management (see Kunreuther, et al., 1990; Clarke, 1989; Nelkin and Brown, 1984; Levine, 1982; Walsh, 1981).

The adversarial legal culture of the United States encourages confrontation--between organizations and their clients, between decision makers and segments of the public, among firms, between firms and government agencies, between firms and labor organizations, and between firms, voluntary associations, and government agencies--over many types of risky decisions (see Jasanoff, 1986). All legal aspects of risk are affected by this legal culture--regulatory rules, legislation, policy, enforcement, and adjudication at federal and state levels, local government handling of risk-related matters, the operation of tort, libel, products liability law, malpractice, and so on. Several of these are noted in the book, for example with the coupling of neoclassical economic theory with tort law (which proves inadequate) as a deterrent to production processes that result in latent injuries (Felstiner and Siegelman). Bankruptcy law permits organizations to protect themselves, but not their creditors, from financial hazards associated with doing business (Delaney). Libel law, designed to protect individuals against defamation, exerts a chilling effect on free expression and on information available via news media (Shapiro). The institutionalization of risk is dominated by legal considerations (Reiss).

Litigation and its threat loom large in all of these matters. Legal scholar David O'Brien attributes this "judicialization" of science-policy disputes to the "deeply imbedded...value of fairness...in our cultural responses to dispute resolution" and its "identification with the judicial process" (1987:vi). He argues, further, that the regulation of risks tends to be judicialized because policy makers face a "vexing trilemma" consisting of the necessity to accommodate "competing demands for scientific certainty, political compromise, and procedural fairness" (x). The research reported in these pages contributes to our understanding of the consequences of the legal contexts of risks as experienced in specific local situations, as well as at the broader level of response to risks by broad sectors of the economy and of national policy.

That legal considerations should prove to be so important to the social construction of risk and risk management is hardly surprising. Scientific and legal communities have become increasingly interdependent, in part because science and technology are such important engines of social change and because law has become the preeminent means of social control in modern nation states (see Thomas, 1983). The need for further systematic--and sustained--attention to this area of inquiry is suggested by findings in virtually all of these chapters.

Conclusion

Clarke ends Chapter 2 with a declaration that good explanations for decision making will center on "structural factors, with significant contributions from scholarship on culture and ideology as well." The specific studies in this book bear out the utility of such explanations, which upend the usual scholarly focus on individuals' preferences, cognitions, decisions, and decision making. These studies bring us closer to understanding how organizations and institutions often make choices with tragic consequences, including how those choices shape the world for the rest of us.

References

Abbott, A. (1988) *The System of the Professions*. Chicago: University of Chicago Press.

———— (1990) "Conceptions of Time and Events in Social Science Methods: Causal and Narrative Approaches," *Historical Methods* 23 4: 140.

Abel, R. (1982) "A Socialist Approach to Risk," *Maryland Law Review* 41: 695.

Abelson, P. H. (1990) "Incorporation of New Science into Risk Assessment," *Science* 250 (December 14): 4987.

———— (1991) "Federal Impediments to Scientific Research," *Science* 251 (February 8): 605.

Adams, F. K., and S. Zuckerman (1984) "Variation in Growth and Incidence of Medical Malpractice Claims," *Journal of Health, Politics, Policy and Law* 9: 475.

Ainslie, G. (1985) "Beyond Microeconomics: Conflict Among Interests in a Multiple Self as a Determinant of Value," in Jon Elster ed., *The Multiple Self*. Cambridge, England: Cambridge University Press.

Akerlof, G., and J. Yellen (1985) "Can Small Deviations from Rationality Make Large Differences to Economic Equilibria?" *American Economic Review* 75: 108.

Akerlof, G., and W. Dickens (1982) "The Economic Consequences of Cognitive Dissonance," *American Economic Review* 72: 307.

Allison, G. T. (1971) *Essence of Decision: Explaining the Cuban Missile Crisis*. Boston: Little, Brown.

Almond, G., and S. Verba (1963) *The Civic Culture*. Princeton: Princeton University Press.

Altman, E. (1968) "Financial Ratios, Discriminant Analysis and the Prediction of Corporation Bankruptcy," *Journal of Finance* 23: 589.

Altman, E. (1971) *Corporate Bankruptcy in America*. Lexington, MA: Lexington Books.

———— (1983) *Corporate Financial Distress: A Complete Guide to Predicting, Avoiding and Dealing with Bankruptcy*. New York: Wiley and Sons.

Altman, L. K. (1987) *New York Times*, Oct. 18: 1.

American Law Institute (1965) *Restatement of the Law Torts 2d*. Pamphlet 2. St. Paul, Minn: American Law Institute Publishers.

American Society of Newspaper Editors (1986) *Newspaper Credibility: 206 Practical Approaches to Heighten Reader Trust*. Washington, D.C.: ASNE.

Anderson, D. A. (1975) "Libel and Press Self-Censorship," *Texas Law Review* 53: 422.

Anderson, J., and J. Spear (1987) "Columnists: Suits Do Censor Media," *Freedom of Information '86-'87*. National Freedom of Information Committee of the Society of Professional Journalists, Sigma Delta Chi: 7.

Ang, J., and J. Chua (1980) "Coalitions, the Me-First Rule, and the Liquidation Decision," *The Bell Journal of Economics* 11: 355.

Anspach, R. (forthcoming) *Decisions at Life's Frontier: Fateful Choices in the Intensive Care Nursery*. Berkeley: University of California Press.

Aoki, M. (1984) *The Co-operative Game Theory of the Firm*. Oxford: Clarendon Press.

Apostolakis, G. (1990) "The Concept of Probability in Safety Assessments of Technological Systems," *Science* 250 (December 7): 1359.

Arkes, H., and C. Blumer (1985) "The Psychology of Sunk Cost," *Organizational Behavior and Human Decision Processes* 35: 124.

Arrow, K. (1985) "The Economics of Agency," in J. Pratt and R. Zeckhauser eds., *Principals and Agents: The Structure of Business*. Boston: Harvard Business School Press.

Arrow, K., and L. Hurwicz (1972) "An Optimality Criterion for Decision-Making Under Ignorance" in C. F. Carter and J. L. Ford eds., *Uncertainty and Expectation in Economics*. Oxford: Basil Blackwell

Ashford, N. A. and C. S. Miller (1991) *Chemical Exposures: Low Levels and High Stakes*. New York: Van Nostrand Reinhold.

Ashley, P. P. (1976) *Say It Safely: Legal Limits in Publishing, Radio, and Television*. (5th edition). Seattle, WA: University of Washington Press.

Aya, R. (1990) *Rethinking Revolutions and Collective Violence: Studies on Concept, Theory, and Method*. Amsterdam: Het Spinhuis.

Bachrach, P., and M. Baratz (1970) *Power and Poverty*. London: Oxford University Press.

Baer, D. (1985) "Insurers to Libel Defense Counsel: The Party's Over," *American Lawyer* 7 (November): 69.

Baird, D. (1987a) "A World Without Bankruptcy," *Law and Contemporary Problems* 50: 173.

_____ (1987b) "Loss Distribution, Forum Shopping and Bankruptcy: A Reply to Warren," *Univ. of Chicago Law Review* 54: 815.

Baldwin, R. (1987) "Rules at Work," Unpublished paper presented to HSE.

Barber, B. (1983) *The Logic and Limits of Trust*. New Brunswick, NJ: Rutgers University Press.

Bardach , E., and Kagan, R. A. (1982) *Going by the Book: The Problem of Regulatory Unreasonableness*. Philadelphia: Temple University Press.

Barker, A., and B. G. Peters, eds. (1992) *The Politics of Expert Advice in Western Europe: Creating, Using and Manipulating Scientific Knowledge for Public Policy.*. Edinburgh: Edinburgh University Press.

Barker, A., and M. Couper (1984) "The Art of Quasi-Judicial Administration: the Planning Appeal and Inquiry Systems in England," *Urban Law and Policy* 6: 363.

Barnard, C. I. (1938) *The Functions of the Executive.* Cambridge, MA: Harvard University Press.

Barnes, B. (1983) "On the Conventional Character of Knowledge and Cognition," in K. Knorr-Cetina and M. Mulkay eds., *Science Observed* . Newbury Park, CA: Sage.

Barrett, D. A. (1986) "Declaratory Judgments for Libel: A Better Alternative," *California Law Review* 74: 847.

Barth, P. S. (1982) "Compensation for Asbestos-Associated Disease" in I. J. Selikoff ed., *Disability Compensation for Asbestos-Associated Disease in the United States.* New York: Environmental Sciences Laboratory, Mt. Sinai School of Medicine of CUNY.

_____ (1984) "A Proposal for Dealing with the Compensation of Occupational Diseases," *Journal of Legal Studies* 13: 569.

Barth, P., and H. A. Hunt (1980) *Workers Compensation and Work Related Illnesses.* Cambridge, MA: MIT Press.

Bartrip, P. W. J. (1987) "The Regulation of Lead Poisoning in the White Lead and Pottery Industries in the Nineteenth and Early Twentieth Centuries," Unpublished paper presented to HSE.

Baumgartner, F. R., and B. Jones (1991) "Agenda Dynamics and Policy Subsystems," *The Journal of Politics* 53 4: 1044.

Beaver, W. H. (1968) "Market Prices, Financial Ratios and the Prediction of Failure," *Journal of Accounting Research* 6: 179.

Becker, H. S., and J. W. Carper (1956) "The Development of Identification with an Occupation," *American Journal of Sociology* 61: 289.

Bell, T. E., and K. Esch (1987) "The Fatal Flaw in Flight 51-L," *IEEE Spectrum* (February): 36.

Bem, D. (1967) "Self-Perception: The Dependent Variable of Human Performance," *Organizational Behavior and Human Performance* 2: 105-21.

Berger P. L., and T. Luckmann (1966) *The Social Construction of Reality: A Treatise in the Sociology of Knowledge.* Garden City, New York: Doubleday.

Berliner, J. S. (1957) *Factory and Manager in the U.S.S.R.* Cambridge, MA: Harvard University Press.

Berman, D. (1978) *Death on the Job.* New York: Monthly Review Press.

Bertin, J. E. (1982) "Discrimination Against Women of Childbearing Capacity," address at Hastings Center (unpublished).

Bezanson, R. P., G. Cranberg, and J. Soloski (1987) *Libel Law and the Press: Myth and Reality.* New York: Free Press.

Biderman, A. D., and A. J. Reiss, Jr. (1967) "On Exploring the 'Dark Figure' of Crime." *The Annals* 374 (November): 1-15.

Bijker, W. E. (1987) "The Social Construction of Bakelite: Toward a Theory of Invention," in W. E. Bijker, T. P. Hughes, and T. J. Pinch eds., *The Social Construction of Technological Systems: New Directions in the Sociology and History of Technology.* Cambridge, MA: MIT Press.

Bingham, G. (1986) *Resolving Environmental Disputes: A Decade of Experience.* Washington, D.C.: The Conservation Foundation.

Black, D. J. (1971) "The Social Organization of Arrest," *Stanford Law Review* 23: 1087.

_____ (1973) "The Mobilisation of Law," *Journal of Legal Studies* 2: 125

_____ (1976) *The Behavior of Law.* New York: Academic Press.

_____ (1987) "Compensation and the Social Structure of Misfortune," *Law and Society Review* 21: 563.

Block, F. (1990) *Post-industrial possibilities,* Berkeley, CA: University of California Press.

Blow, R., and A. Posner (1988) "Adventures in Fact Checking: Are You Completely Bald?" *The New Republic* 199 (13): 23.

Blum, J. D. (1978) "Corporate Liability from In-house Medical Malpractice," *St. Louis University Law Review* 22 3: 433-451.

Boden, L. I., and C. A. Jones (1987) "Occupational Disease Remedies: The Asbestos Experience" in E. E. Bailey ed., *Public Regulation.* Cambridge, MA: MIT Press.

Boisjoly, R. (1987) "Ethical Decisions -- Morton Thiokol and the Space Shuttle Challenger Disaster," paper presented at American Society of Mechanical Engineers Annual Meeting, Boston, December 13-18, 1987.

Boot, W. (1986) "NASA and the Spellbound Press," *Columbia Journalism Review* (July-August): 23-29.

Bosk, C. (1979) *Forgive and Remember: Managing Medical Failure.* Chicago: University of Chicago Press.

Bosso, C. (1987) *Pesticides & Politics: The Life Cycle of a Public Issue.* Pittsburgh: University of Pittsburgh Press.

Bowker, G. (1987) "A Well Ordered Reality: Aspects of the Development of Schlumberger, 1920-39," *Social Studies of Science* 17: 611-55.

Bradbury, J. A. (1989) "The Policy Implications of Differing Concepts of Risk," *Science, Technology, and Human Values* 14 4: 380-9.

Braithwaite, J. (1984) *Corporate Crime in the Pharmaceutical Industry.* London: Routledge and Kegan Paul.

_____ (1985a) *To Punish or Persuade: Enforcement of Coal Mine Safety.* Albany: State University of New York Press.

_____ (1985b) "Taking Responsibility Seriously: Corporate Compliance Systems," in B. Fisse and P. French eds., *Corrigible Corporations and Unruly Law.* San Antonio: Trinity University Press.

Braithwaite, J., and B. Fisse (1983) "Asbestos and Health: A Case of Informal Social Control," *ANZJ of Criminology* 16: 67.

Breed, W. (1955) "Social Control in the News Room: A Functional Analysis," *Social Forces* 33: 326-335.

Brewer, M. B. (1979) "In-group Bias in the Minimal Intergroup Situation," *Psychological Bulletin* 86: 307.

Broad, W. J. (1986) "NASA Had Solution to Key Flaw in Rocket When Shuttle Exploded," *New York Times* (September 22): A-1; B-8.

Brodeur, P. (1974) *Expendable Americans*. New York: Viking Press.

_____ (1985) *Outrageous Misconduct: The Asbestos Industry on Trial*. New York: Pantheon.

Brown, P. (1987) "Popular Epidemiology: Community Response to Toxic Waste-Induced Disease in Woburn, Massachusetts," *Science, Technology and Human Values* 12 5: 78.

Buchanan, J. M. (1968) "Knight, Frank H.," in *International Encyclopedia of the Social Sciences* 8: 424-28.

Bupp, I. C., and J. Derian (1978) *Light Water: How the Nuclear Dream Dissolved*. New York Basic Books.

Bureau of National Affairs (1988a) "Suits, Indictments, Countersuits Spawned by Allegations of False Expert Testimony," *Product Safety and Liability Reporter* 16 19: 446.

_____ (1988b) Simon v. G.D. Searle & Co., DC Minn. No. 4-80-160, *Product Safety and Liability Reporter* 16 19: 439.

Burrows, P. (1984) "Tort and Tautology: The Logic of Restricting the Scope of Liability," *Journal of Legal Studies* 13: 399.

Byrne, J. (1986) "Business Fads: What's In -- What's Out," *Business Week* January 20, 1986: 52.

Calabrese, E. (1986) "Ecogenetics: The Historical Foundation and Current Status," *Journal of Occupational Medicine* 28 10: 1096.

Calabresi, G. (1970) *The Costs of Accidents: A Legal and Economic Analysis*. New Haven, CT: Yale University Press.

Calabresi, G., and P. Bobbit (1978) *Tragic Choices*. New Haven: Yale University Press.

Calfee, J., and R. Craswell (1984) "Some Effects of Uncertainty on Compliance With Legal Standards," *Virginia Law Review* 70: 965.

Callon, M. (1980) "Struggles and Negotiations to Define What is Problematic and What is Not," in K. D. Knorr, R. Krohn, and R. Whitley eds., *The Social Process of Scientific Investigation*, Sociology of the Sciences Yearbook, Volume IV. Boston: Reidel.

_____ (1986) "Some Elements of a Sociology of Translation: Domestification of the Scallops and the Fisherman of St. Brieuc Bay," in J. Law ed., *Power, Action and Belief: A New Sociology of Knowledge?* Boston: Routledge and Kegan Paul.

_____ (1987) "Society in the Making: The Study of Technology as a Tool for Sociological Analysis," in W. E. Bijker, T. P. Hughes, and T. J. Pinch eds., *The Social Construction of Technological Systems: New Directions in the Sociology and History of Technology*. Cambridge, MA: MIT Press.

Callon, M., J. Law, and A. Rip, eds. (1986) *Mapping the Dynamics of Science and Technology*. London: Macmillan.

Campbell, J. (1984) *Nuclear Power and Development*. Unpublished Ph.D. Dissertation, University of Wisconsin, Madison. Department of Sociology.

Canter, E. (1984) "Employment Discrimination: Implications of Genetic Screening Under Title VII and the Rehabilitation Act," *American Journal of Law and Medicine* 323.

Carroll, S. J. (1987) *Assessing the Effects of Tort Reforms.* Santa Monica, CA.: Rand Corporation.

Carson, W. G. (1974) "Symbolic and Instrumental Dimensions of Early Factory Legislation: A Case Study in the Social Origins of Criminal Law," in R. Hood ed. *Crime, Criminology and Public Policy.* London: Heinemann.

_____ (1982) *The Other Price of Britain's Oil.* Oxford: Martin Robertson.

Carter, C. F. (1972) "On Degrees Shackle: Or, the Making of Business Decisions," in C. F. Carter and J. L. Ford eds., *Uncertainty and Expectations in Economics.* Oxford: Basil Blackwell.

Castleman, B. (1986) *Asbestos: Medical and Legal Aspects* (2d ed.). Englewood Cliffs, NJ: Prentice-Hall.

Catton, W. R., Jr. (1980) *Overshoot: The Ecological Basis of Revolutionary Change.* Urbana, IL: University of Illinois Press.

_____ (1989) "Choosing Which Danger to Risk," *Society* (November/December): 6.

Centre for Socio-Legal Studies (1983) *An Agenda for Socio-Legal Research Into the Regulation of Occupational Health and Safety,* Oxford: Centre for Socio-Legal Studies.

Chayes, A., and A. Chayes (1985) "Corporate Counsel and the Elite Law Firm," *Stanford Law Review* 37: 277.

Cherniack, M. (1986) *The Hawk's Nest Incident: America's Worst Industrial Disaster.* New Haven: Yale University Press.

Chin, A. and M. Peterson (1985) *Deep Pockets, Empty Pockets: Who Wins in Cook County Jury Trials?* Santa Monica, CA: Rand Corporation.

Chubb, J. (1983) *Interest Groups and the Bureaucracy: The Politics of Energy.* Stanford: Stanford University Press.

Clarke, L. (1985) "The Origins of Nuclear Power: A Case of Institutional Conflict," *Social Problems* 32 5: 474.

_____ (1988a) "Explaining Choices Among Technological "Risks," *Social Problems* 35 1: 501-514.

_____ (1988b) "Politics and Bias in Risk Assessment," *Social Science Journal* 25 2: 155-165.

_____ (1989) *Acceptable Risk: Making Decisions in a Toxic Environment.* Berkeley, CA: University of California Press.

_____ (1990) "Oil Spill Fantasies," *Atlantic Monthly (November)*: 65.

_____ (1992) "Organizational Risk Perception," unpublished.

_____ (Forthcoming) *Controlling the Uncontrollable: The Organizational Production of Fantasy Documents.* Chicago: University of Chicago Press.

Claybrook, J. (1982) *Reagan on the Road: The Crash of the U.S. Auto Safety Program.* Washington, D.C.: Public Citizen.

Clinard, M. (1983) *Corporate Ethics and Crime: The Role of Middle Management.* Beverly Hills, CA: Sage Publications.

Coffee, J. C., Jr. (1977) "Beyond the Shut-Eyed Sentry: Toward a Theoretical View of Corporate Misconduct and Effective Legal Response," *Virginia Law Review* 63: 1099.

_____ (1980) "Corporate Crime and Punishment: A Non-Chicago View of the Economics of Criminal Sanctions," *American Criminal Law Review* 17: 419.

_____ (1981) "No Soul to Damn: No Body to Kick: An Unscandalized Inquiry Into the Problem of Corporate Punishment," *Michigan Law Review* 79: 386.

Cohen, B. L. (1985) "A Reply to Dr. Otway," *Risk Analysis* 5: 275.

Colangelo, V., and P. Thornton (1981) *Engineering Aspects of Product Liability.* Metals Park, Ohio: American Society for Metals.

Cole, G. A., and S. B. Withey (1981) "Perspectives on Risk Perceptions," *Risk Analysis* 1: 143.

Cole, S. (1975) "The Growth of Scientific Knowledge: Theories of Deviance as a Case Study," in L. A. Coser ed., *The Idea of Social Structure.* New York: Harcourt Brace Jovanovich.

Combs, B., and P. Slovic (1979) Newspaper Coverage of Causes of Death," *Journalism Quarterly* 56(Winter): 837.

Conrad, P. (1987) "Wellness in the Workplace," *Milbank Quarterly* 65 2: 269.

Coodley, C. (1984) "Risk in the 1980's: New Perspectives on Managing Chemical Hazards," *San Diego Law Review* 21: 1015.

Cook, J. (1985) "Nuclear Follies," *Forbes* (February 11th): 82.

Cook, K. S., and M. Levi, eds. (1990) *The Limits of Rationality.* Chicago: University of Chicago Press.

Cooter, R., and T. Ulen (1988) *Law and Economics.* Glenview: Scott, Foresman.

Coser, R. L. (1958) "Authority and Decision-Making in a Hospital: A Comparative Analysis," *American Sociological Review* 23, 1: 56.

Covello, V. T. (1986) "Risk Communication: A Review of the Literature," *Risk Abstracts* 3 4: 171.

Crandall, R., and L. Lave, eds. (1981) *The Scientific Basis of Health and Safety Regulation.* Washington, D.C.: The Brookings Institution.

Cranston, R. (1979) *Regulating Business; Law and consumer agencies,* London: Macmillan

Craswell, R., and J. Calfee (1986) "Deterrence and Uncertain Legal Standards," *Journal of Law, Economics and Organization* 2: 279.

Crouch, E., and R. Wilson (1992) *Risk/benefit Analysis.* Cambridge, MA: Ballinger Publishing Co.

Curley, J. (1983) "'Chilling Effect': How Libel Suit Sapped the Crusading Spirit of a Small Newspaper," *Wall Street Journal* (September 29): 1.

Cyert, R., and J. March (1963) *A Behavioral Theory of the Firm.* Englewood Cliffs, NJ: Prentice Hall.

Daniels, D. M. (1981) "Pre-Complaint Phase: Avoiding Litigation - Preventive Counseling," in *Libel Litigation 1981*: 17-45 New York: Practising Law Institute.

Danzon, P. (1985) *Medical Malpractice*. Cambridge, MA: Harvard Univ. Press.

_____ (1986) *New Evidence on the Frequency and Severity of Medical Malpractice Claims*. Santa Monica, CA: Rand Corporation.

_____ (1987) "The Effects of Tort Reforms on the Frequency and Severity of Medical Malpractice Claims," *Ohio State Law Journal* 48: 413.

Davis, L. N. (1979) *Frozen Fire*. San Francisco: Friends of the Earth.

Davis, O. A., and M. I. Kamien (1970) "Externalities, Information, and Alternative Collective Action," in R. H. Haveman and J. Margolis, eds., *Public Expenditures and Policy Analysis*. Chicago: Markham Publishers.

Dawson, S., P. Willman, M. Bamford, and A. Clinton. (1988) *Safety at Work: The Limits of Self-Regulation*. Cambridge: Cambridge University Press.

Delaney, K. (1989a) "Power, Intercorporate Networks and `Strategic Bankruptcy'," *Law & Society Review* 23 4: 643.

_____ (1989b) "Control During Corporate Crisis: Asbestos and the Manville Bankruptcy" *Critical Sociology* 16 2-3: 51.

_____ (1992) *Strategic Bankruptcy: How Corporations and Creditors Use Chapter 11 to Their Advantage*. Berkeley, CA: University of California Press.

Delong, J. (1984) "Risk and the Legal System," *Journal of Products Liability* 7: 353.

Department of the Environment (1990) *Our Common Heritage*. London: Her Majesty's Stationery Office.

Diamond, S. (1986) "NASA Cut or Delayed Safety Spending," *New York Times* (April 24): A-1; B-4.

Dietz, T., and R. W. Rycroft (1987) *The Risk Professionals*. New York: Russell Sage.

Dietz, T., R. Scott Frey, and E. Rosa (forthcoming) "Risk, Technology, and Society," in R. E. Dunlap and W. Michelson eds., *Handbook of Environmental Sociology*. Westport, CT: Greenwood Press.

Dill, B. (1986) *The Journalist's Handbook on Libel and Privacy*. New York: Free Press.

DiMento, J. (1986) *Environmental Law and American Business: Dilemmas of Compliance*. New York: Plenum Press.

Diver, C. (1983) "The Optimal Precision of Administrative Rules," *Yale Law Journal* 93: 65.

Doeringer, P., and M. Piore (1971) *Internal Labour Markets and Manpower Analysis*. Boston: D.C. Heath and Co.

Doherty, N. (1985) *Corporate Risk Management: A Financial Exposition*. New York: McGraw-Hill Book Co.

Douglas, M. (1985) *Risk Acceptability According to the Social Sciences*. New York: Russell Sage Foundation.

_____ (1986) *How Institutions Think*. Syracuse, NY: Syracuse University Press.

Douglas, M., and A. Wildavsky (1982) *Risk and Culture*. Berkeley, CA: University of California Press.

Draper, E. (1991) *Risky Business*, New York: Cambridge University Press.

Drucker, P. (1986) *The Frontiers of Management*. New York: Dutton.

Dubinskas, F. (1988) "Janus Organizations: Scientists and Managers in Genetic Engineering Firms," in F. A. Dubinskas ed., *Making Time: Ethnographies of High-Technology Organizations.* Philadelphia: Temple University Press.

Dun & Bradstreet (yearly) *Business Failure Record*, New York: Dun and Bradstreet Corporation.

DuPont Employee Relations Department (1981) *Occupational Medicine Program.* Wilmington, DE.

Eads, G., and P. Reuter (1983) *Designing Safer Products.* Santa Monica, CA: Rand Corporation.

Edelstein, M. R. (1988) *Contaminated Communities.* Boulder, CO: Westview Press.

Eizenstat, S., and R. Litan (1984) "Protecting the Confidentiality of Your Audit," in L. Harrison, ed., *The McGraw-Hill Environmental Auditing Handbook: A Guide to Corporate and Environmental Risk Management.* New York: McGraw-Hill Book Company.

Ellsberg, D. (1961) "Risk, Ambiguity, and the Savage Axioms," *Quarterly Journal of Economics* 75: 643.

Elster, J. (1979) *Ulysses and the Sirens: Studies in Rationality and Irrationality.* Cambridge, U.K.: Cambridge University Press.

Epidemiology Resources Inc. (ERI Report) (1982) *"Projections of Asbestos-Related Diseases 1980-2000*, Final report issued August 2, 1982.

Epple, D., and A. Raviv (1978) "Product Safety: Liability Rules, Market Structure, and Imperfect Information," *American Economic Review* 68: 80.

Epstein, R. (1982) "The Social Consequences of Common Law Rules," *Harvard Law Review* 95: 1717.

_____ (1986) "The Temporal Dimension in Tort Law," *University of Chicago Law Review* 53: 1175.

_____ (1987) "The Risks of Risk/Utility," *Ohio State Law Journal* 48: 469.

Erikson, K. (1976) *Everything in Its Path: The Destruction of Community in the Buffalo Creek Flood.* New York: Simon and Schuster.

_____ (1990) "Toxic Reckoning: Business Faces a New Kind of Fear," *Harvard Business Review* 90 1: 118.

Fabrega, H. Jr., and D. Silver (1973) *Illness and Shamanistic Curing in Zinacantan.* Palo Alto: Stanford University Press.

Fazio, R., and M. Zanna (1981) "Direct Experience and Attitude-behavior Consistency," *Advanced Experimental Social Psychology* 14: 161.

Feder, B. (1989) "Asbestos: The Saga Drags On," *New York Times*, 4/2/89: Section 3: 1.

Feeley, M. (1979) *The Process is the Punishment: Handling Cases in a Lower Criminal Court.* New York: Russell Sage Foundation.

Feldman, E. J. (1985) *Concorde and Dissent: Explaining High Technology Project Failures in Britain and France.* Cambridge, U.K.: Cambridge University Press.

Feldman, M. S., and J. G. March (1981) Information in Organizations as Signal and Symbol, *Administrative Science Quarterly*, 26: 171.

Felstiner, W., and R. Dingwall (1988) *Asbestos Litigation in the U.K.*, ABF Working Paper.

Felstiner, W., R. Abel, and A. Sarat (1981) "The Emergence and Transformation of Disputes: Naming, Blaming, Claiming . . . ," *Law & Society Review* 15: 631.

Fenn, P. (1987) *Enforcement Policy and the Impact of Regulatory Controls on the Occupational Absorption of Lead.* Oxford: Centre for Socio-Legal Studies.

Feynman, R. P. (1986) "Personal Observations on Reliability of Shuttle," *Report of the Presidential Commission on the Space Shuttle Challenger Accident* Vol. II; Appendix F: 1-5 Washington, D.C.: U.S. Government Printing Office.

———— (1988) *What Do You Care What Other People Think? Further Adventures of a Curious Character.* New York: Norton.

Fiksel, J. (1990) "Risk Analysis in the 1990s," *Risk Analysis* 10 2: 195.

Finsterbusch, K. (1989) "Community Responses to Exposures to Hazardous Wastes," in D. L. Peck ed., *Psychosocial Effects of Hazardous Toxic Waste Disposal on Communities.* Springfield, IL: Charles C. Thomas.

Fischer, D. W., and R. R. Merton (1975) Perception of Environmental Diseconomies: Technical vs. Economic Invisibility, *Social Science Information*, 14 1: 81.

Fischhoff, B. (1975) The Silly Certainty of Hindsight," *Psychology Today* April: 71.

———— (1991) "Nuclear Decisions: Cognitive Limits to the Thinkable," in Philip E. Tetlock et al., eds., *Behavior, Society, and Nuclear War.* New York: Oxford University Press.

Fischhoff, B., P. Slovic, and S. Lichtenstein (1983) "The 'Public' vs. the 'Experts': Perceived vs. Actual Disagreement About the Risks of Nuclear Power," in V. Covello, G. Flamm, J. Rodericks and R. Tardiff eds., *Analysis of Actual vs. Perceived Risks.* New York: Plenum.

Fischhoff, B., S. Lichtenstein, P. Slovic, S. Derby, and R. Keeney (1981) *Acceptable Risk.* Cambridge, U.K.: Cambridge University Press.

Fisse, B. (1983) "Reconstructing Corporate Criminal Law: Deterrence, Retribution, Fault, and Sanctions," *Southern California Law Review* 56: 1185.

Fisse, B., and J. Braithwaite (1983) *The Impact of Publicity on Corporate Offenders.* Albany, NY: State University of New York Press.

Flink, J. J. (1970) *America Adopts the Automobile, 1895-1910.* Cambridge, MA: MIT Press.

Flood, J. (1988) "All Cretans Are Liars': The Fight Against Corporate Crime," *Law & Society Review* 21: 811.

Ford, D. F. (1982a) A Reporter at Large: The Cult of the Atom-Part I," *New Yorker* October 25: 107.

———— (1982b) A Reporter at Large: The Cult of the Atom-Part II," *New Yorker* November 1: 45.

Fortgang C., and T. Meyer (1985) "Valuation in Bankruptcy," *UCLA Law Review* 32: 1061.

Fowlkes, M. R., and P. Y. Miller (1987) "Chemicals and Community at Love Canal," in B. B. Johnson and V. T. Covelo eds., *The Social and Cultural Construction of Risk: Essays on Risk Selection and Perception.* Dordrecht, Holland: D. Reidel.

Fox, F., and B. Staw (1979) "The Trapped Administrator: The Effects of Job Insecurity and Policy Resistance Upon Commitment to a Course of Action," *Administrative Science Quarterly* 24: 449.

Freedman, D. (1987) "Health and Safety at Work: Perceptions of National Trades Union Officials," Unpublished paper.

Freudenburg, W. R. (1988) "Perceived Risk, Real Risk: Social Science and the Art of Probabilistic Risk Assessment," *Science* 242 (October 7): 44.

———— (1991a) "Risk and Recreancy: Weber, the Division of Labor, and the Rationality of Risk Perceptions," unpublished.

———— (1991b) *Organizational Management of Long-Term Risks: Implications for Risk Safety in the Transportation of Nuclear Wastes.* State of Nevada Agency for Nuclear Projects/Nuclear Waste Project Office.

Freudenburg, W. R., and E. A. Rosa, eds. (1984) *Public Reactions to Nuclear Power: Are There Critical Masses?* Boulder, CO: Westview Press for the American Association for the Advancement of Science.

Friedman, D., and M. Hechter (1988) "The Contribution of Rational Choice Theory to Macrosociological Research," *Sociological Theory* 6 (Fall): 201.

Friedman, L. (1985) *Total Justice.* New York, NY: Russell Sage Foundation.

Friedson, E. (1986) *Professional Powers: A Study of the Institutionalization of Formal Knowledge.* Chicago: University of Chicago Press.

Frohock, F. M. (1986) *Special Care: Medical Decisions at the Beginning of Life.* Chicago:University of Chicago Press.

Funtowicz, S. O., and J. R. Ravetz (1992) "Risk Management as a Postnormal Science," *Risk Analysis* 12: 95.

Galanter, M. (1975) "Reading the Landscape of Disputes," *UCLA Law Review* 21: 4.

Gamson, W. A., and A. Modigliani (1989) "Media Discourse and Public Opinion on Nuclear Power," *American Journal of Sociology* 95 1: 1.

Gannett Center for Media Studies (1986) *The Cost of Libel: Economic and Policy Implications.* Conference Report. New York.

Gans, H. J. (1979) *Deciding What's News: A Study of CBS Evening News, NBC Nightly News, Newsweek and Time.* New York: Random House.

Garbus, M. (1986) "The Many Costs of Libel," *Publishers Weekly* 230 10: 34.

General Accounting Office (1986) *Medical Malpractice: Six State Case Studies Show Claims and Costs Still Rise Despite Reforms.* (GAO/HRD-87-21) Washington, D.C.

Genn, H. G. (1987) "Great Expectations: The Robens' Legacy and Employer Self-regulation," Unpublished paper presented to HSE.

Giddens, A. (1976) *New Rules of Sociological Method.* London: Hutchinson.

_____ (1981) "Agency, Institution and Space-Time Analysis" in K. Knorr-Cetina and A. Cicourel eds. *Advances in Social Theory and Methodology*. London: Routledge and Kegan Paul.

_____ (1984) *The Constitution of Society*. Berkeley, CA: University of California Press.

Ginger, A. F., and D. Christiano, eds. (1987) *The Cold War Against Labor (Vols. 1 & 2)*. Berkeley: Meiklejoh Civil Liberties Institute.

Ginniff, M. (1988) "The Case for Deep Storage," *The Observer*, (15 May): 29

Glasser, T. L. (1984) "Objectivity Precludes Responsibility," *The Quill* 72: 13.

Glasser, T. L. and J. S. Ettema (1985) *A Census of North American Newspaper Ombudsmen: Preliminary Findings*. Minneapolis: Silha Center for the Study of Media Ethics and Law.

Glendon, A. (1987) "Risk cognition," in W.T. Singleton and J. Hovden eds., *Risk and Decisions*. New York: John Wiley & Sons Ltd.

Goffman, E. (1959) *The Presentation of Self in Everyday Life*. Garden City, New York: Doubleday Anchor.

_____ (1974) *Frame Analysis: An Essay on the Organization of Experience*. New York: Harper.

Golden, W. T. (1990) *Worldwide Science and Technology Advice to the Highest Levels of Governments*. Elmsford, NY: Pergamon.

Goldman, M. (1987) "Chernobyl: A Radiobiological Perspective," *Science* October 30: 622-623.

Goldstein, B. D. (1990) "The Problem with the Margin of Safety: Toward the Concept of Protection," *Risk Analysis* 10 1: 7.

Goodin, R. E. (1990) "De Gustibus Non Est Explanandum," in K. S. Cook and M. Levi eds., *The Limits of Rationality*. Chicago: University of Chicago Press.

Gordon, M. J. (1971) "Towards a Theory of Financial Distress," *Journal of Finance* 26: 347.

Gorman, W. M. (1967) "Tastes, Habits and Choices," *International Economic Review* 8 2: 218.

Gould, L. C., G. T. Gardner, D. R. DeLuca, A. R. Tiemann, L. W. Doob, and J. A. J. Stolwijk (1988) *Perceptions of Technological Risks and Benefits*. New York: Russell Sage Foundation.

Grady, M. (1988) "Why Are People Negligent? Technology, Nondurable Precautions, and the Medical Malpractice Explosion," *Northwestern University Law Review* 82: 293.

Grandori, A. (1987) *Perspectives on Organization Theory*. Cambridge, MA: Ballinger Publishing Co.

Green, M. (1988) "The Paradox of Statutes of Limitations in Toxic Substances Litigation," *California Law Review* 76: 965.

Greenhouse, L. (1989) "Justices Reject Challenges to Dalkon Shield Settlement," *New York Times*, 11/7/89: D1.

Grenier, G. J. (1988) *Inhuman Relations: Quality Circles and Anti-Unionism in American Industry*. Philadelphia: Temple University Press.

Grether, D. M., and C. R. Plott (1979) "Economic Theory of Choice and the Preference Reversal Phenomenon," *American Economic Review* 69 September: 623.

Griffiths, R. F., ed. (1982) *Dealing with Risk*. Manchester: Manchester University Press.

Gross, E. (1978) "Organizational Crime: A Theoretical Perspective," in N. K. Denzin ed., *Studies in Symbolic Interaction*. Greenwich, CT: JAI Press.

Grossman, S., and O. Hart (1980) "Takeover Bids, the Free Rider Problem, and the Theory of the Corporation." 11 *Bell Journal of Economics* 42.

Guillemin, J. H., and L. L. Holmstrom (1986) *Mixed Blessings: Intensive Care for Newborns*. New York: Oxford University Press.

Gunningham, N. (1974) *Pollution, Social Interest and the Law*. London: Martin Robertson.

Gusfield, J. S. (1981) *The Culture of Public Problems*. Chicago: University of Chicago Press.

Gustaitis, R., and E. W. D. Young (1986) *A Time To Be Born, a Time To Die: Conflicts and Ethics in an Intensive Care Nursery*. Reading, MA: Addison-Wesley.

Haas, J. E., and T. E. Drabek (1979) *Complex Organizations: A Sociological Perspective*. New York: Macmillan.

Hadari, S. A. (1987) "What Are Preference Explanations? The Interpretive Core of Economic Modeling," *Social Science Quarterly* 68 2: 340-357.

Hannan M., and J. Freeman (1977) "The Population Ecology of Organizations," *American Journal of Sociology* 82: 929.

Hardin G. (1968) "The Tragedy of the Commons," *Science* 162: 1243.

Hargreaves-Heap, S. (1986) "Risk and Culture: A Missing Link in the Post-Keynesian Tradition," *Journal of Post-Keynesian Economics* 9: 2.

Harrison, H., with A. Kositsky (1983) *The Premature Baby Book*. New York: St. Martins Press.

Harrison, L. ed. (1984) *The McGraw-Hill Environmental Auditing Handbook: A Guide to Corporate and Environmental Risk Management*. New York: McGraw-Hill.

Hartman, L. W. (1987) "Standards Governing the News: Their Use, Their Character, and Their Legal Implications," *Iowa Law Review* 72: 637.

Hawkins, K. (1984a) "Creating Cases in a Regulatory Agency," *Urban Life*, 12: 371.

_____ (1984b) *Environment and Enforcement: Regulation and the Social Definition of Pollution*, Oxford: Clarendon Press.

_____ (1987) "Prosecution Process," Unpublished paper presented to HSE

_____ (1988) "Law in a Secular Society," *European Yearbook in the Sociology of Law* (Milan: Giuffre): 263.

Hawkins, K., and P. K. Manning (forthcoming) *Legal Decision-Making*.

Health and Safety Executive (HSE) (1985) Manufacturing and Service Industries, 1984 Report, London: HMSO.

_____ (1986a) *Industrial Air Pollution Health and Safety 1985*. London: HMSO.

_____ (1986b) *Health and Safety at Work: Report By HM Chief Inspector of Factories 1985* . London: HMSO.

Heavner, A. (1985) "Developments in Obtaining Insurance, Changing Terms, and Market Restrictions," in J. Lankenau ed., *Media Insurance and Risk Management*. New York: Practising Law Institute.

Hechinger, F. M. (1988) "About Education," *New York Times* (April 27): 25.

Heimer, C. (1985a) *Reactive Risk and Rational Action*. Berkeley, CA: University of California Press.

_____ (1985b) "Allocating Information Costs in a Negotiated Information Order: Interorganizational Constraints on Decision Making in Norwegian Oil Insurance," *Administrative Science Quarterly* 30 3: 395.

_____ (1988) "Social Structure, Psychology, and the Estimation of Risk," *Annual Review of Sociology* 14: 491. Palo Alto, CA: Annual Reviews Inc.

Henderson, J. (1973) "Judicial Review of Manufacturers' Conscious Design Choices: The Limits of Adjudication," *Columbia Law Review* 73: 1531.

_____ (1981) "Should a 'Process Defense' be Recognized in Product Design Cases?," *New York University Law Review* 56: 585.

_____ (1982) "The Boundary Problems of Enterprise Liability," *Maryland Law Review* 41: 659.

_____ (1983) "Product Liability and the Passage of Time: The Imprisonment of Corporate Rationality," *New York University Law Review* 58: 765.

Henrion, M., and B. Fischoff (1986) "Assessing Uncertainty in Physical Constants," *American Journal of Physics* 54 9: 791.

Hensler, D., W. Felstiner, M. Selvin, and P. Ebener (1985) *Asbestos in the Courts*. Santa Monica, CA: Rand Corporation.

Hensler, P. (1987) "Trends in Tort Litigation: Findings From the Institute for Civil Justice's Research," *Ohio State Law Journal* 48: 479.

Hertsgaard, M. (1983) *Nuclear Inc.* New York: Pantheon Books.

Hertz, D., and H. Thomas (1983) *Risk Analysis and Its Applications*. New York: John Wiley & Sons Ltd.

_____ (1984) *Practical Risk Analysis*. New York: John Wiley & Sons Ltd.

Hickson, D. J. (1987) "Decision-making at the Top of Organizations," *Annual Review of Sociology*, 13: 165.

Hilgartner, S. (1985) "The Political Language of Risk: Defining Occupational Health," in D. Nelkin ed., *The Language of Risk: Conflicting Perspectives on Occupational Health*. Newbury Park, CA: Sage.

Hilgartner, S., and C. L. Bosk (1988) "The Rise and Fall of Social Problems: A Public Arenas Model," *American Journal of Sociology* 94: 53.

Hill, S. (1987) *Corporate Violence*. Totowa, NJ: Rowman & Littlefield.

Hirsch, P. (1987) *Pack Your Own Parachute*. Reading, MA: Addison-Wesley.

Hirschman, A. O. (1970) *Exit, Voice, and Loyalty*. Cambridge, MA: Harvard University Press.

_____ (1977) *The Passions and the Interests: Political Arguments for Capitalism Before its Triumph.* Princeton, NJ: Princeton University Press.

_____ (1982) *Shifting Involvements: Private Interest and Public Action.* Princeton, NJ: Princeton University Press.

Hoenig, M. (1981) "Resolution of Crashworthiness Design Claims," *St. John's Law Review* 55: 633.

Hoiberg, J. E., and D. Uddin (1981) "Sickle Cell Trait and Glucose-6-Phosphate Dehydrogenase Deficiency," *Archives of Internal Medicine* (October) 141: 1485.

Holden, C. (1986) "Air Force Challenge on Sickle Trait Policy," *Science* 211 16: 257.

Holstrom, B. (1979) "Moral Hazard and Observability," *Bell Journal of Economics* 10: 74.

Holtzman, N. (1989) *Proceed with Caution.* Baltimore, MD: Johns Hopkins Press.

Hosticka, C. J. (1979) "'We Don't Care What Happened. We Only Care About What Is Going to Happen': Lawyer-client negotiations of reality," *Social Problems* 26: 599.

Huber, P. (1985) "Safety and the Second Best: The Hazards of Public Risk Management in the Courts," *Columbia Law Review* 85: 277.

Hughes, E. C. (1971) *The Sociological Eye.* Chicago: Aldine.

Hughes, T. P. (1983) *Networks of Power: Electrification in Western Society, 1880-1930.* Baltimore, MD: Johns Hopkins University Press.

_____ (1986) "The Seamless Web: Technology, Science, Etcetera, Etcetera," *Social Studies of Science* 16: 281.

_____ (1987) "The Evolution of Large Technological Systems" in W. E. Bijker, T. P. Hughes, and T. J. Pinch eds., *The Social Construction of Technological Systems: New Directions in the Sociology and History of Technology.* Cambridge, MA: MIT Press.

Hutter, B. M. (1986) "An Inspector Calls: The Importance of Proactive Enforcement in the Regulatory Context," *British Journal of Criminology* 26: 114-28.

_____ (1987) "The Question of Compliance in Health and Safety and Environmental Regulation," Unpublished paper presented to HSE.

_____ (1988) *The Reasonable Arm of the Law? The Law Enforcement Procedures of Environmental Health Officers.* Oxford: Clarendon Press.

_____ (1989) "Variations in Regulatory Enforcement Styles," *Law and Policy* 11: 153-74.

Hutter, B. M., and Lloyd-Bostock, S. M. (1990) "The power of accidents: The social and psychological impact of accidents and the enforcement of safety regulations," *British Journal of Criminology* 30: 409-22.

Hutter, B. M., and Manning, P. K. (1991) "The Contexts of Regulation: The Impact Upon Health and Safety Inspectorates in Britain," *Law and Policy* 12: 103.

Hynes, M., and E. VanMarcke (1976) "Reliability of Embankment Performance Prediction," in *Proceedings of the ASCE Engineering Mechanics Division Specialty Conference.* Waterloo, Ontario, Canada: University of Waterloo Press.

Industry Week, 1987, June 1, p. 44.

Insurance Information Institute (1982) *Attitudes Toward the Liability and Litigation System*. New York: The Institute.

Irwin, A. (1985) *Risk and the Control of Technology: Public Policies for Road Traffic Safety in Britain and the United States*. Manchester, U.K.: Manchester University Press.

Isaacs, N.E. (1986) *Untended Gates: The Mismanaged Press*. New York: Columbia University Press.

Ison, T. G. (1967) *The Forensic Lottery*. London: Staples Press.

Jackson, T. (1986) *The Logic and Limits of Bankruptcy Law*. Cambridge, MA: Harvard University Press.

Jamieson, M. (1985) "Persuasion or Punishment: The Enforcement of Health and Safety at Work Legislation by the Factory Inspectorate in Britain," M.Litt. diss. Oxford University.

Jasanoff, S. (1985) "The Misrule of Law at OSHA," in D. Nelkin ed., *The Language of Risk: Conflicting Perspectives on Occupational Health*. Newbury Park, CA: Sage.

_____ (1986) *Risk Management and Political Culture*. New York: Russell Sage Foundation.

Jasper, J. M. (1988) "The Political Life Cycle of Technological Controversies," *Social Forces* 67 2: 357-377.

_____ (1990) *Nuclear Politics: Energy and the State in the United States, Sweden, and France*. Princeton, NJ: Princeton University Press.

Johnson, C. (1970) "Ratio Analysis and the Prediction of Firm Failure," *Journal of Finance* 25: 1166.

Johnson, W. G., and E. Heler (1984) "The Costs of Asbestos-associated Disease and Death," 61 *Milbank Memorial Fund Quarterly*: 177.

Johnston, H. M. (1983) "In-House Procedures to Reduce Exposure to Uninsured Damage Awards," in *Media Insurance: Protecting Against High Judgments, Punitive Damages, and Defense Costs*. New York: Practising Law Institute.

Julin, D. (1988) "The Tinsel-Town Lawyers," *California Lawyer* 8 8: 54.

Kagan, R. (1978) *Regulatory Justice: Implementing a Wage-Price Freeze*. New York: Russell Sage Foundation.

Kahneman, D., and A. Tversky (1984) "Choices, Values and Frames," *American Psychologist* 39: 314.

Kahneman, D., P. Slovic, and A. Tversky, eds. (1982) *Judgment Under Uncertainty: Heuristics and Biases*. Cambridge: Cambridge University Press.

Kakalik, J., P. Ebener, W. Felstiner, G. Haggstrom, and M. Shanley (1984) *Variation in Asbestos Litigation Compensation and Expenses*. Santa Monica, CA: Rand Corporation.

Kanter, R. M. (1976) "Some Effects of Proportions on Group Life: Skewed Sex Ratios and Responses to Token Women," *American Journal of Sociology* 82 5: 965.

Kasperson, R. E., and J. X. Kasperson, eds. (1987) *Nuclear Risk Analysis in Comparative Perspective.* Winchester: Allen and Unwin.

Kates, R. W., and J. X. Kasperson (1983) "Comparative Risk Analysis of Technological Hazards (a review)," *Proceedings of the National Academy of Sciences USA* 80: 7027.

Katz, M. (1969) "The Function of Tort Liability in Technology Assessment," *University of Cincinnati Law Review* 38: 587.

Kelman, S. (1981) *Regulating America, Regulating Sweden: A Comparative Study of Occupational Health and Safety.* Cambridge, MA: MIT Press.

Kemeny, J. et al. (1979) *The Need for Change: The Legacy of TMI.* Report of the President's Commission on the Accident at Three Mile Island. Washington, D.C.: USGPO.

Kempton, W. (1991) "Lay Perspectives on Global Climate Change," *Global Environmental Change: Human and Policy Dimensions* 1 3: 183.

Kent, T. (1987) "Risk of 'Smoking Gun' Papers Is Outweighed by the Benefits," *Preventive Law Reporter* 6: 12.

Kimmel, M. S. (1990) *Revolution: A Sociological Interpretation.* Philadelphia: Temple University Press.

Kinghorn, S. (1984) *Corporate Harm: A Structural Analysis of the Criminogenic Elements of the Corporation.* University of Michigan: Unpublished Doctoral Dissertation.

Knight, F. (1921) *Risk, Uncertainty and Profit.* London School of Economics and Political Science. New York: Kelley.

Knorr-Cetina, K. (1981) *The Manufacture of Knowledge.* New York: Pergamon.

Kochan, T. A. (1985) *Challenges and Choices Facing American Labor.* Cambridge, MA: MIT Press.

Kornhauser, L. (1980) "A Guide to the Perplexed Claims of Efficiency in the Law," *Hofstra Law Review* 8: 591.

Kraakman, R. (1984) "Corporate Liability Strategies and the Costs of Legal Controls," *Yale Law Journal* 93: 857.

Kunreuther, H. C. (1986) "Hazard Compensation and Incentive Systems: An Economic Perspective," *Hazards: Technology and Fairness*, Washington, D.C.: National Academy Press.

Kunreuther, H. C., W. Sanderson, and R. Vetschera (1985) "A Behavior Model of the Adoption of Protective Activities," *Journal of Economic Behavior and Organization* 6: 1-15.

Kunreuther, H. C., D. Easterling, W. Desvousges, and P. Slovic (1990) "Public Attitudes Toward Siting a High-Level Nuclear Waste Repository in Nevada," *Risk Analysis* 10 4: 469.

Labaton, S. (1989) "Trust May Sell Manville or Shift it to Private Control," *New York Times*, 10/25/89: D1.

Lalley, E. (1982) *Corporate Uncertainty and Risk Management.* New York: Risk Management Society.

Lampert, N. (1984) "Law and Order in the USSR: The Case of Economic and Official Crime," *Soviet Studies* 36: 366.

Landes, W. M., and R. A. Posner (1987) *The Economic Structure of Tort Law.* Cambridge, MA: Harvard University Press.

Langley, A. (1989) "In Search of Rationality: The Purposes Behind the Use of Formal Analysis in Organizations," *Administrative Science Quarterly* 34 4: 598.

LaPorte, T. R. (1991) "Working in Practice But Not in Theory: Theoretical Challenges of High-Reliability Organizations," *Journal of Public Administration Research and Theory* 1 1: 19.

Latour, B. (1983) "Give Me a Laboratory and I Will Raise the World," in Karin Knorr-Cetina and Michael Mulkay eds., *Science Observed.* Newbury Park, CA: Sage.

_____ (1987) *Science in Action.* Cambridge, MA: Harvard University Press.

Latour, B., and S. Woolgar (1979) *Laboratory Life: The Social Construction of Scientific Facts.* Beverly Hills: Sage.

Lave, L. (1981) *The Strategy of Social Regulation: Decision Frameworks for Policy.* Washington, D.C.: The Brookings Institution.

Lave, L., ed. (1987) *Risk Assessment and Management.* New York: Plenum Press.

Law, J. (1987) "Technology and Heterogeneous Engineering: The Case of Portuguese Expansion," in W. E. Bijker, T. P. Hughes, and T. J. Pinch eds., *The Social Construction of Technological Systems: New Directions in the Sociology and History of Technology.* Cambridge, MA: MIT Press.

Layfield, Sir F. (1987) *Sizewell B Public Inquiry. Summary of Conclusions and Recommendations.* Department of Energy. London: HMSO.

Lemert, E. M. (1964) "Social Structure, Social Control, and Deviation," in in M. B. Clinard ed., *Anomie and Deviant Behavior: A Discussion and Critique.* New York: Fress Press.

Lempert, R., and J. Sanders (1986) *An Invitation to Law and Social Science.* New York: University of Pennsylvania Press.

Levine, A. G. (1982) *Love Canal: Science, Politics, and People.* Lexington, MA: Lexington.

Lichtenstein, S., and B. Fischhoff (1977) "Do Those Who Know More Also Know More About How Much They Know?" *Organizational Behavior and Human Performance* 20: 159-183.

Lichtenstein, S., and P. Slovic (1971) "Reversals of Preference Between Bids and Choices in Gambling Decisions," *Journal of Experimental Psychology* 89: 46-55.

Lichtenstein, S., B. Fischhoff, and L. Phillips (1982) "Calibration of Probabilities: The State of the Art to 1980," in D. Kahneman, P. Slovic and A. Tversky eds., *Judgment Under Uncertainty: Heuristics and Biases.* Cambridge, U.K.: Cambridge University Press.

Lichtenstein, S., P. Slovic, B. Fischhoff, M. Layman, and B. Combs (1978) "Judged Frequency of Lethal Events," *Journal of Experimental Psychology: Human Learning and Memory* 4: 551.

Liebenstein, H. (1966) "Allocative Efficiency vs. 'X-Efficiency,'" *American Economic Review* 56: 392.

_____ (1976) *Beyond Economic Man: A New Foundation for Micro-Economics.* Cambridge Mass.: Harvard University Press.

_____ (1982) "The Prisoners' Dilemma in the Invisible Hand: An Analysis of Intrafirm Productivity," *American Economic Review* 72: 92.

Lincoln, A. (1972) "Reading Between the Lines--The Lawyers and the News Desk," in M. Rubinstein, ed., *Wicked, Wicked Libels.* London: Rutledge & Kegan Paul: 54.

Lindblom, C. E. (1958) "Policy Analysis, "*American Economic Review* 48: 298.

Lindblom, C. E., and D. Cohen (1979) *Usable Knowledge.* New Haven, CT: Yale University Press.

Lloyd-Bostock, S. (1987) "A Psychological Study of Responses to Accidents," Unpublished paper presented to HSE.

_____ (1988) *Legalism and Discretion. A Study of Responses to Accidents and Accident Information Systems in the Occupational Safety and Health Administration (OSHA), USA.* Oxford: Centre for Socio-Legal Studies.

_____ (1990) "The Psychology of Routine Discretion: British Factory Inspectors' Responses to Accidents" (unpublished paper).

Locke, L. (1985) "Adapting Workers' Compensation to the Special Problems of Occupational Disease," *Harvard Environmental Law Review* 9: 249.

Lord, M. (1987) A Plea for Corporate Conscience." In S. L. Hills ed., *Corporate Violence.* Totowa, N.J.: Rowman and Littlefield.

Lorell, M., and C. Kelly (1985) *Casualties, Public Opinion and Presidential Policy During the Viet Nam War.* Santa Monica, CA: Rand Corporation.

Love, R. R. (1987a) "The Risk of Breast Cancer in American Women," *Journal of the American Medical Association* 257: 1470.

_____ (1987b) "Misleading Figures" *New York Times* (October 28).

Lowrance, W. (1976) *Of Acceptable Risk: Science and the Determination of Safety.* Los Altos, CA: William Kaufman.

MacAvoy, P. (1982) "You, Too, Will Pay for Asbestos," *New York Times* (February 14) sec. 3: 3.

Machlis, G. E., and E. Rosa (1990) "Desired Risk: Broadening the Social Amplification of Risk Framework," *Risk Analysis* 10 1: 161.

MacKenzie, D., and G. Spinardi (1988a) "The Shaping of Nuclear Weapon System Technology: U.S. Fleet Ballistic Missile Guidance and Navigation: I: From Polaris to Poseidon," *Social Studies of Science* 18: 419.

_____ (1988b) "The Shaping of Nuclear Weapon System Technology: U.S. Fleet Ballistic Missile Guidance and Navigation: II: 'Going for Broke' -- The Path to Trident II," *Social Studies of Science* 18: 581.

MacNeil, R. (1985) "The Mass Media and Public Trust," Occasional Paper, New York: Gannett Center for Media Studies.

Maher, P. (1986) "What is Wrong with Strict Bayesianism?" *Philosophy of Science Association,* 1: 450.

Mann, K. (1985) *Defending White-Collar Crime*. New Haven, CT: Yale University Press.

Manning, P. K. (1980) *Narcs' Game*. Cambridge, MA: M.I.T. Press.

———— (1987) "The Ironies of Compliance," in C. Shearing and P. Stenning eds., *Private Policing*. Newbury Park, CA: Sage Publications.

———— (1988) "Organizational Beliefs and Uncertainty," in N. Fielding ed., *Actions and Beliefs*. Farnborough: Gower: 80.

———— (1989a) "The Politics of Fieldwork on Policy," in D. Silverman and J. Gubrium eds., *The Politics of Field Research*. London: Sage Publications, 213.

———— (1989b) "The Limits of Information," in K. Hawkins and J. Thomas, eds., Making Regulatory Policy. Philadelphia: University of Pennsylvania Press.

———— (forthcoming) *Secularized Dread*. Oxford: Oxford University Press.

March, J. G. (1978) "Bounded Rationality, Ambiguity and the Engineering of Choice," *Bell Journal of Economics* 9: 587.

———— (1991) "How Decisions Happen in Organizations," *Human-Computer Interaction* 6: 95.

March, J. G., and H. A. Simon (1958) *Organizations*. New York: Wiley.

March, J. G., and Z. Shapira (1987) "Managerial Perspectives on Risk and Risk Taking," *Management Science*, 33 11: 1404.

March, J., L. S. Sproull, and M. Tamuz (1991) "Learning From Samples of One or Fewer," *Organization Science* 2 1: 1.

Mark, G. (1983) "Issues in Asbestos Litigation," *Hastings Law Journal* 34: 871.

Marris, P. (1974) *Loss and Change* London: Routledge and Kegan Paul.

Massing, M. (1985) "The Libel Chill: How Cold Is It Out There?" *Columbia Journalism Review* 24 1: 31.

Maynard, D. W. (1991) "Interaction and Asymmetry in Clincal Discourse," *American Journal of Sociology* 97, 2: 448.

Mazur, A. (1985) "Bias in Risk-benefit Analysis," *Technology in Society* 7: 25.

Mazzochi, A. (1980) "Working for Your Life," unpublished lecture in St. Louis, MO.

McCabe, S., and Sutcliffe, F. (1978) *Defining Crime*. Oxford: Blackwell.

McCaffrey, D. P. (1982) *OSHA and the Politics of Health Regulation*.. New York: Plenum.

McCloskey, D. N. (1985) *The Rhetoric of Economics*. Madison, WI: University of Wisconsin Press.

McConnell, M. (1987) *Challenger: A Major Malfunction*. Garden City, NY: Doubleday.

McCulloch, J. (1986) *Asbestos: Its Human Cost*. St Lucia, Australia: University of Queensland Press.

McCullough, D. (1977) *The Path Between the Seas*. New York: Simon and Schuster.

McDougall, W. A. (1985) *The Heavens and the Earth: A Political History of the Space Age*. New York: Basic Books.

McGarrity, T., and E. Schroeder (1981) "Risk-Oriented Employment Screening," *Texas Law Review* 59, 6: 1000.

McGovern, F. E. (1986) "Toward a Functional Approach for Managing Complex Litigation," 53 *University of Chicago Law Review* 440.

_____ (1988) "Resolving Mature Mass Tort Litigation," Working Paper #78. New Haven, CT: Yale Law School Program in Civil Liability.

McGuire, E. P. (1988) *The Impact of Product Liability*. The Conference Board Research Report No. 908. New York: The Conference Board.

McIntyre, L. A. (1989) "A Sociological Perspective on Bankruptcy," *Indiana Law Journal* 65 1: 123.

McKenzie, J. (1977) "Evaluation of the Hazards of Sickle Trait in Aviation," *Aviation, Space and Environmental Medicine* (August) 753-762.

McMahon, A. M. (1984) "The Two Social Psychologies: Postcrises Directions," *Annual Review of Sociology* 10: 121.

Meacher, M. (1988) "The Shameful Rise and Rise of Preventable Deaths at Work," *The Independent* (October 12): 20.

Meidinger, E. (1987) "The Culture of Regulatory Politics," unpublished paper, Baldy Center, SUNY, Buffalo.

Merton, R. K. (1968) *Social Structure and Social Theory*. Glencoe: Free Press.

Messick D. M., and M. B. Brewer (1983) "Solving Social Dimemmas," *Review if Personality and Social Psychology* 4: 11.

Messick, D. M., H. Wilke, M. B. Brewer, R. M. Kramer, P. E. Zemke, and L. Lui (1983) "Individual Adaptations and Structural Change," *Journal of Personality and Social Psychology* 44: 294.

Miller, E. A. (1985) "Reducing the Risk by In-House Procedures," in J.C. Lankenau, ed., *Media Insurance and Risk Management 1985*. New York: Practising Law Institute: 465.

Miller, G. A. (1956) "The Magical Number Seven Plus or Minus Two: Some Limits on Our Capacity for Processing Information," *Psychological Review* 63 2: 81.

Miller, R., and A. Sarat (1981) "Grievances, Claims and Disputes: Assessing the Adversary Culture," *Law & Society Review* 15: 525.

Mintzberg, H. (1973) *The Nature of Managerial Work*. London: Harper and Row.

Misa, T. J. (1988) "How Machines Make History, and How Historians (and Others) Help Them to Do So," *Science, Technology and Human Values* 13: 308.

Misa, T. J., and S. W. ElBaz (1991) "Technological Risk and Society: The Interdisciplinary Literature," *Research in Philosophy and Technology* 11: 301.

Mitchell, R. G., Jr. (1983) *Mountain Experience: The Psychology and Sociology of Adventure*. Chicago: University of Chicago Press.

Moe, T. M. (1979) "On the Scientific Status of Rational Models," *American Journal of Political Science* 23 1: 215.

_____ (1984) "The New Economics of Organization," *American Journal of Political Science* 28 4: 739.

Mogavero, D. T. (1982) "The American Press Ombudsman." *Journalism Quarterly* 59: 548.

Morgenstern, O. (1972) "Thirteen Critical Points in Contemporary Economic Theory: An Interpretation," *Journal of Economic Literature,* 10: 1163.

Morone, J. G., and E. J. Woodhouse (1986) *Averting Catastrophe: Strategies for Regulating Risky Technologies.* Berkeley, CA: University of California Press.

Murphy, M. (1984) *The Airline that Pride Almost Bought: The Struggle to Take Over Continental Airlines.* New York: F. Watts.

Nader, R. (1965) *Unsafe at Any Speed: The Designed-In Dangers of the American Automobile.* New York: Grossman Publishers.

National Academy of Sciences (1975) *Principles of Evaluating Chemicals in the Environment.* Washington, D.C.: USGPO

Nelkin, D., ed. (1979) *Controversy: Politics of Technical Decisions..* Newbury Park, CA: Sage.

Nelkin, D., ed. (1985) *The Language of Risk.* Newbury Park, CA: Sage.

Nelkin, D. (1987) "The Culture of Science Journalism," *Society* 24 6: 17.

Nelkin, D., and M. Pollack (1979) "Public participation in technology decisions: reality or grand illusion?" *Technology Review* (August-September).

Nelkin, D., and R. Pollack (1980) "Problems and Procedures in the Regulations of Technological Risk," in R. Schwing and W. Albers Jr. eds., *Societal Risk Assessment: How Safe is Safe Enough?* New York: Plenum Press.

Nelkin, D., and M. S. Brown (1984) *Workers at Risk.* Chicago: University of Chicago Press.

Nelkin, D., and L. Tancredi (1989) Dangerous Diagnostics: The Social Power of Biological Information. New York: Basic Books.

Nelson, R. (1988) "Ideology, Scholarship and Socio-Legal Change," *Law & Society Review* 21: 677.

Nelson, R. R., and S. G. Winter (1982) *The Evolutionary Theory of Economic Change.* Cambridge, MA: Harvard University Press.

"Newsletter" (1987) *Military Medicine* (November) 152: A6.

Nisbett, R., and L. Ross (1980) *Human Inference: Strategies and Shortcomings of Social Judgment.* Englewood Cliffs, NJ: Prentice-Hall.

Nobel, C. (1986) *Liberalism at Work: The Rise and Fall of OSHA.* Philadelphia: Temple University Press.

Oakes, J. B. (1986) "Comments," *Media Freedom and Accountability: A National Conference.* New York: Gannett Center for Media Studies.

Oaks, J. (1986) "Comments," *Media Freedom and Accountability: A National Conference.* New York: Gannett Center for Media Studies.

O'Brien, D. (1987) *What Process is Due? Courts and Science-Policy Disputes.* New York: Russell Sage Foundation.

O'Connell, J. (1985) "A `Neo No-Fault' Contract in Lieu of Tort," *California Law Review* 73: 898.

O'Connell, J. (1987a) "Tort Versus No-Fault," *Accident Anal. and Prev.* 19: 63.

_____ (1987b) "Balanced Proposals for Product Liability Reform," *Ohio State Law Journal* 48: 317.

O'Riordan, T. (1987) "Assessing and Managing Risk in the UK," in R. E. Kasperson and J. X. Kasperson eds., *Nuclear Risk Analysis in Comparative Perspective.* Winchester: Allen and Unwin.

O'Riordan, T., R. Kemp, and M. Purdue (1985) "How the Sizewell B Inquiry is Grappling with the Concept of Acceptable Risk," *Journal of Environmental Psychology* 5: 69.

_____ (1988) *Sizewell "B": An Anatomy of the Inquiry.* London: Macmillan.

Occupational Safety and Health Administration (1981) *Occupational Safety and Health Reporter* (May 7).

Office of Technology Assessment, U.S. Congress (1983) *The Role of Genetic Testing in the Prevention of Occupational Disease.* Washington, D.C.: OTA.

_____ (1990) *Genetics in the Workplace,* Fall.

Ohio State Law Review (1987) *Symposium: Issues in Tort Reform.* 48 2: 317.

Oi, W. (1984) "Tort Law as a Regulatory Regime: A Comment on Landes and Posner," *Journal of Legal Studies* 13: 435.

Otway, H., and D. von Winterfeldt (1992) "Expert Judgment in Risk Analysis and Management: Process, Context, and Pitfalls," *Risk Analysis* 22 1: 83.

Ouchi, W. (1980) "Markets, Bureaucracies and Clans," *Administrative Science Quarterly* 25: 129.

Overbye, D. (1985) "Success Mid the Snafus," *Discover* 6 11: 54.

Owen, D. (1982) "Problems in Assessing Punitive Damages Against Manufacturers of Defective Products," *University of Chicago Law Review* 49: 1.

Page, J. (1983) "Generic Product Risks: The Case Against Comment K and For Strict Tort Liability," *New York University Law Review* 58: 796.

Parker, (Sir) R. (1978) *The Windscale Inquiry: Report.* London: HMSO.

Patterson, W. (1983) *Nuclear Power* 2nd ed. Harmondsworth, U.K.: Penguin.

Perrow, C. (1984) *Normal Accidents: Living With High-Risk Technologies.*New York: Basic Books.

Perrow, C. (1986) *Complex Organizations: A Critical Essay,* 3rd Edition, New York: Random House.

Peters, T., and R. Waterman (1982) *In Search of Excellence.* New York: Harper & Row.

Peterson, M. (1987) *Civil Juries in the 1980s: Trends in Jury Trials and Verdicts in California and Cook County, Illinois.* Santa Monica, CA: The Rand Corporation

Pfeffer, J., and G. R. Salancik (1978) *The External Control of Organizations: A Resource Dependence Perspective.* New York: Harper & Row.

Pfeiffer, J. (1989) "The Secret of Life at the Limits: Cogs Become Big Wheels," *Smithsonian* 10 4: 38.

Pierce, R. (1980) "Encouraging Safety: The Limits of Tort Law and Government Regulation," *Vanderbilt Law Review* 33: 1281.

Piliavin, I., R. Gartner, C. Thornton, and R. Matsueda (1986) "Crime Deterrence and Choice," *American Sociological Review* 51: 101.

Pinch, T. J., and W. E. Bijker (1984) "The Social Construction of Facts and Artifacts: or How the Sociology of Science and Sociology of Technology Might Benefit Each Other," *Social Studies of Science* 14: 399.

Plott, C. R. (1990) "Rational Choice in Experimental Markets," in K. S. Cook and M. Levi eds., *The Limits of Rationality.* Chicago: University of Chicago Press.

Plott, C. R., and M. E. Levine (1978) "A Model of Agenda Influence on Committee Decisions," *American Economic Review* 68: 146.

Porter, L. W., and L. McKibben (1988) *Management Education and Development: Drift or Thrust into the 21st Century?* New York: McGraw Hill.

Powles, W. E., and W. D. Ross (1966) "Industrial and Occupational Psychiatry," in S. Arieti ed., *American Handbook of Psychology,* Vol. III: 595. New York: Basic Books.

Pratt, J., and R. Zeckhauser (1985) "Principals and Agents: An Overview," In J. Pratt and R. Zeckhauser eds., *Principals and Agents: The Structure of Business.* Boston: Harvard Business School Press.

Presidential Commission on the Space Shuttle Challenger Accident (1986) *Report of the Presidential Commission on the Space Shuttle Challenger Accident.* Vol. I; II; IV; V Washington, D.C.: U.S. Government Printing Office.

Price, C., and A. Danzig (1986) "Environmental Auditing: Developing a 'Preventive Medicine' Approach to Governmental Compliance," *Preventive Law Reporter* 5: 26.

Product Liability Prevention Conference (1979) *Proceedings* PLP-79.

Quinn, J. B. (1978) "Strategic Change: Logical Incrementalism," *Sloan Management Review* (Fall): 7.

Rae, J. B. (1965) *The American Automobile: A Brief History.* Chicago: University of Chicago Press.

Raleigh, J. (1977) "The 'State of the Art' in Product Liability: A New Look at an Old 'Defense,'" *Ohio Northern Law Review* 4: 249.

Rasmussen, J. (1987) "Risk and Information Processing," in W. T. Singleton and J. Hovden eds., *Risk and Decisions.* New York: Wiley.

Ratcliffe, J., et al. (1986) "The Prevalence of Screening on Industry Report from the National Institute for Occupational Safety and Health National Occupational Survey," *Journal of Occupational Medicine* 28 10: 911.

Rathi, M. ed. (1989) *Current Perinatology.* New York: Springer-Verlag.

Rayner, S. (1987) "Risk and Relativism in Science for Policy," in B.B. Johnson and V.T. Covello eds., *The Social and Cultural Construction of Risk.* The Netherlands: Reidel.

Rayner, S., and R. Cantor (1987) "How Fair is Safe Enough? The Cultural Approach to Societal Technology Choice," *Risk Analysis* 7: 3-9.

Reimer, J. W. (1976) "Mistakes at Work': The Social Organisation of Error in Building Construction Work," *Social Problems* 23: 255.

Reiser, S. (1978) "The Emergence of the Concept of Screening for Disease," *Milbank Memorial Fund Quarterly* 56, 4: 78.

Reiss, A. J., Jr. (1974) "Discretionary Justice," in D. Glaser ed., *Handbook of Criminology*. Chicago: Rand McNally.

———— (1983a) "The Policing of Organizational Life," in M. Punch ed., *Control in the Police Organization*. Cambridge, MA: M.I.T. Press.

———— (1983b) "Compliance without Coercion." *University of Michigan Law Review* 4: 813.

———— (1984) "Selecting Strategies of Social Control Over Organizational Life," in K. Hawkins and J. Thomas eds. *Enforcing Regulation*. Boston: Kluwer-Nijoff.

———— (1989) "The Institutionalization of Risk," *Law and Policy* 11 3: 391.

Renner, M. (1988) *Rethinking the Role of the Automobile*. Washington, D.C.: Worldwatch Institute.

Reppy, J. (1984) "The Automobile Air Bag," in D. Nelkin ed., *Controversy: Politics of Technical Decisions*, 2nd Edition. Newbury Park, CA: Sage.

Rescher, N. (1983) *Risk*. Lanham, MD: University Press of America.

Rhoden, N. K. (1984) "The Neonatal Dilemma: Live Births from Late Abortions," *Georgetown Law Review* 72: 1451.

Rhoden, N. K., and J. D. Arras (1985) "Withholding Treatment from Baby Does: From Discrimination to Child Abuse," *Milbank Memorial Fund Quarterly/Health and Society* 63 1: 18.

Richardson, G., A. Ogus, and P. Burrows. (1983) *Policing Pollution: A Study of Regulation and Enforcement*, Oxford, U.K.: Clarendon Press.

Ridder, P. (1980) "There are TK Fact-Checkers in the U.S.," *Columbia Journalism Review* 19 4: 59-62.

Rodgers, W. (1979) "A Hard Look at Vermont Yankee: Environmental Law Under Close Scrutiny," *Georgetown Law Journal* 67: 699.

———— (1980) "Benefits, Costs and Risks: Oversight of Health and Environmental Decisionmaking," *Harvard Environmental Law Review* 4: 191.

Roe, M. (1986) "Corporate Strategic Reaction to Mass Tort," *Virginia Law Review* 72: 1.

Roland, A. (1985) "The Shuttle: Triumph or Turkey," *Discover* 6 11: 35.

Rosen, S. (1986) "The Theory of Equalizing Differences." In O. Ashenfelter and R. Layard (eds.), *Handbook of Labor Economics*. Amsterdam: North Holland.

Rosenberg, D. (1984) "The Causal Connection in Mass Exposure Cases: A 'Public Law' Vision of the Tort System," *Harvard Law Review* 97: 851.

Rosenberg, R. (1975) "Corporate Rehabilitation Under the Bankruptcy Act of 1973: Are Reports of the Demise of Chapter XI Greatly Exaggerated? *North Carolina Law Review* 53 6: 1149.

Ross, H. L. (1970) *Settled Out of Court: The Social Process of Insurance Claims Adjustment*. Chicago: Aldine Publishing Co.

Ross, S. (1973) "The Economic Theory of Agency: The Principal's Problem," *American Economic Review* 63: 134.

Rothstein, M. A. (1983) "Employee Selection Based on Susceptibility to Occupational Illness," *Michigan Law Review* 81: 1379.

_____ (1984) *Medical Screening of Workers.* Washington, D.C.: Bureau of National Affairs.

_____ (1986) "Medical Screening: A Tool with Broadening Use," *Business and Health* (October): 8.

Rowe, M. L. (1982) "Are Routine Spine Films on Workers in Industry Cost- or Risk-Benefit Effective?" *Journal of Occupational Medicine* 24: 41.

Royce, E. (1985) "The Origins of Southern Sharecropping: Explaining Social Change," *Current Perspectives in Social Theory* 6: 279.

Ruhga, V. (1987a) "Insurers Drop Policies; Costs Soar," *Freedom of Information '86-87.* National Freedom of Information Committee of the Society of Professional Journalists, Sigma Delta Chi: 6.

_____ (1987b) "Libel Insurance Crisis: Whose Fault?," *Freedom of Information '86-87.* National Freedom of Information Committee of the Society of Professional Journalists, Sigma Delta Chi: 6.

Rule, J. (1978) *Insight and Social Betterment: A Preface to Applied Social Science.* New York: Oxford University Press.

_____ (1989) *Theories of Civil Violence.* Berkeley: University of California Press.

Sabatier, P. (1978) "The Acquisition and Utilization of Technical Information by Administrative Agencies," *Administrative Science Quarterly* 23: 3: 396.

Sagan, C., and R. Turco (1991) *A Path Where No Man Thought: Nuclear Winter and the End of the Arms Race.* New York: Random House.

Sagoff, M. (1982) "On Markets for Risk," *Maryland Law Review* 41: 755.

San Diego Law Review (1987) *Tort Reform Symposium.* 24 4: 794.

Sanford, B. W. (1985) "Pre-Publication Review," in *Libel and Privacy: The Prevention and Defense of Litigation.* New York: Law and Business, Inc./Harcourt Brace Jovanovich: 35.

Scherer, F. (1981) *Industrial Market Structure and Economic Performance.* Boston, MA: Houghton, Mifflin.

Schmidt, F. D. (1985) "Regulatory Raiders Deflate the Airbag," *Business and Society Review* 52 (Winter): 23.

Schneider, S. H. (1989) "The Changing Climate," *Scientific American* 261(September): 70.

Scholz, J. (1984) "Cooperation, Deterrence and the Ecology of Regulatory Enforcement," *Law and Society Review* 18: 179.

Schrager, L. S., and J. F. Short, Jr. (1978) "Toward a Sociology of Organizational Crime," *Social Problems* 25: 407.

Schuck, P. (1986) *Agent Orange on Trial.* Cambridge, MA: Harvard University Press.

Schuman, H., and M. P. Johnson (1976) "Attitudes and Behavior," *Annual Review of Sociology* 2: 161. Palo Alto, CA: Annual Reviews Inc.

Schwartz, A. (1988) "Proposals For Products Liability Reform: A Theoretical Synthesis," *Yale Law Journal* 97: 353.

Schwartz, G. T. (1983) "New Products, Old Products, Evolving Law, Retroactive Law," *New York University Law Review* 58: 892.

Seiden, M. (1984) *Product Safety Engineering For Managers: A Practical Handbook and Guide.* Englewood Cliffs, NJ: Prentice-Hall.

Severo, R. (1980) "Federal Mandate for Gene Tests Disturbs U.S. Job Safety Official," *New York Times* (February 3, 4, and 6).

Shapiro, M. M. (1986) "Libel Regulatory Analysis," *California Law Review* 74: 883.

Shapiro, S. P. (1990) "Caution! This Story Has Not Been Fact-Checked: A Study of Fact Checking in American Magazines." New York: Gannett Center for Media Studies.

Shapo, M. (1984) *Towards a Jurisprudence of Injury.* Chicago: American Bar Association.

_____ (1987) *The Law of Products Liability.* Boston: Warren, Gorham & Lamont.

Shavell, S. (1980) "Strict Liability Versus Negligence," *Journal of Legal Studies* 9: 1.

_____ (1987) *Economic Analysis of Accident Law*, Cambridge, MA: Harvard University Press.

Short, J. F., Jr. (1984) "The Social Fabric at Risk: Toward the Sociological Transformation of Risk Analysis," *American Sociological Review* 49: 711.

Shrader-Frechette, K. (1985) *Risk Analysis and Scientific Method.* Boston, MA: Reidel.

_____ (1991) "Experts' Errors in Assessing Radwaste Risks: What Nevadans Should Know About Yucca Mountain," Nuclear Waste Program, State of Nevada: unpublished.

Shrivastava, P. (1987) *Bhopal: Anatomy of a Crisis.* Cambridge, MA: Ballinger.

Siliciano, J. (1987) "Corporate Behavior and the Social Efficiency of Tort Law," *Michigan Law Review* 85: 1820.

Simon, H. A. (1952-53) "A Comparison of Organizational Theories," *Review of Economic Studies* 20: 40.

_____ (1955) "A Behavioral Model of Rational Choice," *Quarterly Journal of Economics* 69: 99.

_____ (1959) "Theories of Decision Making in Economics and Behavioral Science," 49 *American Economic Review* 253.

Singer, E., and P. Endreny (1987) "Reporting Hazards: Their Benefits and Costs," *Journal of Communication* 37 3: 10.

Singleton, W., and J. Hovden, eds. (1987) *Risk and Decisions.* New York: John Wiley & Sons Ltd.

Sloan, F. (1985) "State Responses to the Malpractice Insurance Crisis of the 1970's," *Journal of Health, Politics, Policy and Law* 9: 629.

Slovic, P., J. Flynn, and M. Layman (1991) "Perceived Risk, Trust, and the Politics of Nuclear Waste," *Science* 254: 1603.

Slovic, P., and S. Lichtenstein (1983) "Preference Reversals: A Broader Perspective," *American Economic Review* 73 4: 596.

Slovic, P., B. Fischhoff, and S. Lichtenstein (1979) "Rating the Risks: The Structure of Expert and Lay Perceptions," *Environment* 21 3: 14.

_____ (1982) "Response Mode, Framing and Information-processing Effects in Risk Assessment," in R. Hogarth ed., *New Directions for Methodology of Social and Behavioral Science: Question Framing and Response Consistency*. San Francisco, CA: Jossey-Bass.

_____ (1982) "Why Study Risk Perception?" *Risk Analysis* 2: 83.

_____ (1985) "Regulation of Risk: A Psychological Perspective," in R. G. Noll ed., *Regulatory Policy and the Social Sciences* Berkeley, CA: University of California Press.

_____ (1987) "Behavioral Decision Theory Perspectives on Protective Behavior," in N. Weinstein ed., *Taking Care: Understanding and Encouraging Self-protective Behavior*. Cambridge, U.K.: Cambridge University Press.

Smith, D. E. (1974) "The Social Construction of Documentary Reality," *Sociological Inquiry* 44: 257.

Smith, R. S. (1979) "Compensating Wage Differentials and Public Policy," 32 *Industrial and Labor Relations Review* 339.

Smolla, R. A. (1986) *Suing the Press*. New York: Oxford University Press.

_____ (1988) *Law of Defamation*. New York: Clark Boardman.

Soelberg, P. O. (1967) "Unprogrammed Decision Making," *Industrial Management Review* (Spring): 19.

Spence, M. A. (1974) *Market Signaling*. Cambridge: Harvard University Press.

Stallings, R. A. (1990) "Media Discourse and the Social Construction of Risk," *Social Problems* 37 1: 80.

Star, S. L. (1988) "Introduction: The Sociology of Science and Technology," *Social Problems* 35 3: 197.

Starbuck, W. H., and F. J. Milliken (1988) "Challenger: Fine-Tuning the Odds Until Something Breaks," *Journal of Management Studies* 25 4: 320.

Starr, C. (1969) "Social Benefit Versus Technological Risk: What is our Society Willing to Pay for Safety?" *Science* 165 (Sept. 19): 1232.

Starr, P. (1982) *The Social Transformation of American Medicine*. New York: Basic Books.

Staw, B. (1976) "Knee-deep in the Big Muddy; A Study of Escalating Commitment to a Chosen Course of Action," *Organizational Behavior and Human Performance* 16: 27.

Staw, B., and F. Fox (1977) "Escalation: Some Determinants of Commitment to a Personally Chosen Course of Action," *Human Relations* 30: 431.

Stein, J. (1988) "Takeovers and Managerial Myopia," *Journal of Political Economy* 96: 61.

Stern, P. et al (1989) *Perspectives on Deterrence*. New York: Oxford University Press.

Stewart, R. (1987) "Crisis in Tort Law?," *University of Chicago Law Review* 54: 184.

Stigler, G. J., and G. S. Becker (1990) "De Gustibus Non Est Disputandum," in K. S. Cook and M. Levi eds., *The Limits of Rationality* Chicago: University of Chicago Press.

Stinchcombe, A. L. (1990a) "Reason and Rationality," in K. S. Cook and M. Levi eds., *The Limits of Rationality*. Chicago: University of Chicago Press.

_____ (1990b) *Information and Organizations*, Berkeley: University of California Press.

Stinson, R., and P. Stinson. (1983 [1979]) *The Long Dying of Baby Andrew*. Boston: Little, Brown.

Stone, C. D. (1975) *Where the Law Ends: The Social Control of Corporate Behavior*. New York: Harper and Row.

_____ (1980) "The Place of Enterprise Liability in the Control of Corporate Conduct," *Yale Law Journal* 90: 1.

Stone, D. A. "The Resistible Rise of Preventive Medicine," *Journal of Health Politics, Policy and Law* 11, 4: 671.

Sudnow, D. (1967) *Passing On: The Social Organization of Dying*. Englewood Cliffs, NJ: Prentice-Hall.

Sullivan, T., E. Warren, and J. Westbrook (1989) *As We Forgive Our Debtors*. New York: Oxford University Press.

Svenson, O. (1981) "Are We All Less Risky and More Skillful Than Our Fellow Drivers?" *Acta Psychologica* 47: 143.

_____ (1990) "Cooperation and Rationality: Notes on the Collective Action Problem and its Solutions," in K. S. Cook and M. Levi eds., *The Limits of Rationality*. Chicago: University of Chicago Press.

Sweetland, R. C., and D. Keyser, eds. (1986) *Tests: A Comprehensive Reference for Assessments in Psychology, Education and Business*. Kansas City: Test Corporation of America.

Szasz, A. (forthcoming) *Environmental Protection and the Grass Roots*. Newbury Park, CA: Sage.

Tamuz, M. (1988) Monitoring Dangers in the Air: Studies in Ambiguity and Information. Unpublished Ph. D. dissertation, Department of Sociology, Stanford University.

Tate, C. (1984) "What Do Ombudsmen Do?" *Columbia Journalism Review* 23 1: 37.

Tetlock, P. (1985) "Accountability," in L.L. Cummings and B.M. Staw eds., *Research in Organizational Behavior*. Volume 7. Greenwich, CN: JAI Press.

Thaler, R. (1980) "Toward a Positive Theory of Consumer Choice," *Journal of Economic Behavior and Organization* 1: 39.

_____ (1983) "Illusions and Mirages in Public Policy," *The Public Interest* 73: 60.

Thomas, J. E. (1986) "Statements of Fact, Statements of Opinion, and the First Amendment," *California Law Review* 74: 1001.

Thomas, W. A., ed. (1983) *Science and Law: An Essential Alliance*. Published in cooperation with the American Bar Association and the American Association for the Advancement of Science. Boulder, CO: Westview.

Thompson, J. D. (1967) *Organizations in Action.*. New York: McGraw Hill.

Travis, C. C., and S. T. Hester (1990) "Background Exposure to Chemicals," *Risk Analysis* 10 4: 463.

Tremain, I. (1927) "Escaping the Creditor in the Middle Ages," *Law Quarterly Review* 43: 230.

_____ (1938) "Acts of Bankruptcy: A Medieval Concept in Modern Bankruptcy Law," *Harvard Law Review* 52: 189.

Tuchman, G. (1978) *Making News: A Study in the Construction of Reality*. New York: The Free Press.

Tullock, G. (1964) *The Politics of Bureaucracy*. Washington, D.C.: Public Affairs Press.

Turner, B. A. (1976) "The Organizational and Interorganizational Development of Disasters," *Administrative Science Quarterly* 21: 378.

_____ (1978) *Man-made Disasters*. London: Wykeham.

Turner, R. H., J. M. Nigg, and D. H. Paz (1986) *Waiting for Disaster: Earthquake Watch in California*. Berkeley, CA: University of California Press.

Turner-Lewis, S. (1990-91) "Are Merchant Ships As Safe with Smaller Crews on Duty?" *News Report*. National Research Council, XLI 1 (December-January): 2.

Tversky, A. (1981) "The Framing of Decisions and the Psychology of Choice," *Science* 211(January 30): 453.

Tversky, A., and D. Kahneman (1974) "Judgment Under Uncertainty: Heuristics and Biases," *Science* 211: 1453.

_____ (1981) "The Framing of Decisions and the Psychology of Choice," *Cognitive Psychology* 5: 207.

_____ (1982) "Availability: A Heuristic for Judging Frequency and Probability," in D. Kahneman, P. Slovic, and A. Tversky eds., *Judgment Under Uncertainty: Heuristics and Biases*. Cambridge, U.K.: Cambridge University Press.

Twerski, A., A. Weinstein, W. Donaher, and H. Piehler (1976) "The Use and Abuse of Warnings in Products Liability--Design Defect Litigation Comes of Age," *Cornell Law Review* 61: 495.

_____ (1980) "Shifting Perspectives in Products Liability: From Quality to Process Standards," *New York University Law Review* 55: 347.

_____ (1981) "In Defense of Process," *New York University Law Review* 56: 616.

U.S. Code Congressional and Administrative News (1978) *Senate Report on the Bankruptcy Reform Act*, Washington, D.C.: Government Printing Office pp. 5787.

U.S. Congress (1967) "Congress Trims Space Authorization Below $5 Billion," *Congressional Quarterly Almanac* 23 Washington, D.C.: Congressional Quarterly Service.

_____ (1981-82) House of Representatives Subcommittee on Investigations and Oversight of the Committee on Science and Technology, *Genetic Screening and the Handling of High Risk Groups in the Workplace,* 99th Congress, 1st Session, October 14-15, 1981, and 2nd Session, October 6, 1982.

_____ (1986) *Investigation of the Challenger Accident.* Report of the Committee on Science and Technology, House of Representatives. Washington: U. S. Government Printing Office.

U.S. Senate (1982) *The Manville Bankruptcy and the Northern Pipeline Decision.* Subcommittee on the Courts, Committee on the Judiciary.

Uzych, L. (1986) "Genetic Testing and Exclusionary Practices in the Workplace," *Journal of Public Health Policy,* Spring 7, 1: 37.

Van Allen, J. A. (1986) "Space Science, Space Technology, and the Space Station," *Scientific American* 254 (1): 32.

Vaughan, D.(1982a) "Transaction Systems and Unlawful Organizational Behavior," *Social Problems* 29: 373.

_____ (1982b) "Toward Understanding Unlawful Organizational Behavior," *Michigan Law Review* 80: 1377.

_____ (1983) *Controlling Unlawful Organizational Behavior: Social Structure and Corporate Misconduct.* Chicago: University of Chicago Press.

_____ (1990) "Autonomy, Interdependence, and Social Control: NASA and the Space Shuttle Challenger," *Administrative Science Quarterly* 35 2: 225.

_____ (1992a) "The Macro/Micro Connection in 'White-Collar Crime' Theory," in Kip Schlegel and David Weisburd (eds.) *Essays in White-Collar Crime.* Boston: Northeastern University Press.

_____ (1992b) "Theory Elaboration: The Heuristics of Case Analysis," in C. C. Ragin and H. S. Becker eds., *What is a Case? Issues in the Logic of Social Inquiry.* Cambridge, U.K.: Cambridge University Press.

_____ (forthcoming) *The Social Construction of Risk: NASA and the Space Shuttle Challenger.*

Viscusi, W. K. (1983) "Alternative Approaches to Valuing the Health Impacts of Accidents: Liability Law and Prospective Evaluations," *Law and Contemporary Problems* 46: 49.

_____ (1983) *Risk by Choice.* Cambridge, MA: Harvard University Press.

_____ (1986) "The Determinants of the Disposition of Product Liability Claims and Compensation for Bodily Injury," *Journal of Legal Studies* 15: 321.

Vogel, D. (1986) *National Styles of Regulation: Environmental Policy in Great Britain and the United States.* Ithaca: Cornell University Press.

Vogel, E. (1979) *Japan As Number One: Lessons for America.* Cambridge, MA: Harvard University Press.

Wade, J. (1983) "On the Effect in Products Liability of Knowledge Unavailable Prior to Marketing," *New York University Law Review* 58: 734.

Walsh, D. C. (1987) *Corporate Physicians: Between Medical Care and Management.* New Haven, CT: Yale University Press.

Walsh, E. J. (1981) "Resource Mobilization and Citizen Protest in Communities Around Three Mile Island," *Social Problems* 29: 1.

Walters, V. (1982) "Company Doctors' Perception of and Response to Conflicting Pressures from Labor and Management," *Social Problems* 30, 1: 1.

Warren, C. (1935) *Bankruptcy in United States History*. Cambridge, MA: Harvard University Press.

Weait, M (1989) "The Letter of the Law? An Enquiry Into Reasoning and Formal Enforcement in the Industrial Air Pollution Inspectorate," *British Journal of Criminology* 29: 57.

Weber, M. (1919) "Science as a Vocation," reprinted in H. H. Gerth and C. W. Mills eds., (1946) *From Max Weber: Essays in Sociology*. New York: Oxford University Press.

Weber, T., Jr. (1986) "Editors Surveyed Describe Half of All Libel Cases as 'Nuisance' Suits," *The Bulletin* of American Society of Newspaper Editors (January): 38.

Weick, K. (1979) *The Social Psychology of Organizing*, Reading, MA: Addison-Wesley.

_____ (1987) "Organizational Culture as a Source of High Reliability," *California Management Review* 29(2): 112.

Weinberg, A. (1972) "Sciences and Trans-science," *Minerva* 10: 209.

Whelan, E. (1981) "Chemicals and Cancerphobia," *Society* (March/April): 7.

Whipple, C., and V. Covello (1985) *Risk Analysis in the Private Sector*. New York: Plenum Press.

White, J. (1984) "The Bildisco Case and the Congressional Response." *Wayne Law Review* 30: 1169.

Whitney, D. C. (1986) "Begging Your Pardon: Corrections and Corrections Policies at Twelve U.S. Newspapers." Working paper. New York: Gannett Center for Media Studies.

Whyte, G. (1989) "Groupthink Reconsidered," *Academy of Management Review* 14 1: 40.

Wildavsky, A. (1988) *Searching for Safety*. New Brunswick, NJ: Transaction Books.

_____ (1989) "Thanks for the Commentary: Replies to Critics and Critiques," *Society* 27 1 (November/December): 28.

Wilensky, H. L. (1967) *Organizational Intelligence: Knowledge and Policy in Government and Industry*. New York: Basic Books.

Williams, R. (1980) *The Nuclear Power Decisions*. London: Croom-Helm.

Williams, W. (1981) "Firing Women to Protect the Fetus," *Georgetown law Journal* 69: 641.

Williamson, O. (1975) *Markets and Hierarchies: Antitrust Implications*. New York: Free Press.

_____ (1981) "The Economics of Organization: The Transaction Cost Approach," *American Journal of Sociology* 87: 548.

_____ (1985) *The Economic Institutions of Capitalism*. New York: The Free Press.

Williamson, O., and W. Ouchi (1981) "The Markets and Hierarchies Program of Research: Origins, Implications and Prospects," in A. Van de Ven and W. Joyce eds., *Perspectives on Organization Design and Behavior.* New York: John Wiley & Son.

Wilsnack, Richard W. (1980) "Information Control: A Conceptual Framework for Sociological Analysis," *Urban Life* 8: 467.

Wilson, J. Q. (1978) *The Investigators.* New York: Basic Books.

_____ (1980) *The Politics of Regulation.* New York: Basic Books.

Wynne, B. (1982) *Rationality and Ritual: The Windscale Inquiry and Nuclear Decisions in Britain.* Chalfont St. Giles: British Society for the History of Science.

_____ (1988) "Unruly Technology: Practical Rules, Impractical Discourses, and Public Understanding," *Social Studies of Science* (January): 18.

Yates, R. (1987) "Burn Victims--Bic Settlements," *ABA Journal* (June 1).

Yellin, J. (1981) "High Technology and the Courts: Nuclear Power and the Need for Institutional Reform," *Harvard Law Review* 94: 489.

Young, R. (1988) "Is Population Ecology a Useful Paradigm for the Study of Organizations?" *American Journal of Sociology* 94: 1.

Zacharias, F. (1986) "The Politics of Torts," *Yale Law Journal* 95: 698.

Zaltman, G. (1982) "Knowledge Disavowal," paper presented at Conference on Producing Useful Knowledge for Organizations, Graduate School of Business, University of Pittsburgh.

Zemans, F. (1982) "Framework for Analysis of Legal Mobilization: A Decision-Making Model," *American Bar Foundation Research Journal* 4: 989.

_____ (1983) "Legal Mobilization: The Neglected Role of the Law in the Political System," *American Political Science Review* 77 3: 690.

Zey-Ferrell, M., and O. C. Ferrell (1982) "Role-Set Configuration and Opportunity as Predictors of Unethical Behavior in Organizations," *Human Relations* 35: 587.

About the Contributors

Anthony Barker is a Reader in the Department of Government of the University of Essex and has twice been Visiting Professor in the Department of Political Science, University of Wisconsin at Madison. He is co-editor with B. Guy Peters of the University of Pittsburgh of two volumes on information and expertise in public policy making: *The Politics of Expert Advice in Western Europe: Creating, Using and Manipulating Scientific Knowledge for Public Policy* and *Advising West European Governments: Inquiries, Expertise and Public Policy*, both from Edinburgh University Press (1992). Other edited books include *Quangos in Britain* and *Public Policy and Private Interests: The Institutions of Compromise* (both from Macmillan, London).

Lee Clarke is in the Department of Sociology at Rutgers University. He has authored *Acceptable Risk? Making Decisions in a Toxic Environment* (University of California Press, 1989), "Oil Spill Fantasies" (*Atlantic Monthly*, 1990), "Explaining Choices Among Technological Risks" (*Social Problems*, 1988), and other works on organizations, technology, and risk. He is currently writing a book on organizational responses to extreme uncertainty.

Kevin J. Delaney is Assistant Professor of Sociology at Temple University. He received his B.A. degree from Georgetown University and his Ph.D. from the State University of New York at Stony Brook. His research centers on interorganizational action during Chapter 11 bankruptcy, the topic of his chapter in this volume and of his book, *Strategic Bankruptcy* (University of California Press, 1992). He has published in *Law and Society Review*, the *International Journal of Health Services*, and other professional journals.

W. F. Felstiner received his B.A. and J.D. degrees from Yale University. A former Director of American Bar Foundation, he is now a Distinguished Research Fellow at the Foundation. He has published widely in legal and law and society journals.

Keith Hawkins is Deputy Director of the Centre for Socio-Legal Studies at Oxford. He is interested in problems of legal decision making, and has explored the topic in a variety of legal arenas, particularly governmental regulation and the administration of criminal justice. He is the author of many papers, and of *Environment and Enforcement* (Oxford University Press, 1984).

Carol A. Heimer is Associate Professor of Sociology at Northwestern University and Research Fellow at the American Bar Foundation. She received her Ph.D. in sociology from the University of Chicago. Her major publications include *Reactive Risk and Rational Action* (University of California Press), "Social Structure, Psychology and the Estimation of Risk (*Annual Review of Sociology*), and a forthcoming paper on universalism and particularism. She is currently writing two books on responsibility, one a theoretical piece and the second a study of who takes responsibility for graduates of neonatal intensive care units.

Stephen Hilgartner, a sociologist, is Assistant Professor of Social Medicine at the Center for the Study of Society and Medicine, Columbia University. His specialty is the sociology of science and technology. His publications include "The Dominant View of Popularization: Conceptual Problems, Political Uses" (*Social Studies of Science*, 1990) and (with Charles Bosk) "The Rise and Fall of Social Problems (*American Journal of Sociology*, 1988). He is now completing a book, *Who Speaks for Science? Cultural Authority in the Diet-Cancer Debate*, and is conducting a long-term, prospective study of the effort to map and sequence the human genome.

Bridget M. Hutter is a Research Fellow at the Centre for Socio-Legal Studies and Senior Research Fellow in Sociology at Jesus College, University of Oxford. Her recent research has addressed the question of compliance in health and safety and environmental regulation in Great Britain and the impact of these regulations upon industry. She is the author of *The Reasonable Arm of the Law?* (Clarendon Press, Oxford, 1988) and journal articles about regulatory enforcement. She is currently working on a book about "compliance."

James M. Jasper teaches sociology at New York University. Educated at Harvard and the University of California at Berkeley, he writes about the moral, cultural, and psychological dimensions of political action. His publications include *Nuclear Politics: Energy and the State in the United States, Sweden, and France* (Princeton University Press, 1990) and (with Dorothy Nelkin) *The Animal Rights Crusade: The Growth of a Moral Protest* (Free Press, 1992). He is now working on *The Art of Moral Protest*, a synthetic theoretical work on several recent protest movements.

Sally Lloyd-Bostock is a Research Fellow at the Centre for Socio-Legal Studies, University of Oxford. She has published widely in her field of psychology and law. As a member of the Centre's Health and Safety research programme, she conducted a psychological study of responses to accidents and accident reports by the British Health and Safety Executive, incorporating as well a small comparative study of OSHA in the U. S. More generally, her research has explored, in a range of contexts, the perspectives and choices of those using or applying the law: accident victims seeking compensation, factory inspectors enforcing safety regulations, hospital patients pursuing grievances and negligence claims.

Peter K. Manning is Professor of Sociology and Psychiatry at Michigan State University. He received his B.A. from Willamette University, his M.A. and Ph.D. degrees in sociology from Duke University. He is a former Fellow of Balliol and Wolfson Colleges, Oxford, and was a Research Fellow at the Oxford Centre for Socio-Legal Studies, 1984-86. He is author or editor of many books, articles, and chapters in scientific publications, including *Semiotics and Fieldwork* (Sage) and *Symbolic Communication* (M.I.T. Press), and *Organizational Communication* (Aldine).

Dorothy Nelkin holds a University Professorship at New York University where she is also Professor of Sociology and Affiliated Professor in the School of Law. She has been a Guggenheim Fellow and a Visiting Scholar at the Russell Sage Foundation. Her books include: *Controversy: The Politics of Technical Decisions*; *Science as Intellectual Property*; *The Creation Controversy*; *Workers at Risk* (with M. Brown); *Selling Science: How the Press Covers Science and Technology*; *A Disease of Society, The Cultural Impact of Aids* (with D. Willis); and *Dangerous Diagnostics: The Social Power of Biological Information* (with L. Tancredi).

Albert J. Reiss, Jr. is the William Graham Sumner Professor Sociology at Yale University and a Lecturer in Law at Yale Law School. He holds a Ph.D. from Marquette University, M.A. degrees from the University of Chicago and Yale (privatim) and the Ph.D. from the University of Chicago. He was awarded an honorary LL.D. by John Jay College, The City University of New York, and the Docteur Honoris Causa by the University of Montreal. The author of more than 150 books and articles in scholarly journals, law reviews, encyclopedias, and edited volumes, his best known books include *The Police and the Public: Studies in Crime and Law Enforcement in Major Metropolitan Areas*; *Data Sources on White-Collar Law Breaking* (with A. Biderman), and *Crime and Communities* (with M. Tonry).

Joseph Sanders is Professor of Law at the University of Houston. His research interests include expert witnessing, product liability and safety, and the cross-national study of legal structure and legal culture.

Susan P. Shapiro is a research fellow at the American Bar Foundation. The research reported in this book is part of a larger project on the social control of accuracy by news media conducted during a fellowship at the Gannett Center for Media Studies (now the Freedom Forum Media Studies Center) at Columbia University. Related work on the role of newsmagazine fact checkers as "gatekeepers of truth" includes her Gannett Center working paper, "Caution! This Paper Has Not Been Fact Checked!: A Study of Fact Checking in American Magazines." She also writes about the sociology of trust, white-collar crime, social control, and regulation. Her current research explores conflicts of interest in the legal profession.

James F. Short, Jr. is Professor of Sociology at Washington State University. He received B.A. and D.Sc. degrees from Denison University and the M.A. and Ph.D. from the University of Chicago. A former president of the American Sociological Association, his books include *Suicide and Homicide: Some Economic, Sociological and Psychological Aspects of Aggression* (with A. Henry), *Group Process and Gang Delinquency* (with F. Strodtbeck), *Delinquency and Society,* and several edited volumes, including *The State of Sociology: Problems and Prospects,* and *The Social Fabric: Dimensions and Issues.*

Peter Siegelman received his B.A. degree from Swarthmore and his Ph. D. in economics from Yale University. He is a Research Fellow at the American Bar Foundation.

Charles Tilly is University Distinguished Professor and Director of the Center for Studies of Social Change, New School for Social Research. His B.A. and Ph.D. degrees are from Harvard. A member of the National Academy of Sciences (U.S.A.), his work centers on conflict, collective action, the development and dynamics of capitalism, the formation and transformation of national states, and the social organization of demographic processes. His most recent books include *Big Structures, Large Processes, Huge Comparisons* (1984); *The Contentious French : Strikes, Wars, and Revolutions,* with Leopold Haimson (1986); *Coercion, Capital, and European States*; (1989); and *European Revolutions* (in press).

Diane Vaughan is Associate Professor of Sociology, Boston College. She received her Ph. D. from the Ohio State University. Her research interests are the sociology of organizations, deviance and social control, and transitions. She is the author of *Controlling Unlawful Organizational Behavior* and *Uncoupling.* Currently she is writing an historical ethnography explaining NASA's decision to launch the Space Shuttle Challenger. Also in progress is a book on theory elaboration, a methodological strategy aimed at developing general theory by comparative qualitative analysis of organizations that vary in size, complexity, and function.

Author Index

Subject Index

A. H. Robins, 94, 103, 111
"acceptable risk," 208, 300
accident(s), 193-94, 281
   impacts of on perceptions of risk,
   197
   organizational-technical fixes and,
   251
acutane, 83
additional hazard, 208
Agent Orange, 83
Agricultural Inspectorate, British,
   190 ff, 282
AIDS, 120
Air Pollution Inspectorate, British,
   283
American Cyanamid, 124
American Nuclear Society, 225
American Society of Newspaper
   Editors, 140
American Tort Reform Association,
   91
antinuclear movement, 230
asbestos, 83, 94, 97, 108, 294
asset specificity, 63
assets and liabilities, definition of,
   108
Atomic Energy Commission, 314
auto-based transport, 45

bad news, 21
   group context of, 186
   reception, transmision of, 162
   responsibility for, 179
Bankruptcy Act of 1867, 106
Bankruptcy Code, 91
Bankruptcy Reform Act, 104
   bankruptcy, 5, 103

as risk shifting, 115
as strategy, 108
causes of, 107
conceptions of, 105
economic models of, 106
legal claim to, 109
legal context of, 104, 317, 320
morality of, 105
organizational v. individual
   concerns, 17
social construction of, 104
Barker v. Lull Engineering, 69
beliefs, as ideologies and operating
   tenets, 268
bendectin, 83
*Beshada v. Johns-Manville Products
   Corp.*, 71
Bhopal, 98, 209, 263
biases and heuristics, 163
biases, of experts and officials, 34
   cultural, 257
Bic lighters, 94
biological testing, 16
   economic rationality of, 128
   in the armed forces, 126
Boston Globe, 243
bounded rationality, 15, 21, 33, 61,
   87
Britain (British), 207, 215
   inspectorates, 5, 190, 260
British Nuclear Fuels, Ltd. [BNFL],
   217-8, 260
*Brown v. The Superior Court of the
   City and County of San
   Francisco*, 66
Bruce v. Martin-Marietta Corp., 70
bureaucracy, bureaucrats, 224
Business Week, 104

About the Book

Every day, individuals, groups, and organizations make decisions that involve uncertainty and risk—and, often, important consequences for society. Increasingly, our lives are being defined by large-scale organizational decision processes involving governments, businesses, and other institutions. This book examines the nature of decisionmaking by organizations confronted with various risks, focusing on choices in which technology and scientific advances play major roles. The contributors also look at the regulatory agencies that set and enforce standards of health and safety.

Within the literature on risk analysis this book is unique in its integration of social theory with a wide variety of case examples. Theories of rational choice advanced by neoclassical economics and cognitive psychology are critically examined in view of the importance of the *context* for decisionmaking. Specific avenues for the study of the organizational/institutional contexts of decisionmaking and the process of socially constructing risk objects are proposed as a means of correcting the weaknesses of these theories.

The contributors examine the strategies of manufacturing and communications firms, neonatal intensive care units of hospitals, and a major U.S. governmental operating agency. Other examples of governmental strategies are given: how energy choices are made in France and how expert advice and formal public involvement are incorporated into risk-related policy decisions in Britain. Field studies of regulatory agencies in Britain at both policymaking and enforcement levels are also included.